FIANNA FÁIL

A Biography of the Party

ABOUT THE AUTHOR

Noel Whelan is the author or co-author of a number of previous books on Irish politics, elections and electoral law, including the series of Tallyman's Guides to Irish elections. He writes a weekly political column for the *Irish Times* and is a regular contributor on politics and current affairs for the broadcast media. He holds an MA degree in History and a BA degree in History and Politics from University College Dublin as well as a Barrister at Law degree from Kings Inns. He worked previously as a Political Organiser at Fianna Fáil Headquarters and then as Adviser to the Minister of State for European Affairs at the Departments of An Taoiseach and Foreign Affairs. He works currently as barrister on the Dublin and South Eastern Circuits.

FIANNA FÁIL

A Biography of the Party

NOEL WHELAN ∾

Gill & Macmillan

Gill & Macmillan Ltd
Hume Avenue, Park West, Dublin 12
with associated companies throughout the world
www.gillmacmillan.ie

© Noel Whelan 2011
978 07171 4761 8

Typography design by Make Communication
Print origination by Carole Lynch
Index compiled by Cover to Cover
Printed and bound in Great Britain by
MPG Books Ltd, Bodmin, Cornwall

This book is typeset in Linotype Minion 11/13pt
and Neue Helvetica.

The paper used in this book comes from the wood
pulp of managed forests. For every tree felled, at least
one tree is planted, thereby renewing natural
resources.

A CIP catalogue record for this book is available from
the British Library.

5 4 3 2 1

Dedicated to Seamus Whelan, 1935–2008

CONTENTS

ACKNOWLEDGEMENTS

This book is a largely chronological summary history of Fianna Fáil that draws in the main on secondary sources, with a particular emphasis on the accounts of those who were directly involved in the relevant events or close observers of them. The many authors on whose works I have drawn in relevant chapters are identified in the bibliography and notes. There are four in particular I want to thank, namely Stephen Collins, John Horgan, Gary Murphy and Donnacha Ó Beacháin, each of whom also took the time to review large parts of the nearly completed manuscript, providing additional viewpoints, pointing out errors and advising on further points of research.

It would not have been possible to complete this work, and certainly not within the time limit and the changing environment involved, without the substantial assistance of Kathryn Marsh. This is the fourth book on which I have had the pleasure of working with her and she was again a calm force throughout its writing, editing, referencing and proof-reading. She brought a forensic mind and keen eye to bear on the text in its earliest and its latest stages, was always meticulous in her approach to fact-checking and ever insightful in her many valuable suggestions. I owe her a great debt of gratitude.

A very special word of thanks is due also to Brian Murphy, now a doctoral student in the School of History at University College Dublin, concentrating on de Valera and the Presidency of Ireland. He was kind enough to take time off from his studies to apply his skills and knowledge of history to the draft of a number of the chapters, especially those dealing with post-war Governments and the Reynolds years. Because of his proximity to events involving more recent Fianna Fáil leaders he opted not to involve himself in reviewing the last four chapters or the introduction. There is no doubt that he is now destined in his own right to make a substantial contribution to Irish historical research.

I am also grateful to Peter Feeney, Éamonn Mac Aodha, Neil McCarthy, Mary Bailey, Richard Molloy and Michael Marsh for particular assistance in different aspects of this project.

I am obliged to Sean Dorgan, general secretary of Fianna Fáil, and Kathleen Hunt, then at Fianna Fáil head office, for access to the party's documentary and photographic archives and also for permission to use photographs and poster images.

A word of special thanks is also due to all at Gill & Macmillan who both initiated this project and are responsible for the quality of the final production. In particular I would like to thank and acknowledge the forbearance of Fergal Tobin, Publishing Director, and the skills of Deirdre Rennison Kunz, Managing Editor, and her team for the professional and painstaking manner in which this work was edited. Thanks also to Jen Patton, who sourced some fascinating photos, which give a flavour of Fianna Fáil's colourful and complicated history.

I have been blessed all my life with the considerable support of the extended Whelan family, to whom I am again grateful. I am also again grateful to Sinéad McSweeney for her assistance on the book and for so much else besides. Without her encouragement this book, like so much else in my life, would not have been possible. She and Seamus quietly endured the many late nights, early mornings and weekends when Daddy was busy "working at his computer." Their patience and support are again appreciated.

Introduction ᑎ

TALKING TO THE LEMASS
GROUP IN THE COWEN ERA

It was late October 2010, and there was something appropriate about the fact that the event was being held in the audio-visual centre in the modern Leinster House extension, rather than the traditional Fianna Fáil party rooms on the fifth floor of Leinster House itself. There was also something appropriate, poignant perhaps, about the fact that the gathering was called the "Lemass group". As one of those responsible for launching the original Fianna Fáil machine in the late 1920s and early 30s, redeveloping it in the 1950s and leading it in the 1960s, Seán Lemass would have been horrified by what I was about to tell the gathering.

The Lemass group had been set up by a handful of dissident back-benchers. Gradually, in the way that Fianna Fáil leaderships have traditionally managed internal affairs, the group had been gathered into the party's formal structure. Of late even ministers had been invited to address the gathering, most notably Brian Lenihan, Minister for Finance, who had spent two hours the previous week in robust encounters with the deputies about the policies he had implemented to address the fiscal and banking crisis. The format, even the setting, with its tiered seating, lent itself to more fruitful exchanges than the set pieces that the weekly meeting of the parliamentary party had become.

I was somewhat nervous as I rose to speak. I had been surprised ten days earlier to get the invitation. Although I had once worked for the party, it had been years since I had been asked to speak at a party meeting. I was nervous too because, as I reminded them at the start, I, like my father before me, had been an unsuccessful candidate for the party, he in Wexford in 1977, I in Dublin South-East twenty years later. This left me feeling like one of those retired or fired generals who used to irritate Dick Cheney, former Vice-President of the United States, so much. Cheney complained about how these armchair critics, "safely embedded in TV studios," dared to lecture those on the battlefield about how they should conduct the war.

A further reason for my nervousness was that, even though in recent years I had carved out a niche as a relatively independent political analyst in the media, I was, after all, someone from the Fianna Fáil gene pool: I had grown up in a Haughey house in the 1970s and early 80s, when Fianna Fáil homes were divided into Haughey houses and Lynch houses, or later again into

Haughey houses and Colley-O'Malley houses. I had therefore some empathy for the political distress these Fianna Fáil back-benchers were feeling; many of them also were second or third-generation people. A good few had fathers who had been TDS before them; a few even had grandfathers who had served in the Oireachtas. My grandfather had been a cumann secretary for much of the later part of his life. My father had been a cumann secretary in his twenties, a comhairle ceantair (district council) secretary in his thirties and a constituency chairperson and director of elections from his forties to his mid-sixties. I had a sense that these deputies also felt that their grandfathers or fathers, like mine, would turn in their graves at some of the things the party had been doing in recent times.

There was a real sense in the room, as one suspects there was at many Fianna Fáil gatherings around this time, that the present generation of political leaders had squandered the fine inheritance that had been passed on to them. A cadre of able young people, those accidental politicians, had built Fianna Fáil from the ruins of a bitter civil war and from the electoral defeats suffered by the "third Sinn Féin", as historians are wont to call it. They had developed it into one of the most effective political organisations ever to operate in any western democracy. After decades of political dominance and the exercise of power in the interest of the national good, as they saw it, the party was now indicted for economic recklessness, and its support was on the brink of collapse. Like some errant heir, the present leaders had gambled away the family treasures, pillaged the family finances, allowed the party organisation to rot and neglected the gardens, where the grass roots were once so carefully tended.

I was nervous too because what I was about to say was going to be blunt. I took a deep breath and told them that I had recently reviewed all polling data published in the previous eighteen months, had mapped the 2009 local election results to Dáil constituencies, had assessed the impact of boundary re-drawings, had allowed for likely retirements, had looked at the line-up of potential candidates in each of the forty-three constituencies, and had come with one important piece of advice. I told them that the following weekend they should each find some time to sit down and frankly discuss with their wives, husbands or partners how they would psychologically, financially and politically cope with losing their Dáil seat—because that was the fate I saw awaiting more than half of them.

At that point, in October 2010, I and other political commentators had assessed Fianna Fáil's national support at about 24 per cent. From that I had concluded that even with a fair wind at its back Fianna Fáil could not win more than forty-five seats if an election were called any time soon. The party was already well below the tipping-point where it would lose the seat bonus it had achieved in previous elections because of its size.

"Surely things will get better when the election actually comes round," one or two of the deputies in my audience said; but I warned them that there was no reason to assume that there was a floor under Fianna Fáil's vote. There was every possibility that it would fall even further. I felt that the party was being complacent about its survival prospects and reminded them how a former Fine Gael director of elections, Frank Flannery, had bluntly warned his party, after its disastrous 2002 general election, that it should not assume that just because it had always been a large feature of national life that situation would continue. Fianna Fáil, I added, now risked suffering the same fate as the *Irish Press* and other supposed national institutions.

As I came to the end of my presentation one of the deputies joked that what they needed after this political analysis was to hear from a bereavement counsellor. The next time I spoke to that deputy was three months later, when he rang me in a state of panic to ask me my view of his prospects. The election was about to be called, and that day he had been handed polling data by head office that suggested that he had no chance of holding on to his seat. The new party leader was encouraging him to join the hordes of his colleagues who were retiring, so that his running-mate's seat might be saved.

The sequence of events and confluence of factors that had brought Fianna Fáil's vote to a historic low point by that autumn of 2010 will fascinate historians and political scientists for years to come. Later events, which caused it to fall even further in opinion polls a few weeks later, will be equally compelling. How could a party that had risen so high so quickly, and had stayed up for so long, fall so low, and so suddenly?

By the end of 2010 Fianna Fáil had been in government for 60 years of its 84-year existence. Since 1932 it had never polled less than 39 per cent in a Dáil election. Until 1990 it had won all presidential elections. Until 2004 it had always been the largest Irish party in the European Parliament. Until 2009 it had always been by far the largest party in local government.

Yet in the general election of February 2011 Fianna Fáil suffered electoral collapse. Its vote more than halved, and it lost almost two-thirds of its Dáil seats. Not only did it lose power but it came in third, behind Fine Gael and the Labour Party and only just ahead of Sinn Féin. It was an extraordinary political disaster.

The essential determinant in the transformation of Fianna Fáil's fortunes was, as it usually is, economics. It was clear from the anecdotal and polling data available shortly after the acute phase of the banking and fiscal crisis in the summer and autumn of 2008 that the electorate blamed Fianna Fáil for the economic crash. The party had polled 42 per cent in the 2007 general election. In opinion polls from then until the bank guarantee it averaged 37 per cent, but by mid-2009 its share was down to 25 per cent.

The first sharp drop in Fianna Fáil's support coincided with the introduction of the bank guarantee in September 2008, although that single event did not occasion it. The dip was the culmination of months of bad economic news and the gradual realisation among the electorate that not only was the rapid growth of the "Celtic Tiger" years over but the crises in the public finances and banking were going to mean both a severe drop in living standards and a severe rise in unemployment. Fianna Fáil's opinion poll ratings slipped down only a little further as the economic news worsened over the next year and the impact of tax increases and unemployment became even more apparent.

Of course many in the party thought it was unfair that Fianna Fáil was taking all the punishment for the economic crisis. They pointed to international factors or cited a general communal responsibility for overindulgence in the boom times. There can be no doubt, however, that when the international environment deteriorated and the economic road conditions got dangerous, Ireland was speeding and continued to speed even as the bends got sharper. As the party at the wheel when the crash occurred, Fianna Fáil took the lion's share of blame.

Any prospect Fianna Fáil might have had of ameliorating its loss in support by doing a quality repair job on the banking and fiscal damage was always slim but was completely undermined by the falling confidence in its capacity to do so within the international money market. This culminated, inevitably, with the arrival of the European Central Bank and International Monetary Fund in November 2010. By late October 2010 the RED C opinion poll showed that the party's support had fallen into the teens, at 18 per cent. This was followed by a figure of 17 per cent in November and December and only 14 and 16 per cent in two opinion polls in January. Its support never rose significantly from this new low point.

One of Fianna Fáil's principal selling points, especially since the Lemass-led boom of the 1960s, had been that it could provide competent economic management in government. This was the reason—the only reason—that it had secured a third term in 2007. Stripped of that distinctive reputation, the party's support was left perilously close to free fall.

Economic factors were not the only ones at play, however. Just when it was needed most, Fianna Fáil had failed to show strong political leadership. Brian Cowen had looked like a strong figure when he became the seventh leader of Fianna Fáil in May 2008. He had long been a favourite of the party grass roots, particularly at ard-fheiseanna, when his combative orations used to send the clapometer off the scale. He appeared to have been a competent, if not particularly colourful, administrator in his most recent jobs at Foreign Affairs and Finance. For years he had been central to all Fianna Fáil party activity, candidate selection and by-election campaigns. His standing in the party was formalised by his appointment as deputy leader in 2002. More recently he had played a central role in the party's victorious campaign in the 2007 election. At a time when that campaign appeared to have become stuck in the mire of Bertie Ahern's personal finances, Cowen had pulled it out and then given the party some momentum by a systematic destruction of Fine Gael's policy proposals. Shortly after that election he had been formally anointed on national radio by Bertie Ahern as his successor.

When Ahern finally fell, in May 2008, Cowen was the obvious choice to succeed him as Fianna Fáil leader and Taoiseach. Once he decided to run, no-one declared against him, and the parliamentary party elected him unanimously. Colleagues hoped that, as a man of unquestioned political integrity and demonstrated ability who had a deep heritage in the party, he would represent a break from the controversies of the Haughey and Ahern years.

Having coasted into the top job, Cowen suddenly became unlucky. He had no time to establish himself as Taoiseach in the public mind. His capacity to effect a transition was undermined by Ahern's prolonged departure. The Lisbon Treaty campaign was just one of the projects stalled during the peculiar interregnum between the time when Ahern announced he was going and when he actually went. Within weeks of assuming office, Cowen suffered a serious defeat in the Lisbon Treaty referendum. This may explain why he felt the need for a win so badly that he agreed to a new social partnership agreement the following autumn when it was clear that the country could not afford it. As the economic challenges facing the Government worsened, Cowen appeared reluctant to take the necessary steps to address them. There was a constant sense, notwithstanding the efforts of Brian Lenihan, that the Cowen Government was increasingly behind the curve.

As the curtain was drawn back on the real state of banking and the public finances, Cowen's tenure at the Department of Finance came in for closer scrutiny, and inevitable questions were asked about how so much that was wrong could have gone on without being spotted and prevented. This undermined Cowen's standing and may also have undermined his own self-confidence. Throughout his time as Taoiseach, at least in public, he gave off a sense of unhappiness. His disengaged demeanour suggested that he just did not want to be there. There was much to be unhappy about; but an electorate traumatised by bad economic news needed a cheerier and more energetic messenger in chief.

Many in the Fianna Fáil parliamentary party were shocked that Cowen could not provide leadership of a better quality, but, in accordance with party tradition, most of them supported him almost to the end, although not perhaps to the very end. Many of his difficulties stemmed from his attitude to those in the media. He always gave the feeling that he resented having to engage with them at all. Apart from a few notable exceptions, his interviews and public speeches as Taoiseach were less than inspiring. A truculent relationship between Taoiseach and media can be difficult even in good times; such antagonism in a time of crisis, when the electorate needed to hear what the Taoiseach was going to do about the crisis and where he was going to lead them, proved disastrous.

Cowen's Government had had some successes. There were advances in the Northern Ireland peace process, including the transfer of responsibility for policing and justice to the devolved Assembly and Executive. Some of the measures for plugging the hole in public finances were drastic, including a combination of freezes on new hiring, wage cuts and a pension levy; but these came after the damage had been done. The Government could not avoid the scale of the economic crisis or the responsibility that attached to Fianna Fáil for it. Cowen also struggled when it came to coalition management.

After the relatively peaceful inter-party relations that had characterised the Ahern-Harney years, the Ahern-McDowell relationship had been stormy. Ahern's decision to govern with the Green Party after the 2007 election took many by surprise, but, once established, the Government worked surprisingly well at first. With Cowen as leader of Fianna Fáil and the change of economic circumstances, the real strains in the relationship emerged. The Green Party suffered its own convulsions over having to support the tough measures necessary to tackle the economic crisis, and Cowen showed insufficient regard for the need to nurse their concerns. The Green Party's insistence on pushing through some of its own legislative initiatives, including those in the area of climate change and animal welfare, became a focal point for back-bench dissent within Fianna Fáil.

The final weeks of the Cowen Government were chaotic, bordering on the surreal. The Green Party's decision to announce, days after the EU-ECB-IMF deal was negotiated, that it was pulling out of government raised tensions even further, although it agreed to stay for several weeks in order to let the Finance Bill pass.

By January 2011 Fianna Fáil deputies had realised belatedly how much trouble they were in, and the rumblings in the parliamentary party intensified. On 13 January there were rumours that Cowen might fall on his sword, but instead he announced that he would consult parliamentary colleagues before making a decision on whether he would stay or go. At the end of his consultations he announced that he had decided to stay. In protest, Micheál Martin, Minister for Foreign Affairs, announced his intention of leaving the Government.

Cowen survived a no-confidence motion on Tuesday 18 January, only to destroy his Government's and party's last bit of credibility with a botched attempt to replace retiring ministers with new faces at a point when it was obvious to everyone that the Government had lost all public support and an election was only weeks away. The craziness came to its peak the following Thursday, and Cowen, unable to implement his proposed reshuffle and in order to avoid an immediate collapse, was forced to announce that the election would be brought forward to 25 February.

Reeling, traumatised and incoherent, Fianna Fáil then went through the process of a new leadership election, and Micheál Martin emerged as the man chosen to head the salvage mission. He led a competently conducted campaign over the following four weeks but could not assuage the national anger at Fianna Fáil.

If economic and political mismanagement were the most significant reasons for the collapse in Fianna Fáil's support, blame must also be placed on the depleted state of the Fianna Fáil organisation and its inability to provide if not a bulwark then at least some sort of temporary shelter against the storm of protest. By the early 1980s it had become apparent to the more ambitious politicians in Fianna Fáil that the party organisation was so old and its methods so outdated that a new form of political campaigning was required, particularly in the cities and commuter belt. The increasing pattern of urbanisation and the growing scale and intensity of political campaigning, coupled with the fall in the number of political volunteers, meant that the party's traditional reliance on the activists in its cumainn was no longer adequate.

Many Fianna Fáil TDs or aspirant TDs set about building separate personal organisations in their constituencies. During elections, canvassing machines were constructed to carry out door-to-door work not for the party but for an individual candidate. Personalised posters began to appear, most of them erected by paid postering crews. The reliance on local volunteers to deliver campaign literature was supplemented, or replaced, by the use of direct-mail companies.

Whereas such personalised and professionalised campaigning had previously been prohibited by head office, or at least frowned on, during more recent years it not only became standard practice but was actively encouraged by the hierarchy. It could hardly do otherwise, as most of the party's senior politicians were engaged in it themselves. Indeed Bertie Ahern's highly personalised and well-resourced operation in Dublin Central epitomised this new campaigning style. With candidate selection increasingly controlled by head office, new candidates were identified more often on the grounds of their capacity to build and obtain funds for their personal election machine than because they had any useful political or social base in the local constituency. Ministers and TDs literally disorganised the party in their areas, sidelining party structures for fear they might thwart their personal machine. In many areas Fianna Fáil simply became a franchise, its logo affixed to the literature of individual political operations.

With the party organisation weakened dramatically by the 1990s there were insufficient workers to deliver a result for the party rather than the individual candidate in local and European Parliament elections. The particular weakness of the party organisation in Dublin, which had bedevilled Liam Lawlor during his work at head office on "Operation Dublin" in the mid-1980s and which Séamus Brennan had again tried to tackle when he was national director of the party in the 1990s, had actually worsened. It had merely been masked by the political dividend that Fianna Fáil derived from being in government during the economic boom and by the remarkable personal appeal of Bertie Ahern.

The apparatus of modern full-time campaigning is expensive. Building it and sustaining it requires funding—a lot of funding. As personal campaigning grew more competitive, the need for money increased, and so more donations were sought and received. Increasingly, because they were funding a personalised political operation, these donations were handled outside the traditional party financial channels. In the days before the introduction of more stringent controls, many Fianna Fáil politicians channelled the fundraising for their personalised political campaigns through a friendly local cumann, while others simply lodged the money in their own accounts. The intermingling of party and personal money became in some instances a cover for suspect political and financial transactions.

Devoid of its original driving mission, stripped of its reputation for economic competence and economic probity, lacking critical mass in the Oireachtas and depleted in personnel at the local government and local cumann level, Fianna Fáil may now be in terminal decline. It will find it difficult to master the shift from being a catch-all party of power to a niche party of opposition or to define new, credible policy objectives that will give it a space in our complex party system.

Now, when Fianna Fáil's future is so uncertain, it is timely to take a detailed look at its past.

Chapter 1 ~

FROM THE STEPS OF RATHMINES TOWN HALL, 1926

One afternoon in March 1926 two men strolled out of Rathmines Town Hall. The taller of them had just formally resigned as president of Sinn Féin. As he later told it, he turned to his companion and said, "Now, Seán, I have done my best, but I have been beaten. Now is the end for me. I am leaving public life."

The speaker was Éamon de Valera; the man to whom he declared his intention to retire from politics was Seán Lemass. In later accounts de Valera reported that Lemass was shocked to hear what he said and replied, "But you are not going to leave us now, Dev, at this stage. You cannot leave us like that. We have to go on now. We must form a new organisation along the policy lines you suggested at the ard-fheis. It is the only way forward."[1]

De Valera's version of this exchange overstates his reluctance to become involved in establishing a new political party, but it accurately reflects Lemass's enthusiasm for the project. The journey both men had taken to that moment was mirrored by many within Sinn Féin and the anti-treaty IRA who would decide to break away with them. Their relationship was to be if not the rock at least one of the foundation stones on which Fianna Fáil would be built. Together and in turn they would lead the new party for more than four decades.

De Valera's pronouncement that he was leaving public life, if it had been accepted by Lemass, would indeed have been a startling one. When he spoke these words Éamon de Valera was forty-three, but he had been the most prominent face and perhaps the most important personality in Irish nationalist politics for the preceding decade. Ten years earlier he had been the commander of the rebel garrison in Boland's Mill in Dublin during the rising of April 1916 and had avoided execution with the other leaders only because of his American birth. He had been imprisoned in England during the maelstrom that engulfed Ireland in the aftermath of the rising and executions, but when he was released, in June 1917, he emerged as a central figure in the new national independence movement that quickly gathered and grew under the umbrella name of Sinn Féin ("ourselves"). The name was that of a small political group established by Arthur Griffith that had long argued for an emphasis on the need for economic as well as political self-reliance and that had been initially blamed for the 1916 Rising by the British authorities.

As disenchantment with the Irish Party in the British Parliament and antagonism towards Britain increased, further fuelled by attempts to impose wartime conscription in Ireland, de Valera's standing within the movement also grew. The transformation of Griffith's small party into a broad popular front and national independence movement was reflected in de Valera's assumption of the presidency of Sinn Féin at the party's ard-fheis in 1917.

In the 1918 general election Sinn Féin had a landslide victory in Ireland on a policy of abstention from the British Parliament. De Valera had been re-arrested in May 1918 as part of the so-called German Plot and was in jail again in England when the Sinn Féin deputies met in the Round Room of the Mansion House, Dublin, on 21 January 1919 and constituted themselves as Dáil Éireann. Cathal Brugha was elected temporary president in de Valera's absence. Following his escape in February from Lincoln Jail, masterminded by Michael Collins and Harry Boland, de Valera was elected Príomh-Aire (first minister) and president of Dáil Éireann in April 1919. As such he was not only the figurehead of the republic that had been proclaimed in 1916 but was also chairman of the executive council of ministers running the alternative government structure that Sinn Féin now developed throughout the country, and political head of the independence movement. The latter was engaged in a brutal but effective guerrilla campaign, which fought the British forces in Ireland to a standstill, forcing them to enter negotiations in the late summer of 1921.

Although head of the government of the self-declared Irish Republic, de Valera himself did not travel to London as a member of the negotiation team. It was instead led by Arthur Griffith, who was effectually deputy head of the Dáil government, and Michael Collins, who was Minister for Finance as well as commander of the independence movement's guerrilla forces. De Valera was unhappy with the treaty that was eventually agreed between the Irish and British delegations and signed on 6 December 1921. Along with fellow-ministers, including Cathal Brugha and Austin Stack, he angrily rejected the contention that the Anglo-Irish Treaty gave effective independence to the 26 Counties. They railed against it because it provided for the partition of Ireland, and more vociferously because it included a requirement that, although the Dáil would be recognised as an Irish parliament, its members would have to swear an oath of allegiance to the British King. De Valera and the other opponents of the treaty contended that Griffith and Collins and their fellow-plenipotentiaries had signed the treaty without approval from the cabinet in Dublin and that at the time the signatories had been intimidated by a British threat of return to "immediate and terrible war".

As the Dáil, Sinn Féin, the Irish Republican Army and the country followed the cabinet in bitter division over the provisions of the treaty, de Valera led the opposing side. On 7 January 1922 he and his followers narrowly lost the Dáil vote on the treaty and walked out of the assembly, claiming to be the true custodians of the Irish Republic as proclaimed in 1916 and ratified by the first Dáil. They lost the subsequent elections in 1922 and 1923 and were even more decisively beaten in the short but brutal and bitter Civil War, which raged particularly in the east and south from June 1922 to May 1923.

Sidelined by more militant and military leaders during the conduct of the Civil War, and imprisoned for eleven months in its immediate aftermath, de Valera was released in July 1924 and sought to pick up the reins of the depleted and defeated republican anti-treaty political organisation that, though it retained the name Sinn Féin, had lost many of its leading politicians to the pro-treaty side or to death. In the wake of its electoral and military defeat Sinn Féin was a dishevelled organisation, lacking money and manpower; more significantly, by failing to recognise the newly established Irish Free State it was lacking a sustainable political strategy.

From then until he spoke those words to Lemass on the steps of Rathmines Town Hall, de Valera and the other revisionists within the third Sinn Féin who had appreciated the reality of their defeat on the treaty issue and come to recognise the futility of abstention from the institutions established under the treaty sought to move Sinn Féin from a course they knew would only leave it in the political wilderness. His remarks to Lemass were his acceptance that they had failed.

Seán Lemass was considerably younger than de Valera, being only twenty-six in March 1926, but he too had led a dramatic and dangerous life over the previous decade. The son of a hatter in Capel Street, Dublin, the young Lemass had to lie about his age when in 1915 he gained admittance to A Company, 3rd Battalion of the Dublin City Regiment of the Irish Volunteers. Shortly thereafter Éamon de Valera became adjutant of this battalion, and Lemass later recalled his first impression of de Valera's personal magnetism and his "capacity to hold a crowd of volunteers there while he addressed them in inordinate length, as he always did." Notwithstanding his "queer looking appearance", the "long thin fellow" impressed the young Lemass enormously.[2]

Lemass, as a young recruit, would not have been aware that the poet and educationalist Patrick Pearse and the Labour leader James Connolly and others had planned a rising for Easter Sunday, 23 April 1916. All the young Lemass did know was that a parade in O'Connell Street scheduled for that day had been cancelled the night before on the instruction of Professor Eoin MacNeill, titular head of the Irish Volunteers. The following day Lemass and his older brother, Noel, who was also a member of the Volunteers, headed off instead on a bank holiday hike up the Dublin Mountains. A chance meeting en route with Professor MacNeill and his two sons was to prove a turning-point in the lives of both Lemass brothers. The MacNeill boys bore news that, notwithstanding their father's countermanding order, some of the Volunteers had proceeded with the plan for a rising on the Monday and had set about taking control of strategic sites around Dublin. A clearly agitated MacNeill, who had strongly opposed the plan for the rising when he became aware of it, told them that armed unrest had already broken out in the city centre.

Determined to get into the action, the two Lemass brothers hurried back
to town, making their way first to Jacob's biscuit factory in Bishop Street,
where, because nobody knew them, they were refused admission. The
following morning they wandered the various sites where they understood
the Volunteers had taken up position until, when they were passing the GPO
in O'Connell Street, a friend on sentry duty recognised them and brought
them inside, where they were "absorbed into the garrison and given arms." In
a personal account published at the time of the fiftieth anniversary of the
rising in 1966 Lemass recalled that he was given a shotgun and positioned on
the roof of the GPO, where he stayed until the building came under heavy
British shelling on the Thursday.

The rising having collapsed by Friday, Lemass was part of the retreat to
Moore Street, during which, like almost everyone else involved in the
evacuation, he briefly assisted in carrying the stretchered James Connolly,
who had been injured during the fighting. After the eventual surrender
Lemass was arrested but was detained for only two weeks before being
released because of his age. The young Lemass now returned briefly to the
family business and to his studies, in apparent compliance with his father's
wish that he would become a barrister.

Despite writing about his involvement in the rising, Lemass left no formal
account and seldom spoke of his subsequent activities in the War of
Independence between 1920 and 1922 or of his involvement in the Civil War.
We know, however, that he maintained his membership of the Irish
Volunteers and that in late 1917 he became a lieutenant in the 2nd Battalion of
the reconstituted Dublin Brigade—no mean achievement for someone of
his youth. Lemass is said by some historians to have been one of the "Apostles"
or "Squad"—a very effective assassination crew of "tough steel-willed
men from the Dublin Volunteers," hand-picked and directed by Michael
Collins. He was certainly one of those responsible for killing British agents on
"Bloody Sunday", 21 November 1920. Lemass and his company were also
involved in a number of shooting incidents in 1920, including a number of
arms raids.

We know too that during a short visit home in December 1920 Lemass was
arrested and interned at Ballykinler, Co. Down. Always a man to use his time
well, he was an avid reader during his imprisonment and at this time began
his self-directed study of economics. He was released on the signing of the
Anglo-Irish Treaty in December 1921 and was appointed a training officer in
the new Free State police force. However, having reflected on the treaty's
contents, and having realised that his first pay cheque was drawn on the
Provisional Government of the Irish Free State and not on Dáil Éireann, as he
had assumed, he resigned and joined up with other anti-treaty training
officers who had based themselves at the former British army barracks at
Beggars' Bush, Dublin.

Lemass was part of the anti-treaty IRA group that seized the Four Courts in
Dublin on 14 April 1922, and such was the regard for him that he was appointed

adjutant to the garrison's commander, Rory O'Connor. The Provisional Government, headed by Michael Collins, began shelling the building on 28 June, and after two days O'Connor and the garrison surrendered. Although Lemass escaped, he was later recaptured and imprisoned, this time in the Deerpark Camp in the Curragh.

In July 1923 Noel Lemass, also an anti-treaty IRA officer, was abducted in Dublin, it is believed by men connected to the new Free State Special Branch. His mutilated body was discovered the following October dumped on the side of Killakee Mountain in Co. Dublin. Released from imprisonment on compassionate grounds, Seán Lemass returned to work in his father's business but also resumed his active career in the republican movement, although from this point onwards the direction of his involvement "was increasingly political."[3]

Lemass had not previously been a member of Sinn Féin, but now, though still an IRA man, he became increasingly important in the political wing. The ard-fheis of November 1923 was suspended for a period to allow delegates to attend the funeral of Noel Lemass, and when it reconvened Seán Lemass, in his absence and unknown to him, was elected to the party's standing committee. He now advanced rapidly through the party ranks. On 18 November 1924 he was elected to Dáil Éireann on his second attempt in a by-election in the Dublin County constituency.

It was at this stage that his working relationship with de Valera intensified. Within weeks of Lemass's election to Dáil Éireann, de Valera named him Minister for Defence in the notional Republican government that the anti-treaty Sinn Féin maintained. He succeeded Frank Aiken in this political post, but Aiken remained chief of staff of the IRA. Lemass had even less enthusiasm than Aiken for the prospect of another offensive military campaign against the Free State forces. He argued instead for an emphasis on the need to mobilise public opinion, and he set about attempting to reorganise the party in Dublin.

At this time de Valera also appointed Lemass to the organisational and economic sub-committees of the Sinn Féin Ard-Chomhairle. At its meetings Lemass became one of the most ardent advocates for Sinn Féin taking a more pragmatic political approach. More practically, he set about applying his already obvious administrative skills to that end and in particular to revitalising the party's Dublin organisation. In a series of six articles in the party's weekly newspaper, An Phoblacht, between September 1925 and January 1926 Lemass offered an increasingly depressing analysis of the state of the Sinn Féin organisation, finances and membership. He also made increasingly strident calls for a change of direction and for an emphasis on "immediately recognisable political objectives." The Lemass articles were all the more significant because they could not have appeared without the agreement of P. J. Ruttledge, the publication's editor, and because Lemass was widely regarded as a protégé of de Valera.

Lemass became increasingly impatient with political progress, and indeed with de Valera's cautiousness. In one of his articles in An Phoblacht in early

January 1926 Lemass wrote: "There are some who would have us sit at the roadside and debate the true points about a *de jure* this and a *de facto* that but the reality we want is away in the distance and we cannot get there unless we move." It is an observation that some historians have argued was directed as much at the party president as at the membership generally.

The question whether or not those elected as Sinn Féin deputies would take the oath and therefore their Dáil seats was given new impetus by the fiasco over the report of the Boundary Commission. The three-member commission had been established under the terms of the Anglo-Irish Treaty to decide on the precise delineation of the boundary between the Irish Free State and Northern Ireland. Both sides in the treaty debate had expected that substantial areas of Northern Ireland along the provisional border would be transferred to the Free State. However, an authoritative article on what was said to be a draft of the commission's report was published in a conservative English newspaper, the *Morning Post*. This suggested that extensive adjustments to the existing border were to be recommended, which caused consternation among both nationalists and unionists.

Such was the intensity of the public reaction in the South that the Irish member of the commission, Eoin MacNeill, now a minister in the Free State government, resigned from the commission and then from his government position. Fearing further disputes, the Free State, Northern Ireland and British governments agreed to suppress the full report, and in a wider agreement, ratified on 3 December 1925, the head of the Free State government, W. T. Cosgrave, agreed with his British and Northern counterparts that the existing border would be retained.

The case against the anti-treaty deputies' continued abstention from the Free State Dáil was further undermined by this controversy. It did not escape de Valera's notice, or that of the public in general, that if the forty-eight Sinn Féin deputies had taken the seats to which they had been elected the Cosgrave government's proposal on the boundary would have been defeated. Indeed on 8 December 1925 de Valera had led thirty-eight republican deputies in a meeting with the Labour Party deputies and others at which the Labour Party leader beseeched de Valera and his colleagues to take their seats so as to defeat the boundary proposal. However, as Sinn Féin had been elected on a mandate of principled opposition not only to the oath but to participation in the Free State institutions, and facing substantial opposition from within the party, de Valera could not follow this course of action.

In private deliberations and correspondence about this time de Valera commented that while Sinn Féin could not, he felt, renege on its mandate from the last election to absent itself from the Free State institutions, at the next election it should offer the electorate a policy of taking its seats if the requirement for the oath was removed.

Early in 1926, at a meeting in Ranelagh, Dublin, de Valera said publicly for the first time that he himself would be prepared to enter the Dáil if there was no oath of allegiance. A week later, on 9 March, a special ard-fheis of Sinn Féin at the Rotunda in Dublin was called to debate the issue. At this ard-fheis de Valera proposed a motion "that once the admission Oath of the 26 County and the 6 County assemblies is removed, it becomes a question not of principle but of policy whether or not republican representatives should attend these assemblies."

A counter-motion was proposed by Father Michael O'Flanagan, a prominent doctrinaire republican and senior member of the party, to the effect that it would be incompatible with Sinn Féin principles to send representatives into what he described as a "usurping" legislature. Father O'Flanagan's amendment was taken first and was carried by a tiny majority, reported as 223 votes to 218, although in the circumstances of the considerable confusion that prevailed after the votes were cast the figures may not have been accurately counted. De Valera and his supporters then withdrew from the hall and broke formally with the party.

Eighty-five years later there is still some confusion about whether de Valera in fact wanted to win this vote. Lemass and others had already concluded that the shift in political direction could be more easily facilitated by a new political movement. Lemass later reported that de Valera was not upset by the narrow defeat. Indeed Lemass argued that some delegates appeared to have been converted to the new departure but had been advised by de Valera supporters to obey their cumann instructions and vote accordingly.

Gerry Boland, a War of Independence and Civil War veteran and brother of the republican martyr Harry Boland, was another of the organisers on the de Valera side at the special ard-fheis. He later recounted that he had gone around the hall ensuring that some of those committed to voting against Father O'Flanagan's amendment did not in fact do so. De Valera could have won the vote on the motion if they wanted, but "it would not have been advantageous: we wanted a new organisation." The Chief himself later remarked that "it mattered very little to me whether we had a majority or minority at [that] ard-fheis."[4]

As John Bowman sees it, "senior Fianna Fáil politicians were pleased to have left some of their former colleagues in the trenches: they saw them as cranks who were determined to remain strangers to political reality." It is now clear that de Valera was among those who were of this view.[5]

While this dispute over whether opposition to the parliamentary oath of allegiance should be tactical rather than philosophical was the precise occasion of the breakaway from Sinn Féin, many historians have argued that it is unwise to see the factors that led to the birth of Fianna Fáil as being purely issues of a "constitutional and tactical nature". In the view of Richard Dunphy, author of the definitive history of the party's foundation, "Sinn Féin's complete failure to defend the vital economic and social interests of those groups from which it drew its support"[6] was the most significant catalyst leading to the birth of the new party. Sinn Féin's lack of credibility because of its non-recognition of the Free State was rapidly undermining its electoral prospects, but so too was its failure to set out an alternative social and economic policy to the austerity being pursued by the Cosgrave government. Political systems abhor vacuums, and, as Dunphy says, in the infant Irish political system a "political vacuum existed by the mid 1920s which a new party could hope to fill."

The reality was that, having lost the parliamentary vote and electoral battle over the Anglo-Irish Treaty, having been beaten even more comprehensively in the Civil War, and then having lost a further election, the republicans just had to accept that if they were going to achieve their objective it would have to be within the Free State institutions.

Liberated from the "galaxy of cranks" and "nuts" who had dominated the "third Sinn Féin", Lemass now urged de Valera to found a new party. While the pace of the break may have been forced upon him by Lemass and others, de Valera too was happy to move on. Notwithstanding his protestations to the contrary in his conversation with Lemass on the steps of Rathmines Town Hall and to others during those early weeks, it is apparent from private correspondence sent as early as four days after the fateful breach at the ardfheis that de Valera was already clear in his mind that he was setting up a new party, if nervous about its prospects for success. To one correspondent the president of Sinn Féin, soon to be the president of Fianna Fáil, wrote: "What will be the fate of this new venture, I do not know. I have at any rate done my duty and launched the ship on the sea of fate. If favourable winds blow, I may bring her safely to harbour. If not, well I am prepared to go down trying."[7]

Chapter 2 ❧

LAYING THE FOUNDATIONS, 1926–7

If the pace of events within Sinn Féin from December 1925 to March 1926 had been brisk, the speed with which de Valera and his lieutenants now moved to establish a new political party was even more so.

Within two weeks of the special Sinn Féin ard-fheis a number of *ad hoc* meetings had been held to explore how a new party might be organised. The most significant of these meetings appears to have been that held at the home of Colonel Maurice Moore in Dublin on 23 March 1927. Moore was a Co. Mayo landlord who had served with the Connaught Rangers in the Anglo-Boer War, had been a supporter of John Redmond and indeed was credited by some with being the founder of the Irish Volunteers. He was also a keen advocate of the Irish revival and latterly had been associated with the republican cause.

This gathering at Moore's home was attended by many of Sinn Féin's leading lights, including de Valera, Lemass, Seán T. O'Kelly, Seán MacEntee, P. J. Ruttledge, Dr James Ryan and Gerry Boland. A provisional organising committee, chaired by Ruttledge, was established to plan the new venture. It seems that de Valera declined the chair at this initial organising group and did not attend many of the early gatherings that fine-tuned plans for the new organisation. He was still hoping, though not expecting, that differences with Sinn Féin could be resolved.

Lemass showed no such reluctance. On the day after this meeting, as acting secretary of what he was already calling "the Republican Party", he wrote to Seán MacEntee confirming that those supporting de Valera's policy on the oath as advanced at the ard-fheis would no longer attend meetings of the Sinn Féin standing committee.[1] Within a week, on 29 March 1926, ten members of the Sinn Féin standing committee did indeed resign. This was the first slide in an avalanche that saw resignations follow at all levels of the Sinn Féin infrastructure as plans for the new party became definite.

Three days later, on 2 April 1926, an extended meeting to plan the new organisation was held upstairs at the Sinn Féin offices at 23 Suffolk Street, Dublin. Fianna Fáil today recognises this gathering as its private founding event.[2] De Valera was not only present but was the leading personality on this occasion, which decided, among other matters, the name of the new party.

He himself suggested the poetic-sounding title Fianna Fáil (literally "warrior bands of Ireland"), but Lemass argued instead for Republican Party. De Valera's suggestion had the mystic attraction of reaching back to Irish mythology, evoking stories of the legendary hero-soldier Fionn mac Cumhaill and the Fianna. "Fianna Fáil" also suggested continuity with the independence movement, as it had been one of the Irish names proposed for the Irish Volunteers, and the letters FF had been included in the Volunteers' badge. (This design was continued when some of that force was reorganised as the Irish Republican Army and carried forward again to the badge of the army established by the Free State government.) The name also had the advantage, in de Valera's view, of being untranslatable (though that did not prevent it later being incorrectly, and usually derisively, translated as "soldiers of destiny").

Lemass countered that people would not understand an Irish title, and that the word "Fáil" would be distorted by their opponents to the English word "fail". For de Valera, however, the title Fianna Fáil also captured the type of organisation he was anxious to build, or at least to portray his new party as. He later told the press that "the name Fianna Fáil had been chosen to symbolise the banding together of the people for national service, with a standard of personal honour for all who join, as high as that which characterised the mythological Fianna Éireann and a spirit of devotion equal to that of the Irish Volunteers of 1913–16."[3] This depiction of the party's name as suggesting a collegiate gathering in the public interest was reiterated constantly. At the 1927 ard-fheis the honorary secretaries in their address reminded delegates that the party name conveyed "the idea of an association of selected citizens banded together for the purpose of rendering voluntary service to the Irish nation."[4]

More practically, de Valera, in suggesting the name Fianna Fáil, hoped to attract some of those who were not on the anti-treaty side during the Civil War or whose political involvement had since lapsed. He feared they might be put off by the title "Republican", as it had been commonly used to describe those who had politically and militarily opposed the treaty.

De Valera wanted his new party to be seen as a unifying force in Irish politics. Speaking in Waterford in 1931, he said: "The object of founding Fianna Fáil was to try to enable the forces that had been divided by the treaty to come back and begin over again the forward march and to bring back those who believed the Treaty was a stepping stone to freedom." Indeed a number of members of Cumann na nGaedheal—the name adopted by the pro-treaty section of Sinn Féin in 1923—did join Fianna Fáil, among them James Geoghegan, Pádraig Ó Máille and J. J. Walsh. Robert Barton, one of the signatories of the treaty, also campaigned for Fianna Fáil. Some members of other parties, including the National League and the Labour Party, also joined.

A typical de Valera-Lemass compromise ultimately emerged from the Suffolk Street meeting. The "Chief" got his way, and the new party's title would be Fianna Fáil but its sub-title would be the Republican Party.

Within a fortnight the party not only had plans for an inaugural public event but had refined its initial policy statement. On 14 April 1926 the organising committee adopted a national policy that was clearly influenced by Lemass. It proclaimed that the new political departure that was soon to become Fianna Fáil would strive to "bring into one constitutional movement all citizens of good will who realise that national peace is necessary to national prosperity and who are ready to utilise the powers and machinery of Government already gained for national advance."

The party went public in *An Phoblacht* on 16 April 1926 with the announcement that a provisional organisation committee had been set up to establish the new party and that all Sinn Féin branches and officers were asked to contact it.

The next day de Valera gave an extensive interview to the international news agency United Press in which he revealed his plans for the new movement and suggested that the aims of the party he was establishing would be along the following lines:

1. To secure the independence of a United Ireland as a Republic.
2. To work for the restoration of the Irish language and the development of a native Irish culture.
3. To develop a social system in which as far as possible equal opportunity will be afforded to every citizen to live a noble and useful Christian life.
4. To distribute the land of Ireland so as to get the greatest possible number of Irish families rooted to the soil of Ireland.
5. To make Ireland an economic unit, as self-contained and self-sufficient as possible, with a proper balance between agriculture and other essential industries.

Some days later the party's provisional organising committee published a formal statement of fundamental aims. The subtle differences in emphasis between this officially promulgated version and those outlined by de Valera in his interview give some insight into the type of debate about basic aims that had been going on among the party's founding fathers, although it is clear that the Chief himself was the dominant influence on the final text. In the words adopted formally by the party, and indeed carried in the pockets of the party faithful on the back of their membership cards until it was rewritten in the early 1990s, the aims of Fianna Fáil were:

1. To secure the Unity and Independence of Ireland as a Republic.
2. To restore the Irish Language as the spoken language of the people and to develop a distinctive national life in accordance with Irish traditions and ideals.
3. To make the resources and wealth of Ireland subservient to the needs and welfare of all the people of Ireland.

4. To make Ireland as far as possible, economically self-contained and self-sufficing.
5. To establish as many families as practicable on the land.
6. By suitable distribution of power to promote the ruralisation of industries essential to the lives of people as opposed to their concentration in cities.
7. To carry out the Democratic Programme of the First Dáil.

On 16 May 1926 five hundred delegates gathered in Dublin for the formal public launch of Fianna Fáil. The venue was the La Scala Theatre in O'Connell Street, Dublin (where Penney's department store now stands), which had been chosen to emphasise continuity with the republican project, sited as it was next door to the iconic birthplace of the Republic at the GPO.

The proceedings that night were presided over by Constance Markievicz. A daughter of the Anglo-Irish explorer and philanthropist Sir Henry Gore-Booth, who had a large estate in Co. Sligo, Constance had championed the cause of Dublin's working class and had jointly founded (with James Connolly) the Irish Citizen Army. She had actually fought in the 1916 Rising and had gone on to be a minister in the first Dáil government. She had also fought on the anti-treaty side when the Dáil split and the country descended into civil war. She had taken de Valera's side again at the Sinn Féin ard-fheis the previous March. From the outset it was clear that she was to play a prominent role in the new party, and it is likely that she would also have featured in future Fianna Fáil governments had it not been for her early death from a sudden illness in July 1927.

De Valera's address from the La Scala platform not only explained why he had broken with Sinn Féin but revealed more of the content and likely emphasis of the policies of the new party.

> I could not stand by and watch the movement brought into a position in which it must appear to be reduced and to degenerate as time went on to an empty formalism. To allow that when I am convinced that the Republican movement can be restored to its former robust strength would be to prove false to the Republican rank and file and to the nation.

His address included a predictably strong attack on the oath of allegiance and a commitment to the peaceful reunification of Ireland. Although much of the speech was inevitably concerned with how effective independence could be achieved, de Valera also dealt extensively with what he termed "the purpose of freedom" and laid out the central tenets of what would become Fianna Fáil's popular social and economic policy. He strongly attacked the Cosgrave government's economic programme, which had led, he said, to mass unemployment and bad housing.

On a more subtle note he identified himself and his new party with the 1916 martyr James Connolly, founder of the Irish Labour Party. He committed the new party to introducing improved health insurance and social welfare. He promised the protection and development of native industry, the breaking up of large rancher farms and the withholding from Britain of the land annuities (repayments by farmers of loans given under the nineteenth-century Land Acts). His message to the wider electorate was coated with populist attacks on the cost of state bureaucracy, a pledge to reduce the size of the Dáil by more than a third and a commitment to abolish the Seanad.

Even before the public launch Fianna Fáil had taken up occupancy of a temporary head office across the road in premises overlooking the GPO at 35 Lower O'Connell Street, over Jameson's jewellery shop. In his memoir Bob Briscoe gives a vivid account of the setting up of this office.

> The office was as bare as a boneless cupboard—no typewriters, no desks, not even a chair to sit on. Money for all these things as well as the rent and a small staff had to be found. We, the founder members, rushed around collecting donations from our friends and personally pledging what we could.

Among those initial contributors to the seed capital of the new party was the actor Jimmy O'Dea. He was close to Lemass, who had been best man at his wedding, and at his personal request donated the then princely sum of £100 to help start the new party.[5]

A small Information Bureau was quickly established, directed by the former journalist and long-time republican propagandist Frank Gallagher. Its function was to advise cumainn, the party's local branches, on policy and to provide back-up for party spokespersons and deputies. Among the early tasks undertaken by this initial publicity division was the printing of a pamphlet, *A National Policy Outlined by Éamon de Valera*, which included the leader's inaugural address at the La Scala "amplified with complementary matter." This was the first in a series of five pamphlets jointly written by de Valera and Gallagher that were widely distributed to mark the founding of the party.

Gallagher's small team also co-ordinated the organising of chapel-gate meetings throughout the country "to explain policy and enlist supporters." A panel of speakers was compiled and put on tour to address public meetings of the party. More than four hundred such meetings were held throughout the country in the summer and autumn of 1926. "Notes for speakers" issued to these travelling orators by Gallagher and his team urged them to "give wide publicity to those points in the programme of action set out in our printed leaflets especially to social and economic policy."[6] Briscoe recalled that

> meetings were held in all parts of the land. Groups of speakers would be sent to the county towns and village to explain Fianna Fáil and arouse enthusiasm. Then one of us would be left behind to organise a Fianna Fáil Cumann . . . There were then only about twenty or twenty five regular speakers among us and we covered the whole country from

Bantry Bay to Malin Head. I had acquired my first motor car and I remember every Sunday and sometimes on a Saturday evening leaving home with four or five speakers in my car bound for Kerry or Carlow, down to Limerick and west across the Shannon, where some of our supporters would have arranged public meetings. At other times we would just try to catch the crowd coming out of church after Mass.[7]

Briscoe, who was Jewish, gave a memorable account of one such after-mass meeting in Ballyseedy, Co. Kerry.

Our local leader was Willie O'Leary, ex-commandant of the IRA. This Sunday I went with O'Leary and some of his friends to the church. They all went into Mass, while I remained with the car from which we would speak when it was over. O'Leary turned back and said to me, "Will you not go into Mass?"

"I don't go to Mass," I replied.

"Everybody goes to Mass here, you'll have to do likewise."

I began to explain the differences in our faiths, when O'Leary interrupted me. Speaking between clenched teeth he said, "Haven't we enough bloody trouble explaining Fianna Fáil without having to explain you as well? At least go to the door and pretend you're going to Mass!"

I complied.

De Valera himself set out on a tour of the country, addressing larger gatherings in the main county towns. Meanwhile the primary focus of the party's other leading personalities over the late spring and summer months of 1926 was the nationwide exercise of establishing the party's basic organisation. Seán Lemass, Gerry Boland and Tommy Mullins played the most prominent roles in this endeavour, travelling the country, meeting old Sinn Féin colleagues and War of Independence or Civil War contacts and asking them to lead the launch of the party in their localities. The ambitious plan was that they would establish branches of the party in each Catholic parish in the country, so that the organisation had a geographically based hierarchy from the outset. In each district outside Dublin these cumainn were overseen by a comhairle ceantair (district council), and at the constituency level there was a comhairle dáilcheantair (constituency council). The priority, however, was to have sufficient candidates, branches and personnel to contest the next election, which was then seen as imminent.

By the end of August 1926 the party's small head office staff had circulated a pamphlet on voter registration. A full check of the electoral register was in train by the middle of September. By November 1926 more than 450 cumainn had been established, and more than five hundred delegates attended the party's first ard-fheis, held in the Rotunda on 24 November.

At this meeting the roles of those given positions in the provisional organising committee were formalised. De Valera was elected president of the party, while Seán T. O'Kelly and P. J. Ruttledge were elected vice-presidents. O'Kelly, at forty-four only a year younger than de Valera, was one of the veterans of the Sinn Féin leadership and a long-time close colleague of the Chief. He too had been a participant in the 1916 Rising and in 1918 had been elected a Sinn Féin MP for the College Green division of Dublin. He had been ceann comhairle (speaker) of the first Dáil when it met in the Mansion House on 21 January 1919 and was an emissary from the newly declared Irish Republic to the Versailles Peace Conference.

P. J. Ruttledge was a Mayo man who had been educated at St Enda's school, run by Patrick Pearse. He subsequently studied law and was prominent in the Sinn Féin courts. An active member of the 4th Western Division of the IRA, he had been first elected to Dáil Éireann in 1921. As a member of Sinn Féin in the 1920s he was "acting President of the Republic" during de Valera's imprisonment. He had been editor of An Phoblacht and played an important publicity role for Sinn Féin both before and after the treaty split. He would do the same for the new party. During de Valera's absence from Ireland to raise funds in the United States much of the task of building up the new party was directed by Ruttledge.

Seán Lemass and Gerry Boland were formally nominated to the important executive roles of joint honorary secretaries. Like Lemass, Boland had lost a brother during the Civil War. Harry Boland, a close associate of Michael Collins, had been shot by Free State forces during a skirmish at Skerries, Co. Dublin. Gerry Boland, who had fought in Jacob's factory during the 1916 Rising, had become a TD for Roscommon in 1923.

The party's first honorary treasurers were Seán MacEntee and Dr James Ryan. MacEntee was a consultant engineer who had been vice-commandant of the Belfast Brigade during the War of Independence and had fought on the anti-treaty side in Dublin during the Civil War. James Ryan, who was TD for Wexford, had been medical officer in the GPO during the rising, had subsequently been elected to the first Dáil for the Wexford South constituency and had served as commandant of the Wexford Battalion during the War of Independence.

These first national officers would go on, with Frank Aiken, to form the core of all Fianna Fáil Governments over the following forty years.

The first Ard-Chomhairle of Fianna Fáil, elected at this inaugural ard-fheis, included all these officer board members and many other leading lights of the independence struggle. Among these was Frank Aiken. He was a native of Co. Armagh who had been chief of staff of the anti-treaty IRA during the Civil War and at the time of the declaration of the truce in 1923.

The commandant of the Tipperary flying squad, Dan Breen, and of the Mayo flying squad, Michael Kilroy, along with the latter's fellow-Mayoman and fellow-IRA man Tom Derrig, were also members of this inaugural executive. Also elected was P. J. Little, another former editor of An Phoblacht, Dr Con Murphy, who had lost his public service position for refusing to swear allegiance to the Free State, the Co. Mayo secondary teacher Eugene Mullen, who later became a professor and subsequently joined the Carmelite order, and Professor P. Caffrey.

Among the women members were Margaret Pearse, whose two sons, Patrick and William, had been shot after the 1916 Rising, and Kathleen Clarke, widow of an executed signatory of the 1916 Proclamation, Tom Clàrke. The prominent feminist nationalists on the first Fianna Fáil Ard-Chomhairle included Dorothy Macardle, Hanna Sheehy Skeffington, Constance Markievicz and Linda Kearns. The first executive also included the Rev. E. Coyle of Co. Fermanagh, who was one of the few parish priests who openly supported de Valera's new party from the beginning.

In addition to these elections, the first ard-fheis also debated and adopted a relatively comprehensive policy programme, touching in turn on political, cultural and economic objectives and reiterating more of the principles and reusing much of the language in de Valera's La Scala address.[8] It was fleshed out, however, in a policy programme remarkable at the time for its detail and radicalism. Among the policy stances approved at the ard-fheis were the protection of the natural resources of the country and the encouragement of native industry by imposing further tariffs, the creation of an Irish mercantile marine, and measures to effect the reforestation of the country on a national scale and to break up large grazing ranches and distribute them as economic farms among young farmers and agricultural labourers. The platform also included a commitment to full employment, protection for town tenants, proposals for a state bank, and a tax on native capital invested abroad.[9]

After Christmas the frantic organisation and election preparations continued. De Valera was out of the country for much of the early part of 1927. He travelled to New York in March to give evidence in the "Sinn Féin funds case", in which the Free State government was seeking to have money donated by Americans to Dáil Éireann in the early days of the independence struggle handed over to the new government. Once finished in the witness box in New York, de Valera set off on an extended tour of American cities to raise funds for Fianna Fáil. Indeed it was thanks mainly to these fund-raising efforts that Fianna Fáil was established on a relatively sound financial footing, as de Valera collected £20,000 during this tour.

Frank Gallagher, who accompanied de Valera on this trip, recalled one very successful fund-raising event in Boston.

From all parts of the house people came carrying bundles of dollars and five dollar bills. The dais was soon littered with them. Each subscription as it was handed up was announced and the fat ones and those with a ringing covering message roused the audience to new applause. For an hour it went on . . . When the black bag with 5,000 dollars was taken away D. stood up to speak . . . It was magnificent and carried the House off its feet.[10]

De Valera toured the United States again in December the same year. The party's balance sheet in 1927 showed that no less than £29,782 of the total party income of £30,402 that year came from abroad, almost all from the United States.

The ultimate outcome of the Sinn Féin funds case also operated to the considerable advantage of the fledgling party. Mr Justice Peters of the New York Supreme Court decided in May 1927 that money in the relevant accounts, estimated at approximately $3 million, should be returned to the subscribers. At de Valera's request, many of these diverted their returned donations to political purposes nominated by him, and such funds were used to finance, among other things, a move to more spacious offices in Middle Abbey Street and the launch of the party's own national daily newspaper, the *Irish Press*, in 1931.[11]

Other funds came from Australia, where Archbishop Daniel Mannix of Melbourne, who had moved to Australia from Ireland in 1913, gathered donations totalling £1,000, which was one of the earliest large sums received by the party.[12]

During this establishment stage Fianna Fáil also attracted surprisingly strong financial support from the business community. One of the early organisers, Tommy Mullins, a TD and subsequent general secretary, says that the party wrote to two hundred or so "wealthy friends" seeking financial support. Bob Briscoe, who was also one of the party's successful Dublin candidates in the 1927 election, recalled that collecting funds from wealthy backers at the initial stages of the party's existence was easier than he had expected.

If the manner in which the new party laid its financial foundations was impressive, the speed with which the organisation was developed "from a group sitting in Dublin" was extraordinary. The intensity of this initial period of organisation was recounted many years later by Seán MacEntee, who said:

> For more than five years hardly any of us were at home for a single night or any week-end. Lemass bought up four or five second-hand Ford cars, "old bangers" and with them we toured every parish in the country founding Fianna Fáil branches on the solid basis of Old IRA and Sinn Féin members.[13]

Lemass's first biographer, Brian Farrell, comments that while Lemass retained little memory of the original organising of the party, what he did remember was

> careering around Ireland in a tin lizzy [Ford Model T] concentrating on the recruitment of sound republicans around whom local organisations could be developed. With political opinions already being formed around the disagreement on the basic Treaty issue the effort of organisation was not so much to convert people to the Republican

cause as expounded by Fianna Fáil as to get them actively involved in supporting the party.[14]

Writing in the 1980s, Gerry Boland's son Kevin felt the need to emphasise to his readers how difficult a task even town-by-town, let alone parish-by-parish, political organising was in the late 1920s.

> In those days organisational work at ground level involved real hardship. Roads were bad and the transport available was worse. Spare wheels were a luxury not normally carried and punctures which were an unavoidable feature on a journey of any distance had to be repaired on the spot. All the organisers had hair raising stories to tell of their difficulties in travelling but they generally succeeded in getting to their meetings even if they were a few hours late.[15]

Indeed Kevin Boland, who was himself to be a leading organiser for the party before his break with it in the early 1970s, wonders whether the practice of starting a meeting scheduled for 8 p.m. at 10 p.m., which endures in the party in many areas to the present day, was a tradition that began in those early days.

The small fleet of Fords of which MacEntee speaks could cover only some of the country. The bulk of the organisers, including on occasion Gerry Boland himself, travelled by train to central points and from there embarked on lengthy bicycle tours to towns off the railway network.

By 20 February 1927 Fianna Fáil had 571 registered cumainn, and this number rose to 777 by 10 April 1927.[16] By the time of the party's second ard-fheis, in November 1927, the honorary secretaries reported that there were 1,307, although they warned that many of these branches were already in need of reorganisation. By the end of the year the party had also launched a weekly party news-sheet, the *Nation*, under the editorship of Seán T. O'Kelly.

It has been argued that Fianna Fáil's organisation was built on the "ashes of the anti-Treaty wing of Sinn Féin."[17] To an extent this is true. The rise of Fianna Fáil's network of cumainn did indeed mirror the collapse of Sinn Féin's. The number of Sinn Féin affiliated branches fell: for example, almost a hundred closed within a month in March and April 1926. Sinn Féin also haemorrhaged TDs and officials to Fianna Fáil: 17 of the 37 Sinn Féin standing committee members and 21 of the its 47 TDs joined Fianna Fáil in its first months. Initially hesitant, prominent Sinn Féiners such as Oscar Traynor later joined these early defectors.

The scale of defection from the mother party was clearly more extensive than had been expected. The founders of Fianna Fáil were surprised that the apparently evenly divided ard-fheis in March 1926 was "not representative of sentiment within Sinn Féin at [the] local level." Lemass later commented: "It was assumed that the Ard Fheis which rejected de Valera's policy represented the majority of Sinn Féin opinion throughout the country but when we started to organise Fianna Fáil we found this was not so."[18]

Even at this early stage, however, Fianna Fáil drew its leadership, member-ship and organisational base from sources other than Sinn Féin, and in particular from the IRA. Indeed Richard Dunphy, who has conducted sub-stantial research on the launch of the party, argues that "the large pool of disillusioned republicans who had not been politically active since the Civil War" was of greater importance to the party's initial infrastructure than was the mother party.[19]

Both in the selection of candidates and in organisational development the primary emphasis was on contacting local IRA commanders, who, "because of their (real or legendary) exploits during the war of independence and civil war had established themselves as heroic or charismatic figureheads in their localities."[20] Lemass and Boland, during their many separate country-wide tours over these months, would call on such veterans, often repeatedly, seeking to persuade them to join and to stand for the party. Most of the local republican leaders they identified had been soldiers rather than politicians during the War of Independence and Civil War, and their initial reluctance to engage with the senior Fianna Fáil recruiters now calling to their doors arose as much from the military man's distrust of politicians as from doubts about the prospects for de Valera's latest project. This "key men" strategy of targeting well-known republicans also had the advantage that their lieutenants almost always followed them into the new political activity. This approach did not apply only to seeking candidates or constituency leaderships but was replicated right down to the parish level when people were being recruited to staff cumann officer boards.

Perhaps the most studied of the Fianna Fáil organisations was that set up in Co. Donegal. The party's initial development there was typical of that in most other counties. Many years later, on a family holiday in the Rosnakill area, Lemass proudly pointed out to his children the field in which he told them Fianna Fáil had been founded in the county.[21] He was referring to his meeting in late 1926 or early 1927 with Neal Blaney. Blaney had served as commandant of the Fanad Battalion of the 1st Northern Division of the IRA from 1920 to 1922 and had been vice-commandant of Donegal No. 2 Brigade of the anti-treaty IRA during the Civil War. After the Civil War he returned to work his family farm in Rosnakill until his peace there was disturbed by a sustained effort by Lemass to have him return to active service, this time in the political realm as leader of the new party in Donegal. Lemass's recollection was mirrored by that of Neal Blaney's son Neil, later a prominent Fianna Fáil minister, who often recounted his childhood memory of Lemass's first visit. Motor cars were a novelty at the time, and Neil had a clear recollection of the car bearing Lemass, which, having called to the family home, was directed by the young Blaney to a spot two fields away, where his father was at work ricking hay.

Neal Blaney, like quite a few of those ultimately persuaded to stand for Fianna Fáil in those years, was at first opposed to de Valera's actions in setting up the new party but was eventually won over by Lemass.[22] In his study of

Neil Blaney's "Donegal Mafia" the American academic Paul Sacks tells how Blaney's father's organising efforts during the 1927 election drew on several different resources.

> Through his membership of Sinn Féin he drew upon the already established network of party cumainn to form branches for the new organisation. Many of these men were Blaney's old followers from the republican movement. Particularly in the Milford and Letterkenny [areas] membership in the Fianna Fáil cumainn was virtually coextensive with the old Sinn Féin branches. Using his other contacts in the [Irish Volunteers] and the IRA, Blaney established a number of new cumainn between 1927 and 1932. Fianna Fáil's assumption of power in 1932 provided a further boost to the party organisation in Donegal.[23]

At the other end of the country, in Co. Cork, another obvious target for a new party in search of well-known republican candidates was the former commandant of Cork No. 2 Brigade, Seán Moylan. Moylan had gone to the United States after the Civil War but had been back living in Kishkeam, Co. Cork, since late 1924. Despite several personal entreaties from de Valera, Moylan had stayed out of politics since his return and had also ignored invitations to become involved in the new party. Again his initial hesitancy was illustrative of the difficulty de Valera and his colleagues had in getting some War of Independence and Civil War veterans to reactivate and take up politics. Gerry Boland travelled to Co. Cork in at least three unsuccessful attempts to sign Moylan up to the new initiative. In 1928 de Valera went so far as to have Moylan selected as a Fianna Fáil candidate for the Seanad without his knowledge. The party's official notification to Moylan to that effect went unanswered. Moylan ultimately relented, however, probably because of his personal loyalty to de Valera, and was a successful candidate for the party in the 1932 election.[24]

This reliance on prominent local leaders was not the only thing that Fianna Fáil inherited from the IRA network. The "structurally anchored cult of leadership" at both the national and the local level and the strong emphasis on loyalty, which has been called "Fianna Fáil's brand of democratic centralism," also owes more to these military origins and the party's inheritance of IRA power structures than it does to its origins in the break from Sinn Féin.

There was a strong puritanical streak in the party, and one of the most striking features of the founding members was their idealism, their asceticism and their dedication to republican aims. Todd Andrews alluded to this in his autobiography. "We didn't drink. We respected women and . . . knew nothing about them. We disapproved of any kind of ostentation . . . We disapproved of horse racing and everything and everyone associated with it."[25]

From the outset, strong discipline was a central tenet. The oath required from all candidates included an undertaking that if elected to public office and "called upon by two thirds majority of the National Executive [Ard-Chomhairle] of Fianna Fáil to resign that office, I shall immediately do so." Indeed this part of the oath taken by Fianna Fáil candidates persists in almost precisely the same form today.

The sense of political camaraderie within the party and the recognition, at least in its earlier decades, that personal political interest had to be subordinated to the national or party interest owes much to these origins. While Kevin Boland's account of Fianna Fáil's early years includes much romanticising, there was no such overstatement when he described how activists and candidates "voted and canvassed exactly as strategists at local and national level directed." In the early days candidates were not even allowed to canvass. In rural areas in particular the constituencies "were divided among the candidates with almost mathematical accuracy and there were no breaches of the plan." The candidates themselves, having almost all been comrades in arms, worked as a team. In support of this contention Boland instanced Co. Kerry, that most republican of counties, where the original seven-seat constituency was divided exactly among the party candidates, the organisation and panel of candidates were so disciplined that the supporters voted almost exactly as advised, and when the results were announced the Fianna Fáil candidates always came in in a solid block, with only a small difference between the highest and lowest. In the second election, in 1927, the party took the last four seats in Co. Kerry and came close to taking a fifth, while in 1932 it took the first five seats.[26]

Among the political and organisational innovations adopted almost immediately by Fianna Fáil was the holding of a national church-gate collection throughout the country on a single day each year. Requiring each cumann to present itself at the gates of the church or churches in its area to seek contributions from the ordinary citizenry served as a further, if initially limited, source of funds for the party. More importantly, it generated a significant, visible party activity in each parish, and served as a "catalyst for organisational expansion and consolidation." In those early stages of the introduction of the cumann network, and for many decades afterwards, the returns from the national collection also served as a useful indicator of the party's organisational strength and support in each area. The fact that in 1927 the church-gate collection yielded £2,000 and by the early 1930s had risen to £5,000 was indicative of the early strength of its network and the pace of its development.

Electoral advancement, however, rather than financial or policy contributions from membership, was the imperative behind the construction of the nationwide cumann infrastructure. The party organisation had a distinctive electoral orientation from the outset and it maintained this for the whole of its history. To attract the diminished vote that the third Sinn Féin had been able to command and then improve on it Fianna Fáil not only had to garner support from the plethora of smaller parties and independent republicans but also had to inspire the thousands of activists and voters who had withdrawn from elections since the treaty split to re-engage with the political process.

The four Dáil elections held between 1923 and 1932 saw a "rapid and permanent" increase in turn-out,[27] and simultaneously a rapid rise in Fianna Fáil's support. In the first election of 1927 the party managed to displace Sinn Féin and to hold the "republican" share of the vote that Sinn Féin had secured in 1923. In the second election of that year, by which time the party had entered the Dáil, the polarisation of politics saw Fianna Fáil, along with Cumann na nGaedheal, benefit at the expense of smaller parties. By 1932, however, the party was able to increase its vote even further by intensively mobilising new or returning voters not only in rural areas but also, and perhaps more importantly, in Dublin's working-class districts.

The story of the party's extraordinarily rapid electoral rise in those first five years has to be understood in a series of contexts. The first of these was the dramatic increase in electoral participation; the second was a series of significant political events during this period, the most important of which was Fianna Fáil's entry into the Dáil; and the third was the persisting, and indeed worsening, economic deprivation that the Free State endured and to which the Free State government appeared to many to be indifferent. The essential reason for the establishment of Fianna Fáil was to regroup and rejuvenate the republican forces so that their struggle could be continued within the political institutions of the Free State. However, it also happened that Fianna Fáil was by accident well timed and by design well positioned to capitalise on growing social and economic discontent in the emerging state.

Chapter 3 ∽

OVER THE OATH AND THEN INTO POWER, 1927–32

Fianna Fáil's first Dáil election campaign was already in full swing by the time de Valera returned from the United States in May 1927. In the months before the election was formally called there was an attempt by the IRA to ensure a united republican front between Fianna Fáil and Sinn Féin, but this was unsuccessful.[1]

De Valera had no intention of realigning himself with those who had remained in Sinn Féin: he had moved on from them when he established a new republican party. In the event, both Fianna Fáil and Sinn Féin rejected the IRA proposal for a common abstentionist platform. This worked to Fianna Fáil's benefit, because the IRA increasingly threw its weight behind the new party. As a result, a significant overlap in membership between the two organisations began to develop. As Tim Pat Coogan notes, "even during the campaign, in particularly Republican parts of the country such as Clare, Kerry and Tipperary (but by no means confined to these areas) Fianna Fáil Cumainn by day drilled as IRA columns by night."[2]

In the campaign, de Valera's election speeches and the party's canvass generally emphasised its promises to abolish the oath of allegiance, to withhold the land annuities, and to introduce an extensive range of protective tariffs. Fianna Fáil emphasised its promise to withhold the payment of land annuities to the British government, though it was quieter about its intention to continue to require these payments from the relevant farmers.

Just as they had done while standing as Sinn Féin candidates in the previous election, de Valera and his colleagues maintained their policy of not taking their seats in Dáil Éireann until the requirement to swear an oath of allegiance to the British monarch had been abolished. But now, as Fianna Fáil, they presented this as a tactical rather than a principled stance. Fianna Fáil took out full-page advertisements in the *Irish Independent* and regional newspapers headed "Fianna Fáil is going in"—a campaign slogan that left sufficient ambiguity on this defining question. As one historian has pointed out, "there is no doubt that many thousands of electors voted for Fianna Fáil in the belief [that] they would take their seats, Oath or no Oath."[3]

Cumann na nGaedheal campaigned on its performance in office over the previous four years and relied "on loose associations of prominent citizens to get out the vote in each constituency."[4]

Such had been the launching of its organisation that even by this stage Fianna Fáil was in a position to put up 87 candidates for the 153 Dáil seats, contesting every constituency except the universities and North Cork. The party won 26 per cent of the first-preference vote and 44 seats. Cumann na nGaedheal won 46 seats, the Labour Party 22, independents 22, the Farmers' Party 11, and the National League (the remnants of the Irish Party, led by William Redmond), 8 seats.

Although less than fourteen months old, Fianna Fáil had received only 1 per cent less of the first-preference vote and the same number of seats that Sinn Féin had won at the previous election in 1923. Forty-four seats was no mean achievement in the circumstances. Cumann na nGaedheal lost 100,000 first-preference votes, a fall of 11 percentage points, and sixteen seats.

The extent to which Fianna Fáil had displaced its parent party was reflected in the fact that Sinn Féin could manage to nominate only fifteen candidates and polled 3.6 per cent of the vote to win only five seats. Within two years of the June 1927 election Sinn Féin had effectually collapsed. By the time of its 1929 ard-fheis it had only seventy-one branches in the Free State, and its funds after expenses were officially reported to be £3. Sinn Féin would not be an electoral force of any significance again until the 1950s and even then would only be a marginal party.

When the new Dáil assembled, on 23 June 1927, de Valera and the other Fianna Fáil deputies presented themselves at Leinster House but, predictably, were denied access to the Dáil chamber because they had not taken the oath of allegiance. Tim Pat Coogan paints a vivid picture of these events.

> It was a dramatic scene: a large contingent of Gardaí kept back the excited crowd and the excitement in the air was almost a tangible thing. The Gardaí cleared a passage for de Valera. He was armed, not with a weapon, but with a legal opinion prepared by three eminent lawyers, which proved to their satisfaction that he could not be excluded because of not taking the oath. But it was not to the satisfaction of the officiating clerk, Colm Ó Murchadha ... although de Valera pressed the case with his usual forcefulness. The clerk had the doors to the chamber locked and, after some ritual expostulation, de Valera withdrew.[5]

That evening the Fianna Fáil Ard-Chomhairle agreed to a legal action to be initiated by Lemass and O'Kelly against their exclusion. At the same time, at a rally in College Green, Dublin, de Valera announced that Fianna Fáil would force a constitutional referendum on the oath. He launched a campaign to gather signatures calling for this issue to be put to the people in a referendum. This was clever politics. Under article 48 of the Constitution of the Irish Free State, if a petition on an issue was signed by 75,000 electors the government was obliged to hold a referendum. Had such a referendum ever been held, the result would have been a "foregone conclusion," and would have put the Cosgrave government in "a highly awkward position."[6]

On this issue, de Valera sought to make political capital at Cumann na nGaedheal's expense. T. Ryle Dwyer observes:

> De Valera contended that the Cosgrave government was deliberately retaining the oath as a political means of ensuring that conscientious Republicans would not enter the Dáil. In ancient times the walls of Bandon bore the inscription, "Beggar, Jew, atheist may enter here but not a papist." Now, he said, the authorities of the Free State were essentially inscribing their own slogan over government buildings: "Unionist, Orangeman, anarchist may enter here, but not a Republican."[7]

The signatures campaign was also good for party morale and gave a focus to cumann activity in the months immediately following the election; but, as the Cosgrave government still held the power to amend the Free State Constitution by simple parliamentary majority, it was unlikely to allow such a referendum to occur. The reality therefore was that, notwithstanding the electoral success of their new organisation, the Fianna Fáil deputies "laboured under the same handicap which de Valera had feared would asphyxiate Sinn Féin, it was still an abstentionist party."[8]

Getting out of this abstentionist rut was going to require considerable political skill and dexterity on the part of de Valera and his colleagues. It is likely that it would have happened anyway at some point in the following few years, but within three weeks of the election in June 1927 events took a turn that created the circumstances for Fianna Fáil deputies to enter the Dáil and take their seats. This occurred against a background of the highest tensions in the country since the Civil War.

On 10 July 1927 the Minister for Justice and Vice-President of the Executive Council (the government of the Irish Free State), Kevin O'Higgins, was shot and wounded as he walked to mass near his home in Booterstown, Co. Dublin. He died that night. His killing was probably the work of maverick republican gunmen, although suspicions endure that one of the assassins was Timothy Coughlan, who was also a member of Fianna Fáil. Coughlan's possible involvement did not emerge until decades later. There is no doubt de Valera was shocked by the killing and he strongly criticised O'Higgins's murder. "It is the duty of every citizen to set his face sternly against anything of this kind. It is a crime that cuts at the root of representative government, and no one who realises what the crime means can do otherwise than deplore and condemn it."[9]

The Cosgrave government, understandably traumatised by the assassination, reacted with a series of legislative measures required, as they saw it, to protect the institutions of the state from further violent sedition but that also forced de Valera and his colleagues to choose between going into the Dáil and leaving politics altogether.

Firstly, the Free State government introduced a more draconian Public Safety Act, the provisions of which were directed primarily at the IRA. Secondly, it proposed an Electoral (Amendment) Bill, the effect of which was to require all Dáil candidates to sign an affidavit before nomination in which they agreed to take the oath of allegiance within two months of election or forfeit their seat. This was accompanied by a constitutional amendment removing the petition mechanism that Fianna Fáil had hoped to employ in its campaign against the oath.

The pressure on Fianna Fáil to comply with the oath requirement and enter the Dáil had been intense even before these measures forced its hand. The renowned Tipperary IRA commander Dan Breen, who as a Dáil deputy had split from Sinn Féin to join Fianna Fáil in April 1926, resigned from the new party in January 1927, signed the oath, and took his seat. When this new electoral legislation was announced another Fianna Fáil deputy, Patrick Belton, followed Breen's course, signing the oath and gaining access to the chamber on 27 July 1927.

Publicly de Valera denounced Belton and the proposed legislation and reiterated the party's position that "under no circumstances whatever" would it subscribe to the oath of allegiance. "If Mr. Cosgrave's new legislation goes through," he declared, "the effort Fianna Fáil has been making to secure national unity will undoubtedly be frustrated. Mr. Cosgrave's aim apparently is to secure that result and force us to retire. Be it so."[10]

Privately, however, during the intense weeks between the announcement of the measures in the wake of the O'Higgins assassination and the point of their formal passage through the Dáil and Seanad, Fianna Fáil's parliamentarians and its Ard-Chomhairle deliberated on whether or not the party's deputies should or could take the oath. Lemass warned that other Fianna Fáil deputies might take the same course of action as Belton and that the party would become a spent force.[11] De Valera, finding himself "torn between rival principles,"[12] privately consulted political, legal and even theological advisers, both at home and abroad. In reality there was always going to be only one outcome to these tortured deliberations. As de Valera would later admit, taking the oath was "the only alternative to resigning ourselves to gradual extinction as a political force."[13] Having led the breakaway from Sinn Féin in order to avoid the political wilderness of principled abstention, de Valera and his lieutenants were not now, after sixteen months of organisational and electoral effort, going to retreat to the sidelines of political participation in the Free State.

By 5 August it was clear that within the parliamentary party the ground was shifting. At a meeting of deputies that evening the minute-takers noted that a discussion had taken place on "the present situation, the future prospects, the feeling in the country, the question of whether our commitments were such that they precluded us even in the present emergency from deviating from our pledges with respect to non subscription to the Free State formula for entry into the Free State Parliament."[14] A sub-committee of de Valera, MacEntee, O'Kelly, Lemass, Boland and Aiken was established to explore the issue further.

On 9 August, de Valera put the choice facing the party in stark terms to the Ard-Chomhairle. There was, he emphasised, "no alternative between giving up political action and entry into the Free State Dáil." He obtained an overwhelming majority for a shift in policy when the Ard-Chomhairle adopted a resolution, by 44 votes to 7, that the elected deputies of the party as a body would "be given a free hand in the matter of entering Dáil Éireann."

The parliamentary party met the following evening and, after a discussion that concluded about midnight, exercised that free hand as expected when forty-three of them signed a declaration that included the following:

> It has . . . been repeatedly stated, and it is not uncommonly believed, that the required declaration is not an oath; that the signing of it implies no contractual obligation, and that it has no binding significance in conscience or in law; that, in short, it is merely an empty political formula which deputies could conscientiously sign without becoming involved, or without involving the nation, in obligations of loyalty to the English Crown . . .
>
> The Fianna Fáil deputies here give public notice that they purpose [sic] to regard the declaration as an empty formality, and repeat that their only allegiance is to the Irish nation, and that it will be given to no other power or authority.

The procedural requirements on deputies in assenting to the oath were not, of themselves, particularly onerous. Taking the oath was not the hand-raising or Bible-swearing event many may have assumed: in fact the procedure had always been simply that before taking their seats deputies were required to attend at the office of the Clerk of the Dáil and sign the appropriate ledger, on a line under the text of the oath, before they could be allowed take their seats.

On 11 August 1927 de Valera, after what his authorised biographers tell us was a sleepless night caused by a "nightmarish crisis of conscience," led his colleagues into Leinster House. In groups of three they entered the office of the Clerk of the Dáil, signed where required, and gained admittance to the Dáil chamber. They did so with little room for political manoeuvre. However, they were reminded by critics from the Free State establishment and from Sinn Féin that, although they now professed it an empty formula, they and many of their colleagues on the republican side had only four years previously fought, killed and died in a bitter civil war in large part owing to their opposition to symbols such as the oath.

De Valera, accompanied in the first trio by James Ryan and Frank Aiken, noticed a Bible face down on the table near where he was required to sign. He closed it, moved it out of sight to a couch on the other side of the room, and addressed the Clerk of the Dáil with a prepared statement.

I want you to understand that I am not taking any oath nor giving any promise of faithfulness to the King of England or to any power outside of Ireland. I am putting my name here merely as a formality to get the permission necessary to enter amongst the other teachtaí that were elected by the people of Ireland, and I want you to know that no other meaning is to be attached to it.

Having thus unburdened himself, de Valera signed on the required line. Thus, as Joseph Lee memorably if disparagingly puts it, "seeing no oath, hearing no oath, speaking no oath, signing no oath, the Soldiers of Destiny shuffled into Dáil Éireann."[15]

While he was steadfast in his own belief that he had not signed any oath, de Valera nevertheless "felt deeply the humiliation of the situation."[16] He felt also the boon it would give his enemies. He signed the oath, he later stated, realising "its baleful significance and the full realisation of the triumphant shout with which the British propagandists in every part of the world, and every enemy of Irish independence would hail this token of ours."[17] He could comfort himself with one thought: with Fianna Fáil in the chamber there would be a majority or near-majority in favour of removing the oath. The leader of the Labour Party, Thomas Johnson, and the leader of the National League, William Redmond, had also made a commitment to its abolition.

The events of 11 August 1927 were obviously significant in the life of the nascent Irish political system. Forty years later Prof. T. Desmond Williams described Fianna Fáil's subscribing to the oath as a great turning-point in the history of Irish parliamentary government.[18] In 1970 de Valera's biographers, Longford and O'Neill, argued that his decision to bring his deputies into the Dáil, "however one interprets it and assesses it, made it certain that parliamentary democracy would prevail." More recently the political scientist Peter Mair viewed it as arguably the most crucial single event in creating the party system as it exists today.[19]

While agreeing on the event's significance, historians remain unclear about whether the outcome was that intended by the Free State government. There is still debate about whether Cosgrave acted "out of panic or calculation" in introducing the legislation and whether forcing Fianna Fáil into Dáil Éireann or out of politics altogether was his government's objective at the time. In a contribution to the debate on this point Ciara Meehan, in her recent study of Cosgrave's party, mentions that Cosgrave publicly welcomed Fianna Fáil's move into the realm of constitutional politics, heralding it as "the best thing that has happened during the last five years." However, she also points to informed suggestions that when told that Fianna Fáil was taking the oath Cosgrave reacted with shock. For her own part she concludes (although she sounds somewhat unconvinced) that in forcing de Valera's hand on signing the oath "it appears . . . that the Cumann na nGaedheal acted selflessly and in the interests of the state . . ."[20] It can equally be argued that the Electoral (Amendment) Act was designed to destroy the fledgling

supported by Fianna Fáil, the National League, and Breen and
not been for a number of unrelated factors—a decision by
not to call one of its deputies back from abroad, a b
National League, and the curious absence of another N
John Jinks of Sligo, at the time of the vote—the gove
defeated and an alternative government, probably
supported by Fianna Fáil, might have taken p
official biographers "there was no question
pating in the alternative government, b
de Valera had received he was willing t
and National League in office."22
A few days after surviving t
Comhairle's casting vote, Cosg
with such a slim majority, di
Cumann na nGaedheal h
seats held by O'Higgin
public anxiety in the
electoral benefit o
that de Valera'
resources to
time cam
In fa
electi
pa

The 1927 ard-fheis did endorse the
entering the Dáil, but by that stage it was a *fait* accompli.
pertinently, Ó Beacháin notes that,

> having devoted months of research and acres of paper to demonstrating
> that there was no possible means whereby a Fianna Fáil deputy could
> subscribe to the oath while simultaneously retaining their political
> integrity—not to mention their soul—the intellectual resources of
> Fianna Fáil were again employed to trawl afresh through their sources
> and to discover arguments previously thought inapplicable.[21]

Not for the last time, the party's leadership had made a fundamental shift
in policy without an ard-fheis decision or any real consultation with the
membership. Nor would it be the final occasion on which pressing practical
and political considerations would prompt the party leadership to take a
decision contrary to what was previously stated policy.

The arrival of the forty-three Fianna Fáil deputies in the chamber immediately transformed the parliamentary situation. Within days the Labour Party
put down a motion of no confidence in the Cosgrave government, which was

Belton. Had it
the Labour Party
reakaway from the
tional League deputy,
rnment would have been
led by the Labour Party but
wer. According to de Valera's
of Fianna Fáil actually partici-
t on the basis of the guarantees
keep a coalition of the Labour Party

is no-confidence motion by the Ceann
ve, understandably nervous about proceeding
solved the Dáil. He did so with some confidence.
d won two by-elections in late August, to fill the
and Markievicz; so Cosgrave was entitled to feel that
wake of the O'Higgins assassination would accrue to the
his party. He and his colleagues may also have assumed
new party could not have the organisational or financial
ontest two Dáil elections in three months. After a short, harvest-
aign, polling was held on 15 September.
t it was the smaller parties that were squeezed by the demands of two
on campaigns in such quick succession. With Fianna Fáil now in
liamentary opposition, the choice crystallised into one between the two
larger parties. Cumann na nGaedheal regained much of the ground lost in the
June election, increasing its vote from 27 to 38 per cent and the number of its
seats to 62. Fianna Fáil increased the number of its seats from 44 to 57. This
improved performance was mainly at the expense of the party's potential
allies, but, notwithstanding the fact that Fianna Fáil would now be a force in
the voting lobbies, Cosgrave would remain in government. His party entered
a formal arrangement with the Farmers' Party and some of the independents,
which gave it a combined majority comfortable enough to keep it in government for a full five-year term.

Some have contended that Fianna Fáil was fortunate not to have gained
power in 1927. Writing half a century later, Vincent Browne, with typical
bluntness, argued that "had the party come to office in 1927 either on its
own or in coalition with Labour its ignorance of parliamentary procedure,
unsophisticated knowledge of the details of economic and social policies and
its overall unrefined intellectual and administrative abilities could only have
spelt disaster for it, then and maybe for quite a while afterwards."[23]

Indeed Lemass himself later remarked that he and his colleagues were "a
pretty raw lot"[24] when they entered the Dáil in 1927; but the notion of the
parliamentary party needing to serve an apprenticeship does something of an
injustice to the array of parliamentary, administrative and intellectual abilities
within its ranks at that time. Until 1922 de Valera, O'Kelly and MacEntee, for

example, had had career paths in the independence movement similar to, and indeed at a more senior level than, those of many of the Free State ministers; and, while inexperienced in parliamentary affairs, Lemass and his younger colleagues had already shown themselves to be impressive political talents.

Whether or not it was better off in opposition, Fianna Fáil certainly put the next five years to good use. As well as developing their expertise in parliamentary procedure, its leadership set out to further expand and organise the party machinery, securing its financial base and, perhaps most significantly of all, establishing its own press organ.

Again, Lemass and Boland played leading roles on the organisational front. Then, as now, the level of official registration at head office was only one of the indicators of the strength of the party's organisation, but on this measurement it appears that there was first a dip, and then a resurgence, in cumann activity during this period. After the initial excitement of preparing for, and campaigning in, the 1927 elections, the level of cumann registrations became less reliable. By 1928 the number of registered cumainn had declined to 1,033, and by 1929 the number "notified to the Ard Fheis" had fallen to 703, though some of these reductions were explained by the honorary secretaries at the 1928 ard-fheis as being due to amalgamations in some areas.[25]

A sustained organisational drive was maintained, however, and even though in 1930 the party took the risky step of imposing a registration fee for cumainn, by 1932 the number of registered cumainn was back up to 1,404.[26]

In addition to the income now flowing from the cumann registration fee and, more significantly, from continuing fund-raising efforts in the United States led by de Valera, Fianna Fáil also consolidated its financial position by more structured approaches to the business community. The extent of support from business in these years was such that Gerry Boland bemoaned the influx of "big subscriptions". In one particular incident, where an apparently unsolicited donation of the then extremely large sum of £500 was received in 1931 from the former Cumann na nGaedheal supporter Joe McGrath, Boland sought to have it returned, only to be overruled by the Ard-Chomhairle on the insistence of the ever-practical Lemass.[27] The personal papers left by Seán MacEntee, one of the party's first honorary treasurers, include copies of correspondence relating to fund-raising appeals and receipts issued to numerous wealthy business people who donated to Fianna Fáil in the 1930s.[28]

Financial contributions from the United States were also to be central to the party's most significant extra-parliamentary activity of this period, the establishment of the *Irish Press* in the summer of 1931. For de Valera, the idea of a daily newspaper that would be the organ of his party and serve as a counterweight to the anti-republican bias in the *Irish Independent* and *Irish Times* had long been a consuming passion. This period in opposition provided him with the opportunity to achieve it. In December 1927 he visited the United States for six weeks and managed to raise $80,000 for a new national newspaper.[29] He returned for a further six-month fund-raising trip in November 1929. The fund-raising for the project was structured in such a way that shares to the value of £200,000 were issued, half in the Free State and half in the United States.

After a summer of detailed planning directly overseen by de Valera himself, the first editions of the paper rolled off the presses early in the morning of 5 September 1931. Edited by Frank Gallagher, the *Irish Press* went on to have the second-largest circulation in the country, supplemented in the late 1950s by the *Sunday Press* and *Evening Press*. While the title-piece of the new daily paper promised "The truth in the news," it was, at least in this early phase, a purely partisan publication. Its news pages slavishly carried the pronouncements of de Valera and other leading party figures and covered all national events from the party's viewpoint, and its editorials unapologetically propagated the Fianna Fáil message. However, that was only part of the story: the paper also succeeded because of its popular appeal and the accessibility of its editorial style.

It is difficult to overstate the political impact of this new journalistic venture. While a national radio station had been established in 1926, it would be decades before it would have any substantial coverage of political affairs, and at this time, more than three decades before the establishment of a national television channel, newspapers provided the dominant coverage of politics. By establishing its own daily newspaper Fianna Fáil dramatically enhanced its capacity in the political arena. The *Irish Press* became a central component in the electoral emergence of the party. In the short term it did indeed, as Stephen Collins suggests, provide a "powerful battering ram for Fianna Fáil and helped to sour the atmosphere for an already beleaguered government."[30] For the more medium term the assessment of the historian Joseph Lee is that the *Irish Press* played an important part in the Fianna Fáil electoral victories, "not only by confirming the convictions of the faithful but also by converting previous non voters or even unbelievers." Indeed Lee argues that the increase in electoral turn-out from 69 per cent in September 1927 to 77 per cent in 1932 and to 81 per cent in 1933 probably owed a good deal to the popular enthusiasm generated by the *Irish Press*.

In the 1970s Longford and O'Neill characterised the establishment of the *Irish Press* as de Valera's "outstanding contribution to the growth of his own party." That assessment has stood the test of time, notwithstanding the paper's later demise. However, the *Irish Press* and, in particular, its complex and peculiar ownership arrangements were to be the subject of much controversy for de Valera and his family in later decades. As trustee and representative of the American company, Irish Press Incorporated, on the board of directors, de Valera had a controlling interest. Of itself this would not have been controversial were it not for the fact that in the late 1950s he was succeeded as controlling director and editor in chief by his son Vivion de Valera, who was in turn succeeded in 1982 by his own son, Dr Éamon de Valera.

During his long career de Valera always maintained that he "never got one penny"[31] out of the *Irish Press*, but he was deeply conscious of its political value. For this reason he even commented in the paper's formative years that if ever it came to a choice between leading the party and running the paper he believed he would go with the paper.[32]

In his memoir, Joseph Connolly, a member of the first Fianna Fáil government, wrote that for de Valera the day the *Irish Press* was launched was "probably the most memorable date in his diary next to Easter Monday, 1916. The new paper gave an added impetus to the already considerable growth of Fianna Fáil all over the country . . . and as such was zealous in spreading the gospel of Fianna Fáil."[33]

During this period de Valera and his senior colleagues not only had their organisational work load but as sitting deputies had to find time to make their contribution to parliamentary opposition. De Valera himself had been the dominant personality in the pre-treaty Dáil, and he found it easy to take up parliamentary duties again, although for much of this Dáil term he was often absent, either on fund-raising activities in the United States or on *Irish Press* and party political duties at home.

In early 1929 he was also absent for a month because of imprisonment. As well as being a member of Dáil Éireann, de Valera had been elected to the Northern Ireland Parliament for South Down, although he never took his seat there. His visits to Northern Ireland were rare, as he was the subject of an exclusion order dating from 1924. In February 1929 he accepted an invitation to address a cultural event organised jointly by the GAA and the Gaelic League, and he was arrested by members of the Royal Ulster Constabulary as he proceeded towards Belfast. He was sentenced to a month's imprisonment for crossing the border in contravention of an exclusion order. Predictably, this incident caused outrage south of the border, and a protest meeting in Leinster House was chaired by the leader of the Labour Party, Thomas Johnson.

De Valera's imprisonment was a valuable propaganda coup for Fianna Fáil, which used it to remind the public of its anti-partition credentials. In response to de Valera's arrest Seán MacEntee, himself a Belfast man, was quick to remind the public that Fianna Fáil was working for the day that the republican flag would fly over Stormont, and he denounced partition in virulent terms. "Let the grass grow on the streets of Belfast. Let the mills be silent . . . The people who built up Belfast were not Irish but English and Scottish and they would not be Irish until the people of the South showed them they were stronger than they."[34]

Although they participated with some gusto in the parliamentary exchanges in Dáil Éireann, the Fianna Fáil deputies were still hostile to the Free State institutions and indeed towards Free State politicians. All members of Fianna Fáil were prohibited by resolutions of the ard-fheis from attending social functions organised by the Free State government. It was a ban that had many curious implications. It meant, for example, that Fianna Fáil members, though they attended the religious ceremony welcoming the first Papal Nuncio (diplomatic representative of the Vatican) in 1929, could not attend the state dinner given in his honour. It also meant that Margaret Pearse, then a Fianna Fáil deputy, could not accept an invitation to the reopening of the

renovated GPO. The extent of Civil War bitterness during this period is evident
in a motion passed by the Fianna Fáil parliamentary party in November 1928
that laid down the rule that members "should not conduct any business with
Cumann na nGaedheal Ministers or deputies in the bar or restaurant and that
fraternisation under any circumstances be prohibited."[35]

As leader of the opposition, de Valera used these years to attack the
government on a range of economic and constitutional issues, with a
particular emphasis on efforts to abolish the oath of allegiance by legislation
and on the controversy surrounding the payment of land annuities.

After the September 1927 election Fianna Fáil in the Dáil formed
committees to shadow the various government departments. In early 1928 the
chairmanships of these committees were reshuffled into a line-up that was to
reflect the portfolios allocated when the party later came to power. Seán
MacEntee was chairman of the Finance Committee, James Ryan of
Agriculture, Frank Aiken of Defence and Lemass of Industry and Commerce.
It was during this period that Lemass established his position as the party's
principal spokesperson on economic affairs, a role that he was to "consolidate
with ease" when Fianna Fáil entered government. Lemass was not the only
spokesperson in this area, however, as de Valera himself, MacEntee, James
Ryan and the Cork businessman and TD Hugo Flinn were also frequent
contributors in social and economic debates. Even MacEntee's biographer
accepts that, "because Lemass generally took up the argument relating to most
socio-economic issues, MacEntee, more often than not had to defer to his
younger colleague."[36]

Lemass's most famous and most often cited Dáil contribution from these
years was not on the economy but on Fianna Fáil's attitude to the Free State
institutions themselves. Speaking during a Dáil debate in November 1928 on
a private member's motion by P. J. Ruttledge proposing the establishment of
a select committee to, among other things, review the cases of all prisoners,
Lemass described Fianna Fáil as a "slightly constitutional party". The term
passed quickly into the popular political lexicon and was often thrown back
at him by opponents in charged political debate. Indeed it is still frequently
employed by historians seeking a basis on which to analyse the true character
of Fianna Fáil and its commitment to democratic politics in this period. It
benefits, therefore, from some contextualisation.

Lemass's first biographer, Brian Farrell, was careful to mine the Dáil
transcripts before coming to a view on the precise meaning and import of the
"slightly constitutional" characterisation. During the particular debate the
Labour Party deputy William Davin had wondered aloud what the "real
meaning of constitutional activity as interpreted by Fianna Fáil was." He
provoked Lemass to state:

> I think it would be right to inform Deputy Davin that Fianna Fáil is a
> slightly constitutional party. We are perhaps open to the definition of a
> constitutional party, but before anything we are a Republican party. We

have adopted the method of political agitation to achieve our end, because we believe, in the present circumstances, that method is best in the interests of the nation and of the republican movement, and for no other reason.

Another Labour Party deputy, T. J. O'Connell, intervened to say, "It took you five years to make up your mind," a reference to the period from the Anglo-Irish Treaty to the taking of the oath. Lemass responded:

Five years ago the methods we adopted were not the methods we have adopted now. Five years ago we were on the defensive, and perhaps in time we may recoup our strength sufficiently to go on the offensive. Our object is to establish a republican government in Ireland. If that can be done by the present methods we have, we will be very pleased, but if not we would not confine ourselves to them.[37]

While, as Farrell comments, Lemass's remark certainly suggests a "less than wholehearted commitment to democratic process and reflected a pragmatic willingness to go on the offensive and use force to achieve political aims," he also suggests that allowance has to be made for the fact that Lemass, by his own admission, was an impatient and, at this time, inexperienced parliamentarian who on this particular occasion, "provoked into saying more than he meant, had blurted out some of the residual frustration of a defeated armed militancy which at a considered level he had already abandoned."[38]

Lemass's remark and its context touch on an ambiguity that surrounded the very purpose of the Fianna Fáil project. Lemass, de Valera and their colleagues broke from Sinn Féin in part because they were turning their back on violence as a means of achieving their political aim of a more independent and ultimately united Ireland, but it can be argued that they did not do so out of any irreversible conversion to purely political means. De Valera had not been a combatant in the Civil War, but a large number of his leadership in Fianna Fáil, including Lemass, MacEntee and Aiken, had been. De Valera had endorsed—some historians say provoked—that violent confrontation to the authority of the Free State government. These men switched to non-violent political actions out of expediency rather than any abhorrence of violent resistance to the Free State government or even the very existence of the Free State as a political entity. This attitude was clearly set out in the party's newspaper, the *Nation*, in February 1929, which stated:

We entered a fake parliament which we believed in our hearts to be illegitimate and we still believe it; and we faced a junta there which we did not regard as the rightful Government of this country. We did not respect, nor do we now, such a Government or such a Parliament . . . Our presence in the "Dáil" of usurpers is sheer expedience, nothing else.[39]

De Valera and his colleagues were driven into politics by military defeat in the Civil War. Their immediate electoral successes in the political realm under the new Fianna Fáil banner, and the fact that within five years they would come to power in the Free State institutions themselves, meant that these men did not have to revisit the question of whether a resort to violence might again be justified or necessitated in more opportune times.

Fianna Fáil's founding fathers collectively and deliberately opted for non-violent political action in the 26 counties, although they never hesitated to marshal the rhetoric of violent republican heritage in furtherance of their political advance. As Lemass's most recent biographer, Tom Garvin, has noted, while also discussing the famous "slightly constitutional" remark,

> for Fianna Fáil to work [Lemass] and his colleagues were going to have to walk a fine line between Republican radicalism and the demands of civil society, a society that was quietly but relentlessly pushing the Republicans away from the gun and into democratic politics, or "war by other means," to use an Irish inversion of one of Clausewitz's famous quotes.[40]

As the years passed and Fianna Fáil first embedded itself in the Free State institutions and then employed them in government to create a republic in all but name in the 26 counties, de Valera, Lemass and others spoke and acted with even greater clarity to show that they had chosen a constitutional, non-violent path in the South. However, an ambiguity about whether militant action might be appropriate for achieving the party's stated objective of independence for the whole of Ireland if the opportunity arose remained and was implied in much of the rhetoric. De Valera, for example, would warn in 1930 that

> as long as a British soldier remains in Ireland . . . as long as our country is partitioned, no Irishman can say that this is the final settlement of Ireland's claim to nationhood . . . Every Irishman worthy of the name, no matter where he may be, lives in the hope that there will be a Battle of Clontarf for the British as there was for the Danes.

However, for the most part de Valera and Lemass said unequivocally that Ireland could not be united through violence. A party advertisement from 1927, for example, had made this clear.

> What Fianna Fáil Does Not Stand For: Attacking the North East: Fianna Fáil does not stand for attacking 'Ulster'. It will accept EXISTING REALITIES, but will work resolutely to bring Partition to an end.[41]

These clear statements did not stop some in the party, even at its most senior levels, from wanting to, or feeling they were being encouraged to, believe that non-constitutional methods could be used to achieve reunification. It was an ambiguity that was to contribute to the crisis that would nearly tear Fianna Fáil asunder more than forty years later when violence erupted in Northern Ireland.

Chapter 4 ∾

FIRST TERMS IN GOVERNMENT, 1932–9

In the 1932 general election the voters were presented with the starkest contrast in policy options ever proffered by the two main parties in an Irish election campaign.

William Cosgrave dissolved the Dáil on 29 January 1932, announcing that an election would be held on 16 February. He is said to have opted for an earlier date than expected in order to avoid politicising the Eucharistic Congress, which was to be held in Dublin in June that year. On top of this, the budgetary outlook for 1932 was very poor, and Cosgrave may well have calculated that it would be more electorally beneficial to cut and run than to have to implement further spending reductions and taxes.

While they had put some thought into the timing of the election, Cosgrave and his colleagues showed little sign of having put much thought into how they would fight the election campaign. There was no political benefit to the outgoing Cumann na nGaedheal government in standing on its economic record. It had governed in very difficult economic times. The global economic crisis triggered by the 1929 Wall Street crash affected Ireland particularly harshly from 1931 onwards. Those years were disastrous ones for agriculture, the dominant industry, owing to a collapse in bacon, dairy, cattle and sheep prices. From 1929 to 1931 the value of agricultural exports fell by £2½ million.[1]

In a situation where the public finances were under severe pressure, Cosgrave's Minister for Finance, Ernest Blythe, opted for fiscal rectitude rather than a populist approach. Tim Pat Coogan argues that

> de Valera operated in an economic climate ever more favourable to an Opposition leader. Blythe's policies also resulted in a series of electoral lunacies including cuts in pensions for the elderly and the blind. The effects of these were added to by announcements in the run-up to the election that the Government intended to effect economies by cutting the pay of both police and teachers. In addition, married women were to be rendered ineligible to be teachers. With enemies like these, de Valera hardly needed friends.[2]

Not only was Cumann na nGaedheal unable to stand on its economic record but, wedded as it was to *laissez-faire* economic orthodoxy, it could not offer any positive economic programme for the future. It became the party of the austere status quo. Cosgrave himself defined its dilemma: "It was one of the privileges of the opposition that they should table the most attractive and costly programmes and it was one of the disadvantages of the government that they must provide the means or answer for not providing the means."[3]

It was hardly surprising, therefore, that Cumann na nGaedheal devoted only one of the fourteen chapters in its programme for the 1932 election to social and economic policy.[4] Instead the outgoing government's campaign concentrated almost exclusively on law-and-order concerns and on the instability that, as Cumann na nGaedheal saw it, would follow a Fianna Fáil victory. It also launched an energetic "red scare" against de Valera and his party.

On the first evening of the election campaign, at a Cumann na nGaedheal rally in the Mansion House, Cosgrave himself set the tone when he warned that a Fianna Fáil victory would turn Ireland into "a field for the cultivation of those doctrines of materialism and Communism which can so effectively poison the wells of religion and national traditions." One poster warned voters: "The shadow of a gunman—Keep it from your home." Another depicted a red flag partially covering the Tricolour with the caption "We want no Reds here. Keep their colours off your flag." A prominent newspaper advertisement warned: "The gunmen are voting for Fianna Fail—The communists are voting for Fianna Fail." As T. Ryle Dwyer has pointed out, in the emotional atmosphere of the campaign it was not long before de Valera was accused of being at best "a weak Kerensky" who would be toppled by communists in Fianna Fáil once the party came to power.[5]

The government campaign also derided de Valera and his party for their change of mind on the oath of allegiance. The most famous Cumann na nGaedheal poster of this campaign was headlined: "Devvy's Circus, absolutely the greatest road show in Ireland." It depicted "Senor de Valera, World Famous Illusionist, Oath Swallower and Escapologist" and invited voters to see "his renowned act escaping from the strait jacket of the Republic," along with "Frank F. Aiken, fearsome fire eater. Shaunty O'Kelly, the man in dress clothes. Monsieur Lemass, famous tight rope performer, see him cross from the Treaty to the Republic every night. Performing frogs, champion croakers, marvellous trained sheep."[6]

Cosgrave and his colleagues also appeared passive on the other central issue in the election, that of sovereignty. They argued that the Free State now enjoyed all the freedom it needed, not least because of the gradual enlargement of the notion of dominion status, which they had helped to negotiate within the British Commonwealth, culminating with the Statute of Westminster (1931). Cumann na nGaedheal warned that the terms of the Anglo-Irish Treaty could not and should not be repudiated: to do so would be a breach of national honour. Cosgrave was caught, Tim Pat Coogan has argued, in the

honourable, but weak, position of attempting to amend the Treaty by negotiation, for which he needed British co-operation—always an unreliable prospect for Irish moderates. He had to mute his quite substantive triumphs in Anglo-Irish relations, lest he give aid and comfort to both British Conservatives and Irish Republican critics. His defence of the constitutional position, which appealed to Unionist elements, provided de Valera with the opportunity for attacking him as being pro-Unionist. De Valera was in the far stronger position of threatening unilateral action against the ancient enemy.[7]

In contrast to Cumann na nGaedheal, Fianna Fáil put forward a radical policy platform that promised sweeping constitutional change and dramatic economic intervention. It published a series of detailed policy statements, all of which placed at least as much emphasis on tackling unemployment as they did on the constitutional question. The party sought an explicit mandate to remove the oath of allegiance, to retain the land annuities and to implement a full-bodied policy of protectionism. It promised to reduce unemployment, to develop the natural resources of the country and to eliminate waste in public administration. In Fianna Fáil advertisements and speeches prominence was given to a promise that it would "never cease to protest against the iniquity of partition" and "by every peaceful means strive to bring it to an end." It also promised to engage in a "systematic effort" to preserve the Irish language and to make it again the spoken language of the people. However, it gave equal prominence to more practical initiatives, including a commitment to introduce a national housing scheme so as to provide dwellings for working-class tenants at reasonable rents, legislation to enable farm labourers to become owners of their cottages and an intensification of land redistribution by breaking up larger farms.

Fianna Fáil's campaign also contained a large dollop of populist politics. A consistent theme of Fianna Fáil in opposition was attacking the salaries paid to government ministers. One election poster urged voters to "vote for the Fianna Fáil Candidates and End this Colossal Jobbery!" The party astutely recognised that with the economic recession impinging on many people, a tough stance against "waste and extravagance" would be popular. The Fianna Fáil manifesto promised to scale down higher salaries in the public service "till they are more in keeping with the means of the taxpayer"; it proposed a reduction in the number of deputies, from 153 to 100; and de Valera was putting himself on the side of most voters when he argued that "no man is worth more than a thousand pounds [per year]."[8]

Unlike Cumann na nGaedheal, Fianna Fáil's leadership had been able to spend the previous five years in the detailed development both of its party organisation and of its policy positions. It now also had the electoral firepower of a mass-selling daily newspaper. Seán Lemass was director of elections and he ran a lively campaign, which, like those in 1927, was built around a nationwide tour by de Valera. The Chief led evening rallies in the principal towns of most constituencies. Each of these began with a torchlight procession from the outskirts and ended with an address in the central square. Tim Pat Coogan writes descriptively of these occasions.

De Valera's theatrical flair resulted in some spectacular personal appearances. "The Chief", the star turn of the Fianna Fáil circus, entered some country towns "escorted by a volunteer cavalry, the manes of the horses braided with Republican colours," preceded by fife and drum bands. The sight of de Valera in flowing black cloak, mounted on a white horse, sometimes accompanied by a torchlight procession, made a lasting impact on the Irish political landscape.[9]

Fianna Fáil's campaign had its climax in a 30,000-strong rally in Dublin city centre on the eve of the poll.

The result of the election was to set a pattern that did not change until 2011. It not only propelled Fianna Fáil into power for an unbroken period of sixteen years but within eighteen months precipitated a reconfiguration of the anti-Fianna Fáil political forces into a new political party, Fine Gael ("the Irish family").

Fianna Fáil had put up 104 candidates. It increased its share of the first-preference vote by more than 9 points, to 44 per cent. More significantly, it gained fifteen extra seats and now had 72. Six years after its foundation it was by far the biggest party in the Dáil and only five seats short of an absolute majority. Despite a pre-election merger with the remnants of the National League and some independents, Cumann na nGaedheal had lost 3½ per cent of its national vote (5 per cent if the National League vote is included). It lost ten seats and was left with 57 deputies. Internal divisions and the Fianna Fáil surge had led to a collapse in support for the Labour Party, which won only 7 seats. The Farmers' Party won 3, and there were 14 independents.

When the Dáil resumed on 9 March 1932, tensions were high. Fianna Fáil seemed set to form the new government. It was assured of support from the Labour Party, which had become alienated by the increasing conservatism of Cumann na nGaedheal. A wave of wild rumours swirled around the capital suggesting that Cosgrave and his colleagues would not cede power peacefully, or that there would be an army coup. De Valera was accompanied that afternoon to Leinster House by his son Vivion, who, photographs clearly show, had a revolver in his pocket. Frank Aiken had handed out guns to party colleagues, and James Dillon, who was taking his seat in the Dáil for the first time that day, observed that many Fianna Fáil TDs were "armed to the teeth."[10] There are even suggestions that one Fianna Fáil TD assembled a machine gun in a telephone booth near the door of the Dáil chamber.[11]

Weaponry was unnecessary, however. When it came to selecting the President of the Executive Council, de Valera was elected comfortably. In addition to the votes of the Fianna Fáil and Labour deputies he enjoyed the support of three independents, including James Dillon, son of John Dillon, the last leader of the Irish Party, and himself later a leader of Fine Gael. Dillon told the Dáil that the people had voted for de Valera as their leader and he had acted accordingly.[12]

The first crucial handing over of power took place peacefully and without incident. Ireland had reached a benchmark in democratic consolidation. As

Peter Mair notes, "in the Irish case . . . it was especially crucial, since it involved the former losers in a civil war replacing the former winners. Less than ten years after having being defeated in an armed conflict, the loser was finally coming to political power."[13]

De Valera was clearly conscious of the magnitude of what had occurred. In November 1932, at the first Fianna Fáil ard-fheis following the party's transition to power, he said:

> We came into office . . . to take over an army that had been opposed to us in a civil war, a Civil Service that was built up during ten years of our opponents' regime. We came into office determined to be fair to everybody. The army of our opponents loyally came in as the army of the State and are prepared to serve the State loyally. We took over the police force under similar conditions, and, while here and there there are complaints, still, to the credit of the men in the army, to the credit of the Civic Guards and the Civil Service, the civil services and the forces of the State are prepared to serve elected representatives of the people. That is a great achievement.[14]

It is an achievement for which many historians have been reluctant to give de Valera credit. Mair is one of the more recent commentators to criticise the manner in which credit for the peaceful transition has been doled out to one side only. Most historians, he argues, have applauded the "apparent magnanimity" of Cosgrave and Cumann na nGaedheal in "allowing" the change of government to take place. He instances as examples of this one-sided view Joseph Lee's contention that "nothing so became Cosgrave in office as his manner of leaving it," and Tom Garvin's suggestion that "the adhesion of the bulk of the anti Treaty forces to the institutions of the state in 1927" (by Fianna Fáil's entry into the Dáil) was "an extraordinary triumph for William Cosgrave's statesmanship."

Mair argues that the credit for the peaceful transfer of power and the consolidation of Irish democracy is owed to de Valera at least as much as it is to Cosgrave. Although he had repudiated majority will in the months leading up to the Civil War in 1922, de Valera deserves much credit for his actions in 1932 in taking power by democratic means and in 1933 by calling a democratic election as the means to consolidate his power. It was, Mair emphasises, an extraordinary moment in Irish history.

> Those who had been defeated in a bitter civil war less than a decade before were now in office and had displaced those who defeated them. And once in office they were to proceed to follow all the rules of the game—and more. And all this was to take place in the 1930s when Catholic Europe seemed otherwise to abandon its new-found engagement with democracy. In theory at least this was not what might have been expected.[15]

Once elected President of the Executive Council, de Valera named a government that contained few surprises in either personnel or portfolios. Almost all of those named "bore the marks of battle" and had worked closely with him for at least a decade, some since 1916 or before.[16] Most of them had also shadowed their new departments from the opposition benches.

In addition to the position of President of the Executive Council, de Valera retained to himself the Department of External Affairs. Seán T. O'Kelly was nominated Vice-President of the Executive Council and Minister for Local Government and Public Health. Seán MacEntee became Minister for Finance. Seán Lemass was appointed Minister for Industry and Commerce and James Ryan became Minister for Agriculture. Frank Aiken became Minister for Defence and P. J. Ruttledge became Minister for Lands and Fisheries.

Among the others appointed to government were Thomas Derrig, a former secondary school teacher who became Minister for Education. Derrig had been a member of the first and second Dálaí for Mayo but had been defeated in the 1923 election, returning to the Dáil in 1927 as a Fianna Fáil candidate for Carlow-Kilkenny. The new Minister for Justice was James Geoghegan, a barrister, who had been elected in 1930 in a by-election in Longford-Westmeath. He had formerly been a member of Cumann na nGaedheal, and his appointment to this sensitive portfolio was a signal that the new government would not victimise its opponents.[17] The final member of the government was Joseph Connolly, as Minister for Posts and Telegraphs, who became the first member of the Seanad to be appointed to government.

Gerry Boland was appointed Parliamentary Secretary to the government and chief whip, while Dr Con Ward, a Monaghan deputy, became Parliamentary Secretary to the Minister for Local Government and Public Health.

Anxious to set a reforming tone immediately, the new head of government announced that his own salary would be reduced by £1,000, to £1,500, and that those of other ministers would be reduced by £500, to £1,000. The members of the new government also made it known that they would decline to wear the top hat and frock coat that until then had been the required garb for formal occasions.

As well as these stylistic changes, Fianna Fáil began to implement the more radical elements of its election manifesto with a speed and decisiveness that belied its minority government status, disorienting the political opposition at home and setting the party on a diplomatic and economic collision course with the British Government.

It is worth noting, however, that however radical the approach of the new Fianna Fáil government would be in those areas, it was not a revolutionary government. There was, of course, a change in the personnel at the ministerial level, but, with a handful of exceptions, no changes were made to the holders of other public offices. There was no sacking of judges or army officers. The only change to the Garda Síochána was the dismissal of the Commissioner, Eoin O'Duffy. His sacking was not effected until February 1933, by which time there had been a further election and the dismissal had become inevitable because of O'Duffy's hostility to the Fianna Fáil government. Indeed on 10 March 1932, the day after he took up office, de Valera summoned the heads of the departments to a meeting at which he assured them that there would be no dismissals.

The fact that after 1932 a complete continuity of public administration was provided by the same civil service, army and police as had served Cumann na nGaedheal during and since the Civil War was the central achievement. The credit for this, Garret FitzGerald has argued, belongs to the public service itself for establishing its political neutrality, to the Cumann na nGaedheal government for taking steps to ensure that the army, in particular, would be loyal to a future Fianna Fáil government, and to de Valera, who effectually "resisted great pressure to purge the army, the police and the administration he had inherited."[18] As Ronan Fanning puts it, de Valera "wanted to bend the machinery of government for his own purposes not to dismantle it."[19]

Constitutional change was de Valera's priority in government. When initially enacted, the Constitution of the Irish Free State provided that it could be amended by legislation alone for a period of eight years and after that only by plebiscite. However, in 1928 the Cosgrave government had extended the period during which it could be amended by legislation to sixteen years. This meant that until 1938 de Valera could change the provisions of the constitution by the simple adoption of a Constitution Amendment Bill by the Dáil and Seanad. He embarked upon this task with a vengeance, stating that his aim was the removal of

> any form or symbol that is out of keeping with Ireland's right as a sovereign nation . . . so that this state that we control may be a republic in fact, and that when the time comes the proclaiming of the Republic may involve no more than a ceremony, the formal confirmation of a status already achieved.[20]

On 23 April 1932 the Constitution (Removal of Oath) Bill was published, although it took another year for it to pass through Leinster House because the opposition delayed it in the Seanad. Over the next two years the position of Governor-General, the King's representative in Ireland, was gradually downgraded. Members of the Fianna Fáil government boycotted functions to which the Governor-General, James MacNeill, had been invited. MacNeill was effectually humiliated into early retirement in October 1932. His replacement, Domhnall Ó Buachalla, a 1916 veteran and unsuccessful Fianna Fáil candidate in the 1932 election, willingly acquiesced in the reduction of the office's status. He operated as Governor-General in name only, continuing to live in his own surburban home rather than the Viceregal Lodge in the Phoenix Park and exercising his constitutional powers only in the manner directed by de Valera's government.

The Free State Seanad persisted in slowing down some of the new government's constitutional changes and so was itself abolished in 1936.

Ultimately, in December 1936, de Valera skilfully used the sudden abdication of King Edward VIII to amend the Constitution of the Irish Free State to delete all mention of the Governor-General, removing the Crown completely from the internal affairs of the state but preserving it as an instrument of external relations. The Executive Authority (External Relations) Act declared that "the diplomatic representatives of Saorstát Éireann in other countries shall be appointed on the authority of the Executive Council" but that "for the purposes of the appointment of diplomatic and consular representatives and the conclusion of international agreements" the King "may, and is hereby authorised to, act on behalf of Saorstát Éireann for the like purposes as and when advised by the Executive Council so to do."

Though some in Fianna Fáil would have preferred de Valera to declare a republic at this point, he believed it was advantageous to maintain a connection with the Commonwealth in order to resolve partition. He told the Dáil: "I do not propose to use this situation to declare a republic for the 26 counties. Our people at any time will have the opportunity of doing that. We are putting no barrier of any sort in the way. They can do it if they want to do it at any time."[21]

Once in power, Fianna Fáil also moved quickly to reverse some of the coercive measures introduced by Cosgrave's government. On the day that de Valera announced his first government two of his ministers, Frank Aiken and James Geoghegan, went to Arbour Hill Military Prison to visit the IRA prisoners. The following day, honouring Fianna Fáil's election pledge, all "political prisoners" were released. On 18 March 1932 the Public Safety Act was suspended (although, interestingly, not repealed), the Military Tribunal was abolished and the ban on the IRA and kindred organisations was lifted. Many of these newly freed IRA activists immediately began public agitation, concentrating on antagonising Cumann na nGaedheal members and disrupting their meetings.

In its most dramatic move, in June 1932 the de Valera government suspended the payment of the land annuities to the British exchequer. In response, the British government published a secret agreement that had been signed by the Cosgrave government in 1923 in which the Irish side undertook to pay all the land annuities and also certain pensions to former members of the Royal Irish Constabulary. De Valera countered that, as this agreement had been kept secret from the Dáil, his government had no obligation to implement it. He made maximum use of the revelation as political capital against Cumann na nGaedheal.

The British government retaliated by imposing a 20 per cent duty on Irish imports to make up the shortfall. The Fianna Fáil government replied in kind, introducing a high tariff on British goods coming into Ireland, and thus began a tariff battle that became known as the Anglo-Irish Economic War.

The Economic War was devastating for the Irish economy, as 96 per cent of exports at the time went to Britain. However, the economic nationalism it engendered, the diversification in agriculture and the acceleration in protectionism to which it gave rise proved politically advantageous to Fianna Fáil. As the political scientist Warner Moss put it, writing while the Economic War was still raging, "the distress caused to agriculture by the Anglo Irish economic war bore chiefly upon the cattle trade. Yet the reduction in the cost of food and the extension of social services won vast numbers of persons to the Government's support."[22]

The shift in agricultural policy, although it had been intensified by the imposition of tariffs on produce going to Britain, was one on which Fianna Fáil had been set in any case. The cattle trade had hitherto dominated agriculture, but now the government introduced a series of incentives towards tillage farming and especially cereal production.

In wider economic policy the new government embarked on a range of counter-cyclical measures, similar to those being adopted in many other countries. As Brian Girvin has noted, "a radical response to the depression, job creation, enhanced welfare provision and state intervention were all features of reformist governments in the United States and Scandinavia during the decade."[23] Indeed Moss, an American, wrote that Ireland in 1933 was "definitely under the control of the youthful champions of the New Deal and the Irish Five Year plan."[24]

On 8 June 1932 the new Minister for Industry and Commerce, Seán Lemass, launched his first major legislative initiative, the Control of Manufactures Bill, and it had passed both Dáil and Seanad by the end of October. Its provisions were designed to ensure that Irish industry, fully sheltered behind tariff walls, should be as far as possible in the hands of Irish citizens and companies so as to "build up the industries of the country with native capital and organisations and to permit outside control of industries only when the possibility of developing the industries concerned under home control has been exhausted."[25]

The government was also busy enacting social legislation, including an enhanced provision of old-age pensions and unemployment assistance. The Unemployment Assistance Act (1933) was introduced and dramatically increased the numbers of people eligible for the payment.[26] A Housing Act was passed in August 1932 that provided funds for local authority house-building, an initiative that triggered large-scale slum clearance projects and new local authority schemes. An average of twelve thousand houses per year were to be built between 1932 and 1938, in comparison with two thousand per year under the previous government.

De Valera's attention was focused primarily on non-economic concerns. His standing at home and abroad was enhanced by his performance in the role of President of the Council of the League of Nations. He had been fortunate that in September 1932 it became Ireland's turn for the presidency. In his opening address to the Assembly, de Valera had given a blunt but well-received analysis of the weaknesses of the League of Nations. He became a strong advocate of collective security, and he was deeply involved in efforts to secure the withdrawal of Japan from Manchuria. He attempted to get the league to intervene to bring an end to the Chaco War, between Bolivia and Paraguay, but supported a policy of non-intervention in the Spanish Civil War. He advocated membership of the league for the Soviet Union and opposed Mussolini's takeover of Abyssinia.

Through his work with the League of Nations de Valera became a respected international statesman, and this did Fianna Fáil's popularity at home no harm. As T. Ryle Dwyer points out, "de Valera with his vivid political discernment, was quick to appreciate the domestic advantages of a high international profile." Dwyer also notes that he took these stands at the League of Nations even when his actions might have been expected to be unpopular at home.[27]

On the political front, the impact of the 1932 election quickly worked its way through the party system. In late 1932 James Dillon and some other independent deputies joined with four of the five remaining deputies of the Farmers' Party to form a new National Centre Party, led by Frank MacDermot. There followed informal contacts between this new party and leading figures in Cumann na nGaedheal with a view to forming an anti-Fianna Fáil bloc. This process culminated in a meeting between the two groups on 29 December 1932. Four days later de Valera pulled the rug from under these nascent efforts to unite the opposition against him by calling a general election.

De Valera had become increasingly frustrated with his dependence on the Labour Party in Dáil votes. A formalised system of weekly meetings between the parties to agree issues had broken down before Christmas, and the Labour Party had indicated that it would oppose proposals for cuts in the cost-of-living bonus to civil servants. Faced with this uncertainty, and with the prospect of a more coherent opposition developing, de Valera decided to go for a quick election to consolidate his government's position and win an absolute majority. It was indeed "a master stroke of strategy,"[28] the first display of de Valera's uncanny sense of electoral timing.

It remains unclear whether his decision to call the 1933 election was made in consultation with other ministers. Lemass later told Brian Farrell that the idea had been discussed with him, but others, including Gerry Boland and de Valera's official biographers, say that the decision had been taken by de Valera alone and was as much of a surprise to his ministers as it was to the rest of the country.[29] Whatever the circumstances of the decision, the effect was to plunge Fianna Fáil into another whirlwind campaign.

Cornelius O'Leary, the leading historian of Irish elections, has described the 1933 campaign as the bitterest in the history of the country,[30] which is saying a lot when one considers the events of the previous decades. The campaign, he says, was both "brief in its duration and straightforward in its policy content." The economic and constitutional confrontation with Britain was the dominant issue. The parties had less money to spend, so there was less advertising on each side. The weather was bad, so the number of rallies was fewer. The choice, however, was as stark as it had been in February 1932. In presentation, the issues had been simplified. After the government had been only eleven months in office the people were asked to approve again the programme put forward by Fianna Fáil in 1932. De Valera said he needed a new mandate to continue the process of dismantling the Anglo-Irish Treaty and to impress on the British government that this approach had the support of the Irish people. The withholding of land annuities and the abolition of the oath were presented as Ireland v. England. The opposition parties were simply labelled anti-national for opposing these moves, although Cosgrave did attempt to outstrip Fianna Fáil by promising, if he got back to power, to cancel the arrears of land annuities, declare a moratorium on their payment for 1934 and negotiate to have them reduced thereafter.[31] This was portrayed by Fianna Fáil as too little, too late, and it also claimed it was a belated admission by Cumann na nGaedheal that de Valera had been right on this issue all along. The dividing line in Irish politics was now clear to all: the choice was crystallised and personalised as one between de Valera and Cosgrave.

Although the election was conducted at a time of year most inhospitable for campaigning and voting, the turn-out was the highest ever recorded, at 81 per cent. Fianna Fáil did consolidate its position, as de Valera hoped, though perhaps not to the extent he might have wished. He had won a majority, but only just. Fianna Fáil obtained nearly 50 per cent of the first-preference vote and after getting most Labour Party transfers gained five more seats. Cumann na nGaedheal lost nine seats. The Labour Party increased its representation by one, to 8. The new National Centre Party won 11 seats.

Fianna Fáil now had a working majority of one, because it could rely on the precedent that in a tie the Ceann Comhairle would vote with the government, and it could also call on the support of some independents if required.

Even Fianna Fáil's opponents were forced to acknowledge, albeit in private, the organisational superiority of de Valera's party. The future Fine Gael leader Richard Mulcahy, in the spring of 1933, observed that "the politicians had beaten the statesmen and however unpalatable it may be, it was the fault of the statesmen."[32]

Having consolidated its position, the Fianna Fáil government continued even more enthusiastically on the path of radical constitutional and economic change. However, 1933 and 1934 were to prove particularly tense years in Irish politics, and the de Valera government had to face down further challenges to democracy, both from its old comrades in the IRA and from a new quasi-fascist organisation, the Blueshirts.

The Army Comrades' Association had been established during the 1932 election campaign with the aim of protecting Cumann na nGaedheal political activity from IRA intimidation. Headed by Tom O'Higgins, a Cumann na nGaedheal deputy and brother of Kevin O'Higgins, the association was made up mainly of ex-servicemen. Within a few months it had thirty thousand members, and after the 1933 election it became a more prominent and controversial organisation. On 20 July, O'Higgins stepped down as leader, to be replaced by Eoin O'Duffy, recently sacked as Commissioner of the Garda

Síochána. O'Duffy changed the name of the association to the National Guard and had it adopt the blue shirt as its uniform. In both dress and attitudes the Blueshirts, as they now became popularly known, increasingly came to resemble contemporary fascist movements in Europe.[33] While O'Duffy himself may have wished to fashion the organisation's policy and objectives to resemble those of Mussolini's Italian fascists, it is not clear that the mass of the Blueshirt membership shared or appreciated his intentions.

Cumann na nGaedheal had sustained a combined loss of nineteen seats in the 1932 and 1933 elections and was now in crisis. It had at first consoled itself after the 1932 result with the hope that the minority de Valera government would not last long, but the 1933 outcome had shattered any notion that Cosgrave and his colleagues had of returning to government soon. Over the summer of 1933 leading figures of the demoralised Cumann na nGaedheal, the National Centre Party and the increasingly active Blueshirts held a series of meetings to discuss a merger between the three entities to form a new political party.

That summer O'Duffy also set off on a countrywide recruitment campaign, which was to culminate in him leading a march on Dáil Éireann on 12 August, the day scheduled for the annual commemorative parade to Leinster Lawn in honour of Griffith, Collins and O'Higgins. Unsure of O'Duffy's intentions, and fearful that he was hoping to replicate Mussolini's "March on Rome" in 1922, the Fianna Fáil government banned the Blueshirt march the day before, and on 23 August it proclaimed the National Guard an illegal organisation.

The banning of the National Guard served to galvanise the pro-merger elements in both Cumann na nGaedheal and the Centre Party. On 8 September the new political party, Fine Gael, subtitled the United Ireland Party, was formally launched in the Mansion House. O'Duffy was introduced as the new party's president.

Cosgrave became one of three vice-presidents, along with James Dillon and Frank MacDermot, and its parliamentary leader. He had little confidence in O'Duffy's abilities, but, given the demands of the National Centre Party for a new leader, he felt he was left with little option but to step aside. In regard to the merger with the Blueshirts, Maurice Manning notes that "Cosgrave was not especially enthusiastic about the whole idea and it seems that his reservations were shared by some of his front-bench colleagues, most of all by Patrick Hogan."[34] Despite these very real doubts, Cumann na nGaedheal decided to throw in its lot with O'Duffy and the Centre Party as the best means to stop Fianna Fáil.

Lemass "cruelly if not inaptly" called the new three-component party "the cripple alliance".[35] It was certainly handicapped by O'Duffy's eccentricity and his lack of political skill. He was deposed as leader within a year: Cosgrave's and Dillon's patience with him finally snapped when he called on farmers to cease paying to the government the reduced annuities they were now being required to pay.

At this remove the decision of Cosgrave, Dillon and the other deputies to enter any dalliance with O'Duffy seems strange and ill advised. It is hard to disagree with O'Leary's conclusion that

> Cosgrave's original intention may have been to strengthen the opposition and so to force an end to the Anglo Irish economic war . . . Nevertheless, by flirting with an extra parliamentary, quasi fascist movement Cosgrave's party damaged its own prestige, and in effect made it easier for the government to ban extremists both of the Left and the Right.[36]

Meanwhile the IRA was becoming a growing embarrassment for the Fianna Fáil government and a growing danger to the state. It had engaged in violent clashes with the Blueshirts and in raids for arms as well as carrying out a number of murders, which outraged public opinion, including that of a 73-year-old retired British vice-admiral living in Castletownshend, Co. Cork. Gerry Boland told the Dáil:

> The fact that murders have occurred makes it clear that stern action must be taken . . . I now give definite notice to all concerned that the so-called IRA, or any organisation which promotes or advocates the use of arms for the attainment of its objectives, will not be tolerated . . . We smashed them [the Blueshirts], and now we are going to smash the others.[37]

On 18 June 1936 the IRA was declared an illegal organisation. The IRA march to Bodenstown on 23 June was also banned. These were significant steps, given the close ties and sentimental attachment that had existed between Fianna Fáil and radical republicanism, particularly during the opposition years 1927–32.

Above all else, however, it was the continuing tariff war with Britain that dominated government policy during the mid-1930s. In January 1935 an early attempt to resolve the annuities issue in negotiations with the British Prime Minister, Ramsay MacDonald, proved unsuccessful, although an agreement on coal and cattle did relieve some of the hardship.

While the situation in agriculture was still desperate, Lemass's industrial policy succeeded in having industries established behind these protective walls. Between 1931 and 1936 industrial employment rose sharply, from 111,000 to 154,000, and the increase was almost entirely in manufacturing industry. The protectionist industrial policy was "virtually canonised" in 1933 when, in a lecture at University College Dublin, attended by prominent politicians of both parties, the renowned British economist John Maynard Keynes said, "If I were an Irishman, I should find much to attract me in the economic outlook of your present government towards greater self-sufficiency."[38]

Lemass was also busy expanding state-sponsored industry. In 1933 Comhlucht Siúicre Éireann was founded to manufacture sugar from home-grown sugarbeet. The same year the Industrial Credit Company was founded. The Turf Development Board (later Bord na Móna) was founded in 1934 and Aer Lingus in 1936. Lemass was also involved in efforts to sustain and develop the Electricity Supply Board and the railways.

None of these industrial initiatives, however, could take away from the reality that the Economic War had led to spiralling unemployment and emigration, compounded by the continuing international recession.

The crowning achievement of the pre-war Fianna Fáil government was to be the Constitution of Ireland. The enactment of a completely new constitution was the logical next step from the measures it had taken since 1932. In 1935 the Executive Council had decided that a new constitution was necessary, and by early 1937 de Valera had a first version of the text prepared. While he consulted widely on this and later drafts, usually in bilateral engagements with officials, lawyers and sometimes ministers or bishops, the constitution was essentially de Valera's own work. In its final form it gave the state the name Ireland in place of Irish Free State; claimed sovereignty over the whole island; provided for two houses of the Oireachtas, Dáil Éireann and a new Seanad Éireann; renamed the Executive Council the Government and gave its head the title of Taoiseach; provided for a directly elected president as head of state; declared the principle of popular sovereignty; enshrined proportional representation as the system of voting; gave the vote to all men and women over the age of twenty-one; provided for the holding of referendums; and prohibited religious discrimination.

At a time when the lights of democracy were dimming throughout Europe, de Valera's constitution was a profoundly democratic document. Stressing this point, he remarked, when the debate on the second reading opened in the Dáil: "If there is one thing more than another that is clear and shining through this Constitution, it is the fact that the people are the masters."[39]

The constitution was republican in character but did not declare the state to be a republic, as some in Fianna Fáil wished. This was because of the position of Northern Ireland. De Valera himself was to confirm later that "if the Northern problem is not there . . . in all probability there would be a flat, downright proclamation of a republic in this constitution."[40]

The Dáil approved the new constitution on 14 June 1937 by 62 votes to 48. Less than half an hour later de Valera dissolved the Dáil and called a general election for 1 July, to coincide with a plebiscite on the constitution. On this occasion Fianna Fáil's campaign was less confrontational than that of 1933 and the party made a particular effort to appeal to the middle ground. The referendum on the constitution saw the electorate break largely along partisan lines, and it had a comfortable passage, with 685,105 voting for its adoption and 526,945 against.

In the election Fianna Fáil lost its absolute majority. It dropped to 69 seats out of 138 in the newly reduced Dáil but was still comfortably ahead of Fine Gael, which won 48 seats, so de Valera was able to return to government but needed Labour Party support. It was generally expected that a new election would not be long delayed.

The gathering storm in Europe created an environment conducive to the resolution of Britain and Ireland's local economic difficulty. After lengthy negotiations between the two sides, led by de Valera and Neville Chamberlain, the two governments entered into a comprehensive set of agreements collectively known as the Anglo-Irish Agreement of 1938, signed on 25 April. The agreement provided for a final settlement of the land annuities, with the British accepting a payment of £10 million—a tenth of the £100 million they claimed they were entitled to. Significantly, it also provided for the return of the treaty ports of Cóbh, Bearhaven and Lough Swilly, which had been held on to by the British under the treaty. In addition it included a trade agreement that granted Irish goods very advantageous access to the British market.

As far as de Valera was concerned, he had now isolated partition as the one outstanding grievance between Ireland and Britain, and if this issue could be resolved it would open the door to a new era of harmony. He wrote to Chamberlain in these terms at the conclusion of the negotiations on the 1938 agreement.

I have no doubt the happy ending of the disputes in question has begotten a new attitude of mind on the part of our people, and if we could only now succeed in solving the problem created by Partition, a happy future of mutual understanding and fruitful co-operation in matters of common concern lies ahead before our two peoples.[41]

Although for Fianna Fáil partition remained a lingering sore, the end of the Economic War was widely welcomed and the agreement was viewed as a diplomatic triumph for de Valera. He seized his opportunity to dissolve the Dáil four weeks later when he lost a technical vote over civil service salary arbitration.

During the 1938 election campaign Fianna Fáil triumphantly touted its "victory" in the Economic War. Addressing an election rally in Dublin, Seán T. O'Kelly declared: "In the past six years, look how we whipped John Bull every time! Look at the last agreement we made with her. We won all round us, we whipped her right, left and centre, and with God's help, we shall do the same again."[42]

The 1938 outcome was to be Fianna Fáil's best electoral performance yet. Its vote rose to 52 per cent, giving it 77 of the 128 seats and a majority of 16. Fine Gael won 45 seats, the Labour Party 9, and there were 7 independents.

After six years of power Fianna Fáil had lost much of its radical edge and increased its support by becoming a competent centrist party of government. It had also won over many of its former enemies, most notably perhaps the *Irish Times*. During the 1937 election campaign the paper had editorialised: "We are glad to admit that in many ways President de Valera's government has confounded its former critics including ourselves, that it has acted fairly and

uprightly towards political and religious minorities, and that Ministers had
done their job conscientiously and well."[43] Despite this praise, the paper went
on to endorse Cumann na nGaedheal in that election, but by 1938 its editorial
line had come full circle, proclaiming: "We are glad that [de Valera] has been
returned to power."

The industrial policy that the party had adopted since 1932 also had a
political advantage, at least in the short term. According to Michael Gallagher,
"Fianna Fáil was virtually able to create new supporters in that both the
businessmen who set up the protected firms, and the workers they employed
probably looked favourably upon the party thereafter."[44]

In assessing Fianna Fáil's prospects in 1933, Warner Moss identified its
relationship with the Catholic Church as one of the important determinants
of its future, noting presciently that "either the clergy will be won over to the
Republicans because of the fundamental conservatism of Fianna Fáil in the
field of morals and ethics or [they] will be repelled by de Valera's overtures to
extremists of the left." The former was to be the eventual scenario.

In these first terms of government Fianna Fáil developed comfortable
relations with the church. While there had been mutual suspicions in 1932,
each side quickly "satisfied the other of its credentials. On the major issues of
concern to the hierarchy, the government proved willing to legislate where
necessary in a fashion acceptable to the church."[45] Among the matters on
which the party and the church could agree was the Criminal Law
Amendment Act (1935), prohibiting the sale and importing of contraceptives.
The Fianna Fáil Government also proved as enthusiastic as that of Cumann
na nGaedheal in applying the Censorship of Publications Act (1929). The
party and the hierarchy agreed also, in the main, on the text of the new 1937
constitution, which in addition to incorporating much Catholic social and
vocational teaching gave constitutional recognition to the "special position"
of the Catholic Church as "the guardian of the Faith professed by the great
majority of the citizens."

This provision caused de Valera more anxiety than any other article.
Although some suggest that the "special position" clause reflected the supine
nature of Fianna Fáil's relationship with the church, the hierarchy had wanted
de Valera to go further, and indeed an earlier draft recognised the Catholic
faith as "the true religion." This version had caused consternation in the anti-
clerical wing of Fianna Fáil, which lobbied successfully to have it altered. As
T. Ryle Dwyer records,

> Gerry Boland, the Minister for Lands, was appalled. "If this clause gets
> through as now worded," he said, "it would be equivalent to the
> expulsion from our history of great Irishmen." Protestant patriots like
> Wolfe Tone, Henry Joy McCracken, Charles Stewart Parnell, Erskine
> Childers and many others would never have lived in Ireland "under
> such a constitution," he argued. "And I would not live under it either. I
> would take my wife and children and put myself out of it."[46]

The manner in which Fianna Fáil had so quickly become the majority party is remarkable. Brian Farrell remarks on how steady growth in Fianna Fáil's vote in Dublin over the four elections between 1927 and 1933 was particularly noteworthy. In June 1927 the party obtained 22 per cent in Dublin North; in September 1927 that increased to 25 per cent; in 1932 it increased to 35 per cent; and in 1933 it had dramatically increased to 45 per cent. Similarly in the Dublin South constituency Fianna Fáil obtained 29 per cent in June 1927, growing to 35 per cent in September 1927 and to 41 per cent in 1932; by 1933 it had grown to a massive 53 per cent. In fact for the 1937 election the Fianna Fáil vote in Dublin South, which was Lemass's constituency, fell back to 47 per cent but then in 1938 went back up to 56 per cent.[47] On the other hand, as Michael Gallagher has pointed out, Dublin remained Fianna Fáil's weakest area generally. In the six general elections from June 1927 to 1938 its average first-preference vote in Connacht was 50 per cent while in Dublin it was 36½ per cent. Its national average was 42 per cent.

During these years Fianna Fáil became increasingly at ease as a party of power. The Government worked as a tight and cohesive group, helped no doubt by its shared pre-government history and the fact that there were few changes during the period. In addition, until the 1937 constitution was enacted the numbers attending Government meetings were limited to ten ministers.

Seán T. O'Kelly and Frank Aiken were particularly close to de Valera. Aiken's personal closeness to the Chief, coupled with his prominence in the Government and indeed in the party, made him at the time the most obvious candidate to succeed de Valera in the unlikely event of a vacancy suddenly arising. In 1932 Lemass was the youngest government minister in Europe, at thirty-three, but Aiken was only a year older. John Horgan points out that in the 1933 election to the party's Ard-Chomhairle, Aiken topped the poll, with 521 votes, with Lemass second by a wide margin with 421, which reflected the pecking order at least at that point.[48]

Within the Government, as in the party generally, de Valera was "pre-eminent and maintained his dominance almost effortlessly."[49] There were some well-documented disagreements on the thrust of economic policy, particularly between MacEntee and Lemass, but these owed as much, at least at this time, to their different departmental interests as it did to any significant ideological battle within these first Fianna Fáil Governments.

In a pattern that was to endure during later terms in government, matters of state took over from party matters for Fianna Fáil's leading personalities. De Valera was completely absorbed in his dual roles as Taoiseach and Minister for External Affairs and from 1936 onwards as draftsman in chief of the new constitution.[50] He had chaired almost all meetings of the Fianna Fáil Ard-Chomhairle before 1932, but when the party went into government his atten-dance at Ard-Chomhairle meetings became infrequent. Lemass similarly found little time for party activities, except during elections, and even struggled to find time to attend meetings of the parliamentary party. He had resigned his position as honorary secretary on his appointment to the Government, to be replaced by Oscar Traynor, who did not become a minister until 1936.

Notwithstanding this inevitable neglect of their party management duties, de Valera enjoyed near-absolute loyalty within the Fianna Fáil organisation. It was already presenting itself as a "cohesive national party, united at grass roots, regimented in parliament and impeccably monolithic in government," in the manner that, Farrell says, characterised the party's discipline throughout de Valera's tenure as leader.[51]

If the party was united at this time it was because its leaders and activists had much about which to be happy. Party morale was understandably high. From 1927 to 1933 it had been on a dramatic upward electoral trajectory. Now comfortably ensconced in power, it had been effective in government, not least in stripping out the most abhorrent treaty provisions from the Free State constitution. Fianna Fáil had designed in its stead a whole new constitution that would make southern Ireland a republic in all but name. With its political opponents in disarray, it enjoyed popular support for its economic and constitutional battle with the old enemy from 1932 to 1938, and it benefited electorally from the negotiated peace.

The only republican objective on which no progress had been made was the ending of partition. There were, in these and the following years, many equally well-documented disagreements between de Valera and the "interventionist wing"[52] within his Ard-Chomhairle, and within the party more generally, over his refusal to permit the party to organise in Northern Ireland as well as over the lack of progress on the issue of the border. At the 1933 ard-fheis de Valera was heckled by a Fianna Fáil TD, Éamonn Donnelly, when giving his address. Donnelly was a native of Co. Armagh who represented Laois-Offaly and was a strong advocate of Fianna Fáil establishing itself in the North as well as a critic of the leadership's progress on partition.[53]

On this issue the Chief adopted a practical approach. There was little he could do to change the partitioned status quo. His consistent approach was to talk much about the ignominy of the border but in practice to maximise sovereignty for the Southern state, over which he could exercise control. Organising Fianna Fáil north of the border would only complicate his political and diplomatic difficulties and divide Northern nationalists. On this issue, as on all issues, notwithstanding the occasional disputes, the de Valera writ ran within the party.[54]

Chapter 5 ∾

GOVERNMENT IN WARTIME, 1939–48

In September 1939 Europe descended into war for the second time in a quarter of a century. These war years were not nearly as eventful in Ireland as they were elsewhere, nor indeed as eventful as those between 1914 and 1918 had been. Nevertheless Ireland's society, its economy and its politics were altered during the period that Irish people, uniquely and somewhat quaintly, came to refer to as "the Emergency" following the declaration of a national emergency on 2 September 1939.

Deputies were summoned by telegram to an emergency meeting of Dáil Éireann on Saturday 2 September, the day after Nazi Germany invaded Poland. De Valera, as Taoiseach, rose first to address the special session, telling the Dáil:

> Back in February last, I stated in a very definite way that it was the aim of Government policy in case of a European war to keep this country, if at all possible, out of it. We have pursued that policy and we intend to pursue it . . . I know that in this country there are sympathies, very strong sympathies, in regard to the present issues, but I do not think anybody would suggest that the Government policy, the official policy of the State, should be other than . . . what the Government suggests.[1]

His announcement was neither controversial nor unexpected. There was indeed widespread sympathy for the Allied cause among Irish politicians. Most of the Fianna Fáil Government members sympathised with the British against the Nazis, though some, including Frank Aiken and P. J. Little, were convinced that the Germans would win the war and were keen to be on good terms with them. T. Ryle Dwyer quotes Seán MacEntee as saying that, as a result of this conviction, Aiken and Little were "so nervous" that they gave the impression at Government meetings that Hempel, the German minister in Ireland, "might be looking over their shoulders."[2]

From the outset, de Valera was determined that Ireland's neutrality would be as benevolent as possible to Britain. He told Germany that for trade reasons Ireland would have to "show a certain consideration for Britain," but when he first met Sir John Maffey, the British representative in Ireland, he made it clear where his sympathies lay. "There was a time when I would have done anything in my power to help destroy the British Empire. But now my position has changed." There was no doubt the British had right on their side in this struggle. By doing "everything a man could do to prevent this tragedy," Chamberlain had allowed the moral issues at stake to be clearly defined. "England has a moral position today," de Valera said. "Hitler might have his early success, but the moral position would tell."[3]

Among the public the extent of sympathy for the Allies would soon be reflected in the fact that more than 50,000 citizens would join the British armed forces during the war, while another 200,000 would go there to work, replacing British citizens who had been conscripted. Notwithstanding these political and popular sympathies, choosing a policy of neutrality was not difficult for either Fianna Fáil or the political opposition. The arguments for a neutral course were overwhelming.

De Valera had repeatedly argued, most notably as President of the Council of the League of Nations, that small countries should not allow themselves to be used as the tool of any great power. His primary motivation for neutrality was the clear assertion of sovereignty that it would represent: staying out of this war would be the acid test of Ireland's hard-fought-for and newly achieved independence. It would prove conclusively how far Ireland had moved beyond dominion status. In addition, the unresolved question of partition made it impossible for Ireland to pursue any other route. According to de Valera's own assessment, two-thirds of the Irish people were "pro-British, or at any rate anti-Germany," but there was a "very active minority" fundamentally opposed to any co-operation with Britain, because of partition.[4] De Valera had clearly digested the lesson of Redmond's support for the 1914–18 war. He knew that joining the British war effort could leave him vulnerable to those who operated on the principle of England's difficulty being Ireland's opportunity.

Many Fianna Fáil ministers were strongly of the opinion that Ireland was entitled to both neutrality and unity. On at least two occasions during the war the British Government dangled the carrot of unity before the Irish Government in exchange for Ireland's immediate entry into the war. While it is debatable how sincere and ultimately how deliverable the British offers were, what is revealing is the attitude of de Valera and his ministers, who refused to barter neutrality for the holy grail of unity.

In June 1940 the British Minister of Health, Malcolm MacDonald, made a number of visits to Dublin with a view to cajoling the de Valera Government into the war with the offer of a British declaration accepting the principle of a united Ireland. He reported back to the British Government:

Aiken did most of the talking on their side and was even more persistent than de Valera himself had been in urging that the proper solution is a United Ireland which is neutral . . . Lemass seemed to be prepared to discuss our plan in a more reasonable way, but his contributions to [the] discussion were usually cut short by fresh uncompromising interventions from one or other of his colleagues.[5]

On another occasion during the war Frank MacDermot, who had been appointed to the Seanad by de Valera in 1938, visited Belfast to sound out Sir Basil Brooke on whether the Stormont Government might budge on partition in return for an end to Irish neutrality. On his return it was bluntly made clear to MacDermot that the Fianna Fáil ministers were not interested and that for them staying out of the war was more important. "Get this into your head, MacDermot," Aiken told him, "there are no terms for which we would abandon neutrality."[6]

Broad political considerations apart, it is likely that the small size and weakness of the Defence Forces would have rendered neutrality necessary in any case. As the world hovered on the brink of war in 1938, de Valera had reached agreement with Aiken on increasing defence spending. However, MacEntee, as Minister for Finance, objected, arguing that such "heavy commitments" would mean a cut in essential services elsewhere or "an increase in taxation," and de Valera in the end came down on the side of Finance.[7] During the war, in discussions with Allied representatives, de Valera would use Ireland's lack of military strength to his advantage, arguing that this left him with no real choice but to stick firmly with neutrality.

While sovereignty and partition were the primary motivations of neutrality, some writers have pointed to other considerations at work. Garret FitzGerald wrote half a century later:

Among all political parties there was the further powerful . . . consideration that to have entered voluntarily into the conflict on the allied side within sixteen years of the end of the civil war would have created the dangers of a revival of that bitter conflict . . . As was very clear in Spain during the closing period of Franco's rule, a people who have experienced civil war will go to immense lengths to avoid a recurrence of it.

While this basis for neutrality had, for obvious reasons, gone unstated during the war itself, it was a consideration mentioned by both Seán MacEntee and Seán Lemass in retrospective interviews. It also explained, FitzGerald says, the support that his own father, a prominent Fine Gael politician at the time, gave for neutrality despite his deep commitment to the Allied cause.[8]

John Maffey's account of a meeting with de Valera in the aftermath of the spurning by the Government of British overtures on a united Ireland makes it clear that the need to avert civil war was central to de Valera's considerations. Maffey records de Valera as saying: "It had gone hard with him to turn down any scheme which would bring about a united Ireland, the dream of his life. But in the present circumstances acceptance had been impossible. It would have meant civil war."[9]

The policy of neutrality, as announced by de Valera, was met with a cross-party and popular consensus the like of which had never been seen since the Civil War. It was supported by almost all deputies in Dáil Éireann for the full duration of the war. There were some reservations among a minority of Fine Gael deputies, but publicly the party actively supported the policy. The one notable exception was James Dillon, who in 1942 resigned his position as deputy leader of Fine Gael on the principle and became an independent.

Tom O'Higgins summed up the attitude of some in his party when he told the Dáil in late September 1939: "I was never a firm believer in the feasibility and benefits of neutrality . . . I was prepared to adopt it and support it, however, as a policy that appealed to the vast majority of the people and that, at all events, was worth trying."[10]

There was acceptance in the Dáil that any other approach would be hugely divisive and could lead to internal conflict. This is clear from the nightmare scenario set out by de Valera, which was a German invasion of the North, placing intolerable pressure on the policy of neutrality and ultimately resulting in Irish people taking up arms against each other on different sides. John Bowman observes:

> What in particular terrified de Valera was the prospect of a German invasion of nationalist areas north of the border. If he were in charge of German strategy, he told Gray [the American minister in Ireland], he would land in those areas and proclaim himself a liberator. "If they should do that, what I could do I do not know." This contingency was also feared by Richard Mulcahy and was formally raised by another Fine Gael member at the all-party advisory Defence Conference. T. F. O'Higgins asked whether southern troops should be willing to help the north to fight the Germans if they landed there . . . Labour thought any such aid would amount to collaboration with the British in their "occupation and exploitation of the six counties"; Fine Gael, on the contrary, believed that not to assist "would be disgraceful and absurd"; while Fianna Fáil ministers, Aiken and Boland, were non-committal, believing that if the contingency were to arise, any decision would have to be referred to the Dáil. This demonstrated that parties agreed on neutrality could be deeply divided on any deviation from that policy.[11]

While historians may dispute the weight to be attached to the various motivations behind neutrality, all agree on the extent to which the consensus on neutrality healed the divisions of the Civil War. Uniting in a common cause and serving together in the enlarged Permanent Defence Force or the newly established Local Defence Force took some of the edge off the bitterness that had endured between the two sides of the treaty divide.

In his address to the Dáil on 2 September 1939 de Valera also emphasised that neutrality would not be an easy option.

> On another occasion when speaking in this house of that policy, I pointed out how extremely difficult it was going to be. In a sense the

Government of a nation that proposes to be neutral in war of this sort has problems much more delicate and much more difficult of solution even than the problems that arise from being a belligerent.

While the leaders of those countries that were fighting in the war might take issue with de Valera's characterisation of the particular difficulties that neutrals faced, there is no doubt that giving effect to neutrality and charting a safe course through the war would require the Government to exercise particular delicacy and skill, and not only in its international relations.

It would also require it to exercise draconian powers. A First Amendment of the Constitution Bill and an Emergency Powers Bill were rushed through and passed by the Oireachtas in the early hours of 3 September 1939. Later that morning Britain and France would declare war on Germany. It was necessary to amend the constitution to allow the Government to exercise powers during a war in which Ireland was not participating.[12]

The Emergency Powers Act gave the Government sweeping powers. Much to their initial discomfort, de Valera and his new Minister for Justice, Gerry Boland, soon found themselves having to employ these against their former comrades. The IRA marked the outbreak of war by launching a bombing campaign in England and carrying out a spectacular raid on the Magazine Fort in the Phoenix Park, getting away with a million rounds of ammunition. The Government was furious and was fearful that IRA sabotage in England, or suspected links between the IRA and German intelligence, would prompt British retaliation against Ireland's neutrality. Its response was swift and effective. The IRA was tackled head on. The Special Criminal Court established under the Emergency Powers Acts sentenced IRA men to death. Internment was introduced. During the war more than 1,500 IRA activists were interned without trial and hundreds more rounded up and arrested under the Offences Against the State Act.

The resolve of Fianna Fáil ministers on this point did not weaken even when IRA prisoners went on hunger strike. While sympathetic to the prisoners' plight, and at times visibly emotional when talking about the issue, de Valera and other ministers resisted calls to intervene, even when they came from Margaret Pearse, Patrick Pearse's sister, then a Fianna Fáil senator, and from Kathleen Clarke, Lord Mayor of Dublin and widow of the first signatory of the 1916 Proclamation.[13] In response to one such entreaty de Valera countered: "The lesser evil is to see men die rather than that the safety of the whole community should be endangered."[14]

On another occasion, after Paddy McGrath, an IRA member and veteran of 1916, was shot by firing squad on the order of Gerry Boland (who had been interned with him during the War of Independence), Clarke ordered the blinds in the Mansion House to be drawn and the flag to be flown at half mast to demonstrate her sympathy with the family and her disapproval of the Government's action.[15] She subsequently resigned from Fianna Fáil. During the war three IRA prisoners died on hunger strike, six members were killed in gun battles with gardaí, and six more were shot by firing squad after trial in the special courts.

Dealing with IRA sedition was only one of the many difficulties facing the Fianna Fáil wartime Government. Since the mid-1930s the government machinery in Ireland, as elsewhere, had been secretly preparing for the eventuality of war. Among the recommendations of an interdepartmental committee that had been meeting on wartime contingencies since 1935 was the creation of a Department of Supplies. Shortly after war was declared de Valera undertook his most extensive Government reshuffle. Seán Lemass was the obvious candidate to head the new department. Frank Aiken was moved from Defence to become Minister for the Co-ordination of Defensive Measures, with the primary function of implementing wartime censorship. Seán MacEntee was shifted to replace Lemass at Industry and Commerce, and Finance was taken over by the Tánaiste, Seán T. O'Kelly. His vacancy in Local Government was filled by moving Paddy Ruttledge from Justice, to which Gerry Boland was then appointed. Tom Derrig was moved to the Department of Lands and also served briefly in Posts and Telegraphs until P. J. Little was promoted to that position from that of chief whip. Oscar Traynor became Minister for Defence. De Valera added Education to his existing responsibilities as Taoiseach and Minister for External Affairs. Dr James Ryan in Agriculture was the only minister to retain his previous portfolio.

As Minister for Supplies, Lemass had virtually unlimited authority "to control exports, imports and prices of commodities of all kinds and to regulate the treatment, keeping, storage, movement, distribution, sale, purchase, use and consumption of articles of all kinds."[16] Irish Shipping Ltd was established in 1941 to give Ireland a small national merchant fleet and to ensure the availability of basic materials.

Lemass enjoyed the interventionist powers that came with this new portfolio. To keep control over the rationing of consumer goods he made more than six hundred ministerial orders and informed the public of the supply situation in regular radio broadcasts. After a reduction in the butter ration he acquired the nickname "Half-Ounce" Lemass.[17]

Fianna Fáil's drive for national self-sufficiency since it had come to power in 1932 proved beneficial in the wartime situation, but Government policies were now intensified. The existence of native textile and leather industries meant that Ireland could meet its own clothing needs. The Government also strongly promoted the cutting of turf as an alternative to coal, with even the Phoenix Park containing miles of turf ricks.

Dr James Ryan, as Minister for Agriculture, had a central role in ensuring that there would be no severe food shortages. On the outbreak of the war he made tillage compulsory, and by 1942 three-quarters of Ireland's bread requirements were being met at home. Despite having to deal with an outbreak of foot-and-mouth disease in 1941, net agricultural output increased by more than 9 per cent during the war, and the average Irish person was better fed than their British counterpart.[18] Rationing, however, became a fact of daily life. A lack of raw materials hampered industry, and as a result, and because of the availability of work in wartime Britain, emigration soared.

Under the Minister for the Co-ordination of Defensive Measures were three censorship divisions, dealing separately with postal, telegraph and press communications. The bulk of the staff, all of whom were recruited from within the civil service, dealt with postal materials. Under the "rigid and unyielding"[19] Aiken, those dealing with the press were particularly assiduous, and few news stories, photographs or even political advertisements escaped the censor's knife. Aiken set out his approach to the task in a memorandum to the Taoiseach in January 1940.

> There are some self-styled democrats who would hold on to the peace time liberalist trimmings of democracy while the fundamental basis of democracy was being swept from under their feet by the foreign or domestic enemies of their democratic state. Wise men however discard these trimmings when necessary in order successfully to maintain the fundamental right of the citizens freely to chose by whom they shall be governed.[20]

Oscar Traynor was also busy in the Department of Defence, where he oversaw a rapid increase in recruitment to the Defence Forces. The regular army went from 6,000 to nearly 50,000 personnel, supplemented by the volunteer Local Defence Force, while the Garda Síochána was supplemented by the Local Security Force—totalling in all 250,000 people.[21]

During the war years the level of political activity, controversy and debate was inevitably reduced. Newspapers were smaller, because newsprint was rationed. The *Irish Press* had only four pages, and similar restrictions applied to the *Irish Independent* and *Irish Times*,[22] while the news that did appear was heavily censored. Political gatherings and election campaigning, like all gatherings and social activity, were hampered, not least by the rationing of petrol.

In addition to these practical restrictions, politics was less intense because the areas of controversy and competition between parties had narrowed. The enforced consensus on the most important issues at this time of national emergency made it difficult for the opposition; they had to be particularly careful not to be perceived as playing politics with the future of the country. Fine Gael had made the argument that a "national government" (a government of all parties) was the best way to steer the country through the war; but, as Anthony Jordan points out,

> Fianna Fáil rejected this saying that a coalition government would lead to instability. It feared that some of the smaller parties, especially Clann na Talmhan, would make inroads into its own vote should it get into any form of government. Dev believed in single party Government with himself at the head, as the best way of ensuring the future for Fianna Fáil and the country.[23]

Fianna Fáil did agree as a concession to set up a National Defence Conference, composed of three representatives each from Fianna Fáil, Fine Gael and the Labour Party. Fianna Fáil was represented by Frank Aiken, Gerry Boland and Oscar Traynor. Richard Mulcahy, who attended meetings on behalf of Fine Gael, described the attempts of the opposition members to obtain even basic information as like "hens scratching" for facts. Anthony Jordan argues that the conference gave "a public image of national solidarity which was all Dev wanted from it."[24]

In this respect Fianna Fáil enjoyed an obvious and significant advantage as the party in power when the emergency began; it inevitably became the focal point for patriotic fervour at a time of national crisis. As Dónal Ó Drisceoil has pointed out, "the national emergency created a situation in which a single party government effectively became the sole arbitrator of the national interest and the lines between government and state were blurred."[25]

Notwithstanding the practical constraints, there were two general elections during the war. (Sweden was the only other European country to hold an election during the war.[26]) An election was due in 1943, and though there were suggestions that it might be deferred, polling day was set for 23 June, which was almost the latest possible date for an election under the legislation. At the beginning of the war the country had rallied behind the Fianna Fáil Government, but, as the conflict dragged on, the social and economic hardship it was placing on people began to take its toll on the Government's popularity. De Valera, always an astute reader of the public mood, delayed calling the election until the Dáil had run its full course.

During the campaign Fianna Fáil played to its strengths by emphasising the need for stability. "Don't change horses when crossing the stream" was the party's principal slogan, seeking to make a virtue rather than a handicap of the fact that it had been in government for eleven consecutive years. It also emphasised that it was the only party that could offer single-party government. The electorate were encouraged not to gamble with the country's survival. One poster even made the brash claim that "if you vote Fianna Fáil the bombs won't fall."[27]

Seán MacEntee succinctly put the Fianna Fáil case on the need for stability in a speech delivered in Ranelagh, Dublin, on 8 June.

> Sane and sensible people and responsible people will vote for us because they know that if the country is going to be brought in safety and in peace to the end of this war, the government of the state must be in the hands of sane and sensible and responsible men.[28]

The other tactic adopted, at least by some Fianna Fáil speakers, was to prosecute a "red scare" against the Labour Party. In the same Ranelagh speech MacEntee put the charge in typically colourful terms.

> The Comintern has been abolished in Russia but the Muscovites are active in Dublin. I might say they are triumphant in Dublin. They have

captured Mr. Norton [William Norton, leader of the Labour Party] and are holding him a hostage while the Dublin Comintern organisation is infiltrating its advance elements into the Irish Labour Party.[29]

This was the latest in a series of vicious attacks on the Labour Party that MacEntee had delivered in the previous weeks. It attracted immediate censure from Lemass, who, as director of elections, wrote to MacEntee two days later. He said he had been contacted by several Fianna Fáil candidates who had complained about these attacks, saying that the Labour Party was "gaining by them not the reverse."[30] Lemass, somewhat optimistically, offered the view that the majority of the Labour vote would go to Fianna Fáil, "unless we irritate them by unduly severe attacks on the Labour Party."

MacEntee reacted civilly but firmly to the censure and did so again after the election, though this time with one of his ritual threats to resign when, at a meeting of ministers, he was criticised on the same account by several colleagues, including, it seems, de Valera.[31]

The fact that MacEntee felt the need to concentrate his attacks on the Labour Party, and that Lemass felt the need to rein him in, shows which opposition party Fianna Fáil felt it needed to worry about. Fine Gael was suffering from "disconsolate disarray"[32] and appeared to be "drifting into oblivion."[33]

Fine Gael's principal difficulty was that it was a party without a distinctive policy, even without a purpose. Most of the divisive issues arising from the treaty split were no longer alive: they had been resolved in the republicans' favour by the enactment of the 1937 constitution. The remaining divergence between Fianna Fáil and Fine Gael on the national question was muffled by the consensus on neutrality. As Cornelius O'Leary points out,

> the pro-Commonwealth leanings of Fine Gael ought naturally to have made it advocate full cooperation in the struggle in which the very life of the Commonwealth was at stake. For Fine Gael to set itself against neutrality in the face of Fianna Fáil's enormous majority would not only be futile but also might result in a further loss of popularity to the party and a prolongation of its stay in the wilderness . . . By forcing Cosgrave to discard, at least temporarily, his most distinctive policy (pro Commonwealth) the war resulted in a natural closing of the party ranks.[34]

Organisationally Fine Gael had never been strong, but by the early 1940s it had become "a Dublin and Cork Middle Class minor party with a few rural allies."[35] It also suffered inert political leadership. Cosgrave had lost his energy, and many of the party's other leading parliamentarians were juggling opposition front-bench positions with lucrative business or legal careers.

The 1943 election proved a disaster for Fine Gael. It suffered a further drop of 10 per cent in votes, to a mere 23 per cent, losing thirteen seats, a third of its parliamentary party, including the prominent front-benchers Richard Mulcahy and the future Taoiseach John Costello.

Some of the disenchantment with Fianna Fáil that might have been captured by a better-organised and more broadly based Fine Gael was used instead by a new party, Clann na Talmhan ("children of the land"). This organisation was founded shortly after the 1938 election by a Co. Galway farmer, Michael Donnellan, originating as an amalgam of local small farmers' groups in counties Galway, Mayo and Roscommon. At first it seemed to be "more of an agricultural pressure group—perhaps with something of a romantic throwback to the old days of the Land League—than a new political party."[36] Fianna Fáil did not feel in the least threatened by it at first. Indeed Gerry Boland announced that the party did not object to its members becoming involved so long as Clann na Talmhan remained outside political competition.[37] That changed, however, in August 1939 when at a special convention Clann na Talmhan decided to contest elections. As a full-blown, if regionally concentrated, political party its focus remained on representing the interests of smaller farmers—once a bedrock of Fianna Fáil support—whom it claimed the party had neglected in government. Most of the twenty-seven points in its political programme called for Government policy more sympathetic to agriculture.[38]

Clann na Talmhan did well in the local elections held in August 1942 and had an impressive first Dáil contest in the 1943 general election. It secured 10 per cent of the first-preference vote nationally to win eleven seats. Of potentially more concern to Fianna Fáil was the geographical detail within this national vote figure. Clann na Talmhan had won a third of all votes in counties Galway, Roscommon and Mayo. Though it was not to know it at the time, the challenge to Fianna Fáil from this quarter would fizzle out over the next five years, in large part because, as Tom Garvin suggests, Clann na Talmhan's social base was "largely composed of an agricultural stratum which was declining and ageing."[39] In the 1944 election it won two seats fewer; by the time of the 1948 election it had "ceased to have any coherent purpose or corporate identity."[40] In that election it won seven seats and seemed set for gradual demise until its participation in the 1948–51 inter-party Government elongated its life for a period.

In the early 1940s a far greater threat to Fianna Fáil than Clann na Talmhan was the resurgent Labour Party. Wartime hardships, a wages standstill, a municipal workers' strike in Dublin and the weakness of Fine Gael all contributed to a gain in both membership and support between 1939 and 1943. As Ó Beacháin assesses it, the Labour Party

> appeared to be the radical alternative in constitutional politics not so much because of any communist tendencies, as some in Fianna Fáil tried to imply, but simply because Fianna Fáil, previously the champion of the underdog, had moved so much to the right and had become the establishment party.[41]

In the same way that disenchanted small farmers had turned to Clann na Talmhan, disenchanted workers turned to the Labour Party. In the 1942 local elections it won as many seats as Fine Gael nationally and was larger than Fine Gael in Dublin. In the 1943 general election it was not as strong but polled 16 per cent, its strongest vote ever, doubling its representation to seventeen. All these gains were at the expense of Fianna Fáil.[42]

In general, the result of the 1943 election changed little. Fianna Fáil's performance was a disappointment in the circumstances. It lost 10 per cent of the vote and ten seats and was now five seats short of a majority. When the Dáil resumed, Clann na Talmhan abstained on the vote for Taoiseach and de Valera was elected to head a minority Government. The only change in his "new" Government was the appointment of Seán Moylan as Minister for Lands. The 1932 and 1937 precedents suggested that de Valera would go to the country again as soon as a favourable opportunity arose.

Early in 1944 there occurred a series of events that made the electoral climate even easier for Fianna Fáil. In January 1944 W. T. Cosgrave resigned from the leadership of Fine Gael. He was succeeded by Richard Mulcahy, whose capacity to lead the party out of the political mire was hampered by the fact that that he was trying to do so from the Seanad rather than from the Dáil.

In the same week as Cosgrave's retirement there was a sensational development in the Labour Party. Personality clashes and power struggles that had been raging within the trade union movement burst into the political arena, causing a split in the Labour parliamentary party. On 7 January 1944 five TDs left the Labour Party to found the National Labour Party, claiming that the Labour Party was now "infested by communists." All five were members of the Irish Transport and General Workers' Union, whose general secretary, William O'Brien, was the driving force behind the political schism, motivated in part by his antagonism to the controversial Jim Larkin junior, son of "Big Jim" Larkin.

These divisions caused the Labour Party to waste its best opportunity for a real political breakthrough. Much was made then, and since, in Labour folklore about how much the party had suffered because it had waited out the crucial 1918 election in order to give the independence movement a free run and about how it had suffered since because of the dominance of the treaty issue in the late 1920s and 30s. Now, however, with the treaty issue abating, Labour squandered its best chance ever to make a real breakthrough. The window of opportunity that had opened in 1943 was now, in 1944, slammed shut by its own hand. Its enemies were happy to maximise the political damage from the split. Among the sensational *Irish Press* headlines were "Story of the red coup in the party" and "Communist victory over Irish Labour Party."[43]

Then, in February, the troublesome American minister to Ireland, David Gray, wrote what became known as the "American Note" to de Valera, in which the US government demanded the removal of German and Japanese diplomats from Dublin. The note contained an implied threat to Irish neutrality. Reportage of the ensuing controversy reignited real fears that

Ireland's neutral position was in danger, fears that were carefully stoked by Fianna Fáil spokespersons.

The moment was opportune for Fianna Fáil to try to restore its majority. De Valera found his pretext when the Government lost an unimportant vote on a Transport Bill. On 9 May 1944 he dissolved the Dáil, calling an election for three weeks later. The opposition were outraged, believing de Valera was casting aside the inter-party unity of the war years to secure electoral advantage. James Dillon said to de Valera in the Dáil: "There you are; the old warhorse is pawing the ground and sniffing the air. He thinks he is going to secure political advantage in a snap general election."[44]

It was a shorter and duller campaign than that held eleven months earlier, but the outcome was more decisive. Demoralised further by Cosgrave's retirement, Fine Gael ran an even more lacklustre campaign. The Labour Party was distracted by its own internal divisions. Fianna Fáil's was the most active and unified of the campaigns, but it too was more muted. It concentrated on the same themes as 1943, with slogans such as "Keep going ahead," "Don't turn back now," and "Don't stop half way."[45]

The new Fine Gael leader tried to suggest to voters that they were being offered a coalition of his party, the Labour Party and Clann na Talmhan, but the inconclusive outcome of the previous election and the split in the Labour Party served to reinforce Fianna Fáil's argument that only a single-party majority government could provide the necessary stability. *Irish Press* cartoonists helped the party reinforce this theme. On 25 May a front-page cartoon depicted the "Dick Mulcahy Band", all playing out of tune. On the eve of polling another cartoon depicted the proposed coalition as a three-card trickster under the caption "Find the Taoiseach."[46]

With a reduced turn-out of 65 per cent, Fianna Fáil increased its vote by 7 per cent and won an extra nine seats to give it 76 seats in a Dáil of 138. Fine Gael's vote fell again by a further 3 per cent, losing it another two seats. Labour lost all the gains it had made in 1943: the Labour Party and the National Labour Party combined had only 11½ per cent of the vote and 12 seats, while Clann na Talmhan won 9 seats.

Joseph Lee's judgement on this outcome was that Fianna Fáil's victory reflected "despair in the opposition more than confidence in the government."[47] Cornelius O'Leary offers a similar view when he says: "The poor condition of the opposition helped to enhance the apparent invincibility of the government." Yet one may also suggest that in part this victory represented gratitude from the electorate. The Fianna Fáil Government, and de Valera in particular, had performed well during the war. The voters, at least at this point, had much to be grateful for.

One of the reasons that Fianna Fáil's political position was so strong at this time was that it and its leader dominated the two leading means of mass communication. The *Irish Press*, though shrunken in number of pages, was the largest-selling newspaper of the war years. In addition, de Valera as Taoiseach was by far the most prominent politician on the radio, to such an extent that opposition politicians complained that Radio Éireann might as well be called Radio Fianna Fáil, given its tendency to broadcast de Valera's speeches.[48] Shortly after coming to power in 1932 de Valera, like many of his political contemporaries abroad, had come to appreciate the level of intimacy that the new medium allowed politicians in reaching their citizens. Ireland had had its own public-service radio station since 1926, but in 1933 de Valera had officially opened a new high-power station in Athlone, which meant that Radio Éireann could be heard throughout the country.

De Valera was generally regarded as a poor street orator, but his slow delivery, clipped tone and homely style were well suited to the "wireless".[49] While his occasional radio addresses were not as compulsive or as significant as Roosevelt's famous "fireside chats" or Churchill's rallying parliamentary addresses redelivered on radio, they were inevitably significant political events. Two of the radio addresses he gave during the war years stand out for their impact at the time, at least within Ireland, and for the attention they have attracted since in historical commentary. While they were delivered in his role as head of the Government, each is a high point in the statement of Fianna Fáil policy of the era.

The first of these was delivered on 17 March (St Patrick's Day) 1943 to mark the fiftieth anniversary of the Gaelic League. It has come to be de Valera's most famous and most controversial speech, largely because it included the following passage setting out his vision of an ideal Ireland:

> The ideal Ireland that we would have, the Ireland that we dreamed of, would be the home of a people who valued material wealth only as a basis for right living, of a people who, satisfied with frugal comfort, devoted their leisure to the things of the spirit—a land whose country-side would be bright with cosy homesteads, whose fields and villages would be joyous with the sounds of industry, with the rompings of sturdy children, the contests of athletic youths and the laughter of comely maidens, whose firesides would be forums for the wisdom of serene old age. It would, in a word, be the the home of a people living the life that God desires that men should live.

In later decades it became fashionable for commentators to sneer at the vision of Ireland championed by de Valera in what has usually been referred to as his "comely maidens speech."[50] Many historians too have contrasted the idyllic rural life championed by de Valera with the reality of the life that those in Ireland, and more importantly the tens of thousands forced to emigrate from Ireland, were actually living during his tenure and as a consequence of his Government's policies. De Valera's vision inevitably sounded and read as an increasingly outdated aspiration as Ireland became more industrialised, urbanised, liberal and non-sectarian; but, like his other speeches and writings, his St Patrick's Day address must be analysed in the context of its time. As Stephen Collins points out, "at the time de Valera made his remarks most

democracies had fallen under the yoke of fascism or communism . . .
De Valera's vision may seem quaint today but it was a benign one particularly
when compared to the political madness of right and left that engulfed most
of Europe in the 1930s and 1940s."[51] Richard Aldous also notes that, "in the
middle of the Emergency with rationing in full sway, many responded
positively to the call to forsake materialism in favour of the loftier spiritual
and cultural ideals."

Nor was de Valera delusional in what he had to say: he was not describing
Ireland as it then existed but as an aspiration. As Dermot Keogh puts it,

> in retrospect, the imagery and sentiments of de Valera's speech read
> more like the words of a "lay cardinal" than of a politician. However, it
> is not generally pointed out that de Valera did not confuse image with
> reality in the speech . . . It was the "Ireland which we dreamed of . . ."[52]

De Valera's broadcast of 17 May 1945 has also endured as one of his most
famous, and this one was less controversial. It was made four days after
Winston Churchill's victory broadcast on 13 May in which he launched a
bitter attack on the Irish Government's policy of neutrality and on de Valera
in particular.

> Had it been necessary, we should have been forced to come in close
> contact with Mr de Valera. With a restraint and poise to which, I
> venture to say, history will find few parallels, His Majesty's Government
> never laid a violent hand upon them, though at times it would have
> been quite easy and quite natural, and we left the de Valera government
> to frolic with the German and later with the Japanese representatives to
> their hearts' content.

Churchill's remarks were popular in Britain and in America, and indeed
even in Irish America, where de Valera's decision two weeks earlier to call on
the German minister in Ireland to convey condolences on the death of Adolf
Hitler had caused outrage. De Valera had argued that to refuse condolences
"would have been an act of unpardonable discourtesy to the German nation
and to Dr Hempel. During the whole war Dr Hempel's conduct was
irreproachable. I certainly was not going to add to his humiliation in his hour
of defeat." Interestingly, presidential protocol records issued in 2005 revealed
for the first time that the President of Ireland, Douglas Hyde, had also visited
Hempel to offer condolences on 3 May.[53]

Whatever might have been the response among Allied countries,
Churchill's victory broadcast caused fury throughout Ireland, and de Valera's
response was eagerly awaited. When he travelled to the Radio Éireann studio
in the GPO the following Wednesday evening to deliver his reply "everyone in
the country was near a radio to listen."

He began by thanking God for the end of the war and for the fact that
Ireland had been spared. He then thanked the political parties and various

sections of the community and members of the Defence Forces for their united stand. About two-thirds of the way through the speech he turned to deal with Churchill's remarks.

It is indeed fortunate that Britain's necessity did not reach the point when Mr. Churchill would have acted [to invade Ireland]. All credit to him that he successfully resisted the temptation which, I have no doubt, many times assailed him in his difficulties and to which I freely admit many leaders might have easily succumbed. It is, indeed, hard for the strong to be just to the weak, but acting justly always has its rewards.

By resisting his temptation in this instance, Mr. Churchill, instead of adding another horrid chapter to the already bloodstained record of the relations between England and this country, has advanced the cause of international morality an important step—one of the most important, indeed, that can be taken on the road to the establishment of any sure basis for peace.

Noting that Churchill was proud of Britain's standing alone after France had fallen and before America entered the war, de Valera asked:

Could he not find in his heart, the generosity to acknowledge that there is a small nation that stood alone, not for one year or two, but for several hundred years against aggression; that endured spoliations, famines, massacres in endless succession; that was clubbed many times into insensibility, but that each time on returning consciousness, took up the fight anew; a small nation that could never be got to accept defeat and has never surrendered her soul?

Mr. Churchill is justly proud of his nation's perseverance against heavy odds. But we in this island are still prouder of our people's perseverance for freedom through all the centuries. We of our time have played our part in that perseverance, and we have pledged ourselves to the dead generations who have preserved intact for us this glorious heritage, that we too will strive to be faithful to the end, and pass on this tradition unblemished.

As Richard Aldous says, in this response "a man who so often divided opinion on this occasion spoke for the nation."

There was another significant passage earlier in the broadcast to which writers such as Richard Aldous and Stephen Collins have drawn particular attention more recently. Speaking of how many newspapers had contacted him seeking a reply to Churchill's outburst, de Valera told listeners:

I know the reply I would have given a quarter of a century ago. But I have deliberately decided that that is not the reply I shall make to-night. I shall strive not to be guilty of adding any fuel to the flames of hatred and passion which, if continued to be fed, promise to burn up whatever is left by the war of decent human feeling in Europe.

Allowances can be made for Mr. Churchill's statement, however unworthy, in the first flush of his victory. No such excuse could be found for me in this quieter atmosphere. There are, however, some things which it is my duty to say, some things which it is essential to say. I shall try to say them as dispassionately as I can.

It was as close as de Valera had ever come, up to that point, to acknowledging his own role in inflaming tensions in Ireland more than two decades earlier.

The reply to Churchill, while not well perceived internationally, was warmly received in Ireland. Crowds gathered in O'Connell Street to cheer and applaud de Valera as he left the building. His personal secretary recounts that "the 'phone was ringing all night"[54] with calls of congratulation and that telegrams and letters started to flow in the next day complimenting the Taoiseach on his remarks. When the Dáil next met, on the afternoon after the broadcast, de Valera received a standing ovation as he entered the chamber.

Even though he would lead Fianna Fáil for another fifteen years, this was to be the high point of de Valera's political career. In the post-war years things were to continue to be difficult for the country and would become much more difficult for Fianna Fáil.

Chapter 6

PUSHED INTO OPPOSITION BY A PRETENDER, 1948–54

B oth the Government and the public had expected that things would get easier after the war. They didn't. In fact many people's standard of living worsened. In the immediate post-war years many households faced difficulties in their ordinary lives of a type they had not endured even during the war itself. Inevitably, this had political consequences. As Joseph Lee puts it, "many people could not or would not understand why the hardship should continue,"[1] and, understandably, they blamed the Fianna Fáil Government.

With international trade slow to resume, and many raw materials being absorbed by the reconstruction effort in the combatant countries, Ireland suffered continuing shortages. This situation was compounded by a bad harvest in 1946, which, for the first time, caused the rationing of bread in January 1947. The butter ration was reduced from four ounces to two ounces per week.[2] The hardship caused by severe fuel shortages was made worse by a lack of coal supplies from Britain and by the fact that the winter of 1946/7 was the coldest in living memory. Many people referred to 1947 as another Black '47, looking back to the Great Famine. Long-distance trains were cancelled, factories were temporarily closed, and power stations were working at half capacity. On 20 March 1947 even firewood was put on the ration list.[3]

Lemass told people they were now facing a situation "more difficult than at any stage of the war."[4] Emigration rose from 24,000 in 1945 to 40,000 in 1948. In spite of this, the level of unemployment climbed to over 10 per cent.[5] Emigration to Britain was particularly high, as it was in need of workers for reconstruction and nurses for its new national health service. Of course emigration generated its own political resentments.

The industrial relations situation also worsened as pent-up wage expectations now asserted themselves. Teachers went on strike from March to October 1946 for higher pay, but their demand was resisted by the Government, which feared it would open the door to other claims. The Minister for Education, Tom Derrig, and the rest of the Government stood their ground, despite strong public, press and ecclesiastical support for the teachers; but they paid a political price. Derrig's accusation that the teachers were attempting "to hold the country to ransom" and were "challenging the authority of the state" caused much resentment.[6] The teachers were now another group waiting in the long grass for Fianna Fáil.

Soaring prices posed the greatest difficulty for people and Government as the highly dependent Irish economy was exposed to the worst effects of international inflation. Wage standstill orders were issued, and when they were challenged the Government tried to impose wage restraint through the newly established Labour Court. This meant that rising prices caused real cuts in standards of living.

Drastic measures were required, and these took the form of an autumn budget, announced on 14 October 1947. The Government decided to address pressures on the cost of living by increasing food subsidies. It financed these by increasing income tax and imposing a series of extremely unpopular levies on goods such as beer, cigarettes and even cinema tickets.

Since being re-elected in 1944 the Fianna Fáil Government had to deal not only with the continuing economic crisis but with the consequences of three separate corruption allegations levelled at it during these years. In 1946 there was a controversy about transactions in railway company shares on the eve of the adoption of the Transport Bill. It was alleged that business friends of ministers, including Seán Lemass, had been able to make a killing on the stock exchange. A tribunal of inquiry found there was no basis for the claims. One of Lemass's biographers noted: "There was not even a scintilla of evidence to suggest that Lemass benefited in any way from the sale but the sulphur of suspicion was heavy in the air."[7]

Then Con Ward, Parliamentary Secretary to the Minister for Public Health and Local Government, was the subject of allegations about a bacon factory he owned in Co. Monaghan. In this instance a tribunal of inquiry found the more serious charges against him to be unfounded but held that he had made incorrect returns for tax purposes, and he was forced to resign. In an attempt at damage limitation de Valera had sought to announce the tribunal's findings just before the Dáil's summer recess, provoking political and press outrage.

Finally, in October 1947, an even more potent scandal developed about alleged improper authorisation of the sale of Locke's distillery in Kilbeggan, Co. Westmeath, to foreign financiers. Lemass was again the minister who was the subject of the most outlandish of these allegations, which also pointed the finger at de Valera, his son Éamon, Gerry Boland and Senator William Quirke. Under parliamentary privilege, Oliver Flanagan, then an independent deputy for Laois-Offaly, alleged ministerial collusion in the scandal. A tribunal found the charges malicious and rebuked Flanagan; but although it had been exonerated the Government was both distracted and damaged by the controversies.

On the political front Fianna Fáil initially looked comfortable after the war. A few weeks after VE Day the first contested presidential election took place, on 14 June 1945. The Fianna Fáil candidate was its deputy leader and Tánaiste, Seán T. O'Kelly, while Fine Gael nominated General Seán Mac Eoin TD, a former chief of staff of the army. In addition Patrick McCartan, an independent republican, managed to get a nomination from twenty Oireachtas members.

After a campaign that was "raw, robust and redolent with civil war rhetoric,"[8] O'Kelly obtained 537,965 votes on the first count, while Mac Eoin got 335,539. McCartan came in third, as predicted, but with an unexpectedly strong 212,834 first preferences. After McCartan was eliminated his transfers brought O'Kelly to 563,165 and Mac Eoin to 453,425. The size of McCartan's vote and, more importantly, the rate of transfer between the two non-Fianna Fáil candidates should have been seen as a harbinger of the electoral difficulties Fianna Fáil would face in the future, though the party was delighted to have the popular O'Kelly elected with such apparent ease.

In the local elections held on the same day Fianna Fáil did lose some support, but this was to independents rather than to any of the opposition parties, and Fianna Fáil did better than expected in the election to Dublin City Council. It also won four out of five by-elections in 1945–6.

Although Mac Eoin's performance had been respectable, Fine Gael exhibited all the signs of continuing decline. It even failed to contest four of the five by-elections held that year. Labour, meanwhile, continued to war with itself, and Clann na Talmhan remained weak.

In the Government reshuffle occasioned by O'Kelly's departure to Áras an Uachtaráin, Frank Aiken sought and was given the vacancy in Finance. T. Ryle Dwyer has written dismissively of this appointment.

> Aiken had little to recommend him for the position. Although his integrity was unquestionable, he was not renowned for his intelligence. In fact, some people referred to him as "the iron man with the wooden head" . . . In February 1941 after Aiken had expounded on his financial views, which were based on the Social Credit experiment of the provincial government of Alberta, Canada, [David] Gray questioned the Taoiseach, who just laughed. "We don't pay any attention to Frank's ideas about finance," he said. Yet this did not stop him slotting Aiken in as Minister for Finance when the position became vacant in June 1945.[9]

Another interesting appointment was that of Lemass as Tánaiste. After an impressive performance as Minister for Supplies during the war, while simultaneously holding the portfolio of Industry and Commerce from 1941 onwards, Lemass's standing, both in his party and in the country, was very high. His elevation, however, implying as it did that he was now heir apparent, did not meet with universal approval among his colleagues.[10]

In spite of the economic challenges, Fianna Fáil seemed to be comfortable. However, the political situation was changed—and for a period looked as if it might be transformed—by the launch of a new political party, Clann na Poblachta ("children of the republic"), in July 1946.

The new party's founders were, in the main, republicans, although its national leadership was a disparate—one commentator says heterogeneous[11]—

group. The party leader was Seán MacBride, a brilliant senior counsel who was
then prominent as defence counsel in cases relating to the IRA and who had
himself been chief of staff of the IRA in the 1930s. He was a son of Major John
MacBride and Maud Gonne, both of whom had been prominent in the
independence struggle. Another leadership figure was Noel Hartnett, a former
member of the Fianna Fáil Ard-Chomhairle. Among them also was Noël
Browne, a radical young doctor campaigning for improvements in health and
social welfare.[12] Twenty-two out of the twenty-six members of the first
executive committee had been in the IRA at various times since the Anglo-Irish
Treaty of 1921.[13]

From the outset it was clear that, unlike previous pretenders, Clann na
Poblachta was a party whose "ideological and political tentacles reached
inexorably into Fianna Fáil's heartland."[14] Its policies were a mix of left-wing
economics and doctrinaire republicanism. It promised better social services
and guaranteed wage rates, as well as an improved health service, with a
particular emphasis on eliminating tuberculosis. It favoured price controls,
increased old-age pensions, free secondary education and municipally owned
public transport.[15] On partition it was "agitational",[16] promising to invite MPS
from the Six Counties to attend Dáil Éireann and to nominate Northerners to
the Seanad.[17] It proposed the repeal of the Executive Authority (External
Relations) Act and the severing of the link with the British currency.

The new party "quickly attracted the support of many idealists, who had
never been connected with the republican movement but who felt dissatisfied
with the existing parties."[18] Its main appeal, however, as Cornelius O'Leary
assesses it, was

> its professed intention to get away from the *damnosa hereditas*
> [accursed inheritance] of the civil war [and] the irreconcilability of
> Fianna Fáil and to study national problems objectively. This would win
> over the uncommitted mature voters while the rekindling of
> Republican ardours which had cooled under Fianna Fáil was especially
> attractive to the young.[19]

What was most worrying for de Valera and his party was that when they
looked at Clann na Poblachta, its policy mix, the fresh approach to politics it
represented and the political hunger and vitality it exhibited they were
looking in the mirror at a younger version of themselves. MacBride's new
party of the late 1940s resembled Fianna Fáil of the late 1920s. This was no
accident: MacBride had set out to create a "replica" Fianna Fáil. While his new
party would certainly "create waves and set in motion some badly needed
social and political reform," as a political movement it would never even be a
shadow of the organisation de Valera and his colleagues had built, and it
"fatally foundered within a few years."[20]

The years after the foundation of Clann na Poblachta were some of the
stormiest economically and culminated in the budget of October 1947. Two

weeks later three by-elections were held, one each in counties Dublin, Tipperary and Waterford. Two of them were to be the scene of spectacular victories for Clann na Poblachta. MacBride himself was elected in Dublin County and his colleague Paddy Kinane in Tipperary. In Waterford, Fianna Fáil did hold its seat but its vote was significantly reduced. Fine Gael was relegated to third place in all three constituencies.

Lemass was in London when the by-election results were declared. De Valera telephoned to ask, "What would you do?" Lemass replied, "You are not the man I think you are if the Dáil is not dissolved before I get back."[21]

Fianna Fáil had a comfortable majority in Dáil Éireann, holding 77 of the 138 seats, and the Dáil term had another eighteen months to run. De Valera, however, feared that the new party would grow exponentially on the strength of these by-election gains. He announced immediately that the Dáil would be dissolved once certain financial legislation was completed. Shortly before this Seán MacEntee had piloted through the Dáil an Electoral (Amendment) Bill that abolished seven-seat constituencies and increased the number of three-seat constituencies from fifteen to twenty-two.[22] While this should have favoured the large incumbent Government party, the number of deputies was also increased, from 138 to 147, which gave extra space for the new party to grow.

The Dáil was dissolved on 12 January 1948, with the election set for 4 February, and Fianna Fáil embarked on another dreaded winter-time campaign. According to de Valera's official biography some unnamed senior colleagues did not agree with this decision, believing that the party should remain in office until conditions were more favourable for an election.[23]

Clann na Poblachta's slogan for the campaign was blunt: "Put them out." The irony of this was not lost on Fianna Fáil ministers, who had used the same slogan against Cumann na nGaedheal in 1932. In response, Fianna Fáil called on voters to play safe and not to give power to an inexperienced party whose leaders had questionable political pedigrees. The rivalry between Clann na Poblachta and Fianna Fáil was particularly intense. Two incidents illustrate how competitive and bitter the campaign became.

In Longford, Erskine Childers was making a speech outside the courthouse when a Clann na Poblachta lorry pulled up provocatively on the opposite side of the street. Noel Hartnett climbed onto the back of the lorry and began a tirade, jabbing his finger at the Fianna Fáil speaker. Childers retorted: "This is the sort of democracy we can expect from them. They tried to destroy our neutrality during the war, and now they want to destroy freedom of speech."[24]

On another occasion, about an hour before a Clann na Poblachta meeting was due to begin in Dún Laoghaire, the party's banner was stolen from the platform and petrol was poured over the five leather chairs assigned to the speakers. When MacBride belatedly rose to speak he accused de Valera of instructing his henchmen to spread lies that there were "godless communists in Clann na Poblachta."[25] Ó Beacháin says:

Before and during the election Fianna Fáil used the same material that
Cumann na nGaedheal had used against Fianna Fáil during the late
1920s and early 30s to damage the reputation of Clann na Poblachta
and the Labour Party. Since the by-election campaigns in October, Seán
MacEntee had been amassing security files compiled by civil servants
under the Cumann na nGaedheal and Fianna Fáil regimes . . . Fianna
Fáil [also] took out expensive half-page advertisements in national and
local papers headed "A Plan for Safety." It warned of forces working for
the overthrow of democracy . . . Their methods would be "to destroy
confidence in the motives of the Government, and, if possible, by
slander and abuse of political leaders, to weaken public faith in the
democratic system." The advertisement concluded in apocalyptic terms
by claiming that the free election that would bring "the enemies of
Christianity and democracy" to power "is always the last free election
ever held."[26]

Meanwhile Fine Gael was at a low ebb but stayed consistent to its previous
policy course. It ran a lacklustre campaign and appeared doomed to further
losses. "In [the] face of widespread dissatisfaction with economic stagnation,
mounting social discontent, and pressure for change, Fine Gael assured the
electorate that it would be even tougher and more conservative than Fianna
Fáil."[27]

When the result was declared, de Valera's decision to go to the polls early
appeared partially vindicated. Fianna Fáil had lost eight seats, falling to 68 in
the new Dáil of 147. However, the rapid rise of Clann na Poblachta, as
evidenced in the previous autumn's by-elections, which had led some
independent commentators to claim that it might even govern alone after the
election, was abruptly halted. During the campaign the optimism and
euphoria about the new party was widespread. Noel Hartnett, as Clann na
Poblachta's director of elections, predicted on the eve of the poll that it would
get at least 45 and at most 75 seats.[28] After the by-elections in October
MacBride had confidently asserted that Clann na Poblachta would win an
absolute majority.[29] It did nothing of the sort: in the event it won only 10
seats. Fine Gael won 31, the Labour Party 14, Clann na Talmhan 7 and the
National Labour Party 5.

Clann na Poblachta did win 13 per cent of the vote, which was a more than
respectable performance and the best up to that point by any party on its first
attempt, Fianna Fáil excluded. But this was far short of its expectations. It was
probably de Valera's snap election that had the greatest effect on negating the
growth of Clann na Poblachta. As de Valera had intended, it was playing
"catch-up", organisationally and otherwise, throughout the campaign. It ran
too many candidates in too many constituencies, stretching the party's
immature organisation and its limited finances. The policy of running at least
two candidates in every constituency had proved to be a bad idea, as it split the
vote in some places. In all, Clann na Poblachta ran 93 candidates, which meant

its panel was second in size only to that of Fianna Fáil. These candidates, however, were a "scratch group, hastily got together from many different backgrounds."[30] Most of them lacked political experience or electoral drawing power.

It was not a good election for Fine Gael but better than had been expected. Although it fell to a historic low point of 20 per cent, the congratulatory tone of the editorials in the Dublin newspapers—"the remarkably firm stand of Fine Gael" and "Fine Gael polled well"—illustrated how much worse it had been expected to do.[31] The party was still, however, on the very brink of collapse when it was miraculously saved by the opportunity to go into power as part of a diverse coalition.

In 1948 both Labour Parties had secured almost the same share of the poll as they had done in 1944, with a combined total of 11.3 per cent, compared with 11.1 per cent on the former occasion. However, they did much better in number of seats this time: the National Labour Party increased from 4 to 5, while the Labour Party increased from 8 to 14.

In total, Fianna Fáil had one more seat than the combined opposition parties, and there were 12 independents. Fianna Fáil's leaders expected to form a minority Government. They assumed that the National Labour Party, which had campaigned on the understanding that it was going to support Fianna Fáil, would indeed vote for de Valera as Taoiseach. Right up to the night before the Dáil vote they were led to believe that there was no way the National Labour Party would align itself with Clann na Poblachta, or go into government with its despised rivals in the Labour Party. On the day before the vote the *Irish Independent*'s political correspondent anticipated that the National Labour group and about four independents would vote for de Valera and that three or four others would abstain.[32]

The Congress of Irish Unions (a product of the same split that created the National Labour Party) had mandated the National Labour TDs to vote for the Fianna Fáil nominee. However, a meeting between John A. Costello of Fine Gael and James Everett and Dan Spring of the National Labour Party seems to have changed everything.[33] Costello pledged to appoint Everett to the Government. The allure of office was as strong for National Labour as it was for the other four opposition parties; and when the Dáil resumed on 18 February 1948 de Valera was voted out of government by 75 votes to 70, and suddenly Fianna Fáil found itself in opposition after sixteen years in power.

The overriding feeling among the party's TDs was one of being hard done by. A narrative quickly emerged that the loss of power in 1948 was somehow somebody else's fault. They were out because the other parties, united only by their antipathy to Fianna Fáil, had ganged up on them, and also because the National Labour Party had double-crossed them. Alternatively, Fianna Fáil comforted itself with the explanation that it had lost power only because of the newly introduced coalition quirk in the political system.

This was a narrative that endured. It even reappeared twelve years later in an official history published by the party.[34] In a chapter headed "The anti

Fianna Fáil coalitions," the outcome of the 1948 election was explained to supporters as follows:

> Suddenly in 1948 a political move of an unusual kind brought down the government and destroyed the atmosphere of stability, confidence and progress so carefully fostered over the years. The Fianna Fáil government that had carried through the many changes, political, economic and social on which a new Ireland was building, and had kept the country neutral during the war, was replaced by a strange combination of discordant political elements whose only common bond was antagonism to Fianna Fáil and a determination at all costs to get them out of power.

The account continues with a now ironic invitation to future historians and political scientists.

> Such an unusual political phenomenon, in which a majority party is forced out of office by a combination of six minority groups who had nothing discoverable in common except anti-Fianna Fáilism, may have considerable historical interest for future political studies.

The article then explains the loss of power as also being due to false allegations made against the party.

> The story is as follows. Following on the formation of a new party, Clann na Poblachta, an unscrupulous campaign was opened against Fianna Fáil leaders during the year 1947, who were accused of corruption, jobbery, political dishonesty—on all of which charges no evidence was produced either then . . . or since.[35]

Even allowing for the nature of the publication and its proximity to the events it was discussing, the analysis of what happened to Fianna Fáil in 1948 strikes one as delusional.

The reasons for the loss of power in 1948 were manifold. As we have seen, the economic crisis and the manner in which the Fianna Fáil Government responded to it, particularly in October 1947, were major contributing factors, but so too was the fact that the de Valera Government looked tired and was probably exhausted. There was a staleness about this "Government of old men". Of the ten ministers de Valera had appointed to his first government in 1932, six were still ministers sixteen years later. Apart from the extensive reshuffle required by the creation of two specific wartime ministries in 1939, de Valera rarely changed their postings. He himself had held the External Relations portfolio for all sixteen years, while Lemass was in Industry and Commerce for all but two of them. James Ryan had spent all but the last of the sixteen years in Agriculture, and Thomas Derrig had similarly spent fifteen years in Education.[36] While the low turnover in personnel and port-folios may have enabled the Government to function cohesively, after sixteen years it left it looking and acting in an even more lacklustre way than such a long period of incumbency would have accounted for by itself.

There were some in the party who appreciated how tired the Government looked. Among them was Erskine Childers, then Parliamentary Secretary to the Minister for Local Government. Writing to the party general secretary, Tommy Mullins, the week after the 1948 campaign, Childers said:

> There is no question the people are tired of some of the old faces and we may as well make up our minds that something will have to be done, regretfully perhaps, about members of the Party who have given great service in the past but who have become inarticulate between elections and whose personal prestige has been constantly declining.[37]

It is not clear which party figures in particular were the subject of these comments, and Childers would of course have had his own ambitions for ministerial office (soon to be realised), but it was a strikingly candid observation to make to party officialdom.

In private correspondence with Seán MacEntee at about the same time Childers also showed an insight into the underlying reasons for the 1948 defeat that was rare in the party.

> Our TDS were careless, shockingly briefed and a very large number of them simply contented themselves with talking up Dev and down with coalition. This will not do for waverers . . . We underestimated the Clann . . . We underestimated F.G.
>
> There are 250,00 voters of age 21 to 25 who do not believe there is any substantial difference between us and F.G. They chose F.F. because of Dev and other personalities. There is in fact no policy difference save on the Irish Language.[38]

If Fianna Fáil had been complacent during the previous three years in government it continued to be complacent for the next three years about the fact that it was in opposition. The working assumption was that coalitions, "according to some obscure but infallible decree," could not last,[39] and so this five-way Government of such disparate elements could not last long. This period, in Lemass's words, was just an "interlude". Fianna Fáil only had to sit and wait: the Government would soon collapse and another Fianna Fáil reign would begin. It was, of course, to be proved correct in this assumption, though out on the timing by three years.

Niamh Puirséil argues that if Fianna Fáil had suffered a more ignominious defeat in 1948 its response might have been more effective and the party might have begun to renew its policies sooner.[40] Instead, believing itself nudged out of or robbed of power in 1948, Fianna Fáil came to believe that policies had played no part in its defeat and did not require revision. To Lemass, for example, the switch to opposition meant business as usual. He and his colleagues believed that Fianna Fáil would inevitably return to power, so no serious thought was given to the development of new policies. John Horgan, who has studied the minutes of the parliamentary party for this period, says they show ample evidence that the party felt its return to power was inevitable and that it did not need to develop or change its offering to the electorate.[41]

Jack Lynch, who, together with Neil Blaney, was one of the few new Fianna Fáil deputies elected in 1948, was an up-and-coming barrister on the Cork circuit. He later gave an account of his involvement with the parliamentary party in this period, which, perhaps inadvertently, suggests a relatively laid-back and under-resourced approach to research and policy development in opposition. Lynch tells of how "naturally the party took a while to acclimatise itself" to its new circumstances.

> One of its first decisions was to appoint a researcher and secretary to the Parliamentary Party. I was asked to take on both jobs, having been promised that I would still have time for my Bar practice. I agreed, but quickly found that these duties involved me full time, especially as I was expected to help draft speeches for Dev, index Dáil debates and newspaper reports, prepare briefs for front-bench members, etc.
>
> I got on very well with Dev and liked him a lot. One of his traits I noticed particularly was his meticulous attention to the words he used in public speeches. I used to help him on his speeches from 1948 to '49 and I learned a lot of the need for precision in speech, from Dev.
>
> I stayed with the job for a year, but after that I went to Dev and told him that I couldn't afford to continue to neglect my legal duties completely. He understood my position and he took in Pádraig Ó Hannracháin as his own private secretary and this relieved me of most of the work I had been doing.[42]

It is not too harsh to say that de Valera himself did not engage with being leader of the opposition or leader of Fianna Fáil in any meaningful way during those years. Lemass told Brian Farrell that the front bench did not function as an effective shadow cabinet. No firm lines were drawn, all were encouraged to contribute on all topics, and de Valera himself showed "a rather inert attitude" and tended to be the judge of other people's ideas rather than the initiator of policy.[43] By 1948 de Valera was sixty-six and, according to ill-disposed British observers, had "completely lost the sight of one eye and was having problems with the other."[44]

In addition, de Valera was not around for much of the period. Only six of the nearly five hundred pages in his authorised biography are devoted to this opposition term. The relevant chapter is titled "Interlude", and the bulk of it is given over to describing the various trips de Valera undertook from 1948 to 1951. In addition to returning to the United States he visited Australia and

New Zealand, spent the last night of British rule in India as a guest of Lord and Lady Mountbatten, travelled to Strasbourg for the launch of the Council of Europe, attended the commemoration for St Columbanus in France in 1950 and then travelled as a pilgrim to both Rome and Israel.[45]

De Valera's primary focus in opposition and during his travels was partition. He was discomfited by the Government's zeal on this issue and particularly by that shown by Seán MacBride, now Minister for External Affairs. He put the majority of his time and effort into an outspoken if futile attempt to outdo the Government in the anti-partition propaganda effort at home and abroad. During his travels much of his effort in this regard was ineffectual: his speeches appeared to be aimed primarily at the political audience at home and in any case were being delivered to audiences of the converted.[46]

In 1949 de Valera also undertook an extensive tour of British cities, including London, Birmingham, Newcastle and Sheffield, organised by the Anti-Partition League. While many of the meetings were "enormous and enthusiastic," according to the Labour MP Hugh Delargy, who as chairman of the Anti-Partition League shared many of the platforms, "they were all flops." Delargy says:

> They were not political meetings at all. They were tribal rallies, tribes-men met to greet the old Chieftains. The melodies of 1916 were played. A few IRA veterans with their IRA medals, formed guards of honour. Sympathetic Englishmen who attended went away bewildered.[47]

In Ireland, Longford and O'Neill say, "there was a limit to what a Leader of the Opposition could accomplish," and they go on to cite the establishment of the *Sunday Press* as the only significant party achievement of these years. Notwithstanding this inactivity in party matters, de Valera's biographers, probably reflecting the Chief's own view, judge that the party "did not lose its vigour in opposition . . . It was ready to fight an election campaign should the opportunity arise."

De Valera did lead the Fianna Fáil response on the two most significant initiatives taken by the Costello Government, namely the declaration of the Republic of Ireland and the Mother and Child Scheme, although on the latter his strategic approach could be more correctly termed a non-intervention.

When Costello announced, on an official visit to Canada in September 1948, that the Government would repeal the Executive Authority (External Relations) Act, de Valera was as surprised as the rest of the country—and, it appears, some of Costello's own ministers. When the matter came before the Dáil some weeks later there was suppressed fury within the ranks of Fianna Fáil at being outflanked by the Government on a republican issue. De Valera's official biography comments: "De Valera's followers were irate at the manner of Fine Gael's change of policy. It took some persuasion on de Valera's part to achieve unanimity in his party and to prevent some of them voting against the bill."[48]

In the 1930s Fine Gael had opposed Fianna Fáil as it sought to dismantle the treaty. This had a negative effect on Fine Gael's political fortunes, and de Valera understood this. Whatever doubts de Valera had about the wisdom of abandoning the act—and he himself had often offered the view that pending the end of partition some link with the Commonwealth should be retained— he was not going to allow Fianna Fáil to back itself into an electoral cul-de-sac. In the Dáil he welcomed Costello's action and said it showed that all parties now supported the 1937 constitution and the republican status that this had bestowed on the country. Lemass also welcomed the repeal of the act, seeing it, in typically practical terms, as rationalising Ireland's constitutional position and setting relations with Britain and Northern Ireland on a more realistic footing. He wrote: "Whatever opinions were held in our Party regarding the repeal of the External Relations Act—and there was more than one—it was our general view that when it was proposed by the Government there was no alternative to supporting it."[49]

The Mother and Child Scheme, proposed on 6 March 1951 by Noël Browne as Minister for Health, would introduce a largely free health service and health education for mothers and young children. It was vigorously opposed by the medical establishment and the Catholic hierarchy. When the controversy broke, de Valera made sure his party colleagues resisted the temptation to score points or become embroiled in the dispute. He felt that the correspondence between Browne and the hierarchy should not have been published, but he and his party wisely stayed out of the Dáil debate on the matter, save for his disdainful comment "I think we have heard enough." As de Valera saw it, the coalition was falling apart, so Fianna Fáil's best strategy would be to let events take their course.[50]

In 1949 the Government invited Fianna Fáil to join an all-party anti-partition group, which, under Costello's chairmanship, became known as the Mansion House Committee. De Valera's involvement was perfunctory, however. In John Bowman's opinion, "given Dev's lack of enthusiasm for involvement in any anti-partition strategy that he did not control, it seems probable that Costello's private view was fair, that de Valera's support for the Committee's work was 'grudging and unproductive.'"[51]

During this period, and apart from these occasions, it was Lemass rather than de Valera who was effectually leader of the opposition and chief spokesperson for Fianna Fáil in the Dáil. He was the leading spokesperson in the first two significant debates of the new Dáil: the nomination of the members of the new Government and the estimates for the Department of the Taoiseach.[52] Similarly, for a period after the election the parliamentary party was chaired by Lemass rather than by the party leader.

Although he dominated the opposition benches and seemed at times "like a one man party," as Joseph Lee describes it, Lemass was also busy elsewhere. In February 1948, after the election defeat, he was immediately appointed to the board of the *Irish Press* and made managing director. It was a full-time executive position; he was a regular presence at Burgh Quay, where he made a major contribution to the launching of the group's most successful paper, the *Sunday Press*. He even contributed articles to the *Irish Press*, while carrying a major parliamentary responsibility for the party—all of which meant that, even if he had had the inclination, he would have struggled to find the time to lead any substantial renewal of either the organisation or its policies; and indeed, while it is often said that Lemass availed of those years to revamp the Fianna Fáil party machine,[53] there is little evidence that any such revamp happened. Lemass did tell Michael Mills during an interview in 1969 that

> as far as Fianna Fáil was concerned there was a risk which we fully recognised that the great organisation which we founded throughout the Country would begin to disintegrate when it found the Party for the first time in opposition. So we embarked on a very vigorous re-organisation campaign in which the members of the previous Government were free to participate; so that by 1951 we had a much more effective organisation than we had in 1948.[54]

In saying this Lemass was perhaps backdating the party reorganisation that he led in the later 1950s.

Privately to Brian Farrell, Lemass was more critical of his colleagues for their lack of effort during those years. Farrell points out that although the files in the *Irish Press* for this period tell of former ministers addressing party meetings and report the establishment of new cumainn, there was no serious reorganisation and there had been no serious analysis of the 1948 election.[55]

The recent biographies of two other Fianna Fáil front-benchers of the time do not suggest that they were particularly industrious on organisational matters from 1948 to 1951. Tom Feeney's biography of Seán MacEntee deals with these opposition years in one paragraph, most of which is a summary of the Costello Government's economic policy. Otherwise it simply says that "Fianna Fáil returned to government in 1951 after three years in opposition when an unlikely assortment of political opponents introduced the concept of coalition government to Ireland unified by their desire in the words of the sloganeers in 'putting them out'." The writer then moved directly on to deal with MacEntee's reappointment to Finance in 1951.[56]

Aideen Carroll's recent biography of Seán Moylan shows him to have been an able and active minister, both before and after this period; but the years 1948–51 are again dealt with in only one paragraph. This biography tells how in these years Moylan, a deputy for North Cork, now "had more time to enjoy his first grandchild and family life took a slower pace," how he walked most weekday mornings to Leinster House and back each evening to his new home in Clontarf, and how he had time to draft a memoir he had agreed to prepare for the Bureau of Military History.

Erskine Childers, though vocal after the election about the need to reinvigorate the party, used this period in opposition to supplement his TD's salary by taking up a job as Dublin manager of an engineering company,

Blackwood Hodge.[57] We can only conclude that most former Fianna Fáil ministers used this first opposition period to take a badly needed rest.

The first inter-party Government, led by John A. Costello, self-destructed over the controversy surrounding the Mother and Child Scheme in the spring of 1951, with MacBride requesting Browne's resignation. It limped on, but fell when it lost a vote on the price of milk at the beginning of May. Polling day was 30 May 1951, and the new Dáil met on 13 June.

As Fianna Fáil now told voters, the Mother and Child debacle and the collapse of the first inter-party Government showed the correctness of what it had been saying since the 1930s, that is, that coalition governments did not work and that the country needed strong single-party government. Seán MacEntee was in his element. He charged that for government by consent the coalition had substituted "government by convulsion . . . What one of them says today, another is certain to contradict tomorrow."[58]

A Fianna Fáil election advertisement in the *Cork Examiner* on 26 May 1951 was typical of the campaign. It read: "Look ahead—this time—Fianna Fáil." The illustration was of a father holding his son by the hand and striding away as the sun rose behind them. The text of the advertisement spoke of the immediate future, obviously in the context of the Cold War: "Peace or war— Whatever the next five years brings—Ireland will need a Government with a clear policy and capable of effective leadership. Fianna Fáil can establish it." As Dermot Keogh says,

> The alternative, according to the advertisement, was a Government divided against itself, with conflicting and ever shifting policies based on day to day expediency. Fianna Fáil promised an efficient Government and fair play for every citizen and section without fear or favour.[59]

The pitch was sufficient to move marginal voters, while the implosion in Clann na Poblachta also helped Fianna Fáil to regain lost ground. When the votes were counted, the party had increased its share from 42 to 46 per cent but had gained only a single seat. It now had 69 seats, while the combined strength of the other parties was 78; but there were independent deputies. The acrimony between the former coalition partners and within Clann na Poblachta meant that the inter-party Government could not re-form as a majority, at least not for now. De Valera was elected Taoiseach on 13 June 1951 by 74 votes to 69, but only because of the support of independents, including Noël Browne.

Because of his weakening health, de Valera did not resume the External Affairs portfolio; he gave it instead to Frank Aiken, who was to excel at it. Against Lemass's wishes, Seán MacEntee was made Minister for Finance, while Lemass himself returned to Industry and Commerce. Dr James Ryan was sent back to the increasingly sensitive portfolio of Health, where he had spent a year previously. Gerry Boland returned to Justice, Oscar Traynor to Defence and Tom Derrig to Lands, while Paddy Smith took over in Local Government. Among the limited innovations were the appointment of Erskine Childers as

Minister for Posts and Telegraphs, the appointment of the Kilkenny TD Tom Walsh as Minister for Agriculture, and the moving of Seán Moylan to Education. Jack Lynch became Parliamentary Secretary to the Government, with special responsibility for the Gaeltacht and Congested Districts.

The newly returned Taoiseach and his Minister for Health promptly set about seeking to effect reforms in the health service of the type that had proved so intractable for the previous Government. These efforts bore fruit in the Health Act (1953). This raised the proportion of patients entitled to receive either free hospital treatment or such treatment at reduced rates from 30 per cent to 80 per cent. Dr Ryan, like Dr Browne before him, had intended to have no means test but again faced a combination of episcopal and medical opposition. By conceding a modest means test, Ryan managed to get grudging agreement on the changes.

Archbishop John Charles McQuaid of Dublin privately told the Papal Nuncio that he found dealing with the new Fianna Fáil Government a more difficult proposition than dealing with Costello's. He wrote that Fianna Fáil's approach was one of

> distance as far as the Church is concerned. That policy is seen in the failure to consult any bishop on the provisions of a Health Scheme. All the present difficulties result from that failure. In assessing the attitude of Fianna Fáil Governments, one may never forget the revolutionary past of that Party. On so many occasions the Party was on the side opposed to Episcopal directions. While, then, the outward courtesies will be accorded, the inner spirit of sympathetic and open collaboration with the Hierarchy will be missing.[60]

Apart from the success of the Health Act, the Government was weak and ineffective when attempting to deal with the severe economic challenges it faced. Historians have judged it de Valera's worst Government, and some as the worst Fianna Fáil Government ever, at least of the twentieth century. However, one should make some allowances for the fact that it was a minority Government. Lemass later recounted that he did not at all welcome the prospect of coming back into government in the conditions of 1951.

> If we had won a majority on our own in that election it would have been different. Indeed during the period after the 1951 election when it was not certain how the Independents were going to vote I made no personal effort to influence any of them as to how they were going to vote because I realised whoever got their support and became the Government was going to have a difficult time. It was not our most successful period in office, as you know.[61]

Not only was the 1951 Government precarious but it also faced a combination of apparently intractable economic problems, having to deal simultaneously with an acute balance of payments deficit and a severe price crisis. Everything seemed to be going wrong at once. The cost of living was rising rapidly, largely because of factors outside Irish control relating to the Korean War. The Government also faced a series of strikes by, among others, hotel workers and newspaper workers.[62]

The Government response, led by MacEntee as Minister for Finance, was classic fiscal conservatism, culminating in the 1952 budget, which was extremely harsh. It both raised taxes and cut subsidies. In fiscal terms it worked, insofar as it held the public finances in check and solved, at least for a period, the balance of payments problem. However, it had a severely deflationary effect, employment dropped and emigration rose, and the Government's popularity suffered severely as a result.[63]

There were real and, occasionally, destabilising tensions within the Government on how to respond to the economic situation, with a majority favouring the MacEntee approach. MacEntee's policies, however, were too severe, even in the opinion of conservative economists. The deflationary pressures inevitably led to political difficulties, which in the view of many writers not only damaged the Government but wrecked MacEntee's own chances of succeeding to the leadership of Fianna Fáil.[64]

There was a strong sense that the Government could not find, or was not even looking for, a means to resolve the economic crisis. It did not help that de Valera's eyesight was failing along with his political power. He had to spend several months in Utrecht in 1951 and 52, where he had a long series of surgical procedures on his eyes. Lemass too was suffering from ill health and had to take time off to undergo a gall bladder operation.

Lemass himself was sometimes fatalistic. In July 1953 the Government, with the help of independents, survived a no-confidence motion. During the debate Lemass admitted that "the outstanding problem still is unemployment . . . We accept that the work we have done has not been wide enough in its scope or pushed ahead as vigorously as it should have been."

An opportunity to ignite new enthusiasm and to freshen Government and party had been missed in June 1952 when Seán T. O'Kelly's first term of office as President expired. Some in Fianna Fáil, including Lemass in his privately expressed comments, hoped that O'Kelly could be persuaded to step aside from seeking a second term, in which case de Valera might be persuaded to go to the Áras and Lemass could become Taoiseach. Any plan for such a combination of initiatives fell at the first fence: O'Kelly was adamant that he was staying for a second term. The idea of de Valera simply retiring to private life was inconceivable, and nobody in Fianna Fáil would have asked him to do so, let alone pushed him.[65]

It was a particularly frustrating time for new Fianna Fáil deputies. Meetings of the parliamentary party, which had always been lengthy when chaired by de Valera, became even more protracted. Each deputy was simply allowed to speak until de Valera chose the right psychological moment to put a motion to the floor. The Cork North-East deputy John Moher later described party unity under de Valera at this time as "peace by exhaustion".[66]

The debate about the need for a more expansive economic policy, which had continued in differing degrees of intensity in Fianna Fáil Governments since the war, began to get a wider airing in the parliamentary party at this time, but an airing was all it got.

Gary Murphy, who has made a particular study of the shifts in post-war economic policy, says that the minutes of the Fianna Fáil parliamentary party in these years show quite clearly that there was a gulf within the party between the expansionist-Keynesian view, led by Lemass, and the conservatism that MacEntee was implementing in Finance. Murphy tells how one such dispute erupted in late 1952 when Mícheál Ó Móráin urged that "a special meeting be held in the near future for a full discussion of Government policy."

A meeting of the full Fianna Fáil parliamentary party in January 1953 was consequently devoted entirely to economic policy. During the course of the discussion de Valera explained that the policy of the party was "to pay its way and that any additional services called for by the people could only be paid for by taxation" and stressed that "increased production—principally from the land—was the remedy for most of our problems." While this was traditional Fianna Fáil policy it did not satisfy all within the party, and within six months a motion sponsored by twenty deputies was put before the parliamentary party declaring:

> "The party is of the opinion that in present circumstances a policy of financial austerity is no longer justified and requests the government to frame a progressive policy suited to the altered situation, with a view especially to putting an end to the undue restriction of credit by the banks, and making low interest loans available for farmers and house purchasers."
>
> The debate that followed this motion lasted through July, and when no decision had been reached was then postponed until after the summer recess. The topic, however, was not discussed again until January 1954, when the minutes simply record that, after another short debate and an address by de Valera, Deputy Carter withdrew the motion.[67]

Despite these discussions among the parliamentary party, and Lemass's efforts in the Government (which Brian Farrell and others suggest may have been half-hearted at this stage), it is clear that the MacEntee view prevailed. Fianna Fáil would go to the country in 1954 defending a strictly conservative economic record. As a result it lost four seats and would spend another, if more productive, term in opposition.

Chapter 7 ～

| RENEWAL, 1954–9

The 1954 election campaign was low-key and dull, its most memorable moment being Fine Gael's reproduction of a piece of Fianna Fáil election literature from the 1951 campaign. On that occasion Fianna Fáil had distributed a leaflet that showed how the prices of essential commodities had risen during the tenure of the first inter-party Government but had failed to mention the Korean War and its impact on international inflation. Fine Gael republished the leaflet with the prices adjusted upwards to their present level.[1]

For the most part, the contenders in the 1954 election campaign concentrated on the austerity measures, real or imagined, that the main parties might introduce after the election if they were in government. Fine Gael accused Fianna Fáil of "dishonest propaganda" because it had put it about that Fine Gael planned to cut the children's allowance; it said that it was Fianna Fáil that not only had this secret plan but was preparing to cut unemployment assistance once the election was out of the way.[2]

On the day, Fine Gael made a further impressive recovery, gaining ten more seats, to take it from 40 to 50. Fianna Fáil lost three seats and fell back to 65. The newly reunited Labour Party won 19 seats; Clann na Talmhan was still small, with 5, and Clann na Poblachta smaller still with 3. Fine Gael, the Labour Party and Clann na Talmhan put together the second inter-party Government, again headed by John A. Costello, with the backing of independents and the three Clann na Poblachta deputies, who supported the Government from the back benches.

Costello and his ministers were to have an even tougher time of it than their predecessors. The economic crisis they faced was of "daunting severity"[3] and was compounded by the reopening of a large deficit in the balance of payments.

Fianna Fáil came out of the election damaged by a reputation for fiscal conservatism and economic incompetence. It had been overwhelmed by the economic storm it had faced and had appeared unable, and at times unwilling, to look for or find new solutions. More damaging still, by 1954 it appeared even more lacklustre than it had at the end of its last time in government in 1948.

Adjusting again to life on the opposition benches, Fianna Fáil was confident that Costello's coalition would not work, that its constituent parts would again disagree and that the interlude before its return to power would again be short. This time, however, Fianna Fáil had learnt the lessons of 1948–51 and realised that both its organisation and its policies required not just renewal but complete overhaul. It was decided that Lemass would be given the responsibility for the first of these tasks, and the second one he decided to arrogate to himself.[4] But before turning to Lemass's energetic pursuit of both functions it is necessary to say something about how de Valera spent his time as party leader during this term.

De Valera was seventy-two when he became leader of the opposition for the second time. His authorised biographers manage to cover this last opposition period in one page, on which they deal with the important topic of his attitude to the revival of IRA activity in the mid-1950s (discussed later in this chapter). There is nothing in that biography or elsewhere, however, to suggest that, apart from chairing the Ard-Chomhairle or attending at the top table of parliamentary party meetings, he played any active role in, or even appreciated the need for, organisational and policy overhaul in his party. The only new policy issue that he took hold of during this period was a proposal to change the electoral system, about which he became almost obsessive during his remaining years as party leader. In all matters relating to the party organisation and in most matters relating to policy, Lemass was *de facto* leader of Fianna Fáil.

Lemass was already preparing to revamp the party organisation in the period before the loss of power in 1954. During the previous time in opposition, from 1948 to 1951, he had been conscious that the national network of political organisation that he had done so much to develop almost a quarter of a century earlier was in need of overhaul; but he did not have the time, the apparent inclination or the support to conduct such an exercise at that point. Organisational problems continued to be the subject of discussion, both in the parliamentary party and the Ard-Chomhairle, when the party returned to power in 1951, but it was not until November 1953 that any practical steps were taken to do anything about it. On 23 November the Ard-Chomhairle accepted the recommendation of its officer board that a Department of Organisation should be set up, under a director of organisation who would be subject to the authority of the honorary secretaries and "given full executive powers in matters concerning organisation, publicity and propaganda including power to control the activities of all officers engaged in these branches of work."[5] Shortly afterwards Lemass's own constituency organiser in Dublin South-Central, Joe O'Neill, was offered a post as organiser at head office. Shortly after that again Matt Feehan of Dublin North-East was appointed to the newly established position of director of organisation but then, when the election was called, became a candidate. On 8 March 1954 Lemass was appointed director of elections for that campaign.

Following the party's defeat, Lemass himself took over as director of organisation. He also took one of the joint honorary secretary positions again. His reason for returning to the officer board in this position rather than as a vice-president, which would have been more appropriate to his status as a former Tánaiste, was that the position of honorary secretary was the commanding organisational position in the party. It was, after all, the perch from which he had played such a leading role in the party's initial development phase until he became a minister in 1932.

Both positions, director of organisation and honorary secretary, were voluntary posts, but apart from his parliamentary duties Lemass gave the reorganisation task all his time for the next three years. He was voted an allowance for expenses as director of organisation in August 1954, but at £500 per year (€14,200 in today's money) it would, after outlays, have been only a small stipend.[6]

Lemass "fell to his multifarious tasks with an energy he was rarely, if ever, to replicate." The reorganisation project required him to be "a combination of organiser, pacifier, strategist and one man research bureau."[7]

Michael Yeats, who worked in Fianna Fáil head office at this time dealing with publicity, has left a valuable account of the dynamism that Lemass brought to rebuilding the party in the period after the 1954 election.

> He at once took on the task of renewing and revitalising Fianna Fáil, travelling the country with young members of the Organisation Committee, much as he had done thirty years earlier, when the Party was first set up. Very highly organised himself, he had a remarkable capacity to master a brief; in a short time he knew all there was to know about the state of the organisation in each Dáil constituency. Where there were weaknesses, they were dealt with. But this was not enough: he also wanted to know about any local political problems there might be all over the country. Each week, therefore, I read some 45 local newspapers and cut out for him to read any items that might possibly be of political interest. There might be a demand for a new hospital or school, a complaint about the conditions of roads, a wrangle about the Chairmanship of a Council, a farmers' protest about the price of cattle, workers laid off at some local factory. All such items were grist to the Lemass mill.[8]

Yeats also writes glowingly about Lemass's sense of purpose and his ability to get things done.

> His capacity for the taking of instant decisions could be disconcerting. During an election, for example, I might come in of a morning with a list of some 15 decisions that had to be made. I would mention them one by one, getting in each case a one-word or two-word reply. The whole thing would take about one minute, and that would be the end of it. He never went back on a decision, nor indeed did he ever ask whether an instruction had been carried out.[9]

One of the first needs Lemass identified was for day-to-day political management and co-ordination, in addition to that given (or not given) by the shadow cabinet. In June 1954 he proposed to the parliamentary party that an Executive Committee be established to manage day-to-day party affairs. This would consist of the leader, five deputies nominated by the leader and five elected by the parliamentary party from the ranks of those who had not previously held ministerial office. The last condition did not survive, but the Executive Committee was set up, and the principle of some of them at least being elected by the parliamentary party, rather than all being appointed by the leader, was established.[10]

Lemass was given authority to hand-pick an Organisation Committee to work with him on the nationwide renovation. The membership of this committee included many young men who would go on to play a leading role in the party at the national level over the next thirty years. One of these was Kevin Boland, a son of Gerry Boland, who had inherited much of his father's flair for organisational work and some of his contrariness. At thirty-seven he was to be one of the older members of Lemass's reorganisation team. He had already unsuccessfully contested two elections in the Dublin County constituency but would eventually win a seat in 1957.

Also on this Organising Committee was 29-year-old Charles Haughey, a brilliant accountant who was then a member of Dublin City Council and also secretary of the party organisation in Dublin North-East. He had stood unsuccessfully in the two previous general elections and would be again unsuccessful in 1956 but would go on to win a seat—at the expense of the sitting deputy, Harry Colley—in 1957. Haughey was also Lemass's son-in-law, having married Maureen Lemass in 1951.

Another member was 25-year-old Brian Lenihan, a barrister on the Midland Circuit and son of Paddy Lenihan, a businessman in Athlone who had been a Fianna Fáil county councillor since 1942. He had unsuccessfully contested the 1954 election in Longford-Westmeath as Erskine Childers's running mate and succeeded his father as a member of the Fianna Fáil Ard-Chomhairle in that year. With Lemass's help he would soon switch constituencies, despite Gerry Boland's objections, to run in Roscommon for the 1957 election and would ultimately displace the latter in 1961.

Also on the committee, and central to this and many future reorganisation projects, was 34-year-old Eoin Ryan, son of Dr James Ryan. He already had a busy business career and was not interested in full-time politics. He would, however, be elected to Seanad Éireann in 1957, thus beginning a thirty-year career in that chamber, from which he would operate as a central party figure, ultimately becoming honorary secretary, and as a close confidant of both Jack Lynch and George Colley.

Seán Lemass's own son, Noel Lemass, was another committee member. Then thirty-five, he was also a member of Dublin City Council and would be elected a deputy for Dublin South-West in the 1956 by-election.

By early September 1954 Lemass had planned a series of reorganising meetings throughout the country, and by the end of the year an organisation handbook, "Bealach Bua" ("path of victory"), and an election campaigning handbook, "Córas Bua" ("system of victory"), had been printed and distributed to each unit of the party.

"Córas Bua" was a regimental guide to vote-garnering, which included a list of detailed action points that party members were expected to follow without deviation. The foreword read: "The Scheme of Election organisation in this handbook, Córas Bua, should be adhered to as closely as possible in each constituency and there should be no departure from it in any essential detail except with the approval of the Comhairle Dáilcheantair."[11]

"Córas Bua" also placed a special emphasis on the role of local cumainn in achieving electoral success. Its emphasis was on a strong grass-roots campaign over and above the centralised campaign directed from head office in Mount Street.

> The key-stone of the election organisation is the Cumann in charge of each polling station, and wherever an active Cumann does not exist immediate action must be taken to remedy the deficit. The primary concern of the Director of Elections on his appointment is, therefore, to have a Cumann or Group formed in all such areas since it is clear that no Scheme of Election Staff Organisation can produce satisfactory results unless the actual workers are available in every polling area.
>
> Early selection of a Polling Area Director for each polling station is vital to the efficient operation of the election scheme, and the Constituency Director should make it his special business to ensure that this is done—paying as much attention to the most remote districts as to those near his [local] Headquarters.[12]

"Córas Bua" covered every facet of organising a successful election campaign and set out instructions for local activists on how to remedy the state of their local organisation. They should establish a campaign election fund, print local publicity material, organise transport for polling day, organise local campaign offices, organise canvassing, organise public meetings, appoint personation agents, nominate candidates, and provide for the insurance of workers, premises and transport. Its contents reflect Lemass's practical and pragmatic approach to politics, and the document is extraordinary for its attention to detail. For example, it instructs members that on election day

> the Polling Area Director should arrange for meals for the Personation Agent and booth workers who cannot get home during the day. Intoxicants should not be supplied.
>
> He should have as many influential supporters as possible outside the booth during the Poll (and especially between six and nine in the evening) to make a last minute canvass and to give every voter a Card or Specimen Ballot Paper.
>
> He should keep a check on the Poll and see that his Transport Officer is supplied with lists of those who have not voted.

He should arrange to have posters with the names of our Candidates pasted on sheets of wood or cardboard and prominently displayed at the approaches to the booth.[13]

With similar attention to detail Lemass himself carried out a great deal of the initial national survey of the Fianna Fáil machine. Brian Farrell writes:

Once again as in the 1920's Lemass travelled around the country. Originally he had used his old volunteer contacts to seek out men in different localities around whom the new organisation could be built. Now he was probing that organisation, judging its local strengths and weaknesses, preparing where necessary to encourage the substitution of new candidates for the old men he himself had recruited. Companions recall the long journeys through rural Ireland: he could drive for a hundred miles without exchanging a word of conversation concentrating perhaps on the mission at the end of the journey. He was not a man to waste either speech or time. Commonly he carried a bar of chocolate in his pocket rather than be delayed en route stopping for snacks and being buttonholed in casual encounters. Still it was a less intense Lemass than the young man of the twenties: by the mid-fifties if the opportunity arose he was ready to plan his journey to take in a couple of early races at the Curragh before carrying on.

Lemass's band of young organisers travelled the country, with him or separately, conducting a detailed investigation of the state of the party organisation in each constituency and undertaking reorganisation work where required. Charles Haughey recalled of this period:

We were a task force. We travelled the length and breadth of the country at weekends and sometimes during the week. We divided the country up between us covering it area by area, and visiting every cumann, culminating in a meeting of the Comhairle Dáilcheantair which would put our suggestions on stream. I always did a written report for Lemass and he would decide what had to be done.[14]

Their task was to encourage local officers to rejuvenate, disband, amalgamate, reconstruct or realign cumainn as necessary in order to bring them into line with demographic and constituency boundary shifts, as well as with Lemass's diktat that there be one cumann to each 2,500–3,000 people. Where local officers were unwilling to do it, they undertook the work themselves.

Brian Lenihan's biographer identifies another role this team of young political organisers performed. They were not merely organisers: "they also spread the gospel of Keynesianism and economic planning, the Lemass formula for taking the country out of the economic and social trough in which it languished." In crisscrossing the country the young Turks were certainly reorganising, but they were also assuring anyone who would listen "that the power of amelioration lay in the hands of Lemass."[15]

Members of the Organising Committee were required to report back regularly to Lemass on what they found. At least once a week letters passed between these young men and the man they called "the Boss". In this correspondence Lemass set out an itinerary for his own visits to their area or visits he wished them to make to cumainn or constituency organisations in neighbouring areas. Lenihan, for example, "went everywhere, fitting in his Keynesian speeches and his visits to party notabilities with his bar practice and his work in Roscommon politics."[16] Haughey, in one "ebullient" report as secretary of Dublin North-East Comhairle Dáilcheantair, told Lemass how "mé-féiners" were being weeded out: "the self seeker will soon see that Fianna Fáil is an organisation of service and not a ladder for his ambition and he will soon steal away."[17]

These efforts showed immediate results. Lenihan was given the task of proposing the honorary secretaries' report at the 1955 ard-fheis and was happy to report that, even though the cumann registration fee had been increased to ten shillings (50p), there were 1,787 cumainn registered for that year, the highest number in twenty years. There is every reason to believe that, because of the weeding out of paper cumainn and the fact that a detailed cumann membership list had been introduced, each registered cumann now represented a greater degree of active local membership.

In his address as honorary secretary, Lemass told the same ard-fheis that Fianna Fáil had become "too much of an election machine" and was "not fully living up to its responsibilities as a national organisation" and that even as an electoral machine was less efficient in some constituencies than it should have been.

One constituency in which the party organisation was strong then and would continue to be strong was Louth. There a young teacher, Pádraig Faulkner, was emerging as a central figure alongside the veteran deputy Frank Aiken and the local senator, Joe Farrell. Faulkner had been a by-election candidate in 1954 and was to win a seat as Aiken's running-mate in 1957. He later gave a picture of how important the local cumainn were in the Louth organisation when he described the relationship between the deputy and cumann members that operated throughout his Dáil career.

> The cumann is the heart and nerve centre of the organisation. It consists of a group of dedicated people who give their time voluntarily to promote the party and its policies. Such people are real patriots; whatever their political allegiance, men and women dedicate themselves to an ideal—the improvement of living conditions for the people of Ireland—with, for the vast majority no material benefit for themselves. They simply have the fulfilment that goes with a job well done. Over many years I have seen these men and women striving away

year after year. They would be working in elections, taking up the national collection and perhaps most importantly of all defending party policy. Many of them grew old in the service of their party, happy with the contribution they had made. Most were also involved in parish work, in promoting games and in local activity generally. They prove the truth of the saying that busy people can always make time to do more. People so wrapped up in themselves that they have no time for their neighbours' problems find it difficult to understand the enthusiasm of the voluntary worker in the Fianna Fáil organisation, often attempting to attribute it, without foundation to material gain.[18]

Faulkner is describing how the cumann system operated, or was meant to operate, in all constituencies. The local deputy was expected to attend all meetings of the comhairle dáilcheantair and of the comhairle ceantair. In addition he was expected to visit each cumann on its own turf at least once a year, usually for the annual general meeting. In Faulkner's constituency, where the territory was divided between himself in the south of the county and Aiken in the north, he would have had to attend all cumann AGMs in the South Louth district and some of those in north Louth.

The meetings were held in the winter or early spring and were onerous in the sense that the nights were dark; the weather was cold and damp, and more conducive to sitting by the fire than going to meetings. Over the years I came to know what to expect at each individual cumann meeting. A very few had formal agendas but most were informal occasions when we chatted about recent political highlights, or indeed matters not remotely related to politics, the merits of local teams.

Faulkner also tells of attending comhairle ceantair meetings that were then, and in many constituencies still are, held on Sundays at noon. Here they discussed, among other things, the financing of their campaigns.

While we needed money for election purposes, Frank Aiken, Joe Farrell ... and I were careful about the source from which it came and the possible strings attached. In my early days in the Dáil we received a cheque through a supporter from an exporter outside the constituency. The amount though small by today's standards would have been sufficient at the time to cover most of the election expenses. We considered the matter and decided against accepting it.[19]

While Co. Louth may not have needed much attention, Lemass and his team had much with which to busy themselves elsewhere. This exercise not only strengthened the organisation but strengthened Lemass's position within it, preparing the ground for a generational shift in leadership throughout the party. He built relationships throughout the country with those who would lead local activity when he himself became leader. Many of his young team, and others with whom he bonded during these countrywide travels, would themselves make it to Dáil Éireann very soon and would become the reforming core of his Governments when he became leader.

Party reorganisation was only one half of the task Lemass faced. He also had to lead the shaping of new policies. In particular, he knew that the party had to articulate a more sophisticated view of the country's social and economic problems. In this task he was again assisted by the young Turks. Charles Haughey, Eoin Ryan and Brian Lenihan formed something of a vanguard for more modern policies on the Ard-Chomhairle. They found it to be a frustrating place. De Valera, as president of the party, chaired the meetings and had a foolproof method of getting his own way. As Lenihan explained it to his biographer, "proceedings went on for hours, sometimes half the night until such time as de Valera had ground down any opposition or any attempts at innovation."[20]

The Lemass modernisers were joined in their efforts by the former Clann na Poblachta minister Noël Browne, who, along with another former Clann na Poblachta TD, Dr Michael Ffrench-O'Carroll, and a former independent farmer TD, Patrick Cogan, had joined Fianna Fáil in October 1953. An *Irish Times* editorial observed on the occasion:

> Some time ago we commented on Fianna Fáil's lack of young blood: these independent defections will supply a most necessary transfusion. Dr Browne's energy, and the freshness of his ideas, may well be the leaven necessary to leaven the Fianna Fáil lump, and it will be a thousand pities if the lump is content to absorb him and his companions without consenting to be leavened. These are men whose outlook is settled on 1953, rather than 1923, and for that reason alone the Government will do well to accept them as people with a real contribution to make, and not as mere ciphers in the division lobby.[21]

Later in life Browne attributed his decision to join Fianna Fáil to a number of factors. It was, after all, a republican party, like Clann na Poblachta. He had decided that there was no point in staying as an independent, and the Labour Party had refused to let him join. He also admired Lemass's efforts in keeping Ireland fed during the Second World War, and had got more help from Fianna Fáil when he was Minister for Health than from anybody else. (He cited, for example, assistance that Fianna Fáil deputies in Co. Kilkenny had given him in forcing empty fever hospitals run by nuns to take TB patients, contrasting their stance with that of the local National Labour deputy, James Pattison.) Fianna Fáil had introduced the widows' pension, the orphans' pension, and sickness allowances. Having considered the options, he concluded, "there was a seed that could be developed in Fianna Fáil."

Browne tells in his autobiography how he had lost his seat in 1954 because he "innocently" ran for Fianna Fáil in Dublin South-East alongside Seán

MacEntee, then a very unpopular outgoing Minister for Finance, although he came within 382 votes of taking the third seat from MacEntee. As John Horgan points out in his biography of Browne, MacEntee made a determined effort to secure Browne's election in order to obtain an additional seat for Fianna Fáil.

> The election was notable for MacEntee's attitude to Browne. His own position was considerably less secure than it might have been, given the memory of his 1952 Budget and his uncompromising—if occasionally misguided—defence of the public finances. He behaved exceptionally generously towards Browne in the circumstances, operating a primitive form of vote-splitting, and urging Browne to go out and get every vote he could for himself. He also allowed Browne—and this would have been almost unheard of in Fianna Fáil election campaigns—to distribute personalised election literature, as long as his own name was included. Eddie McManus, the tough Belfast man who was MacEntee's right hand in the constituency, was aghast at such unselfishness towards somebody who, he feared, might threaten MacEntee's seat.[22]

Browne stayed in the party after his defeat and proved very popular with the grass roots, coming near the top of the poll for the Ard-Chomhairle at the 1954 ard-fheis.

With Haughey, Ryan, Lenihan, and Michael Yeats, Browne was responsible for the report of an Ard-Chomhairle sub-committee on education that made a number of radical proposals, including the provision of free second-level schooling. These proposals were debated and readily accepted by the Ard-Chomhairle. However, after this decision had been made de Valera intervened to say: "There is one small addendum which I am sure you will accept, that the recommendations will be implemented when financial considerations permit." As Browne himself describes it, "with that handful of words, our valuable and useful work had come to naught; the recommendations would not be implemented so long as de Valera remained leader of Fianna Fáil."[23]

MacEntee, who had become disenchanted with Browne, ensured that the latter did not get a nomination at the Dublin South-East selection convention in 1957. The issue then went before the Ard-Chomhairle and was the subject of inter-generational debate.

> Browne was by no means without supporters in a contest which pitted Fianna Fáil's old guard against its younger, more impatient members with an intensity that this particular forum had never before experienced. Then MacEntee stood up and delivered the coup de grace: if Browne was added to the ticket, he said, he would withdraw. De Valera, whose support for MacEntee in this confrontation was evident, if silent, moved towards closure. Browne's support started to melt away.[24]

When the Ard-Chomhairle took the decision not to add Browne, he resigned from the party, though he later asserted in his autobiography that he had been expelled. He subsequently announced his decision to stand as an independent, and he went on to regain his Dáil seat in the general election of March 1957.

Browne also makes an interesting, if patronising, observation on the Fianna Fáil grass roots as he found them during his tours of the country in his capacity as a member of the Ard-Chomhairle.

> All my life, I have enjoyed the company of the rank and file of Fianna Fáil: they are refreshing, mildly iconoclastic and independent, and given the chance at all would be first class material for a properly developed society. But they are not given that chance by the leadership.[25]

Lemass's own efforts to modernise Fianna Fáil policy within both the parliamentary party and the front bench proved as frustrating as Browne and others had found them to be in the Ard-Chomhairle. He determined, therefore, to circumvent the normal procedures and to find other means of airing policy issues and altering policy stances.

One such initiative was the establishment of Comh-Chomhairle Átha Cliath (Dublin joint council). This was a separate organisation that he established within Fianna Fáil. Although officially "a unit of Fianna Fáil," it allowed associate membership to "any person whether resident in Ireland or not and whether a member of Fianna Fáil or not." Its purpose was twofold: to address the perceived weakness of the party organisation and the flagging support for the party in Dublin and to provide a forum and a means for testing out some of the policy formation going on within the party.[26] It was given the specific task of initiating public discussions about the aims of Fianna Fáil. Two of Lemass's close friends, Dave McIlvenna and Joseph Griffen, were central to the planning of this organisation and the preparations for its inaugural meeting in January 1955.

The Comh-Chomhairle debates proved provocative right from the start. In an address to that inaugural gathering Lemass asked questions about some of the central tenets of what until then had been Fianna Fáil's economic orthodoxy in a manner that suggested, for the first time in a public forum, that they might be up for revision. The following day the *Irish Press* reported that when addressing the lack of industrial development Lemass told the meeting:

> It might be that part of the answer lies in the restrictions which were, for good reasons, placed on the participation of foreign capital in Irish industrial expansion when the industrial drive was first launched. It is now an open question whether these restrictions need to be retained any longer in their present form.[27]

This was a public attack on the Control of Manufactures Acts, which he himself had designed and promoted two decades earlier.

Later the same year Lemass was to deliver one of his most famous speeches to another meeting organised by Comh-Chomhairle Átha Cliath, this time in Clery's Ballroom in O'Connell Street. The speech was scheduled for 11 October and had been well publicised as an important statement of party policy. Its full text was published the next day as a four-page supplement in the *Irish Press*.

Lemass had taken the precaution of presenting a draft in the form of a memorandum to the parliamentary party. At the meeting that considered it, concerns were expressed that the speech was critical of the banking system and that it gave the impression that native resources might not, after all, be sufficient to finance the industrial expansion that was necessary. The minutes of the meeting note "that Mr. Lemass could speak in public in general terms on proposals set out in his memorandum but that reference to the Central Bank should be omitted, it could be pointed out however that our resources are ample to finance agricultural and industrial development."[28] It was indicative of the struggle Lemass faced in trying to shift party policy. John F. McCarthy writes:

> According to Lemass, some of his colleagues argued that his speech was both unnecessary and unwise: unnecessary because [they thought] the coalition was already breaking up and unwise because it would cut off alternative policies. Lemass countered that it "would be politically wise for Fianna Fáil to try to restore the country's morale regardless of the party in power and that there should be political debate on what measures might bring economic recovery."[29]

The speech as delivered on 11 October marked Lemass's public explanation of how much his economic thinking had changed. In his exploration of alternatives to the protectionist policy that he himself had championed for decades he had studied Italy's ten-year employment and income scheme, the Vanoni Plan, and had begun to develop the notion of a similar five-year expansion programme for the Irish economy. By Lemass's own admission the Clery's speech was a "rather amateurish attempt" to emulate the Italian programme.[30] In its very first line the address contained what a recent historian has described as "one of the most important U-turns in the history of the state,"[31] as Lemass began:

> The Fianna Fáil party has accepted that the economic development programme which it initiated 25 years ago, notwithstanding its many and very substantial achievements and its subsequent acceptance by all parties, has not proved to be sufficient to bring about all the economic and social progress which we desired and which we believe can be accomplished.

He told his audience that Fianna Fáil was using the time in opposition (what he called "our present period of release from immediate responsibility for government") to review its programme. As John F. McCarthy has pointed out,

> Lemass's cautious speech caused a small furore at the time, but it was not the far-reaching economic proposal which Whitaker later produced. For one thing, Lemass's main emphasis was on increased public spending for "socially useful projects," rather than on funding successful businesses. Fianna Fáil, as Lemass well knew, was not committed to producing a comprehensive economic plan . . . The "100,000 Jobs Speech," as Lemass later contended, "promoted public acceptance of the idea of programming, planning and active government intervention to eventually produce a pre-defined economic plan."[32]

McCarthy argues that for years such economic planning had been suspect, because of its ties to left-wing ideology and its association with communist regimes, a handicap more compelling in Ireland than elsewhere. In his Clery's speech Lemass set out to cross this Rubicon by proposing a five-year spending programme aimed at attaining full employment. This would involve the Government in giving the economy an initial boost, designed to trigger an increase in private investment activity that would boost private productive enterprise to a level sufficient to generate and sustain full employment.

Lemass accepted that the public expenditure required to finance such an ambitious plan would be considerable, but he expressly rejected the notion that "the sole objective of government policy should be to keep public expenditure at the lowest possible level." He claimed that "the primary aims of Fianna Fáil's policy have been in the past, and will always be, to increase the nation's wealth and to improve the living conditions of the people. These aims over-ride other considerations."

He went on to suggest that an increase in the number of jobs by 100,000 over five years, or an average of 20,000 per year, would result in full employment as ordinarily understood and the end of the high levels of emigration.

In putting a figure on this assessment, Lemass gave 100,000 hostages to fortune. It was, according to John Horgan, rapidly and wrongly interpreted by his opponents as a political promise. Having done this, they then attacked it as a crude attempt to buy the electorate and later would repeatedly taunt Fianna Fáil for failing to deliver the promised full employment. In the debates on Fianna Fáil's budget of 1958/9 a Fine Gael spokesperson asked Lemass why the one-year-old Government had not produced the first instalment of 20,000 new jobs. James Dillon quipped that Lemass would provide 100,000 more jobs, but they would be in Boston and Birmingham.[33]

Lemass's biographers, and other historians, differ in their interpretation of what exactly Lemass was trying to achieve with this speech. Brian Farrell, for example, argues that while this was an important speech in Lemass's effort to formulate new policy it was not a fully formed statement of that policy. He points to a front-page notice in that day's *Irish Press* that set out the purpose of the speech, saying:

> Mr. Seán Lemass will tonight initiate a discussion on National Development at a meeting of Comh-Chomhairle Átha Cliath, Fianna Fáil, having been engaged for some time on a comprehensive programme for the development of the Country's resources . . . Full discussion by the Fianna Fáil organisation on the proposals will continue until the complete programme fully outlined and tested in debate is adopted in full form.

It is also important to stress, Farrell says, that despite the typical assertiveness of Lemass it was the beginning, not the end, of an argument and that it served its purpose in stimulating internal debate. This, however, does not take away from the fact that, delivered as it was by the deputy leader of Fianna Fáil, who had always been its chief economic spokesperson and future leader, the Clery's Ballroom speech was a significant and dramatic policy shift by the party.

Over the course of 1956, in addresses to Comh-Chomhairle Átha Cliath and other groups, Lemass went on to develop the tenets of this new policy and to refine the projected employment figures. These efforts, though he would strenuously deny it, "represented Lemass's determination to get on with economic developments irrespective of Dev's views or feelings which were at best apathetic. It represented a resolution to take command of the situation whether he was Taoiseach or not."[34]

On 17 January 1957 Lemass pushed the boat out further and, in an address to members of Fianna Fáil in Dublin, proposed an increase of 12 per cent in national production. He also suggested that Irish firms might be linked with larger companies that could supply capital, technology and connections, and that smaller companies should be consolidated, with the assistance of the Industrial Credit Corporation. He also urged the setting up of a commercial export board for industry and called for Government investment of £60 million to finance his proposals.

While Fianna Fáil was busy doing all this reorganising and policy repositioning, the parties in government were struggling to tackle the economic situation. Their economic difficulties increased with the deterioration in the balance of payments in 1956. At the same time their political difficulties were further complicated by the outbreak of a fresh IRA cross-border campaign.

De Valera shaped Fianna Fáil's response to this latter development. His authorised biographers say that he was not surprised that, as the British had ignored discrimination and injustices and had failed to protect the nationalist community, quite a few young men had decided that the only way to solve the problem was by the use of force. They also say that that de Valera "felt that [these men] were inspired, for the most part by a sincere love of country, but their knowledge of political reality was minimal." His biographers say that de Valera met some of these men in 1956 (but do not say when, where, or in what context) but that he gave them "not the least encouragement." He was, on the contrary, "extremely forthright with them and impressed upon them his belief often stated publicly that partition could not be solved by force of arms."[35]

In all his public utterances on the topic de Valera was unequivocal in condemning the IRA campaign. At the 1955 ard-fheis, while acknowledging the fundamental injustice of partition, he called on the Costello Government to taken stern action against those involved in the violent activity.[36] Later, in response to a radio broadcast on the topic in which Costello had emphasised the heavy responsibility on those in positions of influence to be on their guard against false comparisons with the past, de Valera declared himself to be in "entire agreement" with the Taoiseach.[37]

The Costello Government's handling of the new outbreak of IRA sedition attracted controversy. It initially played down the danger, but after policemen and civilians had been killed in late 1956 Costello announced a tougher policy in January 1957. This stance was welcomed by the bulk of media and political commentators, but it did not meet with the approval of Clann na Poblachta, which withdrew its support from the inter-party Government. Shortly there-after, Fianna Fáil put down a motion of no confidence in the Government, focusing on economic matters, but, rather than face an inevitable defeat, Costello dissolved the Dáil. Polling day was set for 5 March 1957.

The election campaign was conducted in a tense atmosphere. A newly resurgent Sinn Féin put up nineteen candidates. The IRA's activity and the Government's response to it were a feature of the election, but the economy was the main issue. Whereas party spokespersons widely debated their respective approaches to the economic crisis, the parties were coy on what their attitude to the IRA campaign would be in government.

Fianna Fáil's main tactic was again to emphasise the dangers of coalition. Its advertising campaign in the *Anglo-Celt* (Cavan) was typical. In the second week of the campaign a half-page advertisement warned that national confidence had been "scraped out by three years of coalition government." A week later another half-page advertisement warned voters that "we cannot afford any more experiments in the art of government."[38] Among the Fianna Fáil poster slogans was one promising that "the Dilly Dally Decade is over." The main Fianna Fáil slogan for the campaign was "Let's get cracking," which hinted at Lemass's theme of an expansionist economic programme.

As John F. McCarthy points out, Fianna Fáil's economic platform in this campaign was, at best, ambiguous.

> Although the party's elite had discussed the issue among themselves during the campaign, the party as a whole avoided taking a public position. Privately, Seán Lemass and others had urged support for his "national recovery" plan but according to Lemass no consensus had

been reached: "The general tenor of our campaign was that the serious economic difficulties of the times were curable and that Fianna Fáil had developed ideas for effecting a comprehensive cure," he recalled later. "We did not elaborate on these ideas on which our collective mind was not at the time fully made up."[39]

At this point, winning the election was of much more importance for Fianna Fáil than clarifying or resolving what its policy might be if it was returned to power. McCarthy goes on to argue:

> Clearly, de Valera and Fianna Fáil's conservative wing, especially Seán MacEntee, did not want a growth-oriented, interventionist economic policy creeping into the party's platform. One member of the Fianna Fáil leadership, [the] former Agriculture Minister, James Ryan, said that the party "felt Ireland was not ready for a plan at that time." The Irish economy might have needed such a plan, but the conservative Irish electorate, Fianna Fáil felt, would reject it . . . As Seán Lemass admits, "It is true that we did not seek in the General Election of 1957, a specific mandate for economic planning." The one or two party leaders who did have some ideas on this issue were not allowed to present them to the electorate during the campaign. Perhaps that posture was politically sound, since the 1957 electorate rejected any candidate who voiced support for any form of economic planning.[40]

The inter-party Government brought down the price of tea five days before the election, but it did not help it much. Fianna Fáil increased its vote by 5 per cent and won exactly half the seats, with 78 TDs. Fine Gael lost the ten seats it had gained in 1954 and dropped back to 40. The Labour Party lost seven seats and fell to 12. Clann na Talmhan lost two seats and was left with 3, and Clann na Poblachta lost two (including Seán MacBride's) and was left with only 1. Sinn Féin won 5.3 per cent of the vote and 4 seats. There were 9 independents.

As the Sinn Féin deputies were abstentionist, Fianna Fáil had a working majority. De Valera, at the age of seventy-five, became head of his eighth Government and for the first time since 1944 had an absolute majority.

One of the first things the new Government did was to take on the threat from the resurgent IRA. It reactivated the Offences Against the State Act (1939), including the power to intern suspects without trial. Over the next nine months 130 men suspected of IRA activities were interned, effectually ending the border campaign.[41]

The influence of Lemass exerted itself in the fact that de Valera's new Government included some significant changes from the one he had appointed six years earlier. At Lemass's insistence, Seán MacEntee was not reappointed to Finance but was instead sent to Health. Lemass was also instrumental in having James Ryan elevated to Finance.

It is also said that Lemass told de Valera that he would never again serve in a Government with Gerry Boland. Members of the then parliamentary party say that the animosity between Boland and Lemass was very apparent, although its origins were not clear.[42] This was a difficult situation for de Valera, as he and Boland had a long history together. He had also been particularly close to Boland's brother, Harry, who had been killed during the Civil War. The Chief solved this problem with typical ingenuity by appointing Boland's son Kevin, who had just won a seat in Dublin County, to the Government on his first day in the Dáil.

Other members of the old guard returned to their previous perches: Frank Aiken to External Affairs, Oscar Traynor to Justice; Erskine Childers became Minister for Lands, and Paddy Smith went to Local Government. Seán Moylan, who had lost his Dáil seat to a constituency colleague, was appointed from the Seanad as Minister for Agriculture. It was the fulfilment of a lifelong ambition for him, but tragically he was to die suddenly the following November, at which point Paddy Smith was moved to that post.

In March 1957 de Valera also appointed two younger deputies who had first been elected in 1948. Jack Lynch was appointed Minister for Education at forty-one, while the Donegal deputy Neil Blaney, who was thirty-five, became Minister for Posts and Telegraphs and later that year moved to Local Government. The Mayo deputy and solicitor Mícheál Ó Móráin, aged forty-five, would subsequently be appointed Minister for the Gaeltacht in June 1957.

De Valera also wished to appoint his constituency colleague Patrick Hillery, then thirty-four, to a junior position in this Government, but Hillery, who was more interested in pursuing his medical career, declined the offer. Hillery recalled:

> I made it clear to [de Valera] that my interest was medical practice. I asked him if in the event of taking part in the government, I could apply for a dispensary; he groaned. But I never regarded politics as anything but a temporary derailment—an aberration from which I would one day escape.[43]

It took de Valera three separate meetings to persuade the young Lynch to take a Government position. When he made his initial offer, Lynch replied, "My wife wouldn't like it." De Valera said, "We all have trouble with our wives."[44] Lynch was reluctant to give up his career at the bar for full-time politics. He later stated that he lost £800 in briefs the day he became a member of the Government.

If Lemass had become *de facto* leader of Fianna Fáil during the opposition years, he was now also to become *de facto* Taoiseach in large areas of government.[45]

The issues that dominated politics were those to which Lemass was better suited: the emphasis was no longer on constitutional questions and external relations but on economic concerns. The most significant development of the years 1957–9 was the publication of the first five-year economic plan. This was the brainchild of T. K. Whitaker, an exceptional civil servant who at thirty-nine had been appointed Secretary of the Department of Finance by the previous minister, Gerald Sweetman. Lemass's position was further enhanced by the fact that he chaired the Government's economic affairs committee, which led the new developments.

The new economic thinking that was permeating Fianna Fáil was signalled by James Ryan in his first budget statement in May 1957. He told the Dáil: "The policies of the past, though successful in some directions, have not so far given us what we want . . . Further progress on a worthwhile scale calls for comprehensive review of our economic policy."[46] The ground was clearly being prepared for a fundamental shift in Fianna Fáil's economic policy.

This stepped up another gear on 12 December 1957 when Whitaker addressed a memorandum to his minister, Dr Ryan, requesting authorisation to work on an integrated programme of national development for the next five or ten years. The memorandum was submitted to the Government by Ryan four days later and was immediately approved. The study was prepared by Whitaker, developed in the economic sub-committee and presented to the Government in May 1958. It formed the basis for the First Programme for Economic Expansion, announced by Lemass at the Fianna Fáil ard-fheis in October 1958 and published as a white paper, *Economic Development*, on 12 November.

The fact that the programme was announced by Lemass and not by either de Valera or Ryan is, of course, indicative of the way in which Lemass dominated the Government on economic issues. It dovetailed with, and brought to fruition, most of the thinking on economics that he had been shaping privately since the end of the Second World War and that he had revealed publicly in opposition in 1955 and 1956.

The fundamental principles of the programme marked a sharp break with the policy of previous Fianna Fáil Governments, although de Valera, even twelve years after the publication of the programme, doggedly insisted that it was nothing new and was a continuation of long-established policy. "We set out those policies in 1926 at the formation of Fianna Fáil," he stated.[47] John F. McCarthy argues that

> it was a tribute to de Valera's political genius that he could claim the 1958 Whitaker plan was a continuation of the party's founding principles in 1926. *Economic Development* provided de Valera and his Fianna Fáil party [with] an escape hatch from those 1926 policies which had been tried and found wanting. As an astute politician, de Valera recognised this fact, gave his assent to Whitaker's plan and still claimed with his legendary verbal sleight-of-hand that nothing had changed.[48]

Years later, in an interview in 1986, Whitaker himself gave an interesting explanation of the relationship between de Valera and Lemass and how this explained the shift in Fianna Fáil policy in this period.

First of all one must see that Dev recognised, through the eminence he gave to Lemass, the deficiency in his own viewpoint. De Valera was supplementing his idealistic view of things by a practical go-getter person in Lemass. Dev was still Taoiseach when they decided to publish this piece of official advice, something never heard of before and strongly resisted by Seán MacEntee at the time. One was left thinking that it was his political instinct—it was a way out, a brilliant way out from being imprisoned in the old policies. Dev presumably had the perception to see that change was necessary.[49]

Economic Development marked the beginning of official commitment to economic planning. It provided that a greater proportion of public capital expenditure should be on productive projects and that investment purely for unproductive employment would be discontinued. Savings were to be encouraged and direct taxation to be reduced. It set relatively detailed targets for the main areas of the economy. Protection was to be given to new industries only where it was clear that, after a short initial period, they would be able to survive without protection. The emphasis was to be on a shift to expanding industrial exports rather than catering to the home market. Most significantly of all, perhaps, foreign participation in Irish industry was to be encouraged.

Apart from these shifts in economic policy, the main energy of the de Valera Government in the period 1957–9 was to be spent on a campaign to change the electoral system. This had become a "crusade" for de Valera. In 1958 he announced that a referendum would be held on changing from proportional representation to a single vote and single-seat constituencies. The proposal immediately met with considerable opposition and dragged through the legislative process for months. It was even defeated in the Seanad and thereby further delayed.

The big question that hung over Fianna Fáil and politics generally in these years was when, and even whether, de Valera would step down as Taoiseach. An obvious time suggested itself around the summer of 1958. A presidential election was due by June of the following year, with Seán T. O'Kelly coming to the end of his second term and therefore not eligible to stand again. The question was answered on 15 January 1959 when an emotional de Valera shocked a parliamentary party meeting by announcing his intention to resign as Taoiseach and to make himself available, if the party so desired, as a candidate for the presidency. Several members, including Government ministers, left the meeting with tears in their eyes.

As this was in the days before such matters were the subject of leaks, or before ministers wrote memoirs, we cannot be entirely sure of the extent to which de Valera required a final nudge to retirement in the period after the 1957 general election, or to what extent Lemass faced any serious challenge in the succession. There have been suggestions that some time in late 1958 James Ryan and Seán MacEntee convened a secret *ad hoc* meeting of Government ministers at which the issue of Dev's retirement was discussed. It is said that all those gathered, with the exception of Frank Aiken, felt that Dev should be approached and asked to stand for the presidency the following year. It is also said that MacEntee and Ryan then went to de Valera and told him of the consensus within the Government, and that he agreed to go.[50] Brian Farrell, who undertook a detailed exploration of the circumstances of de Valera's departure and who would have had access, on or off the record, to many of the principal participants, is dismissive of the suggestion that de Valera had to be pushed: in his view, de Valera's timing was his own. Others suggest that the crucial intervention came not from MacEntee and Ryan but as a personal initiative from Oscar Traynor.[51]

The considered view of officials at the British embassy, who obviously had a close interest in these events and communicated their view back to London, was that there was a conflict between Lemass and Aiken that was potentially so deep and divisive that Ryan would be chosen as a compromise candidate for Taoiseach.[52] They revised their view subsequently when de Valera announced his retirement, saying that Ryan, who was close to Lemass, was himself a strong supporter of Lemass's succession and that Lemass would therefore be unopposed.[53]

Whatever British diplomats thought, and whatever the precise machinations at Government level were, there is a consensus among those who were then Fianna Fáil back-benchers that Lemass was the obvious successor and that there was a clear sense that de Valera was facilitating his succession. Patrick Hillery speaks of de Valera "putting his cloak around Lemass."[54] Charles Haughey reported that "Dev set it up for Lemass. He made him Tánaiste, neutralised opposition. I'm sure he talked to the old Guard as well."[55] Brian Lenihan was of the same view, although he suggested that Aiken and MacEntee might not necessarily have been happy about Lemass becoming leader. He also credited James Ryan with having played a central part in securing a unanimous succession. Pádraig Faulkner says simply: "Seán Lemass had served a long apprenticeship and was [the] obvious successor."[56] Michael Yeats makes it clear:

> No one was in doubt that [de Valera] would be succeeded by Seán Lemass. There were perhaps two others whose seniority was such that they might have been eligible to be considered. One of these was Seán MacEntee, who was not, I think, looked on as suitable by anyone in the Parliamentary Party, and who would in any event have been ruled out by his extreme unpopularity throughout the country. The other possibility was Dr James Ryan, who had no interest in the leadership, and was a strong backer of Lemass. There may have been a few rural Deputies who would have preferred someone less closely linked to Dublin, but in the absence of any other possible candidate they had little if anything to say.[57]

Although the announcement had been made in January 1959, de Valera stayed on as leader of Fianna Fáil and Taoiseach for another six months, deciding to run for the presidency without relinquishing his position as Taoiseach. Lemass would have preferred it to be otherwise, but even he "found it difficult, almost impossible to conceive a Fianna Fáil without de Valera at the helm."[58]

This was indeed a surreal and emotional moment for the party. There had never been a Fianna Fáil led by anyone else. There was every reason to be nervous and to doubt whether anyone, even Lemass, could match de Valera's iconic status and hold on to the support of around half the electorate.

While the desire to change the electoral system flowed in part from a concern that it appeared impossible to form stable Governments under the existing system, some in Fianna Fáil were afraid that without the Chief, Fianna Fáil might not be able to sustain a vote that would give it single-party government—minority or majority—under proportional representation.

On 17 June 1959 de Valera was, as expected, elected President, although his victory was surprisingly narrow. In a two-candidate race he defeated the Fine Gael candidate, who was again Seán Mac Eoin, by 538,000 votes to 418,000. On the same day, however, de Valera lost his last political battle, that on the change of the electoral system. The referendum was held simultaneously with the presidential election, and in a poll of 979,675 there was a majority of 33,600 in favour of retaining PR.

In the busy days after de Valera's election victory and the defeat of the constitutional amendment the Fianna Fáil parliamentary party and Ard-Chomhairle met in rapid succession to decide the leadership. At the parliamentary party meeting, when MacEntee proposed Lemass there was, according to the *Irish Press* the next day, a spontaneous burst of applause and cheering, which drowned his concluding remarks. A considerable time elapsed before Frank Aiken could be heard to second him.

Michael Yeats, who even at this point believed that Lemass should have become leader a decade earlier, records the new optimism that his election as leader instilled in many people in the party.

> Though I was not myself at that moment a member of the Parliamentary Party, I was in Leinster House on the day of the election of Seán Lemass as leader. I will always remember the sense of exhilaration that pervaded the place. For years, the Fianna Fáil organisation, particularly the younger people, had been waiting and hoping for this day.[59]

Later that evening, when the veteran Paddy Burke nominated Lemass to the Ard-Chomhairle, he was similarly elected president of Fianna Fáil and a party trustee by loud acclamation.

On the next day, 23 June 1959, Lemass was elected Taoiseach by Dáil Éireann, by 75 votes to 51. De Valera's long tenure at the helm of Fianna Fáil and Irish politics had now come to a close. As Michael O'Sullivan put it, "the age of de Valera had ended and the 'rising tide' of the era of Lemass was about to break."[60]

Chapter 8

A BREATH OF FRESH AIR, 1959–66

Éamon de Valera told at least one early visitor to Áras an Uachtaráin that Seán Lemass becoming Taoiseach would send "a breath of fresh air through the country."[1] This mild self-criticism was an accurate assessment of the impact that the belated commencement of the Lemass leadership would make. Every such change creates a new dynamic, but the arrival of Seán Lemass in the offices of Taoiseach and president of Fianna Fáil created a sense of windows being opened throughout the political and public administration and throughout his party.

Lemass turned sixty three weeks after he took over from de Valera. He had been a TD for more than three decades, a minister for more than two decades and a political organiser in some form or other since his mid-twenties. He had a clear sense of what he wanted to achieve in government, in the civil service and in Fianna Fáil. He was also a man in a hurry to do it.

He was not a man to waste time, energy or words. Above all else Lemass was practical and applied in his approach, which is why he became known in Fianna Fáil as "the Boss" rather than "the Chief". His success as a leader flowed from his focus. He had an incredible ability to concentrate, to absorb information, to reach a decision point and to make decisions. He would have the newspapers read and half the decisions for the day already made before he got out of bed in the morning.[2] All who worked with or for Lemass say that his strongest traits were his direct approach and his capacity to make decisions. It was clear from the outset that he would not be the same kind of leader as his predecessor.

Among the things Lemass did have in common with his predecessor, however, was that he was acutely conscious of the dignity of his office—not of his own position but of the position he held. It was this, for example, that prompted him to give up his favourite hobby of attending race meetings. He did not darken the gates of a racecourse as long as he was Taoiseach.

As we have seen, Lemass had renewed Fianna Fáil's organisation around the country through his reorganisation project a few years earlier, but now he was completely in charge. It was he who would make all the decisions. His opponents on policy or tactics could no longer appeal over his head to the

Chief. He did not have to sit around while de Valera wore down debate to a forced consensus: now, in the party as in the Government, he could just get the decision made and move on to the next.

Those who served in his Governments or have since studied Lemass's style of conducting it say that Government meetings were radically different from those under de Valera. The Government was no longer a forum for lengthy discussions but a decision-making body and a point of final arbitration and determination. One Lemass Government meeting famously lasted only three-quarters of an hour.[3] Kevin Boland pointed to a difference in style at Government meetings, where he noted that under de Valera ministers were "let talk anyway," while Lemass would "cut you off."[4] Neil Blaney concurred, saying he found de Valera a more personal leader than Lemass. "Even if he had little to say to you about politics, he would talk to you about your father, your mother, your children and your grandchildren." He said that "de Valera cultivated the personal," but Lemass did not go in for familial small talk. According to Blaney there were seldom discussions with Seán Lemass outside the Government, and he recalled very few non-Government meetings with him in the time he served as a minister under him. "His attitude was, 'if you're doing the job, well, get on with it; if you're not, well then I'll talk to you.'"[5]

One official close to the Government process said that Lemass "had total control of the Cabinet . . . everything was crisp, he had no patience with waffle."[6] Later, Lemass even had the Government secretariat change the table from a rectangular one to a cigar shape, so that he could have a clear view of all those in attendance, telling his civil servants, only half jokingly, "I want to see who is saying no to me."

He had the same impact at party meetings. At the Ard-Chomhairle more business was done, and it was done in less time. Under de Valera the monthly meetings regularly ran for more than four hours; now they seldom lasted more than twenty minutes.[7]

The approach that the new leader brought to one item on the Ard-Chomhairle agenda demonstrates his new way of doing things. At the beginning of each meeting, after votes of condolence had been taken, the general secretary was in the habit of bringing to the attention of the meeting correspondence of which it should be aware. Among these would invariably be a letter of resignation from some party officer somewhere in the country, complaining about some personal slight or policy change that had offended them. De Valera would take ages over each of these threatened resignations; he would suggest that a delegation be formed to meet the aggrieved officer, and their report would reappear for further discussion at, perhaps, several subsequent meetings, and so the matter would drag on. When, at the first meeting Lemass chaired, a letter threatening resignation came up, Lemass intervened to say: "He's a fine man. I'm very sorry to hear he's resigning; we must assume he knows his own mind. We should send him a letter accepting his resignation with regret." Threats of resignation rapidly dried up.[8]

A story from another Ard-Chomhairle meeting further illustrates the pace at which Lemass made decisions on party matters. Eoin Ryan began to make a presentation on behalf of the Organisation Committee about a proposal to establish a social and events committee within Fianna Fáil, to be known as Cairde Fáil. Lemass cut him short, saying, "Right, you're the chairman; carry on." Decision made, they were sent off on their task.

One area in which Lemass trod with uncharacteristic caution was that of changing personnel and portfolios within the Government. He made very few alterations in ministers or departments when he first took over from de Valera, or indeed when he won his own mandate in 1961. This was in part because de Valera had, at Lemass's instigation, introduced some new and younger faces when appointing his last two Governments, in 1951 and 1957. However, notwithstanding these changes there were seven veterans of the 1916 Rising, War of Independence or Civil War serving when Lemass appointed his first Government in June 1959, including himself. Four of them—Lemass, MacEntee, Aiken and Ryan—had been members of all de Valera's governments since Fianna Fáil first took power in 1932. Lemass was now Taoiseach, and the other three retained the important portfolios of finance, external affairs and health, respectively; indeed MacEntee was now given added responsibility for social welfare. Oscar Traynor, who had first been appointed to the government in 1936, again became Minister for Justice and Paddy Smith stayed on as Minister for Agriculture. Even two of the younger men who had been promoted in recent years and were now retained by Lemass, Kevin Boland and Erskine Childers, were the sons of 1916 veterans.

The only changes in portfolios or personnel that Lemass effected when he first became Taoiseach were those necessitated by de Valera's departure and his own elevation, as well as the simultaneous retirement on health grounds of the Minister for Posts and Telegraphs, Seán Ormonde, who Lemass had tried to persuade to remain on.[9]

Lemass promoted Seán MacEntee to the position of Tánaiste. British embassy officials—having wrongly guessed that Ryan might be Taoiseach—reported in a later despatch that Ryan would be Lemass's Tánaiste.[10] They could be forgiven the latter mistake, however, as many contemporary commentators had also assumed this. Lemass himself had given serious consideration to appointing Ryan. Ten years later he told Michael Mills:

I considered whether I should make Jim Ryan Tánaiste not because of any personal consideration but because I felt that in the Government as it is the Seniority of the Minister for Finance should be marked in some way. In effect he does sit at the Cabinet table in a much stronger position to criticise or to veto proposal of other Ministers than even the Taoiseach because every proposal involves Finance of some kind. However MacEntee was the Senior Minister and it would have seemed a rebuke to him if I did not appoint him as Tánaiste. It is far more important to maintain goodwill and harmony than seek a more effective distribution of responsibility.[11]

Making the decision solely on the basis of seniority displays a surprising caution for a man like Lemass, who had such a reputation for innovative decision-making. It reveals the extent to which party cohesion was as important to him as it had been to his predecessor.

Lemass's elevation also left a vacancy in the position he himself had occupied at the Department of Industry and Commerce. Before moving to Government Buildings he sent for Jack Lynch to his office in Kildare Street and told him, "I want you to sit at this desk."[12]

To fill Lynch's shoes at the Department of Education, Lemass set his sights on the young Clare deputy, Dr Patrick Hillery, who had up to this point inevitably been overshadowed by his constituency colleague and mentor, de Valera. In fact Hillery was planning to leave politics but had put his departure on hold because of de Valera's move to the presidency. As the only remaining Fianna Fáil TD in Co. Clare he felt an obligation to his local party organisation and his constituents, but he remained uncertain of his future in politics.[13] Lemass was to change all that.

Hillery tells how he had originally decided not to go to the parliamentary party meeting that would select de Valera's successor, because he knew the outcome was a foregone conclusion. He was due instead to be on the golf course at Portmarnock, where he was taking a break with his wife. His first game was washed out, so he made his way to Leinster House, and when the meeting was over he was accosted by his friend Michael Hilliard, deputy for Meath, who told him that the Taoiseach-elect wanted to see him. When they went up to the top table Lemass told him, "I want you in the cabinet . . . You're not escaping this time." Hillery tried to demur, citing his wish to continue his medical practice, as he had done when de Valera offered him ministerial office previously, but Lemass was having none of it.[14]

Michael Hilliard, who had fought in the War of Independence as a teenager, was himself appointed to the vacancy in Posts and Telegraphs. A month after these initial appointments Lemass promoted Gerald Bartley, another War of Independence veteran, from his position of parliamentary secretary to that of Minister for the Gaeltacht.[15]

A year later Lemass appointed Charles Haughey to be Parliamentary Secretary to the Minister for Justice. Oscar Traynor had asked for the assistance of a parliamentary secretary to deal with statute reform. Lemass's Government colleagues told him Haughey was the obvious choice. Conscious of Haughey being his son-in-law, and perhaps also feeling that, as he had been a TD only since 1957, Haughey might not be ready for office, Lemass resisted, wishing instead to appoint the Mayo deputy Seán Flanagan. However, he then relented. When he called Haughey in to tell him the news he famously told him, "As your Taoiseach it's my duty to offer you the post of parliamentary secretary; as your father-in-law it's my duty to advise you not to accept it." Haughey took it.

Lemass, of course, also brought a new policy approach to Fianna Fáil in government. He not only put an emphasis on a different range of policy areas from those that had dominated in de Valera's time but brought a reforming zeal, a pragmatism and a youthful outlook that belied his age.

Four days before de Valera formally stepped down, a British embassy analyst sent the following pen picture to London of the man everyone knew would soon be the Taoiseach:

> [Lemass] is without doubt the ablest of the Fianna Fáil Ministers. He is regarded as one who is anxious to get away from the barren political controversies of the past. He is no orator but his public speeches are usually very much to the point, and he is certainly less inclined than his colleagues to wander at large over the fields of Ireland's ancient wrongs. He has a special standing in the country as the chief architect of Irish economic development, and it may be hoped that once he is firmly in the saddle as leader of the Fianna Fáil party, we may see a gradual shift of policy towards a more practical approach to current problems including particularly the cultivation of friendlier relations with the North.[16]

It proved a prescient assessment, not least in its last point. Once he was in the saddle Lemass quickly jerked the reins of Ireland's politics and economics on a whole range of fronts, including policy towards Northern Ireland.

Right from the start, Lemass was determined to set a new policy tone. His policy statements did repeat the traditional Fianna Fáil emphasis on national independence, but they set that struggle in the context of economic development. In a significant speech made only three weeks before he became Taoiseach, Lemass set out the more practical approach to sovereignty that would be a feature of his tenure. "The historic task of this generation," he said, "is to secure the economic foundation of independence."[17] He warned that if there was a failure in the economic aims of the country the political gains would be lost. The primary aim must be the economic one, he argued, beyond all others. He promised that patriotism would take a new form, in that love of country and language would inspire new heights of economic endeavour. He suggested that "state concerns" would be extended to new activities and that new state units would be formed. Some of these would be handed over to private enterprise when they had achieved their purpose, others would co-operate with private enterprise. In addition, he warned that "the industrial forest must be cleared of deadwood to create new growth." He warned also that there would be no more "hiding behind tariff walls but, if necessary exporters must surmount tariff walls."[18]

Central to Lemass's policy framework was his determination that Ireland should join the European Economic Community and should be readied for the rigours that membership would impose. Support for membership of the European Union, as it was to become, and for the greater European integration project would become a central tenet of Fianna Fáil policy from this starting-point. Given the party's nationalist origins, it could easily have been otherwise. The fact that Ireland's largest party was to become so enthusiastically pro-Europe owes much to Lemass's leadership and that of his protégés, such as Jack Lynch and Patrick Hillery.

At the point when Lemass became leader, Britain was expected to apply for membership of the EEC, and Lemass was determined that Ireland would do the same. This was not only because of the ties the Irish economy had with the British market but because for Lemass, now a fully converted advocate of free trade, it would be the means of overhauling Irish industry. It also had the advantage that it would be beneficial to Irish agriculture. The drive to tear down tariff barriers and remove the dependence on the domestic market, which was the focus of the First Programme for Economic Expansion and would be a central tenet of the Second Programme when Lemass launched it in 1963, was part of preparing for the eventuality of EEC membership. But the realist in Lemass knew that Ireland's application was not feasible if Britain's floundered. On 18 July 1961, after meeting Harold Macmillan in London, Lemass said:

> If Britain should not, for any reason, acquire membership, we would be faced with a situation of very great difficulty . . . It is obvious that our interest requires the preservation of arrangements with Britain which would facilitate mutual trade, and that whatever course we take must be such as to permit this.[19]

At the end of July the British Government announced its decision to apply for membership of the EEC. This was followed within twenty-four hours by the announcement that Lemass's Government would also make a formal application.

Meanwhile Lemass continued to make political preparations for membership. In October 1961, when he appointed Brian Lenihan Parliamentary Secretary to the Minister for Justice, he asked Lenihan, whom he knew to have an interest in Europe, to prepare himself for the role of Minister for European Affairs.[20] Lemass later told one interviewer that he envisaged a separate Government department that would handle Ireland's relations with the EEC.[21] He predicted that the EEC would develop a political character and said that Ireland's decision to seek membership was "a political decision".[22] Interestingly, he put a brake on suggestions that Fianna Fáil should join a Europe-wide political grouping in preparation for EEC membership, seeing this as premature and likely to create a distraction from the substance of the issue, which was to have Ireland's application accepted.[23]

In the short term, however, it was the President of France, Charles de Gaulle, who put the brake on Lemass's ambitions. In January 1963 de Gaulle vetoed the British application, and the Irish application was collaterally rejected.

The rejection was a body blow to Lemass's plans. Because of it, he switched his attention to seeking a new economic relationship with the British market that would reflect Ireland's surge towards free trade and alter the unfair trading relationship on agricultural produce. Progress on this matter was also delayed and had to await a change of government in Britain. Following the British election in October 1964, Lemass and Lynch opened negotiations with Harold Wilson's new Labour Government, and these culminated in the Anglo-Irish Free Trade Area Agreement (1965), signed on 14 December that year. It provided for the freeing of industrial trade between the two countries within ten years and a more general guarantee of access for Irish agricultural products to Britain. The agreement was approved by the Dáil without division and was, according to Lemass, "by far the most important trade agreement we have concluded."[24]

Although Lemass busied himself with the trade aspects of Ireland's foreign relations, concentrating in particular on Europe and Britain, he was content to let the Minister for External Affairs, Frank Aiken, who showed little interest in European affairs, pursue his own passions at the United Nations. As the historian T. Desmond Williams has argued,

> Lemass and Aiken each represented different strands of the Sinn Féin and Fianna Fáil position. Lemass was more concerned with issues such as economic growth and development. Aiken viewed his role as being primarily concerned with the cultivation and development of a separate Irish foreign policy at the u.n. Lemass increasingly thought in terms of London and Europe.[25]

Aiken had broken new ground and demonstrated Ireland's non-aligned foreign policy when he supported China's membership of the United Nations in 1957. During Lemass's tenure as Taoiseach, Aiken continued to ensure a relatively strong profile for Ireland on such issues as nuclear non-proliferation, the Algerian war and un peacekeeping while being a passionate supporter of decolonisation in Africa and Asia. He once told the General Assembly that the Irish people "know what imperialism is and what resistance to it involves."[26] Ronan Fanning, however, says of Aiken's role as Minister for External Affairs under Lemass and beyond that

> the Irish public's rapturous fascination with the Kennedy presidency in the us and the Atlanticist predilections of Lemass, curtailed his freedom of manoeuvre. Indeed, Ireland's United Nations policy on Cold War issues during the mid to late 1960s was typically formulated within a United States oriented pro-Western context; the most striking example was the Vietnam War, on which Aiken was eloquent only in his silence.[27]

While Lemass was generally supportive of Aiken's stances, he resisted the elevation of Irish neutrality to the level of an overriding principle of Fianna Fáil's or Ireland's foreign policy. As he saw it, neutrality during the war had been tactical. It was in Ireland's best interests then to prove its sovereignty and stay out of the war. He was not prepared to have the principle of a permanently enshrined neutrality get in the way of Ireland pooling its sovereignty as necessary, for example to be fully fledged members of the EEC. During Ireland's first EEC application campaign Lemass famously told the *New York Times* in July 1962: "We are prepared to go into this integrated Europe without any reservation as to how far this will take us in the field of foreign policy and defence."[28]

The factor that had most impact on political outcomes in these years was the economic boom. The economy was doing well, and as a result Fianna Fáil, as the party in government, did well and in the two elections of this period did better than might otherwise have been expected.

The Lemass years were a time of rapid industrial expansion. Unemployment fell by a third. The First Programme for Economic Expansion had projected growth of 2 per cent per year from 1959 to 1963; in the event the favourable international economic climate meant that an average growth of 4 per cent was achieved. This surge was already setting the economic backdrop to Lemass's first big electoral test, which came in the general election of 1961.

As it happens, all three of the main parties had changed their leaders since the 1957 election. In 1959 James Dillon had become leader of Fine Gael in succession to Richard Mulcahy, while in 1960 Brendan Corish had replaced William Norton.

Lemass had decided that he would seek a mandate as Taoiseach in his own right in the autumn of 1961. Events, however, seemed to be conspiring against him. His initial plan for an election was delayed because of an ESB strike and the Government had to fast-track special legislation through the Dáil to handle the issue. When the election was called, an unfounded rumour spread that 150 Irish soldiers on UN duty in the Congo had been killed. To compound matters further, the rumour suggested that most of the casualties were from Athlone, the town in which Lemass had chosen to launch Fianna Fáil's campaign.[29] It was not the start Fianna Fáil would have wished for; but events soon settled down, and the rest of the election campaign was dull. Lemass's main theme was the benefits of Ireland's EEC application, and he urged his ministers and deputies to persuade the electorate to buy into this.[30]

As Fianna Fáil had done particularly well in 1957, and this was the first contest without de Valera on the posters, it was expected that Fianna Fáil would lose some ground. In the event it dropped from 48 to 44 per cent of first-preference votes and lost eight seats, leaving it with 70; Fine Gael gained seven to return with 47; the Labour Party gained nine, giving it a total of 22; and there was a further reduction in the strength of the smaller parties.

Lemass's Government held on to power with the support of Frank Sherwin, a Dublin deputy, and Joe Lenehan of Mayo North, an independent from the Fine Gael "gene pool" who had failed to secure a nomination and then took the seat as an independent. Although it was a minority Government it was to end up being perhaps the most effective and productive Fianna Fáil Government ever.

Immediately after the election Lemass made another gradual adjustment in the age profile of his Government. Jack Lynch retained Industry and Commerce and Patrick Hillery remained in Education. The party veterans Ryan, MacEntee, Aiken and Smith stayed in Finance, Health, External Affairs and Agriculture, respectively. Michael Hilliard remained in Posts and Telegraphs, Neil Blaney stayed at Local Government and Erskine Childers at Transport and Power. Mícheál Ó Móráin returned to the Gaeltacht, although he was now also given responsibility for Lands. Gerald Bartley moved to Defence and Kevin Boland to Social Welfare. Charles Haughey was brought into the Government as Minister for Justice, succeeding Oscar Traynor, who had retired at the election. Significantly, two of Lemass's young protégés, Donogh O'Malley and Brian Lenihan, were given parliamentary secretary positions as a means of preparing them for full Government rank.

The greatest test to the slim majority enjoyed by this second Lemass Government came with the introduction of the 2½ per cent direct tax, known as turnover tax, in the 1963 budget. The tax was opposed vehemently by both Fine Gael and the Labour Party and, as it was inevitably going to increase the cost of living, it proved particularly unpopular. The Government's difficulties were not helped when Brian Lenihan added what a colleague called "confusion and spice" to the debate by publicly stating that he did not know why ordinary people should concern themselves about the tax, as it applied only to "fur coats and Jaguar cars."[31]

The day after the budget announcement Lemass strongly defended the new tax in a contribution to the budget debate in the Dáil, in which he flaunted his own left-wing leanings. The speech also set out the extent to which Lemass and his Government favoured greater Government expenditure and the degree to which he appreciated that this increased social support and economic activity would require greater taxation.

The speech began with what became an iconic phrase. "I believe that the time has come when national policy should take a shift to the left." Lemass then set out what he meant by such a shift. Firstly, there would be improved social services, benefit payments, educational access and health services; secondly, there would be more Government intervention to "keep the economy on an even keel"; thirdly, they would maintain a high level of state investment; and fourthly, there would be more detailed planning of economic activity. Lemass went on to say that he also believed that the budget just announced by Ryan

> rested on the proposition that economic and social progress required higher social spending. The realisation of higher levels of employment, the extension of health, education and social welfare services, the provision of more houses, the improvement of communications, better living in town and country—all had to be financed through the Budget. One beneficial effect of the Budget is that it will help to clarify the really fundamental differences in approach to national problems between

Fianna Fáil and Fine Gael. Fine Gael is negative, deflationary, timorous and political in the extreme. The Fianna Fáil approach is positive, constructive and national.[32]

The Government had only a tiny majority, and for this Fianna Fáil needed the support of independents, so it was an act of political courage for Lemass to follow his convictions on this issue. As Brian Farrell points out, "while much of the credit for securing a smooth parliamentary passage of the measure must go to Ryan's shrewd handling, responsibility for committing a minority government to the measure was Lemass's."[33] Though the measure passed through the Dáil, there was a massive swing against Fianna Fáil in a by-election the following month, in which Fine Gael retained the late Jack Belton's seat in Dublin North-East.

Apart from this temporary dip in the aftermath of the turnover tax, the Lemass-led Government was generally very popular, as the economy continued to boom. National morale was also improved by the visit of President John F. Kennedy to Ireland in June 1963.

The economic expansion did bring other tensions, and in particular there developed, within Fianna Fáil and elsewhere, resentment among those championing agricultural interests. Jack Lynch, then Minister for Industry and Commerce, later attributed the resignation of Paddy Smith as Minister for Agriculture in October 1964 to "a growing tension between the industrial and agriculture sectors, as the industrial one boomed under the expansionary Fianna Fáil policies at the time and the agricultural sector lagged behind." Smith had threatened resignation several times, but the trigger on this occasion was his objection to the settlement of an eight-week building strike as being surrender to "not only a tyranny but a dishonest incompetent one." Smith phoned the Government Press Office that morning to tell them he proposed releasing the news of his resignation. When Lemass got word of this he captured the initiative by announcing a surprise appointment of the Dublin deputy Charles Haughey to Agriculture. Reflecting on this, Haughey later said:

> Lemass was a great politician. He had a great capacity to anticipate things, to be ahead of developments, not having to react to them. On that occasion he had the new appointment made before the general public were aware of the resignation. He didn't allow any atmosphere to build up; it was all over and done with before most people knew what was happening.[34]

At the same time Brian Lenihan was promoted to become Minister for Justice and George Colley was appointed to the resulting vacancy for a parliamentary secretary.[35] The tensions between the traditional agricultural community, which had always been heavily represented in Fianna Fáil at all levels, and the emerging industrial sector might have become even more intense and potentially dangerous for the party over the next decade had it not been for the extensive benefits that flowed to agriculture when Ireland ultimately joined the EEC in 1973.

From the start of his leadership Lemass also adopted a fresh approach to Northern Ireland policy. His vocabulary, his tone and his emphasis on practical co-operation were ground-breaking for Fianna Fáil. From his first press conference as Taoiseach he abandoned the old vocabulary of "anti-partition", limited his use of phrases like "restoration of the national territory" and spoke more often of the need for greater co-operation on practical economic matters between Dublin and Belfast. In an early interview with the *Belfast Telegraph* he said:

I have no illusions about the strength of the barriers of prejudice and suspicion which now divide the people, but given good will nothing is impossible. Meanwhile better relations can be fostered by practical co-operation for mutual benefit in the economic sphere. Even at present, and without reference to any wider issue, we would be prepared to consider and to discuss proposals as to how policy might be directed so as to ensure that economic progress of both parts of the country will be impeded as little as possible by the existing political division.

In October 1959 Lemass spoke on the theme again at an address to the Oxford Union (the prestigious student debating society closely associated with the University of Oxford). When dealing with the need to recognise the different cultural traditions of the mass of Northern Protestants he spoke of how arrangements might be hammered out "which would give them effective power to protect themselves very especially in regard to educational and religious matters."

In June 1963, when President Kennedy during his visit to Ireland raised the issue of partition, Lemass told him: "What we would like to see happening now would be a clear statement by the British political leaders that there would be no British interest in maintaining partition when Irishmen want to get rid of it."[36]

From the vantage point of Ireland after the Belfast Agreement, Lemass's remarks to Kennedy, though made in private, show extraordinary foresight and mark the evolution of a strategy that would be followed by successive Governments right up to the Downing Street Declaration in 1993, when the British Government declared that it has "no strategic, selfish or economic interest in Northern Ireland."

In what was perhaps his most important speech on the topic, given in Tralee on 29 July 1963, Lemass said:

We recognise that the Government and Parliament there [Northern Ireland] exist with the support of the majority of the Six County area—artificial though that area is. We see it functioning within its powers . . . We believe that it is foolish in the extreme that in this island

and amongst people of the same race there should persist a desire to avoid contacts, even in respect of matters where concerted action is seen to be beneficial. We would hope that from the extension of useful contacts at every level of activity a new situation would develop which would permit of wider responsibilities in accord with our desires . . . The solution of the problem of partition is one to be found in Ireland by Irishmen, and as we move towards it we can be sure that there is no power or influence anywhere which can prevent its implementation when the barriers of misunderstanding and suspicion which have sustained it have been whittled away.

Speeches such as these marked important shifts in policy from the crude anti-partition position that Fianna Fáil, and indeed the inter-party Governments, had adopted and promoted so actively since the end of the war. The significance of the shifts was not perhaps appreciated by the public, nor by the Fianna Fáil party, until January 1965, when they were given practical expression in an actual meeting between Lemass and the Prime Minister of Northern Ireland, Terence O'Neill.

The meeting had been secretly arranged through contacts established by T. K. Whitaker, who had become friendly with O'Neill and his private secretary, Jim Malley, having met them on numerous occasions at World Bank meetings when O'Neill was the Northern Ireland Minister of Finance. When Whitaker came to Lemass with the news that O'Neill was proposing a cross-border meeting, Lemass immediately agreed. He shared news of the proposed initiative with Frank Aiken and perhaps a handful of other colleagues. Apart from this, the meeting was arranged in circumstances of great confidentiality and with no advance publicity. When details and photographs of the meeting were released afterwards, the initiative was met with overwhelming—though by no means unanimous—support north and south of the border. O'Neill told the Northern Ireland House of Commons that he attached significance to the visit because "if Mr Lemass was prepared to drive through the gates of Stormont and to meet me here as Prime Minister of Northern Ireland he was accepting the plain fact of our existence and our jurisdiction here." In Lemass's Government only Neil Blaney argued that Stormont had been legitimised.[37] O'Neill paid a return visit to Dublin the following month. Thus began the first faltering steps towards cross-border economic co-operation.

A month later Lemass called another election. On 10 March a by-election was due to be held in the Mid-Cork constituency, and on the 5th of the month Lemass told a party meeting in Carrigaline that if Fianna Fáil was defeated he would consider it his duty to call a general election, so that the whole people could decide whether they wanted the Government to fulfil its programme.[38] If the by-election went against the Government, its majority would have been dangerously narrowed in any case.

In the event the Fianna Fáil candidate, Flor Crowley, topped the poll on first preferences, but the party's vote had dropped by 1,100, and Eileen Desmond won the seat for the Labour Party with the assistance of a large transfer from the Fine Gael candidate. True to his word, on 11 March 1965 Lemass announced that the Dáil was to be dissolved. Polling day was to be 7 April.

The economic context for the election, although not as favourable as it had been in 1961, was still benign. The Second Programme for Economic Expansion, launched in 1963, was more detailed and technical than the first and had more precise targets. Like the first, it was successful, though growth was a little more sluggish; but the impact of the balance of payments difficulties, which would have to be countered by deflationary methods and were to slow the growth rate in 1965 and 1966, had not yet been felt.

However, the 1965 election was significant for Fianna Fáil because it saw the retirement of some senior party members and ministers. Dr James Ryan, who was then in the Department of Finance, did not contest the election and retired instead to the Seanad, while Gerard Bartley in the Department of Defence stood down completely. However, the veterans Seán MacEntee and Frank Aiken ran again. MacEntee was seventy-six and went to the back benches after the election. He had resisted Lemass's suggestion that he should not contest the election and make room for a younger candidate, reminding the Taoiseach: "You're no chicken yourself."[39] His insistence on not standing down was vindicated by the result in Dublin South-East, where he and his running-mate, Seán Moore, provided two of the three seats for Fianna Fáil.

The party's campaign was fronted primarily this time by the newer and younger ministers. Charles Haughey, then a man "with a growing reputation within the Party,"[40] was made director of elections for the campaign. The Fianna Fáil slogan was "Let Lemass lead on," and the party campaigned on a theme of continuing economic growth, emphasising its proposal that Ireland should become a member of the EEC.

David Thornley, then a political scientist at Trinity College and later to be a Labour Party TD, captured the impact Lemass had on Fianna Fáil and its supporters succinctly when he wrote in the *Irish Times* during the campaign:

Since 1959 Mr Lemass has worked wonders with [the party]. He has cemented the loyalties while refurbishing the image. Thirty years ago this was a party of republicanism, language revival, economic protection, today it is a party of realism, talks with Captain O'Neill, growth and planning, free trade . . .[41]

The campaign was the first since the national television channel, Raidió-Teilifís Éireann, had been established in December 1961. The first party political broadcasts on television during that election attracted a third of the population.[42] Within Fine Gael the most significant developments since the 1961 election had been the party's adoption of the "Just Society" document, written by Declan Costello. It called for a much higher level of social spending and a national incomes policy. Its adoption by Fine Gael suggested that the party had made a spectacular move to the left of Fianna Fáil, even Lemass-led Fianna Fáil, when it came to social policy. When Fianna Fáil made noises about social justice and equality during the campaign this gave James Dillon the chance to brand Lemass, in a memorable phrase, "a political Annie Oakley, tooting 'Anything you can do, I can do better.'"[43]

The other significant factor in the election was that the Labour Party, under Brendan Corish, declared against participation in any coalition after the election. This meant there was no apparent realistic alternative Government on offer.

Lemass argued that a strong Fianna Fáil majority was needed to save the country from "political confusion". This appeal for an absolute majority was a constant refrain during the Fianna Fáil campaign.

> Jack Lynch warned the electorate that if they failed to deliver a working majority there would be another election to follow, and then another if required . . . Seán MacEntee jibed that Labour's sitting TDs were happy to take their Dáil salaries but not the responsibility of government. Labour, he said, was the Peter Pan of politics, unwilling to outgrow its short pants.[44]

Elections were a deadly serious business for Lemass, especially now when he was a Taoiseach in pursuit of an absolute majority. This may in some part explain a rare public flash of anger. The subject was an *Irish Times* prank editorial on April Fools' Day, which claimed that Fianna Fáil intended to introduce prohibition and quoted Lemass as saying: "If I make it on April 7th the boozer will have to go abroad for his drink in the future. He won't get it here."[45] Initially not getting the joke, Lemass made a scathing response.

> The *Irish Times*, which seems to have passed under the control of a group of crypto-Reds supporting Left Wing elements in the Labour Party, has now, for the first time in this country, introduced the Communist tactic of attributing to its political opponents, statements which they never made.[46]

Fine Gael pounced on Lemass's response, and Gerard Sweetman accused him of "going berserk" and asking the electorate to consider whether they could trust a man who in response to a joke "flings out wild accusations."[47]

The turn-out for the election, which had been 70 per cent in 1961, increased to 75 per cent, reflecting a much more vigorous campaign. The three main parties all increased their share of the vote, Fine Gael by 2.1 per cent, attracting much of the former Clann na Talmhan vote, the Labour Party by 3.8 per cent and Fianna Fáil by 3.9 per cent. The Labour Party obtained six more seats than in 1961; Fianna Fáil gained two seats and Fine Gael remained unchanged.

Fianna Fáil was now at 48 per cent of the vote, one of the highest proportions it had ever achieved, with Ireland's new-found economic success doing much to shore up the party's support in this post-de Valera era. Although Lemass was never to achieve an absolute majority, he had held the party's share of the vote at about where de Valera had left it. Over the course of ten elections from 1932 to 1957 Fianna Fáil, with de Valera as leader, had polled between 42 and 52 per cent of the first-preference vote. In his two elections Lemass managed to hold an average of 46 per cent. Stephen Collins puts it well:

> Fianna Fáil reinforced its hold on power as it became identified as the Party which had finally brought economic success to the Country. To the twin virtues of Nationalism and Social cohesion it had added another, the reputation of the party as the one best fitted to run the economy.[48]

Lemass took advantage of his new mandate to promote younger TDs to Government positions. Frank Aiken became Tánaiste while retaining his External Affairs portfolio, Jack Lynch succeeded James Ryan as Minister for Finance, and Patrick Hillery replaced Lynch in Industry and Commerce. On 13 July 1966 Hillery was moved to the new Department of Labour and George Colley was then made a full minister and given Industry and Commerce. Neil Blaney became Minister for Local Government, Charles Haughey remained in Agriculture and Kevin Boland remained in Social Welfare. The Donegal TD Joe Brennan was promoted from chief whip to Minister for Posts and Telegraphs, Donogh O'Malley also got a full ministry for the first time and was given Health. In July 1966 O'Malley was switched to become Minister for Education.

In 1965 Fianna Fáil had "a young Government with an old Taoiseach."[49] Looking back almost a decade and a half after Lemass had appointed his last Government, Jack Lynch, a central figure in all of them, argued that

> it is little appreciated with what ease and tranquillity Seán Lemass effected the transfer of power, from his generation, to another. In all countries, there are painful transition processes when such developments occur, but Lemass achieved this here with fairly considerable ease, although it might be said that his successor as Taoiseach, was the one to bear the full brunt of these difficult adjustments.[50]

Lemass's third term in government and his remaining time as Fianna Fáil leader is memorable for four politically significant events: the fiftieth anniversary of the Easter Rising, the June 1966 presidential election, the announcement in September 1966 of universal free secondary education, and Lemass's own departure.

The first of these, the week-long series of events beginning on 10 April 1966 to mark the anniversary of the 1916 Rising, has recently attracted much controversy. Critical attention has focused on the triumphant manner in which the anniversary was commemorated and how this may have affected both national sentiment in the Republic and, more seriously, nationalist and unionist sentiment north of the border. Within the Republic, and within Fianna Fáil, which is the scope of this work, the political impact was less controversial and less significant. The party felt it proper to mark this important milestone, as it was in power in a fully fledged republic, which represented the fulfilment of the dream to which the 1916 leaders aspired, at least in the South. The party also felt a particular pride that two of its own, de Valera and Lemass, both of them veterans of the rising, were holding the positions of President and Taoiseach, respectively, at the time of these celebrations.

With regard to these leaders Mary E. Daly makes an interesting assessment that, while President de Valera was the most prominent figure in the 1966 commemorations, their intellectual character was determined by the Taoiseach, Seán Lemass.

> Lemass despite being a veteran of the Rising interpreted 1966 in terms of the present and the future. The message of the commemoration was that what Ireland needed was not military action, or an anti-partition campaign, but a new and different form of patriotism designed to enhance the statehood won by the 1916 Rising. At the press conference setting out the official programme of commemoration, Lemass presented the golden jubilee as an opportunity to further enhance the status of our nation in the eyes of the world, emphasising both our pride in the past and confidence in our future. More specifically, he saw the 1916 anniversary as an opportunity to reinvigorate his drive to transform Ireland's economy and society.[51]

The fact that men of the vintage of de Valera and Lemass were still the leading political figures in 1966 might have been of more concern had it not been for the youthful outlook of Lemass as Taoiseach and the fact that the handing over to a younger generation had now been effected at the Government level. The reality was also, as Dermot Keogh says, that even "politicians such as Lemass and Éamon de Valera had liberated themselves from the shibboleths of an earlier generation. They viewed the challenge to end Partition as something other than a matter of restoring lost territory."[52]

De Valera, having decided that he wished to serve a second term in the presidency, chose not to nominate himself, as was his constitutional entitlement, but instead to be nominated again by the party he had founded. As serving President he did not believe it proper to engage in political campaigning on his own behalf. The reality, however, was that, as President and also as the last surviving leader of the 1916 Rising, he was the guest of honour at almost all the events held around the country to mark the fiftieth anniversary. These therefore became a useful series of quasi-campaign events. While formally structured and non-party-political, the commemorations became the centrepieces of de Valera's re-election campaign.

Notwithstanding the recognition that these events brought, de Valera's last election effort came dangerously close to disaster. The Fine Gael candidate was the relatively young deputy Tom O'Higgins (forty-nine at the time, compared with de Valera's eighty-three). O'Higgins managed to achieve a near-miracle by coming within 1 per cent of beating de Valera. More than a million people voted, but de Valera's margin over O'Higgins was less than 11,000 votes.

Donogh O'Malley's announcement of free secondary education is probably still the most-cited and most-celebrated policy declaration by Fianna Fáil. While in tune with, if certainly louder than, the expansionist, left-of-centre mood music of the Lemass era, it was also a break with previous party policy, or at least with the approach to the provision of social services and government expenditure in general of Fianna Fáil Governments in the 1940s and 50s. The free universal provision of any social service would have been contrary to the MacEntee-led conservative orthodoxy that had dominated Fianna Fáil in those years. Even the free medical care for mothers and children provided for under James Ryan's Health Plan of 1953 included a means test, albeit a relatively low one.

One might have thought that such a dramatic announcement would have been the culmination of months or years of internal wrangling within the party, or at least within the Government, or of months of deliberation and preparation. It was nothing of the sort. O'Malley appears to have discussed the idea with only a handful of colleagues, including Lemass, just decided on it and then announced it.

His speech still ranks as one of the most dramatic ever made in Irish political history. The date was 10 September 1966, the Royal Marine Hotel in Dún Laoghaire was the venue, and members of the National Union of Journalists were the audience. The timing was carefully chosen, a Saturday evening, so as to catch the mass-circulation Sunday newspapers and to dominate the high-listenership Sunday lunchtime radio news.

On being appointed Minister for Education a few months earlier O'Malley had come across a study commissioned by one of his predecessors, Patrick Hillery, on a proposal for free secondary education with a means test. O'Malley was astonished to discover that the scheme would cost much less than he and most politicians had previously assumed. For several weeks he tossed the proposal around with his fellow-ministers Brian Lenihan and Charles Haughey, who, along with Eoin Ryan, Michael Yeats and Noël Browne (then in Fianna Fáil), had unsuccessfully pushed for this and other important changes in education policy when they were a reforming cohort on the party's Ard-Chomhairle during the later years of de Valera's leadership. Now the pair, along with O'Malley, were among the cadre of new young ministers promoted by Lemass, and they urged him on. Instead of bringing the proposal to the Government, O'Malley first suggested it to Lemass, who—nervous, as he often was, of the conservatism of his own Government and of the civil service—encouraged O'Malley to float the idea in the media.

Indeed John Healy, the legendary journalist and a friend of O'Malley, claims that when the latter had secretly brought a draft of his speech to the Taoiseach's office the previous Thursday it was Lemass who had effected a crucial amendment. The significant paragraph spoke of setting up a universal secondary education system on the basis of a means test. Lemass took his pen and drove it through the reference to a means test, saying, "This is 1966, the anniversary of the Proclamation. It's about time we treated all the children of the nation equally." Healy was close to O'Malley, and there is every reason to believe that his account of this event is an accurate reflection of what O'Malley told him. Whether O'Malley was overstating Lemass's level of involvement and advance knowledge is not clear; Lemass chose never to reveal the extent of his knowledge, and O'Malley did not survive long enough to share his account with historians or journalists other than Healy.

What we do know is that when the speech was delivered by O'Malley two days later the crucial paragraph read: "I propose for the coming school year, beginning in September of next year, to introduce a scheme whereby up to the completion of the Intermediate Certificate course the opportunity for free post primary education would be available to all families."

The strategy of using the media to force the initiative through the Government worked beyond O'Malley's expectations. All three Sunday newspapers printed it on their front pages, as did all Monday morning's dailies, accompanied by extremely supportive editorials. Among those who privately greeted the proposals with consternation was the Minister for Finance, Jack Lynch, who became aware of it for the first time when he read the press coverage at Dublin Airport on his return from a visit to Turkey.

In the following days the Secretary of the Department of Finance, Dr Whitaker, wrote to the Taoiseach expressing astonishment "that a major change in Educational Policy should be announced at a weekend seminar." He continued in a clinical tone:

> This free schooling Policy has not been the subject of any submission to the Department of Finance, has not been approved by the Government, has certainly not been examined from the financial (whatever about the educational) aspect and therefore should have received no advance publicity particularly of the specific and definitive type involved in Mr. O'Malley's statement.[53]

Lemass issued a formal written reprimand to O'Malley on the Monday following his speech for not giving his Government colleagues the opportunity to consider and discuss the matter before its announcement. Healy is among those who suggest that in sending this letter Lemass was merely covering his own tracks. P. J. Browne, O'Malley's biographer, argues that Lemass was certainly aware of O'Malley's intention, even if there was ambiguity about the wording and the implications surrounding the announcement.

O'Malley replied to Lemass:

It was my understanding that I had your agreement to my outlining these lines of action, particularly in view of the fact that Fine Gael were planning to announce a comprehensive educational policy this week ... If I was under a misapprehension in believing that I had your support for my announcement, I must apologise. I would hope, however, that what I have said will persuade you that I was right in making it and that you will give me your full support in getting my plans approved by the government.[54]

As P. J. Browne points out, this cleverly crafted letter took the pressure off Lemass and allowed him to maintain his tacit support for O'Malley's initiative. During sharp exchanges at the next Government meeting, Lynch and others criticised O'Malley's cavalier disregard for Government procedure and questioned how the initiative might be funded. However, as O'Malley told it to Healy, in the face of a tidal wave of press and popular support for the proposal, and knowing, or suspecting, the Taoiseach's hand in its announcement, those ministers with reservations had no option but to accept it as a *fait accompli*. Brian Farrell, writing in 1983, says that several members of that Government told him that they suspected Lemass had advance knowledge of what O'Malley proposed to announce. Whatever they thought, they relented and looked forward to the educational transformation and to the electoral advantage the initiative might generate. Between 1966 and 1969 the number of pupils attending second-level education rose from 104,000 to 144,000.

The following year O'Malley also announced a plan to extend the school transport scheme, commissioned the building of new non-denominational comprehensive and community schools and introduced the regional technical colleges, which later evolved into the institutes of technology and in his native Limerick into a full university. Sadly, he himself was not to witness the electoral and educational dividends that flowed from his reform programme. In March 1968 he collapsed while campaigning during a by-election in Co. Clare and died on arrival at Limerick Hospital.

When discussing the last days of Lemass's leadership it is necessary to deal with one important feature of the Fianna Fáil he handed over to his successor, namely the increasingly close relationship that the party, and in particular some of his new young ministers, came to have with the emerging business elite. A close relationship, which was on occasion very public, began to develop between some of the party's most colourful personalities, such as Blaney, Haughey, O'Malley and Lenihan, and the brasher elements not only of the emerging Irish business leadership but also of Dublin's lively 1960s social scene. Haughey, O'Malley and Lenihan were increasingly attracting publicity for their social antics, particularly at Groome's Hotel in Cavendish Row and other prominent venues around the city centre. In this era of emerging social diarists and a trend towards a more colourful form of political coverage they generated much copy and were often depicted as "the three musketeers".

Patrons of Groome's included many politicians, not exclusively of the Fianna
Fáil persuasion, along with actors and directors from the Gate Theatre
opposite, journalists, intellectuals and writers such as Peadar O'Donnell, Seán
Ó Faoláin, Kate O'Brien and Ulick O'Connor.[55]

At about the same time Fianna Fáil formalised its funding relationship
with the business community when it established a support group called Taca
("support"), which came into existence in late 1966. Taca's principal activity
was the organising of large dinner events at which business people paid £100
a plate for the opportunity to socialise with some of the party's leading
figures. The precise effect the events had on the party's finances is unclear,
and, given the secrecy surrounding these matters, may never be known, but
they attracted much controversy, as it was suggested that ministers were
favouring their business friends. Many of the new generation of property
developers were prominent at these events which became the subject of
extensive media comment.[56]

While Taca was obviously successful in its financial objective, at least in
Dublin, it was not universally popular within the Fianna Fáil organisation. At
the 1968 ard-fheis a motion criticising Taca and the damage it was doing to
the party's reputation was defeated only after Neil Blaney, one of its leading
figures, intervened from the podium to defend the initiative.

Pádraig Faulkner tells of the reaction in Co. Louth when the organisation
there got a notice from party headquarters asking them to set up a Taca
branch in their area.

> We were unhappy with the new fund-raising scheme in Louth. Joe
> [Senator Joe Farrell] received a letter from Headquarters outlining how
> the Taca scheme should be put into effect. At the following North
> Louth Comhairle Ceantair meeting Joe presented Frank Aiken with the
> letter. Frank read it and then removed the lid of the solid fuel heater in
> the meeting room and dropped the letter into it. Thus Taca died in the
> Louth constituency.[57]

The fact that Fianna Fáil embraced the businessmen and developers just
when the party was expressing what Stephen Collins has called a "proudly
philistine" support for many of the developments that were destroying
Georgian Dublin made the engagement all the more suspect in the mind of
many contemporary commentators and did the party even further damage.
One of the more sober assessments of the damage the Taca escapade did to
Fianna Fáil is that given by James Downey, who concludes:

> It was an extraordinary and a foolish move to parade the party's
> business links in this manner. The expensive dinners at the very least
> signified an exceptional degree of arrogance and carelessness of
> scrupulous standards. At worst they indicated that the diners regarded
> themselves as new masters and permanent masters with no respect for

the public or for propriety. Naturally and quite rightly but not accurately they attached the tag to the entire party.[58]

Taca, which was only just taking root as Lemass was taking his leave of the leadership of Fianna Fáil, would be a problem for Lemass's successor. Arguably an even bigger problem would be the manner in which Lemass managed his own departure. In November 1966 he surprised political observers with his decision to retire, which he explained thus: "It is time I moved on. I don't want to become a national monument around the place."[59]

The decision created tensions within Fianna Fáil, as he had no obvious successor. In later years Lemass justified his decision not to "groom a successor" by stating that

this can cause difficulties. If the Taoiseach begins to indicate whom he wants as a successor then, of course, it could be discouraging to a lot of people who felt that they could grow to take the office. This is a very difficult decision to take; to sort of indicate who was going to be the choice of the retiring Taoiseach as successor, because everybody's entitled to feel the office is open to him, providing he works hard enough, providing he's open enough.[60]

While Lemass may have had qualms about being seen to publicly identify a successor, he also seems to have been alive to the need for Fianna Fáil to avoid a divisive and damaging leadership contest. In the months before he announced his resignation he had discreetly sounded out both Patrick Hillery and Jack Lynch and had separately asked them to consider taking on the leadership. Hillery's biographer writes:

Lemass and Hillery regularly met for lunch in the government dining room and at one of these lunches Lemass raised the issue of the succession. He told the younger man that he was retiring soon and quietly sounded him out about taking over as Taoiseach: "He said, 'You could do it,' and I said I wouldn't. He was the type that would just accept what you said." Lemass also approached Jack Lynch around the same time as his overture to Hillery; Lynch, too, initially rejected the prospect of becoming Taoiseach. Lemass was seeking a candidate who would unite the party and appeal effectively to the wider electorate; it was significant that he considered Lynch and Hillery the potential successors who would best accomplish these objectives.[61]

Both before and after Lemass had made known his decision to stand down, Lynch made it clear privately and publicly that he would not be seeking the leadership. This was not what Lemass had intended. He later confided to Michael Mills, political correspondent of the *Irish Press*, that by announcing his retirement he believed he was creating a breathing space for a successor to emerge. Instead Fianna Fáil now stood on the precipice of a bruising free-for-all for its leadership.

In response to Lynch's declaration that he would not be a candidate, both George Colley and Charles Haughey threw their hats into the ring. Meanwhile Pádraig Faulkner sought to persuade Frank Aiken to put his name forward, but Aiken declined, because of his age. Kevin Boland, who had also approached Aiken, now sought a candidate to block Haughey and Colley, both of whom, he maintained, had to be stopped "at all costs."[62] Boland considered Colley a "nincompoop" and thought that Haughey was not to be trusted.[63]

Believing that a Colley victory was a distinct possibility unless another minister emerged, Boland discussed the situation with Blaney. The Donegal man said, "There's only you or I," to which Boland replied, "Well, that's you." Blaney now entered the race.[64]

At this point the choice on offer seems to have left much of the parliamentary party underwhelmed. Colley had been a minister for only eighteen months and was not a known vote-getter, having been elected at the last election only on the ninth count. Haughey was not favoured by party traditionalists, some of whom saw him as brash, while others rejected him because he came from a Free State family. When Haughey had sought his support Boland had bluntly told him, "No, Charlie, you haven't got the background."[65] For others, Blaney was not an attractive candidate for leader. His biographer Kevin Rafter notes:

> Despite his long standing within the party and his renowned organisational abilities, Neil Blaney would have faced the difficulty that his colleagues might have perceived him as a single issue or two issue candidate. The perception was one of Blaney as the Northern Republican or that perception in combination with the kind of business associations which he had. In many ways, his biggest problem was that he may not have been perceived as having the appeal of say either Lynch or Haughey.[66]

The Haughey-Colley contest had left TDs cold, and Hillery appealed to Lemass to approach Lynch and ask him to reconsider.

> When I got talking to Lemass he asked me what I thought; so I said, "You're in a fix now, because the party is divided between these two boys and they are not wanted." Jack was ahead of me in the government. He was popular with the party, terribly popular with the country. I said, "You'll have to ask him."[67]

The pressure for Lynch to declare for leadership grew even stronger when Blaney entered the race. If some senior TDs were cool on a Haughey or Colley leadership, the prospect of Blaney taking over was viewed with positive alarm. The fear was that, with Dublin TDs divided between Haughey and Colley,

Blaney, with a significant rural backing, would win a three-way contest. Martin Corry and Tom McEllistrim, both of whom saw Blaney as a "loose cannon", approached Lemass and made it clear to him that party stability would not be served by the type of contest that was now looming.[68] Meanwhile Cork TDs, with the support of the Clare deputies Patrick Hillery and Seán Ó Ceallaigh, began a "draft Jack" campaign, and Lemass decided to persuade Lynch to stand. Lynch has left a description of the encounter.

> Lemass again invited me to his room, informed me that several backbenchers wanted me to run and that the party generally favoured me as his successor. He pointed out to me that I owed the party a duty to serve, even as leader. He gave me to understand that the other contenders to whom he had already spoken, were prepared to withdraw in my favour.[69]

At this point Lynch famously went off to consult his wife, while an exasperated Lemass went to work on trying to clear the field for him. He said to Boland: "What kind of people have I got when one man has to get his wife's permission to run and the other [Colley] has to get his wife's permission to withdraw?"[70]

When Lynch finally entered the race, both Blaney and Haughey withdrew after consulting Lemass. Colley, who had been assured by Lynch of his support until the latter's entry into the race, decided to push the contest to a vote. Lynch's victory was decisive—52 votes to 19—but division, disappointment and distrust were now widespread in the parliamentary party because of the failed leadership attempts.

Lemass's election may have been a breath of fresh air, but his departure was tainted with bitterness. He had inherited a united, cohesive party but he left Lynch with a party increasingly at odds with itself. As Bruce Arnold writes,

> Lemass allowed himself too much time in the drawn-out process of succession. It had got out of hand. If there was a design to it, then the leadership contest should have delivered up a united political weapon of invincible strength and purpose to the new leader. It did not fulfil this necessary purpose. In fact, it did the opposite . . .[71]

The debate on the leadership at the parliamentary party meeting was also bitter and divisive. MacEntee criticised Lemass sharply for stepping down at all, while Boland attacked Aiken with a "barrage of abuse". As Boland and Blaney saw it, then and for years afterwards, they had rowed in behind Lynch on the grounds that if they put him in they could, if need be, take him out. Kevin Boland says their backing of Lynch "wasn't out of any assessment of Lynch, from the point of his suitability or ability at all. I remember distinctly saying to Blaney, 'Lookit, let him on, so long as he does what we tell him.'"[72]

Pádraig Faulkner sensed that the great majority of the parliamentary party accepted Lynch as leader, but there was a vague underlying feeling, however, that some senior ministers, who had declared their intention of seeking the leadership, could be biding their time. My theory was that there was a small group who voted for Jack largely because they believed he was too soft to continue for long in the position. They believed that their opportunity would come sooner rather than later.[73]

The genie of frustrated ambition was now well and truly out of the bottle within Fianna Fáil. The party, from the point of Lemass's departure, faced into a long and increasingly bitter period of internal combustions, heaves and leadership challenges. Jack Lynch would be the first leader of Fianna Fáil to have to contend with a divided party.

| A WEAK START, 1966–9

J ack Lynch was elected third leader of Fianna Fáil on 10 November 1966. Because of the controversy that surrounded his election he moved quickly to quash any suggestion that he was in some way an unwilling occupant of the post. On his first day he told the Dáil that, while he had been reluctant to let his name go forward for nomination as Taoiseach for personal reasons, he had now put these aside. He went on to say:

> I can assure the deputies opposite that I shall not be a reluctant Taoiseach. On the contrary, I shall be a vigorous and progressive one. Neither am I here in a caretaker capacity. As I told my party, I shall stay as long as I am able to hold down the job.

Lynch's remarks were more protestations than assurances, and in reality they were aimed as much at the deputies beside and behind him as they were at those opposite.

Many could be forgiven for believing Lynch reluctant. As we have seen, he had been unwilling to become a minister, and it had taken an inordinate amount of pressure from Lemass and from back-bench colleagues to persuade him to become leader of his party. As his political career progressed up the various rungs, Lynch always seemed to resent the further encroachment on the private life he and his wife so enjoyed that went with each promotion.

He had even appeared unenthusiastic about getting into politics to start with. Most of the previous generation of Fianna Fáil ministers had come to politics through their involvement in the War of Independence and the Civil War, while many of the next had family connections with that earlier generation, including Boland, Blaney, Colley and Childers. More recently a new cadre of deputies had emerged through what was to become an established route, namely years of local political activity or involvement in local government.

Jack Lynch's path to politics was through hurling. Long before he was known as a politician he became a household name as a GAA star. He remains today the only player to win medals in six successive all-Ireland finals, five of them in hurling and one in football. Alongside his friend Christy Ring, Lynch is considered one of the greatest hurlers ever, and he was named on the GAA's

Hurling Team of the Millennium in 1999, Team of the Century in 1984, the Cork Millennium Team, and Hurling Captain of the Forties.[1]

It was this status as a GAA hero that made Lynch such an attractive political candidate. He had worked as a civil servant before leaving the public service to become a barrister in 1945. Within a year he was approached by the Brother Delaney Cumann in Blackpool, Cork, to be the Fianna Fáil candidate for the Borough constituency in the 1946 by-election but declined in favour of his friend Pa McGrath. He spoke at a meeting for McGrath during the by-election campaign but had no other political involvement from 1946 to 1948. In early 1948 he was the subject of indirect approaches from Clann na Poblachta, but he told them his interest was in Fianna Fáil.

Closer to the 1948 election he was again approached by the Blackpool cumann, and this time he agreed to allow his name to go forward to the selection convention. He did not, however, attend the convention, because it clashed with a law dinner. When word reached him at the dinner that he had been selected, he went to the convention "clad in dinner jacket" and addressed the delegates, thanking them for their confidence in him. He had not even joined Fianna Fáil before being nominated.

He went on, however, with the significant assistance of friends and colleagues from Glen Rovers, his local club, to receive the highest proportion of the Fianna Fáil vote in that constituency and to take a Dáil seat that he was to hold on to with considerable ease in all subsequent elections.

In time Lynch's status as a sports hero, his apparent lack of political ambition and the very fact that his background and outlook were broader than a narrow Fianna Fáil heritage were among the factors that made him so popular with the public and contributed to his becoming the most electorally successful Fianna Fáil leader. At the outset, however, many of his Government and parliamentary colleagues sneered at his lack of party pedigree and played on his lack of enthusiasm for the political fray. Neil Blaney would later tell his biographer Kevin Rafter: "My experience of him would have been a man who didn't have any conviction about anything . . . Lynch literally didn't have a Fianna Fáil background at all—it would have been the reverse, if anything."[2] According to Rafter,

> Blaney and Boland saw themselves as torch-carriers of the tradition of Fianna Fáil. Pure, unstained Fianna Fáil blood ran through their veins. Men like Lynch, who lacked a history with the party or a link to the fight for political freedom in the 1920s, were in the eyes of Blaney and Boland, only partial Fianna Fáil. Jack Lynch may have been chosen as leader of Fianna Fáil but only after receiving Blaney's and Boland's mark of approval and they still remained the big organisational men within the party who sought to call the shots.[3]

Lemass's departure from the leadership was a watershed for Fianna Fáil, as it was for Irish politics. The 1916 veterans and founding fathers of Fianna Fáil, bonded by their common experience in the War of Independence and the Civil War, handed over power. The previous Fianna Fáil succession, from de Valera to Lemass, "the youngest of the old guard,"[4] had been seamless. Lynch, who after all had been born the year after the 1916 Rising, was somewhat daunted to be succeeding the likes of de Valera and Lemass.

> I . . . found it difficult to visualise myself assuming the mantle of the likes of Éamon de Valera and Seán Lemass. They were both towering figures in my mind and the thought that I could adequately fill their place seemed to me the height of presumption.[5]

Even though the majority of 32 he secured from the parliamentary party suggested that Lynch had a substantial mandate from his colleagues, the reality behind those figures was a deeply divided party. In Pádraig Faulkner's view there was a sizeable contingent in the party who clearly saw Lynch as an interim leader. This group were busy keeping an eye on their rivals while simultaneously waiting for Lynch to slip up. Faulkner felt, because of this prevailing mood, that "the next general election would do much to determine the future."[6]

If the divisions within the parliamentary party were unprecedented, so too were those among Lynch's ministers. The Government was a hotbed of naked and now frustrated ambition. The potential for division was apparent not only to the opposition but to the country at large. James Dillon, who was then Fine Gael's leading orator in Dáil Éireann, was wont to call Haughey, Blaney, Lenihan, Boland and O'Malley the Camorra (a Mafia-like secret society). He suggested in the debate on their renomination as ministers that Lynch was going to be "as expendable as an old shoe in their eyes" and that the "Camorra" would already be "sharpening their knives and whirling their tomahawks, not only for their enemies but for one another."[7]

Lynch's difficulties were compounded by the fact that he had become leader in the middle of a Dáil term and therefore without his own direct electoral mandate. On the day Lynch was elected Taoiseach, Gerard Sweetman of Fine Gael reminded the Dáil that Fianna Fáil had fought the previous year's election on the slogan of "Let Lemass lead on." He suggested that the honourable thing for Fianna Fáil to do was to hold an election, as their slogan was "no longer operative."[8] The new Taoiseach was also hamstrung by the fact that his ministers owed their appointment not to him but to his predecessor. Lynch himself later explained the situation as follows:

> There was inevitably no radical changes in the composition of the Government once I took over. Seán Lemass had already effected the transition from one generation to another and I had merely to endorse the changes he had made . . .While superficially this made life easy for me it did cause problems for I was thereby deprived of one major strength every Prime Minister usually enjoys: the power of Cabinet. Of

course I had that power formally but in effect most Ministers knew that they owed their position to Seán Lemass not to me.

Lynch reappointed all the outgoing Lemass ministers. He continued the seniority approach by retaining Frank Aiken as Tánaiste and Minister for External Affairs. The need to fill his own vacancy at the Department of Finance gave rise to his most dramatic and indeed most successful appointment, that of Charles Haughey. Some have seen this as a reward for Haughey's having agreed to step aside during the leadership contest, but it is more likely to have been a recognition that Haughey was the ablest of the ministers and of the need for a strong personality in Merrion Street to contend with the many strong personalities in the big-spending departments.

As leader of the Government and of his party, Lynch appeared disengaged when compared with Lemass. Lynch and his admirers argue that this was only a change of style and speak of how he wished to be less of a manager than Lemass had been, wanting to marry the Lemass style with that of de Valera. However, it is clear that the most striking aspects of the early years of Lynch's leadership were "conservatism, lack of control over cabinet and loss of the momentum that had characterised the Lemass era."[9]

Bruce Arnold, an admirer of Lynch's conduct during his later terms, agrees with the view that Lynch was a relatively weak leader during his first term.

It could not be said that Jack Lynch's first period as Taoiseach showed him either in firm control of his party, or successfully achieving the target he set himself. He had wanted to create a team spirit among his ministers, to achieve greater cohesion in the Government's operation and, he naturally wished to exert his personal authority. A question mark hangs over the fulfilment of each of these objectives.[10]

Notwithstanding this, it should be acknowledged that Lynch's first Government did clock up some significant policy achievements. On the very day that Lemass revealed his decision to resign, the British Prime Minister, Harold Wilson, announced that Britain intended to apply again for membership of the European Economic Community. Lynch was already convinced that Ireland's future lay in engaging with Europe, not in isolationism, and the British action confirmed his determination that Ireland should join. He put the issue colourfully:

The choice is between taking part in the great new renaissance of Europe or opting for economic, social and cultural sterilisation. It is like that faced by Robinson Crusoe when the ship came to bring him back into the world again.

He engaged in allaying fears at home about the EEC, including those within his own party, and to this end the Government published a white paper on the EEC in April 1967.

Charles Haughey was also to the forefront, outlining the economic arguments in favour of EEC membership. T. Ryle Dwyer writes:

> One of the more attractive aspects of membership of the EEC, he explained, was the budgetary freedom it would provide by relieving the national exchequer "of the burden of supplementing the export of agricultural surpluses." At the time, over 26 per cent of the agricultural budget went on export subsidies. Removing this burden from the exchequer would, he said, provide "very great scope for the development of social services, health services and education services to European levels."[11]

On 10 May 1967 Ireland again formally applied for membership of the EEC. Lynch, Haughey, T. K. Whitaker and Hugh McCann, Secretary of the Department of External Affairs, went on a tour of European capitals to generate support for an Irish application. In Paris they were received cordially by de Gaulle, but his opposition to Britain meant that the Irish application would not be accepted at that time. Lynch continued to work hard in pursuit of Irish membership, but it was not until de Gaulle's dramatic resignation in April 1969 that the expansion of the EEC became again a realistic possibility.

Back home, the Censorship of Publications (Amendment) Act was passed on 11 July 1967, which resulted in the unbanning of thousands of books and put a more liberal face on Fianna Fáil. This was a triumph for the Minister for Justice, Brian Lenihan, who had to overcome departmental and clerical opposition.

In the Department of Finance, Haughey showed real flair and proved a popular success. In his first budget he announced significant increases in social welfare benefits that more than compensated for inflation. He also announced a dramatic extension of the farmers' dole. He began a pattern of particular supports for pensioners by introducing schemes such as free bus and rail travel during off-peak hours, free electricity and free telephone rental, as well as duty-free petrol for disabled drivers of all ages.[12] He also attracted much international attention when he announced tax exemptions for artists and creative writers.

On Northern Ireland policy Lynch continued Lemass's rapprochement with the Stormont government, although Terence O'Neill did not accept the new Taoiseach's invitation to a joint meeting for more than a year. This meeting was held in Belfast on 11 December 1967. Unlike the previous O'Neill-Lemass meetings, it was publicised in advance, thereby enabling Ian Paisley and some followers to avail of the opportunity to throw snowballs at the Taoiseach's car as it rounded the statue of Edward Carson on the drive leading up to Stormont.[13] T. K. Whitaker, who was in the car with Lynch, recalled that the Taoiseach was completely unperturbed. When Paisley's booming voice was heard insisting, "No Pope here!" Lynch mischievously asked Whitaker, "Which one of us does he think is the Pope?"[14]

Initially Lynch tended towards a more hands-off approach on party matters. When compared with his immediate predecessor and his most prominent Government colleagues, Lynch had never really been an organisation man. This left him with no real base in the party outside Cork.

Neil Blaney, who was soon to emerge as Lynch's nemesis, was chairperson of the then powerful Organisation Committee of the Fianna Fáil Ard-Chomhairle. He was also renowned for his efforts during national elections and particularly in by-elections. The American academic Paul Sacks, writing in the early 1970s, told how the Blaney machine assisted in developing his base in the national party.

> In addition to providing him with a local power base (and an impressive majority) the machine aided Blaney in a number of ways. As a central figure within both party and government hierarchies, Blaney was frequently required to assist colleagues in re-election battles. With the aid of skilful henchmen from the machine, Blaney travelled the country to fight in electoral battles far afield from Donegal; the skill and efficiency with which his travelling band operated gained for them the epithet "The Donegal Mafia". The gratitude Blaney earned in this process became an important foundation for his growing national faction. The machine also provided Blaney with vocal support at various national forums [including ard-fheiseanna].[15]

Kevin Boland, like his father before him, was one of the party's two honorary secretaries. He was also *de facto* vice-chairperson of the party's Organisation Committee. This, coupled with his role as director of elections for various by-elections, gave Boland a similar standing to that of Blaney among the party grass roots. Indeed a pattern of holding two by-elections on the same day developed, with Blaney and his Donegal Mafia directing one and Boland and a cadre of regular workers running the other. Boland recalled:

> Blaney would not be content with ensuring that everything in the constituency which he had responsibility over was running smoothly. After canvassing was completed in his own area, Blaney would "come over to pay us a visit to reassure himself that everything was running smoothly." These "semi-official inspections" would occur late in the night and Blaney might have travelled half way round the country to get to wherever Boland was stationed. Then, having reassured himself that all was in order, he would return to his own area of responsibility with another day of canvassing ahead of him.[16]

Haughey was another darling of the grass roots and, like Lenihan and O'Malley, was seen as a force for modernisation and reform in the party and in government. Although not the oldest he was the most senior deputy in Dublin and had a particular responsibility for the party organisation throughout the city. Haughey had also been national director of elections for the 1965 general election and the 1966 presidential election, and he would go on to perform this role in the 1968 constitutional referendum on the voting system and in the 1969 general election.

Blaney, Boland and, particularly, Haughey were also the central figures in the establishment of Taca. Haughey was the primary focus of press comment on the activities of the organisation. He had, for example, organised the first Taca dinner in the autumn of 1966,[17] which was a particularly lavish event in the Gresham Hotel attended by the whole Government. Kevin Boland recalled of this: "We were all organised by Haughey and sent to different tables around the room. The extraordinary thing about my table was that everybody at it was in some way or other connected with the construction industry."[18]

George Colley meanwhile was cultivating a different niche in the party. A favourite of Aiken and other party grandees, Colley was seen as one of their own. His reputation for public probity was in sharp contrast to the controversies that were already surrounding Haughey and the other ministers who were prominent in Taca. Speaking at a Fianna Fáil youth conference in Galway in May 1967, Colley urged those in attendance not to be dispirited "if some people in high places appear to have low standards." The speech caused a sensation at the time, not least because Colley's remarks were widely regarded as a reference to Haughey. Colley denied that it was meant to be taken in that way, but it was indicative not only of the tensions between the two men but of deepening divisions in Lynch's Government.

If Lynch's base in the organisation was narrow, his popular appeal was extraordinarily wide. In time he would be referred to frequently by such accolades as "the most popular Irish leader since Daniel O'Connell." Michael McInerney, political correspondent of the *Irish Times*, dubbed Lynch "the Lord Mayor of Ireland". Patrick Hillery once described electioneering with Lynch as akin to "campaigning with Cú Chulainn." On becoming Taoiseach he had inherited a minority Government from Seán Lemass; within eighteen months he led Fianna Fáil to the remarkable feat of turning this into an absolute majority.[19] There were seven by-elections between December 1966 and May 1968, six of them won by Fianna Fáil, with four seats taken from opposition parties. Blaney, as Fianna Fáil's by-election king, felt entitled to take some of the credit for this tremendous run of victories. Despite his later differences with Lynch, he said with some credibility: "Organisationally, I worked my heart out to make him an acceptable, credible and successful leader by fighting by-elections beyond and above the call of any person in Fianna Fáil."[20]

It was during the Clare by-election that Donogh O'Malley had died suddenly. The resulting Government reshuffle saw Brian Lenihan become Minister for Education. Mícheál Ó Móráin moved to Justice, and Pádraig Faulkner became Minister for Lands and the Gaeltacht. On becoming Taoiseach, Lynch had retained Pádraig Faulkner, Jim Gibbons and Paddy Lalor as parliamentary secretaries, even though it was widely known that they had voted for Colley, and Lynch had faced considerable pressure not to reappoint them.[21] Faulkner remained close to Colley and to Frank Aiken, who had also supported Colley in the leadership race. Faulkner's promotion is significant in that it indicates that Colley and his supporters had become loyal supporters of Lynch, and that his hold on the leader's position had strengthened.

On 22 May 1968 Donogh O'Malley's 29-year-old nephew Desmond O'Malley held Donogh's seat comfortably. His selection as a candidate, rather than the minister's widow, was controversial.[22] The battle for credit within Fianna Fáil for this particular by-election victory was indicative of the tensions. While many attributed the victory to Lynch's popularity, other commentators gave credit to Neil Blaney and his "Donegal Mafia", who were said to have run the campaign with military precision.[23] Once in the Dáil, Des O'Malley quickly emerged as a close confidant of Lynch. Blaney was dismissive of the qualities of the young O'Malley as a candidate, claiming that his main task during the by-election had been to keep O'Malley away from the electorate. He also regularly disparaged O'Malley's lack of party pedigree, both privately and publicly. In the aftermath of the Limerick by-election he told Brian Lenihan that O'Malley, the candidate he had just helped to elect, was "not one of ours" and "not a real Fianna Fáiler."[24] It was in a sense a cultural and a generational gap. Similarly, O'Malley's view of Blaney was that the Donegal man had

> a feel for Fianna Fáil in its more primitive aspects but with huge emphasis on its historic roots and genesis rather than on its contemporary or future strategies: this constant harping back to the past and especially to the Civil War which kind of obsessed him, in a sense. Even in private conversation, he'd be making all these allusions and references to things that happened in Donegal during the Civil War. He used to be constantly alluding to the incident at Drumboe. It was one of the things that drove him on.[25]

Emboldened by these by-election victories, buoyed up by an all-party report on the constitution that recommended change, and, urged on in particular by Boland, the Government decided to hold another referendum to alter the electoral system. Although some have portrayed Lynch as having been reluctant to hold the referendum, he himself later wrote:

> It has been suggested that I wasn't to blame, as others in the party had pushed the proposal through the Government, but the fact of the matter was, that I was as keen on the change, as anyone else . . . I had been very impressed by de Valera's reasons for proposing the change, in 1959. Several European countries had experienced protracted periods of political instability, with disastrous economic consequences, precisely because of the proportional representational system and with the experience of the two coalition Governments here, there were fears that this might happen in Ireland too.[26]

Privately, the leader of Fine Gael, Liam Cosgrave, also favoured a change in the electoral system, so Fianna Fáil had hoped for at least lukewarm support from Fine Gael for the proposal. Any chance of this dissipated when the Trinity College political scientists Basil Chubb and David Thornley published a study that estimated that Fianna Fáil would stand to win more than ninety seats if a general election were held under the proposed straight-vote system.

The Fianna Fáil campaign for the referendum was weak. Michael Mills reported in the *Irish Press* that there was no sign of the famed Fianna Fáil machine mobilising in favour of the referendum. "Is it not all a great illusion?" he mused. Haughey, Fianna Fáil's campaign director for the referendum, was quoted at the time as saying privately, "We are going to lose it, and they are going to blame me."[27] Haughey's involvement in the campaign was cut short, however, when on 20 September he sustained a serious knee injury when his official car hit a wall outside Arklow. He spent the rest of the campaign in the Mater Hospital.[28] After the referendum Michael McInerney in the *Irish Times* estimated that 150,000 supporters of Fianna Fáil had voted against it and claimed that "the grass roots had turned against the leadership of the party."[29]

This proposal, along with one to vary the constitutionally prescribed ratio of TDS to population in rural areas, was defeated by 61 to 39 per cent. The defeat was seen as a dramatic reverse for Fianna Fáil and a significant setback for Lynch personally. It did not augur well for the party's prospects in the general election that was due some time within the following eighteen months.

One consequence of the referendum defeat was that Lynch moved to restrict Taca. Those members of the party who had been out canvassing for the referendum proposal had been met with a barrage of criticism of the Taca dinners and the unseemly public interaction between ministers and developers. In December 1968 Lynch announced changes. Taca was to be reconstructed, and the maximum membership fee would be £100, while the minimum would now be £5.[30]

The party still needed funds, however, and Lynch appointed a young party activist and businessman, Des Hanafin, to take charge of fund-raising. Hanafin stopped the Taca dinners but continued to tap businessmen privately for donations.[31] In a move that was controversial within the party, he transferred the fund-raising operation from Fianna Fáil head office to a city-centre hotel. He kept a strict record of each donation received, but these records have never been published. Hanafin says, however, that Jack Lynch "had no hesitation in returning donations that he felt might compromise the freedom of the party."[32]

In those days before sophisticated opinion-polling, many commentators extrapolated the referendum results to assume that Fianna Fáil would also suffer a bad defeat in the 1969 election. Not for the last time, Fianna Fáil under Lynch was to defy electoral expectations. Even though the party had been in power for twelve years, the economic context was still very favourable for

Fianna Fáil. So too was the constituency map, cleverly redrawn in a partisan way by the Minister for Local Government and referred to by the opposition as "Boland's gerrymander" or "Kevinmandering".[33] Fianna Fáil also had in its new leader a particularly valuable electoral asset.

Fianna Fáil's prospects in the 1969 election were greatly assisted by the stance that the Labour Party adopted towards coalition. Liam Cosgrave had made overtures to the Labour Party to form a loose electoral pact but had been spurned by its leader, Brendan Corish. Having been rejuvenated at the grass-roots level over the previous two years, and having managed to attract a host of celebrity intellectuals as candidates, the Labour Party had taken a sharp turn to the left and ran an independent and ambitious campaign. The new candidates included the commentator, historian and former UN diplomat Conor Cruise O'Brien, David Thornley of Trinity College, the television presenter Justin Keating, and the former minister Noël Browne. This wave of fresh candidates was dismissed by Fianna Fáil's Minister for Justice, Mícheál Ó Móráin, as "new Left Wing political queers who have taken over the Labour Party from the steps of Trinity College and Teilifís Éireann."[34]

Corish fell prey to wishful thinking and argued that if it got enough strength in the Dáil the Labour Party would be in a position to force the setting up of a coalition government of Fine Gael and Fianna Fáil. In the words of Dermot Keogh,

> The alternative might be another general election, out of which the Labour Party might emerge as an actual or embryo Government. The logic was fanciful and the electoral mathematics impossible, the strategy was less practical than millennial, the naïve logic and clueless political analysis that lay behind the Labour slogan "The seventies will be socialist" determined that the socialists would be seventy before they came to power as a single party government or as a majority party in a coalition government.[35]

The Labour Party manifesto, which was markedly more socialist than any before or after, provided Fianna Fáil with lots of ammunition for a renewed red scare. Fianna Fáil also made much of remarks by Conor Cruise O'Brien, who, in January at the Labour Party conference, had suggested that Ireland should close its diplomatic mission in Catholic, authoritarian Portugal and open one in Cuba. One full-page Fianna Fáil newspaper advertisement was repeated in several publications during the campaign and spoke of how there were really two Labour Parties. "One is made up of the traditional Labour supporters. The other is made up of extreme left wing socialists who are preaching class warfare and who want state control and all that goes with it."[36] Fianna Fáil relentlessly stoked up fears of widespread nationalisation under the Labour Party.

Lynch himself, addressing an eve-of-poll rally in Cork, asked what the Labour Party's call for a "new republic" would mean.

Election poster for Fianna Fáil's first election campaign, 1927. (*Fianna Fáil*)

The Fianna Fáil parliamentary party, June 1927. Pictured on de Valera's right is Constance Markievicz and on his left is Kathleen Clarke. (*Fianna Fáil*)

The First Fianna Fáil government took office on 9 March 1932. Standing, from left: Seán MacEntee, Seán T. O'Kelly, Joe Connolly, Seán Lemass, Gerry Boland. Seated from left: Frank Aiken, P. J. Ruttledge, Éamon de Valera, Dr Jim Ryan, Tom Derrig, James Geoghegan. (© *TopFoto*)

1930s general election poster. (*Fianna Fáil*)

1940s general election poster. (*Fianna Fáil*)

Éamon de Valera greets
delegates on his way into
the Mansion House,
Dublin, for the 1949 ard-
fheis. (*Fianna Fáil*)

WIVES!
GET YOUR HUSBANDS OFF TO WORK
VOTE
fianna fáil

1950s general election poster.
(*Fianna Fáil*)

President de Valera welcomes Princess Grace of Monaco and her daughter Caroline to Áras an Uachtaráin, 1961. (*Fianna Fáil*)

1960s general election poster. (*Fianna Fáil*)

Presentation of *The History of Fianna Fáil* to the Taoiseach, Seán Lemass, in the boardroom of 13 Upper Mount Street, Dublin, 1960. (*Fianna Fáil*)

Charles Haughey and Neil Blaney pictured outside the Four Courts, October 1970. (© *Irish Times*)

Fianna Fáil poster for the 1972 referendum on membership of the European Economic Community. (*Fianna Fáil*)

Dr Patrick Hillery as President presents Charles Haughey with his seal of office as Taoiseach, March 1982. (© *Irish Times*)

Erskine Childers pictured in 1973 when, as Tánaiste, he successfully contested the presidential election. (© *Victor Patterson*)

Jack Lynch takes the applause of delegates at the 1978 ard-fheis beside two of his closest lieutenants, Des O'Malley and George Colley. (© *Irish Times*)

Government colleagues Ray MacSharry and George Colley on the platform at the 1980 ard-fheis. MacSharry was parliamentary secretary to Colley in the Department of Finance when he seconded Haughey's nomination for the party leadership in November 1979. (© *Victor Patterson*)

Charles Haughey and Jim Gibbons on the campaign trail in Carlow-Kilkenny in the early 1980s. (© *Irish Times*)

Máire Geoghegan-Quinn, who was appointed Fianna Fáil's first female Government minister in 1979. (© *Victor Patterson*)

Charles Haughey signs autographs for admiring delegates at a 1980s ard-fheis. (*Fianna Fáil*)

Friends and long-time colleagues Brian Lenihan and Charles Haughey at the launch of Lenihan's presidential election campaign, 17 September 1991. (© *Irish Times*)

Albert Reynolds meets Gerry Adams of Sinn Féin and John Hume of the SDLP on 6 September 1994, days after the IRA announced what was expected to be a permanent ceasefire. (© *Irish Times*)

Mary McAleese seeks to console Albert Reynolds after she defeated him for the party's nomination for the 1997 presidential election, 17 September 1997. (© *Irish Times*)

Bertie Ahern chats to Charlie McCreevy after his address to the 2003 ard-fheis. (© *Irish Times*)

Bertie Ahern at the launch of the party's manifesto for the 2007 general election campaign. (© *Irish Times*)

Brian Cowen and party colleagues following his ard-fheis address, February 2009. (© *Irish Times*)

Will it involve the confiscation of industrial firms such as Guinness and Waterford Glass, in which many workers have shares? . . . Who will compensate these shareholders? Will Labour take over the banks and the building societies?[37]

When not attacking the Labour Party, and arguing that only Fianna Fáil could realistically provide single-party stable government, the campaign, for which Charles Haughey was again director, was built around Lynch. He undertook a triumphal presidential-style summertime election tour, visiting almost every constituency. On one day during the campaign he travelled from Donegal by helicopter to Dublin for a television appearance and then flew on to Ballina. It was the first time a party leader had used a helicopter in an election.[38]

Haughey himself was the focus of one of the noisier controversies of the campaign when it was revealed that he had sold his house and lands at Raheny, Dublin, to the builder Matt Gallagher, from whom he had originally bought the property. The figure reported for the sale was £205,500, or £5,000 per acre. Haughey had then gone on to buy the nearby Abbeyville estate and its 250 acres for £140,000. Gerard Sweetman of Fine Gael and Conor Cruise O'Brien, who was the Labour Party candidate in Haughey's constituency of Dublin North-East, sought to make political hay of the issue. Cruise O'Brien repeatedly raised the issue throughout the campaign in an effort to expose what he described as "the Fianna Fáil speculator-orientated oligarchy".[39] Haughey considered it a private matter and refused to comment. In the election he topped the poll and increased his share of first-preference votes by 8 per cent. Cruise O'Brien was a distant second, being more than four thousand votes behind Haughey on the first count.

One feature of Lynch's nationwide tour that attracted particular comment was the number of visits he made to convents. Cruise O'Brien accused Fianna Fáil of "making use of Catholicism for party political purposes, similar to the use by the Northern Unionist Party of Protestantism." He claimed that Lynch had used his "tour of the convent parlours" to make snide suggestions that the Labour Party was tainted with communism and that the reverend mothers then spread the word among mothers of the children in their schools. "The press and media were not present for the series of convent chats," Cruise O'Brien pointed out, "but the word came through all the same." As conspiracies go it was entertaining. Convent visits had long been a feature of Irish election campaigns; and, as Dermot Keogh points out, nuns are also citizens with votes.

In the 1969 election Fine Gael held its ground against the Labour Party's hoped-for surge, obtaining 34 per cent of the vote and moving from 47 to 50 seats. The Labour Party actually dropped, from 22 seats to 18. Although it gained four seats in Dublin, rising from 6 to 10 (including seats for Cruise O'Brien, Thornley and Keating), the party's total outside Dublin was halved, from 16 to 8. The Fianna Fáil vote actually fell by 3 per cent, to 45 per cent, but it gained two seats, to finish with 75. It was the party's best result since 1957.

As a result of the election success Lynch was in a much stronger position in his party. He had won an impressive popular mandate, which gave him a comfortable Dáil majority and set Fianna Fáil up for another full term in office. He could no longer be perceived as a stopgap leader. His improved confidence was reflected in the selection of his second Government. Erskine Childers was made Tánaiste, Frank Aiken retired to the back benches and Patrick Hillery was moved to External Affairs. Pádraig Faulkner was moved to Education and Joseph Brennan was made Minister for Labour. Seán Flanagan was given Lands. Lynch also promoted the parliamentary secretaries Jim Gibbons and Paddy Lalor, who had been in the Colley camp during the leadership contest, to Defence and Posts and Telegraphs, respectively. He also appointed Des O'Malley, who had been in the Dáil for only fourteen months, as his chief whip.

There was one hiccup in the selection of this new Government. Kevin Boland had proved a controversial Minister for Local Government, and Lynch wished to transfer him to Social Welfare. In response to this suggestion Boland wrote to Lynch on 27 June 1969 asking to be left out of the Government, as he had felt for some time that he would be a lot more use as a back-bencher and claiming that there was a great danger "for the future of the Party in what appears to me to be a distinct tendency to move to the Right." Lynch, however, persuaded Boland to remain in the Government but had to agree to leave him with both Local Government and Social Welfare.

The disdain that Boland had for Lynch, and the increasingly difficult relationship between them, was highlighted by Conor Cruise O'Brien, who wrote about his first day in the Dáil following the 1969 election. He said that at the debate on the nomination of ministers it became apparent to him that Lynch was not in full control of his party. He recalled that during the debate opposition members had made some criticisms, as is par for the course, of the ministers that Lynch had nominated, including Boland. Lynch was due to deliver the Government's collective response, but instead Boland

> rose in his place and started to make a vigorous polemical reply to the Opposition members who had criticised him and others. The Taoiseach was seen to write a brief note, which was then passed along, through the line of candidate-Ministers, to Boland, who was the furthest away from the Taoiseach . . . When the Taoiseach's missive reached the person to whom it was addressed, Kevin Boland read it with an expression of flagrant contempt, crumpled the Taoiseach's missive in his hand and tossed it to the floor . . . The Taoiseach swallowed the public insult and meekly proceeded with the appointment of Boland . . . Why did Jack Lynch show such apparent weakness in the face of such insolence? I think the basic reason is that he felt isolated within the party which he nominally led. He was not a born Fianna Fáiler but had been recruited into the party as an electoral

asset because of his enormous popularity in Co. Cork, and also as a well-known and popular name throughout the country. He was very useful to the Party, but he seems never to have been felt to be fully of the Party.[40]

The debate on the nomination of the new Government was also memorable, among other things, for Lynch's defence of Fianna Fáil's intellectual prowess. Replying in particular to a gibe from Noël Browne, who had claimed that the Labour Party was smaller in number but could beat Fianna Fáil in many respects, Lynch said:

> I knew what he was referring to, this so-called superior intellectual capacity. There are two attributions I just cannot stand. The first is an intellectual and the second is a worker. I regard everybody who is doing a job in this Country as a worker, whether he works with his head, his hands or anything else. Whether a person is an intellectual or not often means that one has not had the advantage of going to a University or having gone to University, has not had the means or facility of taking a secondary degree. The intellectual capacity on this side of the house is as good as on any side of the house. The people have proved that by returning Fianna Fáil governments in successive elections since 1932.[41]

There has always been a suggestion that, though Lynch was a skilful hurler, he was prone to bouts of laziness on the pitch. A contemporary hurling source even claimed that one of his own players was often deputed by the trainer to hit Lynch in the course of a match in order to rouse him into top form.[42] It is also likely, however, that the more difficult the game got, the more Lynch was inclined to get stuck in.

If Lynch had been relatively easy-going in his first term as Taoiseach, this was about to change. In his second term he would face national challenges not confronted by any Government since the Second World War. Unlike de Valera, however, Lynch had to face them without a united Fianna Fáil party. In responding to dramatic developments in Northern Ireland and to the passions those developments created in the Republic, Lynch was not only to face concerted and sustained opposition from within his party but even a conspiracy within his own Government. The intensity of the challenge, coupled with the attacks he suffered from those who were supposed to be his team-mates, were to rouse Lynch to a display of political skill and leadership that some had come to suspect he did not possess. It was also to prove the most challenging time ever for Fianna Fáil. Its unity was shattered, and its very survival was to be severely tested.

Chapter 10 ~

ARMS AND INTRIGUE, 1969–70

The months between the Apprentice Boys' Parade in Derry on 12 August 1969 and the Fianna Fáil ard-fheis in Dublin on 20 February 1971 were some of the most dramatic and traumatic in Fianna Fáil's history. While the political eruptions within Fianna Fáil pale into insignificance when compared with the violent events in Northern Ireland, it was those events that shaped them.

This was Fianna Fáil's most volatile episode—at least until the twenty-first century—and for that reason it has attracted more attention from academics, authors and documentary-makers than any other period. A detailed consideration of the period would be beyond the scope or capacity of this book, but it is necessary to discuss some of the principal events in order to illustrate their effect on the country at the time and to get some measure of the bitter legacy that they left within the party.

The tensions within Fianna Fáil arising from differing attitudes to events in Northern Ireland burst fleetingly into the public domain even before the 1969 election. The previous October, in the aftermath of an attack by the Royal Ulster Constabulary on a small civil rights march in Derry on 5 October, Neil Blaney, speaking in Letterkenny, dismissed Lynch's meetings with the Northern Ireland Prime Minister, Terence O'Neill, as futile and called for the territorial claim over the North to be reasserted.[1]

Blaney was mildly reprimanded for this outburst by the Taoiseach, and thereafter there appeared to operate an unspoken agreement between the emerging factions within the party that the issue of Northern Ireland would be put aside for the months leading up to, and during, the campaigning weeks of the general election. Shortly after the party's election victory the situation in the North began to deteriorate as the traditional marching season rolled into late July. Nonetheless, on 9 August 1969 Jack Lynch and his ministers, no doubt exhausted after their electoral exertions, headed off for their holidays, in Lynch's case to west Cork.

They did not get to holiday long. In the wake of the Apprentice Boys' march in Derry communal riots erupted in the Bogside area of the city, leading to widespread violence and a complete breakdown of law and order in the city and in many parts of Northern Ireland. Dramatic pictures of the RUC and loyalist mobs attacking rioters in Derry, and of Catholic communities being attacked in other parts of the province, filled television screens in the Republic and beyond. Northern Ireland seemed on the verge of civil war. The coverage caused outrage in the Republic. Emotions ran high, especially within the ranks of Fianna Fáil. According to Pádraig Faulkner,

> it was understandable that Fianna Fáil supporters were touched to the quick as they watched the violent assaults on nationalists which were regularly portrayed on television. Some party meetings demanded that the government rush to the aid of the beleaguered Nationalist community. A small minority demanded armed intervention.[2]

On 13 August, ministers gathered for an emergency meeting. It was to be the first of nine such crisis meetings over the next ten days as the Government met in near-permanent session. At this point it was deeply divided on policy grounds. On the more republican and interventionist side of the spectrum were Neil Blaney and Kevin Boland. Charles Haughey's position was close to theirs, though he may not have been acting in consort with them. Seán Flanagan and Brian Lenihan, as well as the Minister for Justice, Mícheál Ó Móráin, also supported the stance of Blaney and Boland, to varying degrees at different times.

Lynch himself favoured a more moderate position. Up to this point he had followed the Lemass policy of seeking to actively engage with the Northern Ireland government. When the violence erupted in the summer of 1969 he favoured a cautious reaction by his Government, wishing to avoid doing anything that might inflame tensions further. As the violence worsened, it became very difficult to maintain that stance.

Lynch's view was strongly supported by his Tánaiste, Erskine Childers, and the Minister for External Affairs, Patrick Hillery. He also received strong backing from George Colley. Lynch and Colley were growing increasingly close, despite the fact that they had contested the leadership three years earlier. Other ministers who supported a more moderate stance were Pádraig Faulkner, Joe Brennan, and Paddy Lalor, as well as the chief whip, Des O'Malley.

The Government meeting on 13 August was dominated by discussion of what Lynch should say that night in a televised broadcast. Their deliberations were taking place in an atmosphere of heightened emotions and when only limited information was available from intelligence and other sources about precisely what was happening in the North. Dermot Keogh describes the circumstances in which the Government considered the proposed televised address.

> Those who were present that day were part of a Government that was not well prepared for dealing with the unfolding crisis. While the

official diagnosis had been accurate, the contingency planning was poor or non-existent. The atmosphere in the room was charged as reports continued to reach Dublin that violence and disorder were spreading.[3]

Lynch came to the meeting with a draft text for his broadcast prepared by his civil servants. Several ministers, including Blaney, Boland and Haughey, dismissed the text, demanding that he take a much tougher stance. Lynch and his allies in the Government were minded to react more cautiously to events, but the outcome—at least of this first in the series of Government meetings— greatly favoured the more hawkish position. Lynch's speech was reworked several times during the lengthy meeting. With his party and the country in such an emotional state, the Taoiseach was not able to control his Government or to hold to his preferred policy position.

The statement as broadcast by Lynch that night reflects the tough stance adopted at that meeting. He began:

It is with deep sadness that you, Irish men and women of good will, and I have learnt of tragic events which have been taking place in Derry and elsewhere in the North in recent days. Irishmen in every part of this island have made known their concern at these events. This concern is heightened by the realisation that the spirit of reform and inter-communal co-operation has given way to the forces of sectarianism and prejudice. All people of good will must feel saddened and disappointed at this backward turn in events and must be apprehensive for the future. The Government fully share these feelings, and I wish to repeat that we deplore sectarianism and intolerance in all their forms wherever they occur. The Government have been very patient and have acted with great restraint over several months past. While we made our views known to the British Government on a number of occasions, both by direct contact and through our diplomatic representation in London, we were careful to do nothing that would exacerbate the situation. But it is clear now that the present situation cannot be allowed to continue . . . The Stormont government is evidentially no longer in control of the situation . . . Indeed the present situation is the inevitable outcome of the policies pursued for decades by successive Stormont governments. It is clear also that the Irish Government can no longer stand by and see innocent people injured and perhaps worse. It is obvious that the RUC is no longer accepted as an impartial police force. Neither would the employment of British troops be acceptable, nor would they be likely to restore peaceful conditions, certainly not in the long term.

He went on to say that his Government had

requested the British Government to apply immediately to the United Nations for the urgent despatch of a peacekeeping force to the Six Counties of Northern Ireland and have instructed the Irish Permanent Representative to the United Nations to inform the Secretary-General of this request. We have also asked the British Government to see to it that police attacks on the people of Derry should cease immediately.

He announced that, in the light of the high number of casualties and the need to provide assistance, his Government had "directed the Irish army authorities to have field hospitals established in County Donegal adjacent to Derry and at other points along the border where that may be necessary."

Some subsequent reports maintained that Lynch had said that his Government could no longer "stand idly by." It seems that while this phrase was included in the earlier drafts, it was not included in Lynch's final speech as broadcast.

Many recent histories of this period, when describing the events of that evening, give Desmond Fisher's account of Lynch's mood at the time. Fisher was deputy head of news at RTE and had greeted Lynch on arrival and escorted him to the hospitality suite. When Lynch arrived, Fisher saw the text in his hand. It had been "badly typed, with corrections and ink scrawled all over it," apparently because of last-minute changes. Fisher arranged to have it retyped in larger type and with double line-spacing. While this was being done, Lynch asked for the use of a phone. He called home, and Fisher could overhear him consulting his wife, Máirín, on the final changes to the address. Fisher's account suggests that Lynch was vulnerable and isolated, with few he could trust to advise him. At one point, while they waited, Fisher says Lynch asked him what he thought would happen if he ordered the army into Northern Ireland, "as some of his advisers had counselled him." Fisher replied that the British army "would massacre them within twenty miles of the border." Lynch smiled wanly in response and said he had come to the same conclusion.[4]

Lynch's questions to Fisher reflected some of the discussions of the day within the Government and elsewhere, but it seems that while some of the hawks argued that the army should have been deployed across the border in order to internationalise the crisis and precipitate a UN intervention, the option was never given serious consideration. The Government knew that its army was not in a fit state for such an operation, even as a limited exercise to hold some nationalist areas until international pressure was brought to bear on Britain. A majority also foresaw that soldiers from the Republic crossing the border would give rise to immediate and terrible retaliatory attacks on Catholic communities in other parts of Northern Ireland.

Pádraig Faulkner recalls in his memoir that the question of an army incursion was raised but quickly dismissed. "As far as I can remember, the matter was raised in a rather haphazard way and was given little or no consideration."[5] In mentioning it to Fisher, it seems Lynch was doing no more than "thinking out loud".[6] Even Kevin Boland, who was among those taking a hard line, knew it would be disastrous for the army to become involved. He felt that

> places contiguous to the border could obviously be assisted effectively but to do so would mean the wholesale slaughter of nationalists in other areas where there was no defence available. I feel reasonably certain that the others saw this and that none of them visualised an actual incursion.

If members of the Government saw the risks of retaliation that would result from an incursion across the border, they gave insufficient consideration to the possibility that the rhetoric used by Lynch on television would have some of the same consequences. The broadcast had an immediate and incendiary effect north of the border. Rumours of an "invasion" swept Northern Ireland. The suggestion that the Irish Government "would not stand by" was seen by many Protestants as a threat and provoked further violence against Catholic communities, most seriously in the Bombay Street area of Belfast. Lynch was criticised then and since for contributing to this escalation.

Faulkner is among those who have come to Lynch's defence on this point. "Some commentators may now find part of the final versions of the speech to be less than diplomatic but it must be remembered that it was a very emotional time."[7] In his biography of Lynch, Dermot Keogh makes a similar plea for the broadcast to be seen in its context.

> Lynch's speech was not a detached philosophical statement written in a calm and serene atmosphere, his primary objective was to have the violence stopped immediately without any further loss of life or damage to property, if necessary he wanted to shame the British Government into discharging its Constitutional responsibilities in Northern Ireland by drawing International attention to a deteriorating situation already being reported as if parts of the North were like a scene from the film *Mississippi Burning*.[8]

The British Foreign and Commonwealth Office issued a swift rebuttal of Lynch's speech, and reaffirmed Britain's commitment to remaining in Northern Ireland so long as the majority there demanded it, maintaining that "the border is not an issue."[9]

Among the further steps decided on by the Government at its meetings in August 1969 were that the Minister for External Affairs, Patrick Hillery, should seek a meeting with the British Foreign Secretary or Home Secretary to ask that the British Government agree to a proposal that a UN peacekeeping force, or even a joint Anglo-Irish force, be deployed in Northern Ireland. Hillery only got to see a junior minister and received what was reported at the time as a "courteous brush-off". Government papers released thirty years later reveal that in fact it was far from courteous.[10] The British Government rejected any suggestion that it should listen either to the Irish Government or to international opinion on the affairs of Northern Ireland and had already ordered the British soldiers onto the streets, where they had relieved the siege in Derry and were warmly welcomed.

During these meetings the Government also decided that the Minister for Defence would send soldiers to the border to protect the field hospitals, and also that secret contingency plans would be made in case a further deterioration required the sending of soldiers in to protect Catholic communities. The moderate wing, however, managed to resist a proposal that the FCA, the second-line reserve, be called up. Such a public mobilisation would have further inflamed the situation. The Government also rejected a proposal that Irish units serving with the UN peacekeeping force in Cyprus be brought home. This provoked a threat to resign from Kevin Boland. For Boland the eruption in the North was "the moment of truth for the Fianna Fáil Party, the time for the solution to the final problem."[11] Boland simply stopped attending Government meetings, because, as he saw it, "after a few days of interminable wrangling it became apparent to me that a policy of 'to preserve what we have down here,' and to restore normality up there had prevailed."[12] Boland's resignation was not made public or, it seems, even recorded in the Government meeting files. The threat of resignation at this point was real, however, and according to contemporaries it was only after the intervention of President de Valera that Boland was persuaded back into the Government.

Paddy Lalor, who was then the most junior member of the Government, later explained how for him, as for many in the party, the crisis challenged his deepest beliefs about the meaning of Nationalism and Republicanism.

> I grew up firmly believing that the Island of Ireland would never be truly independent until all Unionists were expelled—or at least driven into the North Channel on the way. My difficulties in 1969 and 1970 when then a member of the Government will therefore be appreciated. I had at Government meetings to hear and absorb lessons on the undoubted need for all Irish men and women at the troubled time to accommodate and make proper provision to embrace the two traditions which must be merged on this Island or at least be enabled to live peacefully together.[13]

In another significant decision, on 16 August the Government gave Haughey, as Minister for Finance, control of a fund for providing "aid for victims of distress" in the North, leaving both "the amount and the channel of this disbursement" to be decided by the minister.

After the deployment of the British army on the streets, the situation in Northern Ireland eased somewhat, and the political convulsions in the

Republic began to calm down. On 21 August there was again a full meeting of the Government, but after that ministers did not meet formally for eight days, by which time Northern Ireland was not a significant issue on its agenda.

It is important to note that the public were largely unaware of the internal struggle over policy that had gone on at the top of Fianna Fáil during the summer of 1969. In the following months two policies effectually operated from Government Buildings. The official policy, endorsed by formal Government decision-making, was enunciated by Lynch in a number of speeches over the autumn and winter of 1969. Ultimately, he had won the battle for a more moderate policy. Meanwhile Blaney and Haughey, separately, it appears, but at times in parallel, ran an independent policy, which in its public rhetoric and in the use of public funds was more interventionist and more republican. It also involved them in secret contact, usually through intermediaries, with many of the individuals who were to lead what subsequently became the Provisional IRA.

On 20 September 1969, a month after the "Battle of the Bogside" had ended, Lynch gave a speech in Tralee that was specifically designed to set out in clear and simple terms the basis of the Fianna Fáil Government's thinking and policy on Northern Ireland. It was the most lucid statement of Fianna Fáil's support for the principle of unity by consent made by any party figure up to that point, and it was designed to calm tensions. In it Lynch set out in some detail the framework for what has been Fianna Fáil's policy on Northern Ireland ever since.

Lynch reminded his audience that "the historical and natural unity of Ireland was also a political unit until this was artificially sundered by the Government of Ireland Act passed by the British Government in 1920." He emphasised, however, that

> the unity we seek is not something forced but a free and genuine union of those living in Ireland, based on mutual respect and tolerance and guaranteed by a form or forms of government authority in Ireland providing for progressive improvement of social, economic and cultural life in a just and peaceful environment . . . Of its nature this policy—of seeking unity through agreement in Ireland between Irishmen—is a long-term one. It is no less, indeed it is even more, patriotic for that. Perseverance in winning the respect and confidence of those now opposed to unity must be sustained by good will, patience, understanding and, at times, forbearance . . . It will remain our most earnest aim and hope to win the consent of the majority of the people in the Six Counties to means by which North and South can come together in a reunited and sovereign Ireland, earning international respect both for the fairness and efficiency with which it is administered and for its contribution to world peace and progress.
>
> Finally, a few words on recognition. It is quite unreasonable for any Unionist to expect my Government, or any future Government, to

abandon the belief and hope that Ireland should be reunited. It is unnecessary to repeat that we seek reunification by peaceful means. We are not seeking to overthrow by violence the Stormont Parliament or Government but rather to win the agreement of a sufficient number of people in the North to an acceptable form of reunification. In any case the Stormont Government, being the executive instrument of a subordinate Parliament, cannot receive formal international recognition.

It is also, for similar reasons, unreasonable and unnecessary to expect those living in the Six Counties who share our desire for unity to renounce their deepest hopes. We and they have accepted as a practical matter the existence of a government in the North of Ireland exercising certain powers devolved on it by the British Parliament. We have had many fruitful contacts with that Government in matters of mutual concern. I hope that this co-operation between North and South will continue.

On 22 October 1969 the Dáil held its first substantive debate on Northern Ireland since before the summer recess. The Government had resisted demands for a recall of the Dáil over the summer months for fear it would only add to the emotion and tension. In his speech during the October debate Lynch reasserted that

> our legitimate desire for a unified Ireland will be realised by peaceful means. First of all we want to see peace and tolerance restored in the Six Counties so that Catholics and Protestants, minority and majority, can live side by side with co-operation and in understanding based on equal citizenship. Ultimately we want to see all Irish men and women in all parts of Ireland, irrespective of class creed or politics, living in that same peace and harmony and unity . . . I feel it my duty to repeat again what I said on a number of occasions recently, namely that the Government in this part of Ireland have no intention of mounting an armed invasion of the Six Counties. We could give a number of reasons for this attitude, but the most cogent in our conviction is that the use of force would not advance our long-term aim of a united Ireland. Nor will the Government connive at unofficial armed activity here directed at targets across the Border.[14]

The more moderate Lynch view was now clearly Fianna Fáil policy, although there were occasional public disagreements with it, from Blaney in particular. On 8 December 1969, addressing the Fianna Fáil faithful gathered in Letterkenny to celebrate his twenty-one years in Dáil Éireann, he said:

> I believe, as do the vast majority, that the ideal way of ending partition is by peaceful means. But no-one has the right to assert that force is

irrevocably out. No political party or group at any rate is entitled to predetermine the right of the Irish people to decide what course of action on this question may be justified in given circumstances. The Fianna Fáil party has never taken a decision to rule out the use of force, if the circumstances in the Six Counties so demand . . . If a situation were to arise in the Six Counties in which the people who do not subscribe to the Unionist regime were under sustained and murderous assault, then, as the Taoiseach said on August 13th, we "cannot not stand idly by."[15]

Apart from Blaney's speech in Letterkenny, relations between the factions in the Fianna Fáil Government appeared calm over the winter and into the spring of 1970; but away from the public gaze some extraordinary developments were taking place.

Many aspects of what occurred from the summer of 1969 to May 1970 have been, and still are, hotly contested. We will never truly know what happened, and who knew what and when, though we may discover more when the Department of Justice files and others relating to the period are put into the public archives. For the moment, however, we can only seek to piece together a narrative based on the more credible accounts of contemporary politicians and commentators and the subsequent research done and assessments made by mainstream historians. The sequence of the principal events over this period appears to be as follows.

On 20 August 1969 the Secretary of the Department of Justice, Peter Berry, told his minister, Mícheál Ó Móráin, about intelligence that suggested that an unnamed Government minister had met a prominent member of the IRA. When the matter was raised at a subsequent Government meeting Haughey volunteered the information that the report could concern him: he had been asked to see someone casually, and "it transpired to be this person. There was nothing in it; it was entirely casual." In subsequent Garda reports it was suggested that Haughey had promised this IRA leader at this meeting £50,000 in assistance.

Captain James Kelly, an army intelligence officer, happened to be in Derry when violence erupted there in mid-August 1969. His report on the events proved invaluable to his superiors, who asked him to keep up his contacts in the North. In the following months Kelly also began to develop contacts on the Continent with a view to importing arms into the Republic in order to have them ready to distribute in Northern Ireland for the purpose of the defence of Catholic communities if and when the need arose. In doing so Kelly was acting with the full authority of Colonel Michael Hefferon, head of army intelligence. It also seems that the Minister for Defence, Jim Gibbons, was kept informed, at least to some degree, about Kelly's activities.

Kelly also reported regularly to Neil Blaney. Blaney was Minister for Agriculture, but as the most senior deputy from the border region and a member of the Government sub-committee on Northern Ireland set up in

August 1969 he had a particular interest in, and was assumed by many to have a particular knowledge of, developments in Northern Ireland. There is no doubt that Blaney was aware of Kelly's activities, and it seems that in reality Kelly may have worked to his orders. Blaney certainly arranged an interpreter for Kelly on his Continental trips in the person of Albert Luykx, an Irish businessman of Belgian origin. Kelly also had a base for a period in the Department of Agriculture, so that he could have direct access to Blaney.

Haughey, as Minister for Finance, was prepared, it seems, to authorise the importing of the arms without the usual customs clearance. He admitted later that a particular consignment was expected from the Continent in April 1970 that Kelly and others had asked him to clear through customs without being inspected. He said that he presumed it included material that the army wanted to have at the ready as part of its contingency planning for a doomsday situation in the North. He claimed, however, that he did not know that this consignment contained arms; this is despite the fact that his civil service private secretary, to whom he had communicated the decision about the consignment being given clearance, knew it contained arms and understood that Haughey knew that it included arms.

In this period Haughey and Blaney also appear to have had access to large amounts of cash for their efforts on behalf of Catholic communities in the North. Haughey had control of the Government's funds for the "relief of distress". In addition there were rumours, even at the time, and firmer suggestions since, that Haughey and others involved with him were the conduits for substantial sums donated by businessmen and party donors for these purposes. As Stephen Collins puts it, "from the very beginning official Government action mingled with private Party action and official funds with private funds."[16]

The Special Detective Unit began to become aware not only of Captain Kelly's efforts to import arms but also of contacts he was forming with members of the Citizens' Defence Committees in the North who were also leading figures in the IRA. This intelligence was communicated in various degrees of detail and to various people, including Peter Berry at the Department of Justice. Berry says he communicated this intelligence to his minister, Mícheál Ó Móráin. The situation was complicated, however, by the fact that throughout this period Ó Móráin was physically and emotionally unwell, a condition either caused or exacerbated by his heavy drinking. In the view of almost all historians, this made him largely ineffective as Minister for Justice during this crucial period.

Garda intelligence officers were also getting some disturbing reports about the activities of Pádraig (Jock) Haughey, a brother of Charles Haughey. Charles Haughey later claimed that he had appointed Jock to go to Britain as part of an official team to liaise with "those disposed to be friendly" to the efforts to help relieve distress in Northern Ireland. Garda intelligence, however, believed that while in London Jock Haughey engaged in negotiations for the purchase of arms.[17]

Berry later said he was uncertain whether his minister was communicating the intelligence information to the rest of the Government, and to the Taoiseach in particular. As a result, when he received intelligence in mid-October 1969 that a meeting between Captain Kelly and prominent IRA leaders was to be held in Ballieborough, Co. Cavan, he decided to talk to the Taoiseach directly.

On 17 October 1969 Berry was an in-patient in Mount Carmel Hospital, Dublin, about to undergo a surgical procedure, but he asked Jack Lynch to come and see him. Berry maintained that at this meeting in his hospital room he told Lynch about the intelligence relating to Captain Kelly's activities. In particular, he said he told Lynch that Kelly had met the chief of staff of the IRA, Cathal Goulding, and that he had set up a meeting for that weekend in Ballieborough with persons from both sides of the border with a known history in the IRA.

What Lynch was in fact told by Berry at this meeting has been one of the most contentious questions in recent Irish history. In a diary that Berry later claimed had been written almost contemporaneously he wrote:

> No person with a scrap of intelligence could doubt that the Taoiseach was made aware by me on the 17th October, the date of my medical test is verifiable in the hospital records, of information of a most serious kind in relation to a plot to import arms and yet he avoided making any more than a cursory inquiry. Indeed I formed the impression from time to time that he was consulting me to find out how much I did not know and that he was not thankful to me for bringing awkward facts to his notice.[18]

After Berry's death this diary and other items were published by the news magazine *Magill* over four months during the summer of 1980. In the light of the quotation above, and other contents and commentary that suggested that he had been informed of this detail in October 1969, Lynch was provoked into breaking the silence he had maintained since his retirement. Speaking in the Dáil as a back-bencher in November 1980, he said firstly that the conversation between himself and Berry on the date in question was chaotic, because members of the medical staff kept coming in to attend to Berry, and secondly that the message conveyed by Berry was not in the order and of the detail that Berry later suggested in his diary. Lynch also emphasised that "at no stage during the interview on this date, 17th October 1969, did Mr Berry mention the name of any member of the Government nor that he tried to implicate them in any way. I may add that there was no suggestion in *Magill* or otherwise that he did."[19]

Lynch's denial that the significance of the intelligence about Captain Kelly was reported to him is disputable, not least because Jim Gibbons later gave evidence that in late October 1969 Lynch had raised Kelly's name and the suggestion of meetings with the IRA and asked him to look into it. However, it is now accepted by almost all historians that, irrespective of what he was told in October 1969, Lynch did not know that his Minister for Finance and Minister for Justice were involved in a conspiracy to import arms until Berry told him so at a meeting in Government Buildings in late April 1970.

It later emerged that, on Haughey's instructions, the Department of Finance had provided £500 to meet Captain Kelly's expenses for the Ballieborough meeting.

On 17 April 1970 Berry learnt of a plan to bring 6.8 tonnes of arms and ammunition into Dublin Airport four days later. In consultation with senior gardaí, he took action to ensure that detectives would be present in the airport, with instructions to seize the cargo. He told Ó Móráin what was happening.

The following day at 6:30 p.m. Berry received a telephone call at home from Haughey. Berry's account of their phone conversation is as follows:

"You know about the cargo that is coming in to Dublin Airport on Sunday," asked Haughey.

"Yes, minister," replied Berry.

"Can it not be let through under a guarantee that it would go direct to the North?"

"No."

"I think that is a bad decision," said Haughey. "Does the man from Mayo [Ó Móráin] know?"

Berry told Haughey that his minister did know.

"What will happen to it when it arrives?" Haughey then asked.

"It will be grabbed," Berry told him.

"I'd better have it called off," said Haughey, and the conversation ended.

In his diaries, Berry says that the telephone conversation with Haughey clarified an important issue for him. "I had a lingering doubt that all this could not have gone on for several months without the knowledge of the Taoiseach unless he was wilfully turning a blind eye, but it now seemed evident that at most a caucus was involved and the Government was not behind the conspiracy."

Berry then took the strange step of consulting President de Valera by telephone to get his advice on what he should do. Many have interpreted this peculiar move as Berry, apparently not confident that Lynch would act, making use of de Valera's status to put pressure on the Taoiseach. Berry did not share the specifics with de Valera but asked him what he should do if he had significant security information that he feared was not being communicated by his minister to the Taoiseach. The President told him he had a duty to tell the Taoiseach.

Berry saw Lynch on 20 April and briefed him fully on what Garda intelligence knew and on what had happened regarding the consignment of arms over the previous days. Lynch, according to Berry, was visibly shocked.

During this meeting he reacted angrily to a comment from Berry that suggested that the latter had believed that the whole Government might be secretly involved in the conspiracy to import arms.

At a later meeting Lynch told Berry about his reaction to his comment. "I saw red: I was not able to speak to you I was so furious."[20] When the two met again the next day Lynch told Berry that he had decided he would have to confront Haughey and Blaney about the plot.

Lynch now hesitated, however, and delayed raising the issue with the two men. There is no doubt that what he was about to do, given its legal and political consequences, would have to be reflected on carefully. He would have to be sure of his information and careful how he brought matters to a head. Lynch's position in the party was difficult. Haughey and Blaney were two of the most senior, most able and most popular of the Fianna Fáil ministers. Sacking them was likely to cause open warfare at all levels of the party. His position as Taoiseach was also difficult. He had a relatively slim majority, and he would have realised that a split in Fianna Fáil would bring about the collapse of his Government and throw Fianna Fáil into an election in what could only be nightmare circumstances.

In trying to decide what to do, Lynch consulted some of the party's leading figures, including his predecessor, Seán Lemass, and Frank Aiken. Lemass told him: "You're the Taoiseach: do what you have to do."[21] Aiken was still a back-bencher. When Lynch outlined the situation in confidence to him Aiken was equally unequivocal. "You are the leader of the Irish people—not just the Fianna Fáil party. The Irish people come first, the party second and the individual third. If you are asking me what I would do, the whip would be off these men from now."[22] Notwithstanding this advice, Lynch still delayed.

Dermot Keogh argues that those who judge Lynch for this initial vacillation should remember that "the dismissal of Neil Blaney and Charles Haughey from the cabinet entailed the most dramatic and difficult decision ever faced by a Taoiseach." He also makes the point that the quality of the information available to Lynch, even at this stage, was sketchy and that much of it had come from "a source known for its exaggeration," by which he obviously means Berry.

There was another complicating factor. On 22 April, Haughey had been badly injured in what was said at the time to have been a horse-riding accident but was later rumoured to have been as a result of an assault. He was due to make his budget speech that day, and Lynch had to deliver it in his stead. Haughey was now an in-patient in the Mater Hospital, and Lynch did not get to see him for several days.

Finally, a week later Lynch called Blaney to his office and told him what he knew of the plot to import arms and asked for his resignation. Blaney denied some of the detail, and refused to resign. Lynch then went to the Mater Hospital, confronted Haughey with the facts, and asked him to resign. Haughey also denied involvement but asked for time to consider the matter. Having been met with these denials and refusals to resign, Lynch did nothing.

Although he felt unable to take action about Haughey or Blaney at this point, Lynch did resolve to address the problem of ministerial ineffectiveness in the Department of Justice. Ó Móráin was in a nursing home after a very public alcohol-induced collapse at a budget night dinner. On 30 April, Lynch asked Berry to accompany him to the nursing home, where he asked the clearly ill Ó Móráin to resign. Ó Móráin agreed.

Blaney attended the next Government meeting, on 1 May. Haughey was still in hospital. At this meeting Lynch told stunned colleagues about the plot to import arms and about how allegations had been made that two ministers were involved. He told them that Blaney and Haughey had denied their involvement and that the matter was closed for the present. Then the Government simply continued dealing with its routine agenda. Pádraig Faulkner recalls:

> Nobody made any comment and we then turned to an item on Agriculture. I can still clearly recall Neil Blaney, Minister for Agriculture vigorously arguing the point on the subject. It was as if the Taoiseach had said nothing of significance.[23]

None of these matters had yet become public, but at this point Liam Cosgrave, leader of Fine Gael and of the opposition, had received information about the plot to import arms and about the suggested involvement of Government ministers. This had come from retired Detective-Superintendent Philip McMahon, who was still heavily involved with Garda intelligence and whose activities in recent months had included monitoring developments concerning the attempts to import arms. Shortly afterwards Cosgrave received separately an anonymous note written on Garda stationery outlining most of the same details. Cosgrave, who was obviously stunned by the information, made efforts to have it published by the *Sunday Independent* or *Irish Independent*, but editors there decided against publication, because the information was unconfirmed and the story was potentially so damaging to national security.

When the Dáil next met, on Tuesday 5 May, Lynch announced that Ó Móráin had resigned. Cosgrave asked Lynch, "Can the Taoiseach say if this is the only ministerial resignation we can expect?" Lynch, apparently not realising what Cosgrave knew, replied: "I do not know what the deputy is referring to." Cosgrave responded: "It's only the tip of the iceberg."

With no other ministerial resignations forthcoming, and having consulted senior party members, Cosgrave went to Lynch at eight o'clock that evening and told him what he knew. Lynch confirmed that the story of a plot to import arms was essentially true, as was the suggestion of the involvement of Blaney and Haughey.

He was now forced to act decisively. He again summoned Blaney and this time demanded his resignation. He then telephoned Haughey with the same request, and when they each refused, he sacked them. Shortly thereafter Kevin

Boland and his parliamentary secretary, Paudge Brennan, resigned their positions in sympathy with Blaney and Haughey. Lynch then went home to consult his wife and other close advisers. At about 2 a.m. he phoned the head of the Government Information Bureau, Eoin Neeson, to issue a statement in the following terms:

> I have requested the resignation of Mr Neil T. Blaney the Minister for Agriculture and Mr C. J. Haughey Minister for Finance because I am satisfied they do not subscribe fully to government policy in relation to the present situation in the Six Counties as stated by me at the Fianna Fáil Ard Fheis in January last.

On the morning of 6 May 1970 the country woke to hear and read the dramatic news that three ministers had been sacked or had resigned from the Government, with no real explanation of the reasons. The Dáil met at 11:30 that morning, by which time deputies on all sides had barely had time to grasp what had occurred. With the need for an immediate meeting of the Government to discuss the situation, and a Fianna Fáil parliamentary party scheduled for the early evening, Lynch proposed that the Dáil be adjourned until 10 p.m. Cosgrave agreed, with some reluctance.

It was to be Lynch's most impressive day as leader of Fianna Fáil. He gathered his remaining ministers for a Government meeting and told them he proposed to fill immediately the four vacancies left by the departure of Ó Móráin, Blaney, Haughey and Boland. Faulkner had a vivid recollection of seeing four vacant chairs, like black holes around the Government table.

> As I looked at the four empty chairs my mind was in turmoil. I was filled with a mixture of incredulity at the alleged activities of colleagues, surprise at Kevin Boland's resignation, regret at the resignation of [Ó Móráin] and sadness at the break-up of a united party. I also felt an element of fear for the future of the country and the party.[24]

Faulkner says that the unease at the parliamentary party meeting at 6 p.m. that evening was also palpable. Lynch managed the meeting with skill, however, confining the motion before it to one about the Taoiseach's constitutional right to appoint and dismiss ministers. He got unanimous support. Appreciating the scale of the crisis for the party, and the disastrous prospects if the Government was to collapse, even those deputies opposed to the sackings, including Blaney, backed the motion. Haughey sent in a statement of loyalty from the hospital.

As Dick Walsh has noted, it was "probably the most remarkable example of an Irish Party's instinct for self preservation overcoming its internal divisions, an example of pragmatism without parallel in the history of constitutional nationalism in Ireland."[25]

Lynch's parliamentary strategy that evening was equally impressive. When the Dáil met at 10 p.m. he confined the debate to one on a motion approving the appointment of Des O'Malley to replace Mícheál Ó Móráin as Minister for Justice. O'Malley was then thirty-one and so became the youngest person ever appointed to ministerial office, beating Seán Lemass's record by a matter of weeks.

Lynch himself spoke for only five minutes, telling the Dáil that he had been made aware of "an alleged attempt to import arms from the Continent," and that these reports involved two members of the Government. He then quickly went through the sequence of events that had led to his asking Haughey and Blaney to resign a week earlier and to sack them the previous night. He had done so because "I was convinced that not even the slightest suspicion should attach to any member of the Government in a matter of this nature."[26] He also told the Dáil that Liam Cosgrave had brought certain information about the plot to him the previous evening.

The debate that night was at times stormy and emotional. It was not over until 3 a.m., with all Fianna Fáil deputies present voting for the motion, giving the Government a comfortable majority.

By the time the Dáil met again, at 10:30 a.m. on Friday 8 May, Lynch was clearly in command of the chamber and of his party. He now moved to ensure the absolute loyalty of his Government, proposing the appointment of three new ministers to fill the three remaining vacancies, namely Gerry Collins, Bobby Molloy and Jerry Cronin. Collins, who was thirty-two, had been in the Dáil only since 1967. His father, Jimmy Collins, had been a deputy from 1948. Gerry Collins had worked for two years as assistant general secretary in Fianna Fáil's head office before contesting the by-election occasioned by his father's death. As well as being a minister in all subsequent Lynch Governments, Collins was from this point a central figure in exerting Lynch's control over the party organisation. Notwithstanding this, he would also go on to be a senior minister in all Haughey's Governments.

Bobby Molloy, at thirty-four, was also a relatively young appointment. He had nominated George Colley against Lynch in the leadership election but, like many Colley loyalists, had become a Lynch loyalist against the Haughey and Blaney factions.

Jerry Cronin was a forty-year-old TD for East Cork who had first been elected to the Dáil in 1967 and had served as parliamentary secretary to Blaney.

Lynch promised an open-ended debate on this motion, and it lasted for 36½ hours, until 11 p.m. on Saturday. When the vote was finally called, Lynch's new ministers were approved by 73 votes to 68. Haughey, Boland and Blaney were among those who voted for their successors.

The next twist came on 27 May 1970 when Captain Kelly, Albert Luykx and John Kelly, a Belfast republican, were arrested and charged with conspiracy to import arms. Blaney and Haughey were similarly arrested and charged the next day, Haughey suffering the ignominy of being arrested in his house while he had guests to dinner, including the Supreme Court judge Brian Walsh, and of being transported by Garda car to the Bridewell.

Infuriated by the arrests, Boland publicly lashed Lynch, accusing him of "felon-setting" and "unparalleled treachery," and demanded a special ard-fheis to remove him as leader. In response Lynch sought a special meeting of the parliamentary party to expel Boland. On 4 June the party whip was removed from Boland in a secret ballot, by 60 votes to 11. Among those supporting Boland were Flor Crowley from West Cork, Lorcan Allen from Wexford, Des Foley, and Seán Sherwin.[27] In June, Boland resigned as honorary secretary. Patrick Hillery replaced him in this post until the ard-fheis. Kevin Boland's father, Gerry Boland, resigned his positions as vice-president of the party and trustee.

In July the charges against Blaney were dismissed in the District Court, on the court's determination that he had no case to answer. Haughey and the others were sent forward to the Central Criminal Court, where their trial began on 22 September. The charge was one of conspiracy to import 500 guns and 180 rounds of ammunition the previous April. The first trial collapsed after six days of prosecution evidence when the judge, Aindrias Ó Caoimh, took exception to being accused of bias by counsel for Luykx. He discharged the jury and ordered a new trial.

The second trial was presided over by Mr Justice Séamus Henchy and opened on 6 October. It continued for fourteen days. The main thrust of the evidence was damaging to the prosecution and to Jim Gibbons. The case turned on the question whether the attempted importing of arms was legal. It would have been legal if Gibbons, as Minister for Defence, had approved it, either formally or by implication. Captain Kelly gave evidence in his own defence, saying that his superiors, including the Minister for Defence, were fully aware of what he was doing. Colonel Hefferon, who was called as a prosecution witness in the first trial but whom the court itself had to call at the second trial, supported Captain Kelly's version of events.

Haughey distanced himself from the other defendants and denied all knowledge of any involvement in the attempt to import arms. There was a particularly significant conflict of evidence between him and Gibbons, relating to a conversation between them on either 17 or 20 April 1969. Gibbons had said that he made it clear in that conversation that the Departments of Defence, Justice and Transport and Power were aware of the plan to import arms through Dublin Airport, and that Haughey's answer suggested that he knew about it. Gibbons said that, in reply to his raising it with him, Haughey had promised to stop the process "for a month". Gibbons said that he then replied, "For God's sake, stop it altogether." Haughey, in evidence, acknowledged that the meeting had taken place but denied that he had said these things to Gibbons or Gibbons to him. In his summation to the jury Mr Justice Henchy said that the only conclusion about this fundamental conflict of evidence was that either Gibbons or Haughey was guilty of perjury.

That was not the central question for the jury, however. If the jury accepted that Captain Kelly was acting under orders, or even within Gibbons's knowledge without restraint, there was no illegal importing of arms and there could be no conspiracy, so all four would be acquitted. The onus was on the prosecution to prove the contrary, that is, that Kelly was a rogue operator and that the Minister for Defence had not even implicitly approved what he was doing, and to prove this beyond reasonable doubt.

After deliberating for an hour, the jury found all four defendants not guilty.

When the verdicts were announced there were dramatic scenes inside and outside the Four Courts. Like the other three defendants, Haughey was carried shoulder-high, surrounded by supporters shouting, "We want Charlie!" and "Lynch must go!" At a press conference in the nearby Four Courts Hotel shortly afterwards Haughey, who had been quiet since the night of his sacking, attacked Lynch, though at first he avoided mentioning him by name. "I was never in any doubt that it was a political trial," he said. "I think those who were responsible for this debacle have no alternative but to take the honourable course that is open to them." "What is that?" a journalist asked. "I think it is pretty evident," Haughey replied. He went on to say: "There is some dissatisfaction with the Taoiseach at the moment. The Taoiseach's position is something that will be decided by the parliamentary party." In the highly charged atmosphere in the wake of the verdict, Haughey had now thrown down a very public gauntlet to the Taoiseach.

Lynch was out of the country at the time to address the United Nations General Assembly in New York. He held a press conference there the next day and issued statements to the Sunday newspapers saying he would strongly resist any challenge to his leadership and was confident that he would see it off. His return to Dublin was delayed until Monday evening. Over the weekend Lynch's allies, including a prominent party activist, Dan Mullane, as well as Colley, Faulkner and Lalor, had been busy ringing around supporters, encouraging them to travel to the airport on Monday evening to welcome the Taoiseach home. When Lynch disembarked he was met by all his ministers, apart from the two who were out of the country, fifty Fianna Fáil TDs, including Frank Aiken, and twenty-seven Fianna Fáil senators. A large crowd of well-wishers, who included party dignitaries such as Seán MacEntee and Paddy Smith, joined them. Also present was the secretary to the Office of the President, which was taken as indicating de Valera's support. The welcoming party was a dramatic expression of the support Lynch enjoyed and a blunt rejection of Haughey's challenge. By the time the Dáil reconvened, the threat to Lynch had again dissipated.

Seeking to capitalise on the conflict of evidence between Haughey and Gibbons at the trial, in November the opposition put down a motion of no confidence in Gibbons as Minister for Defence. Fianna Fáil responded by tabling an amendment that effectually turned the motion into a vote of confidence. On the night of the vote all the attention inevitably focused on what Haughey would do. In the event he "swallowed his pride and marched through the lobby to vote confidence in a Taoiseach he despised and a Minister whose evidence under oath had run directly contrary to his."[28] By comparison, Kevin Boland took the extraordinary step of resigning his Dáil seat on principle rather than vote for Gibbons. He unsuccessfully contested the seat in the 1973 general election.

All these events generated intense turmoil in Fianna Fáil throughout the country. There was a widespread emotional attachment in the party ranks to the traditional anti-partition policy. There were also many with a simplistic view of what the Fianna Fáil Government's response to the outbreak of the conflict in the North should be. Pádraig Faulkner captures the mood at the time among some elements of his local organisation.

All through these momentous events the Fianna Fáil organisation was in ferment in my Louth constituency as elsewhere. Strangely enough however while the Taoiseach was still attacked for inaction there was little or no support for the dismissed Ministers. The more extreme elements focused on the end of partition, which they believed was right. Among such elements the affectionate names for the Old IRA— "the Boys"—were used to describe the new IRA and their exploits were greeted with a certain pleasure. When asked if they agreed with violence these individuals replied that they didn't but . . . the but meaning that in these circumstances they might do so. As the death toll in the North mounted, however, there was a bit of backtracking but at Cumann and Comhairle Ceantair level whenever calls for practical armed support were made, some acclamation still invariably followed. To these people Jack Lynch would never be aggressive enough.[29]

While the immediate political crisis within Fianna Fáil had settled, the long-term struggle for dominance in the party was far from over. In the following months Lynch, with a tight cohort of Government colleagues and advisers, began to do what he should have done in 1967, namely take command of the party organisation. This effort concentrated initially on preparations for the ard-fheis, which was scheduled for the weekend of 20 February 1971.

Lynch's team used and manipulated the accreditation rules to maximise the attendance of his personal supporters. They campaigned within the party to ensure that Lynch supporters would hold as many of the leading Ard-Chomhairle positions as possible, and they managed the agenda to contain the possibilities for mischief-making. While they succeeded in ensuring a pro-Lynch majority for the event, they could not avoid the knowledge that a substantial majority in the party favoured a tougher Northern Ireland policy and near-idolised Boland and Blaney in particular.

More than five thousand delegates attended in the RDS Main Hall in Ballsbridge, Dublin, where the competing factions were gathered in large numbers in one room for the first time. The ard-fheis was to be an acrimonious affair, characterised by bitter verbal exchanges and physical clashes on the floor. Boland, though out of the parliamentary party, was still a member of Fianna Fáil and therefore entitled to be present. Blaney was still a Fianna Fáil TD. Both were determined to maintain the agitation against Lynch and his policy and had been as busy as Lynch's supporters in mobilising the well-established personal machines they had previously used for elections to shore up their position.

Jim Gibbons was shouted down when it was his turn to speak as Minister for Agriculture. Some delegates called him a "Judas", "perjurer" and "traitor". The tensions reached their peak, however, when Patrick Hillery was called to the platform. At the same time Kevin Boland appeared at the podium to the side of the platform, as if to speak. When Hillery began his speech there was uproar. There were shouts of "Free speech!" and competing shouts of "We want Jack!" and "We want Boland!" Tussles and fist-fights broke out as stewards sought to remove Boland from the podium area. Lynch appealed for calm. Shouting to be heard over the noise, Hillery said that the Lynch policy was that of de Valera and Lemass. He told the hall that those shouting him down were not going to prevent the ard-fheis from deciding policy, and the Government would continue the party policy despite "the bullyboys in the organisation."

Then, in a passionate outburst that became a defining television moment and in more recent years a Youtube hit, Hillery, flanked by Lynch on one side and Gerry Collins on the other, faced down the agitation for Boland.

> We can no longer stay silent. We have been silent since last May for the sake of this organisation. We've been silent for the sake of our country. But now if they want a fight they can have it. And I tell ye something: if ye ever succeeded in getting rid of one of us there'll be more of us, and we'll keep comin', we'll keep comin' as long as ye're there. And Fianna Fáil will survive, as it did before.

As elements of the crowd continued shouting "We want Boland!" Hillery screamed back: "Ye can have Boland, but ye can't have Fianna Fáil!"[30]

Boland curled his index finger at Hillery, baiting him to come on. The podium was toppled over as Boland was led down to the floor of the hall amid further exchanges of punches between rival delegates.

Later that evening, when Lynch went to the podium to give his address, Kevin Boland was carried shoulder-high around part of the hall. He was then carried to the back and outside.

There were many bursts of applause for Lynch's speech, but there were also occasional slow handclaps and shouts of "Union Jack!" When he was about half way through his speech Boland returned and took up a seat at the back of the hall, which gave rise to more scuffles and fist-fights. Throughout it all, Lynch stayed focused on his address. Among the points he made was that each member of Fianna Fáil was entitled to express their own views but "then must accept as party policy whatever the party decides."[31]

The 1971 ard-fheis was to be the last stand for the Boland and Blaney faction. In the elections Joseph Groome, who had supported Lynch during the crisis, was comfortably re-elected as one of the joint honorary secretaries, while Patrick Hillery was confirmed by a similar margin in the other post, which had been vacated by Boland the previous June. George Colley was very comfortably elected to the post of joint treasurer, and Anthony Hederman, another supporter of the leadership, retained the other position, just ahead of Blaney.

Some weeks later all sides in the party, and politicians from across the spectrum, came together to pay tribute to Seán Lemass, who died on 11 May 1971. He was given a state funeral on 13 May. Lynch gave the graveside oration before a large attendance, which included President de Valera.

In his tribute to Lemass in the Dáil, Lynch said that "even in his retirement from active public life, Mr Lemass continued to give unstintingly of his counsel."[32] Both de Valera and Lemass, in their own distinct ways, had quietly offered Jack Lynch support and advice during the events of the Arms Trial; but at the end of the day Lynch was on his own. De Valera and Lemass had led united, disciplined and cohesive parliamentary parties; they had never experienced the division and mistrust that characterised Lynch's time. Fianna Fáil was now a political hot-house.

In late 1969 Patrick Hillery had been for one of his regular private visits to his former constituency colleague President de Valera at Áras an Uachtaráin. He asked the President to compare the politics of the day with what it had been like when he was Taoiseach. De Valera replied: "The difference between then and now was that there was no intrigue in the party in my day."[33] De Valera's remarks predated the Arms Crisis; and the intrigue in the party was to deepen further in the wake of these dramatic events.

Chapter 11

BACKING JACK, 1970–77

fter the Arms Crisis, Jack Lynch had wisely rejected demands by the opposition for a general election to clear the air and had concentrated instead on governing the country for another two-and-a-half years. Among Fianna Fáil's achievements during this time was the successful negotiation of Ireland's membership of the European Economic Community. Patrick Hillery played the leading role in this, with Lynch chairing the relevant Government sub-committee. The fact that this Government managed to complete the negotiations for membership on what were generally viewed as favourable terms, except for the fishing rights conceded, and that it did so against the background of such domestic political turmoil, was no mean achievement.

In January 1972 Lynch and Hillery went to Brussels to sign the treaty of accession. In May that year a referendum was held to effect the constitutional changes necessary for membership. Fianna Fáil and Fine Gael both campaigned for a Yes vote. While the active campaigning did not come close to that for an election, it was relatively vigorous for a referendum, with Patrick Hillery and Garret FitzGerald being the most active and prominent for their respective parties. The Labour Party campaigned against membership, although some prominent Labour Party politicians, including Barry Desmond, were in favour. Most commentators expected the proposal to pass comfortably, but in the event the Yes vote was beyond even the Government's most optimistic expectations, at 83 per cent.

In relation to the economy generally, the years 1970–73 were mixed. George Colley took over from Charles Haughey as Minister for Finance, and although he lacked Haughey's flair he was a safe pair of hands in the post. Unemployment was on the rise, however, as was inflation. In 1972 Colley presided over the country's first budget deficit, though it was only 0.2 per cent; nonetheless this was a milestone that, in Joseph Lee's opinion, made that budget "stand as a symbol of breakdown in national discipline."[1]

Over these two-and-a-half years Lynch also worked to further consolidate his position in the Fianna Fáil organisation, mainly through proxies such as Gerry Collins and Eoin Ryan. While he was strengthening his grip his enemies were leaving the party, being thrown out, or keeping their heads down. Kevin

Boland left the party in June 1971. Three months later he founded a new party, Aontacht Éireann ("Irish unity"), of which he was president and Captain James Kelly vice-president. The new party was launched at a rally in Dublin on 19 September 1971 attended by 1,100 people. The young Ballyfermot deputy Seán Sherwin was the only Fianna Fáil Oireachtas member to join the new party. It ran thirteen candidates in the 1973 election, including Sherwin, who lost his seat; the other twelve were also unsuccessful. In total, Aontacht Éireann obtained 0.9 per cent of the national first-preference vote.[2] Boland himself polled only 2,142 votes in Dublin South County, less than half what he had secured when he ran there as a Fianna Fáil minister in 1969.

For a while Neil Blaney continued to snipe at Lynch and his Northern policy from within Fianna Fáil. He was eventually expelled from the parliamentary party in November 1971 and from Fianna Fáil entirely on 26 June 1972, after the Ard-Chomhairle, where he had once been a linchpin, found him guilty of "conduct unbecoming a member of the organisation." Blaney also went on to set up his own party, Independent Fianna Fáil, which was almost exclusively organised in Co. Donegal. This organisation was strong enough to ensure that Blaney himself was always comfortably re-elected to Dáil Éireann and later to the European Parliament, but he never again posed a threat of any substance to Lynch's position.

Haughey's approach differed from the honourable if truculent one adopted by Boland and the confrontational one adopted by Blaney. He stayed silent and avoided provoking the leadership. Any support within the party that he had lost because of his challenges to Lynch were more than compensated for by the new followers he acquired from those who admired his newly revealed republican credentials.

At the ard-fheis of 1972 Haughey was re-elected as one of the five honorary vice-presidents of Fianna Fáil. When his victory in that contest was announced he was, in accordance with tradition, invited to take an appropriate place on the ard-fheis platform. As he made his way along the platform party he received perfunctory congratulations and handshakes from the front-bench members present, with one exception: Erskine Childers deliberately continued reading his newspaper and refused to acknowledge Haughey's arrival on the stage.

In both party and governmental matters Lynch, whose trust in his colleagues had been badly damaged by the Arms Crisis, came to rely on a small core group of ministers and advisers. This group included George Colley, Des O'Malley, Eoin Ryan and Gerry Collins. He also increasingly looked to Martin O'Donoghue for advice. O'Donoghue was a professor of economics in Trinity College when, in April 1970, he received a handwritten note from the Taoiseach asking him to phone his office. Fearing that the letter was a joke, O'Donoghue dialled the number nervously, but when the Taoiseach's private secretary answered he was asked to come over to meet him that afternoon. Having realised that he was going to be swamped by the fall-out from the arms conspiracy, about which he had just learnt, Lynch had decided, on T. K. Whitaker's recommendation, to ask O'Donoghue to become an adviser. In particular he wanted him to oversee the handling by the Department of Finance of Ireland's application for membership of the EEC and other economic matters. O'Donoghue agreed.

O'Donoghue recalls the moment when he crossed over from being strictly an economics adviser to becoming a political speech-writer and strategist for Lynch. On the night before the debate on the motion of censure against Gibbons he realised that Lynch was himself writing the speech he was due to deliver during the Dáil debate the next day. O'Donoghue offered to assist, Lynch gladly accepted, and thus began an increasingly intensive involvement in the political affairs of Fianna Fáil. O'Donoghue became one of Lynch's closest political confidants. He continued to be an adviser when Fianna Fáil went into opposition, was himself a Dáil candidate in 1977 and then an important, perhaps even the most important, minister in Lynch's last Government.

The Northern Ireland issue was to remain a constant concern for Lynch's Government. On Sunday 30 January 1972 British soldiers shot twenty-six unarmed demonstrators and bystanders in Derry. Fourteen of them, including seven teenagers, were killed. Almost immediately the day became known as Bloody Sunday, and passions again ran high throughout the Republic. Faced with blanket denials by the British Government that its forces had done anything wrong, the Government strove to show restraint. Lynch denounced the shootings as "unbelievably savage and inhumane," and the Government recalled the Irish ambassador from London in protest.

The following Wednesday was declared a national day of mourning. On that day more than sixty thousand people gathered in protest outside the British embassy in Merrion Square, Dublin. The building came under attack and was eventually burnt to the ground.

Over the course of 1972 Des O'Malley, as Minister for Justice, set about strengthening the state's security framework and its criminal legislation in response to the new threat presented by the Provisional IRA. In May 1972 he established the Special Criminal Court. In the autumn the Government proposed a new Offences Against the State (Amendment) Bill, which provided, among other things, for a person to be convicted of membership of the IRA on the uncorroborated word of a Garda chief superintendent. The Labour Party opposed the bill on civil liberties grounds. A number of Fianna Fáil deputies and former deputies antagonistic to Lynch's Northern policy, were also expected to vote against it. If Fine Gael opposed it there was every possibility that the bill would be defeated. Appreciating this, Lynch felt that it would be an opportune issue on which to go to the country.

What he had not expected was that the legislation would give rise to convulsions within Fine Gael, where, although the majority wanted to join the Labour Party in opposing the bill, seven deputies, including the party leader, Liam Cosgrave, wanted to vote for it. Fine Gael's spokesperson, T. F. O'Higgins, spoke for the party in the Dáil during the crucial stages of the debate, while his party colleagues gathered upstairs in emergency session to decide what stance to take on the bill when the vote came. Pádraig Faulkner describes what happened next.

> I remember standing in the corridor in Leinster House, looking out over Dublin City and wondering if the Bill would plunge us into an election so shortly after we had weathered the storm and controversy of the Arms Crisis. It was December 1, 1972. As I stood there I heard a muffled explosion across the city. For the first time bombs had gone off in Dublin . . . Fine Gael changed its position and decided to abstain from voting on the Offences Against the State (Amendment) Bill and the immediate threat of a general election had been averted.[3]

The Fine Gael parliamentary party had actually voted to oppose the bill when the bombs went off, which would have made Cosgrave's position untenable, but the explosions in Dublin transformed the political climate.

On 1 January 1973, when Ireland formally joined the European Economic Community, Patrick Hillery resigned from the Government and the Dáil to become Ireland's first member of the European Commission, where he took up the Social Affairs portfolio.

At this point the Lynch Government had a year of its term to run, but its majority had shrunk. The Arms Crisis and its aftermath meant there were four votes on which it could no longer rely. Hillery's departure meant that Lynch was now leading what was technically a minority Government. Conscious of his vulnerability, anxious to exploit the difficulties in Fine Gael and confident that Fine Gael and the Labour Party would again be unable to put an agreed alternative before the electorate, Lynch decided that this was a good time to go to the country. On the last day of the Dáil's extended Christmas and New Year recess, 5 February 1973, he asked President de Valera to dissolve the Dáil and named 28 February as the election date.

To Lynch's surprise, and that of most commentators, Fine Gael and the Labour Party managed, within thirty-six hours of the election being called, to put together a joint programme. It was a short document, which they named "A Statement of Intent"[4] but which came to be known as the "fourteen-point plan". If truth be told, Cosgrave and Corish were able to agree a platform so rapidly because they had each decided at the time of the Arms Crisis that there must be a real alternative to Fianna Fáil whenever the next election came. The pact instantly made the campaign very different from that of 1969, when the Labour Party had run an independent strategy. More importantly, it also significantly strengthened the pattern of transfers between the two opposition parties.

If Lynch was surprised by the outcome of the Cosgrave-Corish deliberations he was to get an even greater shock when he was made aware of developments concerning his party's own selections for the Louth constituency. The day after the election was called, a dinner was held in

Leinster House to commemorate Lynch's twenty-five years in the Dáil. Sitting next to him at the event was the veteran Louth deputy Frank Aiken, who, although he was seventy-five, had already been selected to contest the election again. Aiken told Lynch at the dinner that he would not contest the election if the Ard-Chomhairle ratified Charles Haughey's candidature in Dublin North-East. More worryingly for Lynch, Aiken had drafted a letter to the newspapers, setting out why he would not be standing. He proposed sending it should Haughey run.

In the days before the close of nominations there were frantic efforts behind the scenes to dissuade him from doing this. The notion of Aiken, a founding father of the party and former Tánaiste and Minister for External Affairs, announcing his retirement and citing Haughey as the reason three weeks before an election was a terrifying one for party strategists. It would not only have hobbled the party's campaign from the outset by reminding voters of the Arms Crisis divisions but threatened to split open all those old wounds.

Among those pressed into service in the effort to change Aiken's mind were his fellow-veteran Paddy Smith and even President de Valera. Smith was the more persuasive of the two. Stephen Collins tells how Aiken wrote to Smith to inform him of his intentions and to tell him that he proposed to approach John Hume to stand for the Dáil in his place as an independent with the promise of Fianna Fáil support. Smith replied:

> I understand now what is in your mind. It is at least two years too late in my view . . .[Haughey] has voted and worked with the party and is chairman of one of its committees. At the last Ard Fheis of the party while I was in the chair he was proposed as one of our vice-presidents and he was approved with acclaim by all the delegates. I did not arrange all this but neither of us tried to stop it. He has attended party meetings; he has attended the Dáil and voted with us on all issues . . . I have no brief for the man. I am not trying to be his case-maker but I know I have no course open to me but to do the only logical thing left to me and you are just as guilty as I am and every other member of the party is. The time to take action or propose the taking of such action was before this history I have so crudely outlined here. It is the truth, Frank, and it does not change the story to attempt to slip away from it. I think this is worth trying to read before taking such a foolish course. The proposal for a Hume walk-over I regard as far too childish.[5]

Faulkner, who had assumed that Aiken would again be on the ticket, was not impressed that he had left it until after the convention to step down. He was even less impressed with Aiken's notions about who should succeed him.

> We found out later that when Frank had decided not to stand, he had then involved himself in a strange venture. He had travelled to Dungannon with his daughter Emer to ask John Hume to stand for

election in Louth in his place. Apparently Frank intended to request the
Fianna Fáil convention in Louth to endorse Hume's candidature as an
independent.[6]

Ultimately it was Joe Farrell, the long-time Fianna Fáil director of elections
in Louth and all-round right-hand man to Aiken, who managed to persuade
him from going public. On 13 February, Lynch stopped off on his election tour
at an event in Dundalk to mark Aiken's seventy-fifth birthday, where he
announced that Aiken was retiring from Dáil Éireann "on doctors' orders." Joe
Farrell was then quickly selected to run alongside Faulkner.

While the Fianna Fáil campaign was deflected by these concerns, all the
momentum was with Fine Gael and the Labour Party. Their joint programme
"in effect became the basis of the campaign."[7] In the words of Joseph Lee, the
fourteen-point plan contained "promises for virtually everyone."[8] Among the
inducements offered were increases in welfare benefits, reductions in the
pension age, and the abolition of death duties. The two parties also promised
the "progressive abolition of domestic rates" (local authority property tax).[9]

Like most outgoing Governments, Fianna Fáil ran on its record. On the
economy it promised more of the same, with the added dimension of EEC
membership. It also argued that Fine Gael and Labour social policies were
unworkable and unaffordable and that the abolition of rates was simply
impossible. Fianna Fáil tried to switch some of the focus of the campaign to
Northern Ireland, arguing that only a Fianna Fáil Government led by Lynch
could give stability on policy in this area. Fine Gael and the Labour Party
countered that they did not suffer from internal divisions of the type that had
characterised Fianna Fáil during the term of the outgoing Government.

Fianna Fáil soon realised that its dull policy offering was not working: all
the attention and energy of the campaign had been generated by the
opposition parties. It decided to try to out-promise the coalition. George
Colley announced that Fianna Fáil would use the exchequer saving from EEC
membership to increase social welfare benefits and children's allowance. He
also promised a pound of butter a month for 8 pence for every family
receiving social welfare payments.[10] More controversially, on 21 February 1973
Lynch announced that domestic rates could and would be abolished after all.
The move was a step too far, and both opposition and media punished Fianna
Fáil mercilessly for it. Cornelius O'Leary tells of one dramatic example of how
the U-turn on rates damaged Fianna Fáil's credibility.

A few days later, in one of the regular television confrontations, Garret
FitzGerald was able to produce before an almost speechless George
Colley (Minister for Finance and Fianna Fáil Director of Elections) an
advertisement from the *Limerick Leader* on behalf of the local Fianna
Fáil candidates (including a Minister) which had appeared after Mr
Lynch's statement, attacking as nonsensical the Coalition pledge to
abolish rates! The volte-face dominated the last days of the campaign.[11]

In 1973 the central plank of Fianna Fáil's campaign was, as it had been in every election since 1932, that it alone could form a stable single-party Government, and that the hastily put together coalition alternative could not work.

Fianna Fáil won 69 seats, a loss of six, while Fine Gael and the Labour Party combined had 73. There were only two independents, Neil Blaney and Joe Sherwin. In all the circumstances Fianna Fáil's performance was impressive: it received a slightly higher proportion of the vote than in 1969, nudging it up from 45.7 to 46.2 per cent. Fine Gael improved from 34 to 35 per cent, while the Labour Party dropped from 17 to 14 per cent. Fianna Fáil obtained fewer seats despite its increased first-preference vote, because the pact between the two opposition parties helped Fine Gael. The latter even took seats from the Labour Party, but these were largely compensated for by Labour wins from Fianna Fáil, achieved with improved Fine Gael transfers.

Among the Fianna Fáil poll-toppers were Lynch himself in Cork, where he obtained 12,427 first preferences, and Haughey in Dublin North-East, with 12,900. Among the Fianna Fáil casualties were Mícheál Ó Móráin, Michael Hilliard and Brian Lenihan. Lenihan had been promoted to the position of Minister for Foreign Affairs after Hillery went to Brussels but had lost his seat in Roscommon to his running-mate. He would transfer his political base to Dublin West before the next election.

Six years later Lynch made the following reflections on the result of the 1973 election:

In the event, we lost by a mere handful of votes. Had about 2,000 votes spread throughout key constituencies swung to us, then we would have ended up with the two-seat majority, instead of a two-seat minority. In the event, I think that 1973 election result was probably Fianna Fáil's greatest electoral achievement with me as leader, although the party was the loser. We increased our total first votes by almost 24,000 and pushed up our percentage vote from 45.7 in 1969, to 46.2—never before had a political party, or combination of parties, won such a high vote and lost the election.

Remember what we had been through over the previous 4 years. There was a time during that period, when it was widely believed we would be decimated at the polls, whenever an election took place.[12]

Fianna Fáil's second sixteen-year stint in power had ended. On 14 March 1973 Liam Cosgrave was elected Taoiseach and with Brendan Corish put together a "national coalition" Government. A selection of new faces arrived at the Government table, the most prominent of whom were to be Garrett FitzGerald of Fine Gael and Conor Cruise O'Brien for the Labour Party.

Just as Fianna Fáil was beginning to realise that it was in opposition it faced another electoral contest. At the age of ninety President de Valera retired on 24 June 1973 at the end of his second term. On 6 April the Tánaiste,

Erskine Childers, was nominated as the Fianna Fáil party's candidate. He was the son of Robert Erskine Childers, who had been executed by the Free State during the Civil War. Despite this, he had always been a moderate on Northern policy and related issues. He was a member of the Church of Ireland, and Fianna Fáil presented a Childers presidency as one that could echo that of Douglas Hyde and send a significant signal to the majority in Northern Ireland.

Childers was not particularly popular among his fellow-deputies, many of whom regarded him as aloof. He had also never been a particularly strong vote-getter at constituency level. He was, however, liked and admired among the national electorate. He undertook an extensive tour of the country in a campaign bus that was dubbed the "Wanderly Wagon" by the Labour Party deputy Michael O'Leary, after a popular children's television programme. The Fine Gael candidate was again Tom O'Higgins, whose candidature was also endorsed by the Labour party.

O'Higgins had come within eleven thousand votes of beating de Valera seven years earlier. This time the Fianna Fáil candidate won more comfortably, with Childers obtaining 52 per cent of the vote, compared with O'Higgins's 48 per cent. Childers went on to be "an exceedingly energetic and popular but unhappy President"[13] until his untimely death on 17 November 1974.

The victory in the presidential election helped soften the blow of going into opposition; but Fianna Fáil remained disoriented. Pádraig Faulkner captures the sense of dislocation he and his colleague felt in opposition in 1973.

> For many years Fianna Fáil Ministers had been in the full glare of media attention and had become household names. Suddenly, with defeat at the polls, these well-known figures all but disappeared from public view and were replaced. The Fianna Fáil organisation found it almost impossible to cope with the new situation and party morale plummeted. Complaints flowed into headquarters about the alleged inactivity of our new front bench, of our failure to get publicity and of our propensity for letting the Government away with everything. It took quite some time to make our people accept the reality of political life.[14]

Even Jack Lynch suffered a loss of credibility in the late summer of 1973 because of the Littlejohn Affair. The Littlejohns were two English brothers who sought immunity from prosecution for a bank robbery by claiming to be British agents acting to provoke the Government into introducing internment. In July 1973 the issue of whether the previous Government had been aware of contacts between the British authorities and these two men became a matter of public controversy. Lynch claimed he had never seen any communication from the British Government acknowledging that there had been such contact. The then Attorney-General, Colm Condon, supported Lynch's account. However, the coalition subsequently published documents that proved that Lynch's recollection had been wrong, and he had to apologise publicly.

Lynch later told of how this, together with a boating injury shortly afterwards, prompted him to reflect on his position.

> When the Littlejohn affair arose in July '73, I felt that my position had been compromised to the extent that I should reconsider my position, as leader of Fianna Fáil. It had quite escaped my mind that I had been informed that a junior British minister had had some contact with the Littlejohn brothers before they came to Ireland—the information was passed to me almost as I was boarding a plane for America and I had simply directed that the papers be handed over to the relevant minister to let him deal with the matter. I had begun to give my position some thought when I had the boat accident, in which my right heel bone was broken. I was in too much pain for several weeks thereafter to give resignation or anything else much consideration and when I returned to a party meeting, there was such an obvious flow of sentiment emphatically in favour of my carrying on, that I committed myself to leading the party into the following general election.[15]

Friends and colleagues quickly persuaded Lynch to stay on, and the question mark over whether he might resign triggered a flow of reassuring support.

Ironically, at about the same time that Lynch was having these doubts he and a close group of advisers had begun, over the summer recess in 1973, to design a recovery strategy for the party. The group, or more correctly groups, were *ad hoc* and never became a formal part of the Fianna Fáil structure. Historians of the party in this period speak variously of the "reorganisation group", "advisory group" and "Saturday group". It seems, however, that these were three different groups, whose membership overlapped to a certain extent but each of which performed a distinct function.

The first meeting of the "reorganisation group" was held in July 1973 at Lynch's house in Garville Avenue, Rathgar, Dublin. *Magill* dates the meeting to 18 July 1973, which was a Saturday. It seems that the only other politician present was Senator Eoin Ryan, who was later to be director of elections for the 1977 campaign. Vincent Browne identifies some of those present as Martin O'Donoghue, Hugh O'Flaherty, then a prominent barrister, and Noel Mulcahy, then a lecturer at the Irish Management Institute. There were others present that day whose identities Brown says "are protected even now."[16]

At this first all-day meeting the reorganisation group identified and discussed the party's needs under three broad headings: people, policies and propaganda. In its final form, developed in the following weeks, the revitalisation plan involved the deliberate recruitment of young men (or, potentially, women) to three new positions that were needed for the reorganisation effort. These were a new general secretary, a press officer and a new head of research. In each case the group decided that the young man chosen should ideally have no connection to any of the existing factions within the party.

The party treasurer, Tony Hederman sc, later suggested a name for the research post, and within weeks Lynch announced to the shadow cabinet that he had appointed a young barrister, Esmond Smyth, "to co-ordinate the support service for the party and to set up a library at head office." This deliberate understating of the role was to be a feature of all three appointments. Lynch and his advisory group were conscious of the resentment that the appointment of a cadre of young full-time party officials might engender among the parliamentary party.

It took a little longer to appoint a press officer. The Fianna Fáil frontbench minutes show that on 30 October 1973 a sub-committee was established to recruit for this position. It is interesting to see who Lynch trusted to undertake this task. The interview panel was Brian Lenihan, Paddy Lalor, Hugh O'Flaherty and Ruairí Brugha. Brugha, a son of the War of Independence hero and Civil War martyr Cathal Brugha, had been elected to Dáil Éireann for Wicklow the previous July and was close to Lynch. In 1974 he was to be given the important post of spokesperson on Northern Ireland.

The outcome of the selection process was the appointment of Frank Dunlop, then a young journalist with RTE, who was to have a colourful career in the party and a controversial one afterwards. Dunlop gives an entertaining account of his first days in the job.

> Jack Lynch in his innocence . . . decided that if I was to work with his TDs and senators, I should meet them formally. When he introduced me at a parliamentary party meeting, there was total silence. Everyone stared at me as if I had just landed from an alien galaxy. Having thanked Jack for the welcome, I spoke briefly to what could only be described as a suspicious, even hostile audience. More silence. Then Jack asked if anybody had anything to say. The great vista of what was ahead of me opened up when Paddy Smith—a veteran of many governments under de Valera, Lemass and Lynch [sic]—asked, "What is it exactly you will be doing for us, young fella?"[17]

Dunlop's assessment of the condition of the party at the time accords with that of many members, although Dunlop puts it more bluntly.

> The truth is that the party was suffering from what would now be seen as post-traumatic stress and it was in a time warp. It had come through the arms crisis, the subsequent trial, the acquittals and the inevitable recriminations. Senior members had started laying the foundations on which they would construct their versions of what had happened. In doing so they were also creating the fissures that would eventually widen and split the party.[18]

Dunlop also provides a description of the frame of mind of members of the front bench at this time. It echoes the attitude that had been prevalent on previous occasions when the party was in opposition.

> From the moment of their defeat at the polls the majority of these men, and they were all men, believed that they were not required to do very much in opposition and that when the general election was called they would be returned to power automatically. Holding to the Fianna Fáil mantra that coalitions did not work, they were convinced that the new government would disintegrate or implode within less than two years.

Dunlop also bemoaned what he saw as a lack of commitment from those who held the senior front-bench positions.

> Fianna Fáil as a parliamentary party was totally lost. At sea. Rudderless. There was little, if any coordination in its stances to government policy or action. Everything was *ad hoc*. People who . . . had become accustomed to the trappings of office such as chauffeur driven cars, instant advice from civil servants, prepared scripts and the like found it difficult to operate politically on a TD's salary and therefore they had reverted to their previous professions. Politics—at constituency level and at national level, for those who were members of the front bench— took second place. George Colley and Des O'Malley resumed their solicitor's practices, Michael O'Kennedy and David Andrews returned to the Law Library, Jim Gibbons and Brian Lenihan were appointed to the European Parliament. And Charlie Haughey continued on in isolated splendour in his mansion in Kinsealy.

As Dermot Keogh points out, allowances must be made for Dunlop's "understandable desire to build up his own role in the turnaround of the party's fortunes."[19] Some allowance must also be made for a general tendency on Dunlop's part to dramatise every story, and his own part in it. However, there is no doubt that his assessment of the state of the party's parliamentary operation at the time was essentially accurate. Indeed this assessment was shared by Martin O'Donoghue and others, which is why they had suggested the appointment of qualified outsiders to these posts.

Dunlop depicts the party in the early part of its term in opposition, but by the time he arrived major reorganisation, at least at the head office and parliamentary party level, was already under way.

When it came to the post of general secretary the brief was to find "a dynamic person" to succeed the veteran Tommy Mullins, who was retiring. According to Michael Woods, who, as a member of the Ard-Chomhairle, was one of those involved in the selection process, "Fianna Fáil was operating on a shoestring but we needed to develop the party. We needed a real go getter."[20]

They didn't have to go far to find one. Séamus Brennan, then twenty-five and working as an accountant in Galway, had impressed the leadership since he had come onto the party's Ard-Chomhairle about a year earlier. He applied, and by all accounts he sailed through the interview process. He immediately set about a dramatic revitalisation of head office and an overhaul of the party's campaigning techniques. Among his innovations was the establishment of a youth wing, Ógra Fhianna Fáil.

Setting up a youth wing was not just a cosmetic exercise. The cumulative effect of the reduction of the voting age from twenty-one to eighteen, which would be implemented at the next election, and the demographic shift arising from the 1960s baby boom meant that new voters were likely to account for about a fifth of all voters, depending on when the Dáil was dissolved. Those who became prominent at Ógra Fhianna Fáil's inaugural events included Bertie Ahern and Mary Hanafin.

The original plan devised by the "reorganisation committee" was that, in addition to these strong executive appointments at head office level, a twofold policy support and development system would be established. Once Esmond Smyth was in position this was inaugurated. Firstly there were what was known as "fire brigade" committees assigned to each front-bench spokesperson. These groups were to provide the spokespersons with assistance on parliamentary questions, legislation, private members' bills, and topical issues in their policy areas. The system was structured on a "need to know" basis: each member knew only of the involvement of those within their own group. The conveners or rapporteurs of each of these groups, if trustworthy, also performed the function of co-ordinating the work of another, more *ad hoc* group, through which the party obtained access to expertise in each area, whether through the universities, representative bodies or otherwise. A committee of these rapporteurs met regularly and became known as the "Saturday group". According to Dermot Keogh, this committee was chaired initially by Anthony Hederman, and its members included Dónal Barrington, Hugh O'Flaherty, John McKenna, Michael Woods, Esmond Smyth, Brian Hillery, Eoin Kenny, Noel Mulcahy, J. O'Connor, Nicholas Kearns, Barry Early and Neville Keary.

In this way the party tapped into new ideas. Overseeing all this flexibly structured policy development were Esmond Smyth and an overarching committee chaired by Martin O'Donoghue. This latter committee, often called the "advisory group", was secretly drafting the party's manifesto for the next election.

Immediately after the 1973 election Lynch left the former ministers in their equivalent portfolios on the front bench. However, in September 1973 he reshuffled his spokespersons in preparation for the autumn Dáil term. The new line-up included David Andrews as spokesperson on justice, Joe Brennan on industry and commerce, Gerry Collins on agriculture and Bobby Molloy on local government. George Colley retained his former brief on finance, as did Pádraig Faulkner on social welfare. Des O'Malley, however, was moved to health. Among the new TDs promoted by Lynch at this time was John Wilson, a lecturer in Greek and Roman civilisation at UCD who was a new deputy from

Cavan. He was given responsibility for shadowing education and the arts. Also promoted was the Sligo deputy Ray MacSharry, first elected in 1969, who was given responsibility for the Office of Public Works, and the Tipperary North deputy Michael O'Kennedy, also first elected in 1969, who became spokesperson on foreign affairs. Brian Lenihan became party leader in the Seanad and Paddy Lalor returned to his previous role as chief whip.

Having joined the EEC, Ireland was entitled to representation in the European Parliament, which at that time was appointed rather than directly elected. All those nominated from Ireland were sitting Oireachtas members who doubled up in this new role. As well as his Seanad duties Brian Lenihan became leader of the Fianna Fáil delegation in the European Parliament; Michael Herbert TD was another member of the delegation. One of the first tasks was to identify a European political grouping with which the party could align. The Labour Party was already in the Socialist bloc, and Fine Gael had stolen a march on Fianna Fáil by joining the Christian Democrat bloc. Lenihan managed, however, to negotiate membership of a group known as the European Progressive Party, which it joined in June 1973. The group was dominated by the French Gaullists and was the first incarnation of a series of relatively marginal European groupings with which Fianna Fáil was to be aligned until it switched to the much larger European Liberals bloc in 2009.

While others were reading themselves into their portfolios in the autumn of 1973, Charles Haughey continued to busy himself touring the party organisation around the country. On this tour, soon to be dubbed the "rubber chicken circuit", Haughey's objective was to appeal to the grass roots over the heads of the leadership and the parliamentary party. His almost constant companion on these escapades was a constituency worker, P. J. Mara. Liam Lawlor, another friend, was also occasionally among the travelling party.

Curiously, the newly appointed press director, Frank Dunlop, was another occasional companion on some parts of Haughey's tour. He describes the approach that Haughey took to the task.

> He was on a mission, a focused campaign that had only one objective and all else was irrelevant. Most of the encounters were embarrassing. The crowd was usually small, the personnel were known dissidents within the party; the discussions were stilted; and the food, if any, was diabolical. But Haughey didn't mind. During a visit to a cumann meeting in Castlebar we were entertained by a local party bigwig, one Padraig Flynn. Flynn was a publican and teacher. We ended up in his house after the meeting, where we were introduced to the intricacies of west Mayo politics and whiskey . . . Yes Haughey knew that to a certain extent he was demeaning himself by accepting invitations to address cumainn throughout the country that would never expect to be graced by a member of the party's front bench let alone a former finance Minister. That Charlie was manipulating the vanity of those on the lower rungs of the party is undeniable.

Of course Lynch knew what Haughey was doing, but he was either powerless to prevent it or not interested. He was also aware that Dunlop was accompanying Haughey on some of these trips, but when he finally got around to confronting him about it he did not reprimand, or forbid, but merely warned Dunlop to watch his back, because others were criticising him.

Lynch's attitude to Dunlop's frolics with Haughey suggests that even at this stage he failed to appreciate the challenge to his leadership. While Haughey was always either silent or publicly supportive of Lynch, in private he continued to harbour intense resentment and ambition. Dunlop captured Haughey's *modus operandi* succinctly.

> He remained within the party fold. Nobody could seriously question his activities. He broke no rules. He maintained a dignified silence and spoke only in that circumlocutory way in which politicians who don't want to say anything become adept. On the surface everything was calm and nothing was said or done to give his enemies ammunition against him. There were dangerous outbursts but all within the confines of a small circle of loyal supporters.

When Erskine Childers died, in November 1974, Lynch again found it difficult to suppress speculation that he himself might move to the Park. Then, as previously, the suggestions were given momentum by those interested in taking the job that Lynch was then holding. For obvious reasons, Haughey was suspected of being the author of these rumours. In the event, it was on Lynch's suggestion that the coalition Government agreed to the nomination of a former Chief Justice, Cearbhall Ó Dálaigh, then a judge in the European Court of Justice in Luxembourg. On 19 December 1974 Ó Dálaigh was proposed and unanimously elected.

If Lynch's failure to reign in Dunlop showed naïveté, the decision by a leader who had been attacked as Lynch had been to reappoint Haughey to the front bench in 1975 seems astonishing, at least on first inspection. However, Haughey was very able; although only a back-bencher, he was one of Fianna Fáil's best performers in Dáil exchanges, and Lynch had a dearth of front-bench talent at the time. Secondly, there was a relentless and obviously well co-ordinated campaign among the party rank and file and among some back-benchers to have Haughey restored to the front bench. This pressure was both the objective and the outcome of Haughey's working of the rubber-chicken circuit, and it intensified in the latter part of 1974.

Counter-balancing the pressure from the grass roots, however, was the resistance from senior front-benchers. Of these Jim Gibbons was obviously the most antagonistic. He had made it known that he would not serve there if Haughey were put back on the front bench. Colley too was strongly opposed.

Lynch decided to ignore their advice and to discuss the matter with Haughey. He had decided to allow a Haughey come-back but that it would have to be on his terms. In an extensive and authoritative account of

Haughey's rise published in *Magill* in 1980, Vincent Browne recounts what happened next.

> There were two major problems. The first was that Haughey had represented since 1970 a silent challenge to the leadership of the party and the other was that, since his repudiation of Lynch's line on Northern Ireland at the United Nations in October 1970, he had never retracted that repudiation nor had he issued any statement of support for official party policy on the North. Lynch decided to ignore the leadership issue and at a private meeting with Haughey, asked the former arms trial defendant, if he would agree to issue a statement affirming his support for declared Northern policy, in advance of his return to the front bench. Haughey demurred, pointing out that this would look as though he was buying his way back. Lynch saw the point and restored Haughey to the front bench, after which, Haughey did make a statement agreeing with Northern policy.[21]

On 13 January 1975 Lynch reshuffled his shadow cabinet. Haughey returned as spokesperson on health. Despite his previous protestations, Jim Gibbons accepted the post of spokesperson on agriculture.

On the opening night of the 1975 ard-fheis, standing with Lynch to his left, Haughey declared: "There is no leadership crisis in Fianna Fáil. We are not casting around for a leader. We have a leader democratically chosen and as such commanding the respect, support and allegiance of the party."

Haughey quickly established himself as one of the most effective front-bench performers. Notwithstanding the fact that his portfolio was, in those days, seen as a relatively unimportant one, he managed to garner much media attention and was very effective in the role. Dermot Keogh says of him: "On an under-performing front bench Haughey's ability, his work rate and his presidential-style politics made him stand out well."

That Haughey would use his front-bench position to further develop his power base in the party, and would ultimately challenge again for the leadership whether Lynch departed or not, was entirely foreseeable. This made Lynch's decision all the more curious. Pádraig Faulkner spoke for many of his fellow-frontbenchers when he later wrote:

> Notwithstanding Haughey's ability and capacity for hard work and innovation . . . his well-known antipathy to the party leader made it difficult to understand what motivated Jack Lynch in making his decision. I believe it may be that he thought the move would make for greater unity in the party or he was simply signalling that bygones were bygones. Whatever the motivation the party leader had made his decision and as such it wasn't questioned, though not everybody was happy with it. It was rumoured afterwards that Haughey had been offered Foreign Affairs, but had rejected it.[22]

There was a poignant milestone in the party's history on 29 August 1975, when Éamon de Valera died, at the age of ninety-two. After a state funeral that attracted large crowds to the streets of Dublin, "the Chief" was laid to rest with military honours in a modest grave in Glasnevin Cemetery beside his wife, Sinéad, who had died the previous January.

The other significant development in the parliamentary life of the party in 1975 was that Lynch lost control of his party's Northern policy, albeit temporarily. In a number of speeches and interviews that autumn the party's foreign affairs spokesperon, Michael O'Kennedy, proclaimed that the majority in Northern Ireland did not have the right to determine the direction of the relationship of Northern Ireland with the Irish state, and he called on the British Government to make a declaration of intent to leave. When asked whether these remarks represented a shift in the party's policy from the policy of unity by consent that had been espoused repeatedly by Lynch, O'Kennedy claimed it represented "a conflict of expression rather than policy." However, what Stephen Collins has called the "British withdrawal" lobby within the front bench managed to overcome the more moderate Lynch-Brugha position at that point. A formal policy document along the lines called for by O'Kennedy was actually adopted by the front bench on 30 October 1975. It said that the British Government should "declare Britain's commitment to implement an ordered withdrawal from her involvement in the Six Counties of Northern Ireland." At the time many commentators interpreted this shift in Fianna Fáil policy as a crude attempt to curry favour with the supposedly republican electorate in Mayo East, where a by-election was in train. If it was, it failed to work. Notwithstanding the fact that Fine Gael was in government, its candidate, Enda Kenny, won the by-election comfortably.

While Fianna Fáil busied itself with renewal, the Cosgrave Government struggled with large economic and security challenges. In the aftermath of what was to become the first oil crisis of the 1970s it had to contend with rampant inflation. It also had to contend with an intensification of the IRA campaign, which included the assassination of the British ambassador, Christopher Ewart-Biggs, in July 1976. In the wake of the killing the Cosgrave Government introduced emergency legislation, and there was much speculation that it might even call an early election. Fianna Fáil argued that the declaration of an emergency was unnecessary and that the accompanying legislation was excessive.

Fearing an imminent election, Fianna Fáil now brought forward its policy development and rushed out a document entitled "The Economic Emergency", the tone and content of which were designed to emphasise that the real emergency was the economic one. This document was to be the precursor of the eventual 1977 manifesto; its publication, "coupled together with the very formidable legal case made by Gerry Collins, assisted by Des O'Malley, George Colley, Charlie Haughey and Michael O'Kennedy, against the coalition emergency powers legislation, grasped the initiative."[23]

The major components of "The Economic Emergency", and ultimately of the 1977 manifesto, included a dramatic increase in Government spending of £100 million in the first year of government, which, it was predicted, would provide twenty thousand immediate jobs. It also promised a reduction of a fifth in income tax and a reduction in employers' social welfare contributions to parity with that of employees, and it made a commitment to negotiate an agreement between trade unions and employers to substitute tax cuts for pay rises. It repeated the 1973 promise to remove rates from private dwellings.

While the proposal to abolish rates subsequently proved the most controversial, there were significant flaws in the system then operating, which was regressive, as rates of tax were not related to a household's capacity to pay, house valuations for rates purposes were outdated, and those whose houses were appreciating in value but whose incomes were stagnant were caught in a particular bind.

Just when things were going well for Fianna Fáil, the coalition sustained serious self-inflicted wounds. In accordance with his powers under the Constitution, but much to the annoyance of the coalition Government, President Ó Dálaigh referred the Emergency Powers Act to the Supreme Court for consideration of its constitutionality. On 18 October 1976 the Minister for Defence, Patrick Donegan, while speaking at a function in Columb Barracks, Mullingar, described President Ó Dálaigh as "a thundering disgrace". Offended at the remark, and at the failure of the Taoiseach to accept Donegan's offer of resignation, Ó Dálaigh himself resigned on 23 October, saying he was doing so in order to protect the integrity of the office.

The ensuing controversy badly damaged the Cosgrave Government. In an effort to ameliorate his political difficulties Cosgrave then approached Lynch to see if an agreed candidate to replace Ó Dálaigh could be found. Patrick Hillery, after some persuading by Lynch, agreed to return from Brussels and on 3 December 1976 became the sixth President of Ireland.

On 25 May 1977 Cosgrave dissolved the 24th Dáil, nine months early, thereby firing the starting shot in what was to be one of the liveliest election campaigns in a generation. Polling day was to be 16 June.

Fianna Fáil's campaign hit the ground running. It launched the manifesto on the first day of the campaign, and it dominated the subsequent debate. A few days later Lynch said to the media:

> The first public presentation of the manifesto was not just the opening of a carefully prepared election campaign. It was the culmination of four years of research and political reappraisal, sure in its purpose and unassailable in its costing and coherence, received as such by you, the press. It has stood up equally well to the critical scrutiny of economic commentators and the business community. We know it is an election-winner.[24]

The consensus is that, although the manifesto was an election-winner, as Lynch had hoped, this overstates the situation. Many of the contemporary commentators, embarrassed perhaps by their own failure to foresee a Fianna Fáil victory, came to attach greater significance to the impact of the proposals in the documents drafted by O'Donoghue. The manifesto certainly contained many goodies, but not perhaps many more than both parties had offered in 1973. The reason it subsequently became controversial was that the next Government went on in fact to implement those policies.

The real election-winner for Fianna Fáil was Lynch himself. The party general secretary, Séamus Brennan, had gone to the United States to study the 1976 Nixon-Carter presidential contest and brought home a range of lively new campaigning techniques, which he now employed in a campaign built around Lynch's popularity. Fianna Fáil campaigns had always been leader-focused, but in 1977 the level was unprecedented. "Bring back Jack" was the theme of posters showing Lynch in a relaxed pipe-smoking pose. "I'm backing Jack" was on lapel stickers and cardboard hats distributed at each stop on Lynch's barnstorming election tours. It also featured on T-shirts worn by Ógra Fhianna Fáil squads that did the advance work in each town. "Jack will be back" was the title of internal party manuals describing in detail how the campaign was to be executed. "Jack will fly back" was the confident prediction on trailers dragged across the sky behind hired aircraft.

"Your kind of country" was the slogan for a campaign aimed at new and young voters. It was also the title of the party's election song, sung by Colm Wilkinson, then in the early, pre-Eurovision and pre *Les Misérables* phase of his career. It was an upbeat pop ballad, the chorus of which ran:

Let's make it your kind of country.
Go out there and vote, show them that you're free.
Show them that you give a damn and that we'll win somehow.
It's time to make it your country now.

Most commentators in the last week of the campaign predicted that the coalition would be re-elected comfortably. These predictions were informed in part by their analysis of the new constituency map that had been implemented by the outgoing Minister for the Environment, Jimmy Tully. All were predicting that the "Tullymander", as it was dubbed, would guarantee a return of the Cosgrave Government.

In the most dramatic election result for more than a generation, Fianna Fáil won the support of slightly less than 51 per cent of the electorate to win 84 seats in a Dáil of 144. Fine Gael fell from 53 seats to 43 and the Labour Party from 20 to 17. It was the biggest majority in the history of the state. On the night of the count Lynch himself suggested that it might be too big.

Chapter 12

THE TURBULENT
TRANSITION, 1977–81

When Jack Lynch realised the size of his majority after the 1977 election he said that one had to be careful when carrying a full jug; but if he was conscious that fifty-seven back-benchers would take some handling, he showed little sign of it.

On the night of the count one journalist asked Charles Haughey if he was unhappy that Lynch had secured such a large majority. Haughey's answer was: "Those are all my men."[1] During his wilderness years Haughey had spoken at their local cumann or comhairle ceantair meetings and supped late into the night in their kitchens, even before they became Dáil candidates. Now he set about nursing these new back-benchers assiduously as they found their feet. Neither Lynch nor indeed George Colley—his presumptive and somewhat presumptuous heir—made much effort to shore up their relationship with existing deputies or to get to know the new ones.

However, it would be wrong to see either Lynch's slightly premature retirement in December 1979, or Haughey's succession, as having being determined solely by the competition for the affections of the expanded Fianna Fáil back benches. The principal motivation of these men and women, in leadership machinations as in all things, was their personal electoral survival. The "class of '77" had been elected on the strength of Lynch's extraordinary personal appeal, but within two years they, and most of their more established back-bench colleagues, were watching nervously as deteriorating economic conditions and questionable political management led to a sharp drop in Fianna Fáil's support. They wanted a more modern, vibrant leader. Haughey, again an effective and popular Government minister, fitted the bill.

There was one dramatic innovation in Lynch's last Government. On his first day in the Dáil, Martin O'Donoghue, who had decided only at the last moment to stand as David Andrews's running-mate in Dún Laoghaire, became head of a new department carved primarily out of the Department of Finance. He had designed the Department of Economic Planning himself, and he was also given responsibility for negotiations with the employers and trade unions, liaison with international organisations, and general co-ordination of policy and public-sector reform.

The other newsworthy, if less surprising, aspect of Lynch's new ministerial line-up was the return to the Government of Charles Haughey. Having performed well as opposition spokesperson on health, Haughey felt he was entitled to expect that portfolio in the Government. He was pleasantly surprised, however, to be given responsibility also for the Department of Social Welfare. The same factors of party and public popularity that had persuaded Lynch to reappoint him to the front bench two years earlier now brought him back into the Government.

Lynch's ministerial line-up was otherwise predictable. George Colley, Tánaiste and Minister for Finance, Des O'Malley at Industry and Commerce; the Taoiseach himself and O'Donoghue formed an inner cabinet that made all the main economic policy decisions. Jim Gibbons, as Minister for Agriculture, and Gene Fitzgerald, as Minister for Labour, were also members of the Government economic sub-committee but had much less influence. Pádraig Faulkner became Minister for Tourism and Transport and Minister for Posts and Telegraphs, which would give him responsibility for the modernisation of the telephone system as well as the construction of the DART Dublin suburban railway system. Brian Lenihan, who had regained his seat, was disappointed to be appointed only Minister for Fisheries. Gerry Collins went for the first of his stints in the Department of Justice. John Wilson was made Minister for Education. Bobby Molloy was given Defence, Denis Gallagher the Gaeltacht and Sylvester Barrett the Environment. Ruairí Brugha had lost his seat in Wicklow, so Michael O'Kennedy became Minister for Foreign Affairs, sharing responsibility for Northern Ireland with the Taoiseach.

Grounded in the 1977 election manifesto, the economic policies of Jack Lynch's last Government were among Fianna Fáil's most controversial. They included an expansion of both capital and current expenditure that, if the economic conditions had remained favourable, might have been affordable. In the event the decision to implement non-productive taxation giveaways was not only contentious but led cumulatively, once a further economic downturn came in 1979, to a severe crisis in the public finances.

In 1999 James Downey, in his biography of Brian Lenihan, argued that the 1977 manifesto was "not only economically disastrous but electorally unnecessary." He went on to recount how Brian Lenihan himself privately derided it: "Blessed are the young, for they shall inherit the national debt."[2] Albert Reynolds, then newly elected for Longford, would later boast that he had read the document only after the election.

In his biography of Lynch, Dermot Keogh argues that the 1977 manifesto was "a breakthrough in what later became known as auction politics," which "helped to fuel a growing sectionalism in society and an unfounded fear of Irish politics that it was necessary to 'buy off' sections of the electorate in order to be returned to power." Keogh also argues, however, that this perception of the manifesto's political influence has "eclipsed a careful analysis of the years between 1977 and 1979 and of the longer-term strategies implemented by that Government."[3]

In his assessment of the 1977 campaign Brian Farrell, arguably the leading political scientist of the period, wrote that the emphasis on "consumer politics", which had been a significant feature of the 1977 campaign,

> seemed likely to displace the old rhetoric of nationalist politics and the newer invocation of expansive but vague economic promises. Traditional party loyalties still dominated, but that had been diluted by a more calculated approach to voting. Self-interest and a demand for tangible results would be more likely to determine future elections results. Irish society was changing; the face of Irish politics could not remain static.[4]

Initially the Lynch-Colley-O'Donoghue expansionist economic plan seemed to be working. In a defence of this policy, published in 1990, O'Donoghue pointed out that at the time Fianna Fáil took office unemployment was approximately 106,000. The number of people at work in April 1980 had risen by 80,000 from this level. Inflation fell from 18 per cent in 1976 and 15 per cent in the first half of 1977 to 7½ per cent in 1978.[5]

While O'Donoghue may be accused of bias, he is not alone in his views. In January 1980, in an extended article for *Magill* covering the last years of Lynch's reign and the Haughey succession, Vincent Browne argued that

> the new Lynch administration shaped up in its first year to be the best government the state had known. In 1978 the economy leapt ahead with a 7 per cent growth rate and inflation almost halved from the 13 per cent when the government came into office. Most impressive was the government record in job creation [in its first year]; this crept up towards the 20,000 mark, which was the manifesto target.[6]

Browne goes on, however, to argue what became the consensus view, which was that the 1977–9 Lynch Government undermined recovery and accentuated the downward spiral of the economy.

In early 1979 another global oil crisis induced by OPEC hit the open Irish economy particularly hard. An outbreak of intense labour unrest, including a postal workers' strike that ran from February to June, also undermined the Government's policy. Lynch and O'Donoghue had gambled on both growth and wage restraint but could sustain neither.

The February 1978 budget abolished domestic rates. This has since been seen as one of the most controversial decisions taken by any Government and is regularly cited as an example of Fianna Fáil's reckless policies during this period and as a wanton destruction of the fiscal autonomy of local government. Pádraig Faulkner—so far the only member of that Government to publish a memoir—mounts a strong defence of the abolition of domestic rates, arguing that the system was riddled with anomalies and was inequitable.

Outdated valuations ensured that there were substantial differences in rates charged on the same houses in the same areas. When a family went to the trouble of improving their residence their house's valuation rose and so did their rate. An old lady living alone on a modest income in a large house would pay higher rates than a family size dwelling with several members working and so it went on. Carrying out a total revaluation of the country would take too long . . . so Fianna Fáil abolished them.[7]

Faulkner trenchantly rejects the suggestion that abolishing rates was an election gimmick, pointing out that not only had Fianna Fáil "been dealing with the issue of the abolition of rates in public for many years" but that

all the major parties had committed [themselves] to abolishing rates on domestic dwellings before the election. In the lead up to it the Fine Gael party had first promised to remove rates over a four year period. Then a subsequent manifesto issued by Fine Gael and Labour had promised to abolish rates over a two-year period.

Faulkner examined the newspaper reportage in the immediate aftermath of the 1977 election and found that none of the defeated coalition members interviewed the day after they lost power gave the rates policy as a reason for their defeat. They blamed it instead on the unpopularity of their own Government's policy on the farm tax, on the high level of inflation, on unemployment and on the timing of the election. The newspapers also attributed the defeat of the outgoing Government to other factors.

The *Sunday Press* observed that a government could not expect to win on soaring prices and high unemployment; a theme echoed by the *Sunday Independent*. Only the *Irish Times*, the following day, made a reference to voters being able to calculate the benefit to themselves of the abolition of domestic rates, as part of a more general résumé of the reasons for the coalition government's defeat."[8]

Faulkner also says that both the opposition parties and Lynch's opponents within Fianna Fáil had their own motives for subsequently blaming the 1977 manifesto. They made it the scapegoat, he says, "for their later failures in government to deal positively with critical problems which subsequently arose such as the OPEC crisis in 1979 and the consequent deterioration of the Irish economy."[9]

While Lynch, O'Donoghue and Colley were implementing these economic policies and attracting the blame for the downturn, Haughey was maintaining a high profile in the Departments of Health and Social Welfare. In Social Welfare he built on his previous reputation as a reforming Minister for Finance and friend of the elderly by easing the five-year residence requirement for old-age and other pensions, making provision for those who qualified to get free gas in lieu of free electricity, and giving free telephone rental to pensioners who lived alone. In Health he dramatically enhanced the role of the Health Promotion Unit and launched imaginative campaigns, many of which he himself fronted. Typical of these was the initiative to give a free toothbrush to every schoolchild as part of a National Dental Week. He also introduced ground-breaking legislation to control tobacco advertising and sponsorship, and announced improved free access to hospitals for those earning less than £5,500 per year.

In late 1978 Haughey introduced a Family Planning Bill that would allow those with a medical prescription to purchase condoms for bona fide family planning or medical purposes. Liberals saw this bill as restricting the availability of contraception, while conservatives, including many in Fianna Fáil, viewed it as too liberal. In the Dáil, Haughey argued that his proposal was a "sensible, middle-of-the-road type of solution"[10] and that the legislation sought "to provide an Irish solution to an Irish problem."[11] Today these restrictions seem absurd, but Haughey's handling of the bill, which passed on 17 July 1979, gained much political credit at the time, not least because, as Dermot Keogh puts it, Haughey "showed his adroitness in finding a way out of a legislative cul de sac that had confounded the National Coalition."

Four Fianna Fáil deputies, including Jim Gibbons, defied a three-line whip and failed to vote on the second stage of the bill. At a subsequent parliamentary party meeting the others apologised, but Gibbons remained defiant. When Lynch refused to discipline him it was the first time that a Fianna Fáil TD had been allowed to defy the party whip unpunished. Vincent Browne wrote: "The affair called seriously into question Jack Lynch's ability to control the cabinet, let alone his Parliamentary Party. It also raised unsavoury memories of the arms crisis of 1970 and the role of Gibbons in that affair."[12]

By the summer of 1978 Lynch had decided that he would step down as leader of Fianna Fáil in early 1980, after Ireland had completed its presidency of the EEC. Although he did not announce it, there was wide speculation within the party that he would do this.

In his budget speech in February 1978 George Colley not only announced the abolition of rates and reductions in motor tax but stunned the Dáil by announcing a 2 per cent levy on agricultural produce. The proposal caused consternation among the farming community, which, of course, was instantly reflected within the Fianna Fáil parliamentary party. The internal opposition was led by Tom Meaney, deputy for Mid-Cork, while among the other prominent rebels was the new Kildare TD Charlie McCreevy. The handling of the ensuing controversy illustrates the gap that was opening between the Government and Fianna Fáil back-benchers. Meaney put a motion down at the parliamentary party, and following the discussion it was assumed that there would be some minor adjustments to Colley's proposal. Vincent Browne takes up the story.

Eventually, late on the eve of the Fianna Fáil Ard Fheis, George Colley
agreed to significant modifications . . . While the backbenchers were in
general still quite worried about the electoral consequences of the levy,
they were nonetheless prepared to wear it, in acknowledgement of the
fact that the farming sector was going to have to pay its fair share of the
tax burden. There was a general welcome for the changes announced by
Colley at the Ard Fheis, although the farming organisations reiterated
their continued vehement denunciation of the entire scheme. A meeting
with the farming organisations was arranged for the following Tuesday
and to the amazement of everybody, including even the organisation
involved, the Government agreed to suspend the operation of the levy
pending agreement with the farming bodies on a fair system of farming
taxation. It was this change which infuriated the backbenchers. They
were prepared to shoulder the political consequences of the modified
levy and many of them had defended the scheme at party meetings on
the Monday and Tuesday nights. At least two TDs were involved in
tortuous defences of the plan at cumann meetings when they were
interrupted from the floor that there had just been a television
announcement to the effect that the levy had been suspended. Even a
cabinet minister, Brian Lenihan, was in the throes of such a defence at a
party meeting in Lucan when he was informed by an outsider what his
colleagues had agreed on. There was black fury among the backbenchers
that they should be treated so contemptuously . . . It was a blunder of
truly massive proportions. Already there was building up a resentment
among the PAYE sector about the unfair share of the tax burden which
it was carrying. It was merely adding insult to injury to appear to give
in so cravenly to the farmers. At one stroke, the Government had
alienated both the farming and urban voter.[13]

This debacle over farm tax, the lengthy postal strike, the more severe
budget that Colley had to introduce in early 1979 and the queues at petrol
stations all contributed to a sharp decline in Fianna Fáil's support. This
slippage became very evident in both the local elections and the first elections
for the European Parliament, which were held on 7 June 1979. The Fianna Fáil
vote plummeted from 51 per cent in the general election of 1977 to 35 per cent
in the European Parliament elections. Two independents were elected:
T. J. Maher, a former president of the Irish Farmers' Association, won a seat in
Munster, while Neil Blaney took a seat in Connacht-Ulster, "sending shock
waves through the Parliamentary Party."[14] Fine Gael, now led by Garret
FitzGerald, and the Labour Party, now led by Frank Cluskey, won four seats
each.

On the Fianna Fáil back benches there had been serious rumbling against
Lynch since the spring of 1978. The plotting centred around a group who
frequented the late bar and Coffee Dock restaurant in Jury's Hotel in
Ballsbridge and in lodgings shared by rural deputies when attending Dáil

sessions. According to Vincent Browne, "a house in Harold's Cross, occupied during Dáil sessions by MacSharry, Mark Killilea and Senator Bernard McGlinchey, was where much of the plotting took place." Two long-serving deputies, Jackie Fahey of Waterford, first elected in 1965, and Tom McEllistrim of Kerry, first elected in 1969, were the leading participants in a series of *ad hoc* gatherings and social encounters at which the weaknesses of Lynch and the strengths of Haughey were the main subject of conversation. These two were joined in the conspiracy by three new deputies: Seán Doherty of Co. Roscommon, the colourful Pádraig Flynn from Co. Mayo, and the more restrained and strategic Longford businessman Albert Reynolds. Collectively they later became known in media commentary as the "Gang of Five".

After the June 1979 electoral setbacks the manoeuvres intensified. By now Lynch and his senior ministers were not only absorbed in the worsening economic situation but were simultaneously running the Irish presidency of the European Union. They also had to deal with increasing tensions in Northern Ireland, which again spilled south of the border when, on 27 August 1979, the Provisional IRA blew up Earl Mountbatten's boat at Mullaghmore, Co. Sligo, killing him and his fifteen-year-old grandson and a fifteen-year-old local boy. At the end of September, Lynch and his Government also played host to Pope John Paul II on the first papal visit to Ireland.

All this time a growing number of Fianna Fáil back-benchers were busily scheming against their leader. On 5 July they held a caucus meeting in Dublin to discuss a strategy for displacing Lynch. At the subsequent parliamentary party meeting Lynch, who "was infuriated when informed by a Dublin deputy of the caucus,"[15] demanded to know who had attended it. Only Flynn owned up, though there had been more than twenty back-benchers at the meeting.[16]

In early September the tensions in the party again burst into the public arena when one of the new deputies, Síle de Valera, who had also just been elected a member of the European Parliament, delivered a hard-line speech on Northern Ireland at the Liam Lynch Memorial in Fermoy, even though the Taoiseach had previously asked her to moderate her planned remarks.

In later years the view was expressed that Haughey was behind these various moves. However, in January 1980 Vincent Browne concluded:

> It is not clear exactly how much Charlie Haughey knew of these happenings. Certainly he had no knowledge of the caucus before it happened . . . It seems that he discussed the leadership issue with some members of the five at this stage and compared estimates with them on how individual TDs would vote. But it does not appear to be the case that at this time—i.e. July—he was part of the conspiracy to get rid of Jack Lynch.[17]

The attention of the parliamentary party next shifted to two by-elections to be held in Co. Cork on 7 November, one of them in Lynch's own constituency of Cork City. Fianna Fáil was widely expected to win both seats comfortably.

Lynch had spent four consecutive weekends in Cork campaigning vigorously, and the bookies were offering odds of 1 to 6 on a Fianna Fáil win in the city constituency. Lynch was on a visit to New York in his capacity as president of the European Council when he received the by-election results and was visibly shaken by the news. Fianna Fáil had lost both contests. In his own constituency the party vote had dropped a staggering 22 per cent from June 1977 and in Cork North-East it had dropped by 12 per cent.

By the time he arrived home, Lynch's position had been further undermined by Colley's botched handling of a motion to expel a back-bencher. When, at the Washington Press Club, Lynch claimed that a security deal allowing British military aircraft to overfly the Republic involved only a slight deviation from the air control regulations, the Clare deputy Bill Loughnane told a journalist that Lynch was a liar. When this appeared in the paper, Colley, who was in charge during the Taoiseach's absence, moved a motion at a day-long and at times chaotic parliamentary party meeting to have the whip removed from him. Loughnane claimed he had been misquoted, and his parliamentary colleagues refused Colley's request.

On his return from the United States the following Monday, Lynch was met at the airport by many of his Government and some of his back-benchers. Haughey's absence was interpreted by many as presaging a move against the leader, and Dermot Keogh observed that Lynch had proved to be resilient in 1970, 73 and 77 but observed that on this occasion the size of the welcoming party at the airport was "a signal of distress rather than a triumphant celebration."[18]

In the weeks after his return, however, it was Lynch's own supporters, and in particular Colley and O'Donoghue, who persuaded him to go before Christmas. They were confident that this would deny Haughey further time to organise and would ensure the succession for Colley. On 5 December, Lynch shocked most of his parliamentary party when he announced, at a scheduled meeting, not only that he was stepping down but that the contest for his successor would be held two days later.

The ensuing forty-eight hours were among the most intense in the history of Fianna Fáil. The contest between Haughey and Colley was, in the words of Brian Farrell, "sharp and extremely divisive".[19] Colley was seen from the outset as having the entire Government behind him, except for Haughey. His campaign, however, was low-key. Afterwards some of his supporters suggested that this was a deliberate strategy. "I don't think George Colley ran any sort of campaign," Bobby Molloy later told Stephen Collins. "We were all taken by surprise. Haughey had been campaigning from two years before that but George didn't campaign. He was doing his job as Minster for Finance."[20]

Pádraig Faulkner also recalls a lacklustre Colley campaign during the crucial forty-eight hours.

> George as far as I know rarely left his office and his supporters generally took too much for granted. They relied on the accepted wisdom that he

had the full support of the Cabinet and that Ministers would persuade many deputies to vote for him. Apart from a hazy recollection of one gathering, I know of no meeting to plan strategy or to assess the situation.[21]

The Government press secretary, Frank Dunlop, who appears to have stuck close to both sides for the duration of the short contest, says:

There is no question but that [Colley's] campaign was amateurish in the extreme. It epitomized an attitude then prevalent among some senior ministers—Colley himself, O'Malley, Gibbons, Faulkner and Collins—that back bench TDs would vote for Colley out of deference, almost from a sense of being honoured to do so.[22]

His campaign may have been haphazard, but Colley did have several leading figures, including O'Donoghue, O'Malley, Molloy and the party's general secretary, Séamus Brennan, active on his behalf; but with the exception of Brennan none of these were particularly popular with, or accessible to, back-benchers.

Haughey had the advantage of years of planning and of having had back-benchers working on his behalf for months. He announced his candidature immediately and, to the surprise of the opposing faction, also announced that Colley's minister of state, Ray MacSharry, would propose him. On the morning of the vote it emerged that Michael O'Kennedy, Minister for Foreign Affairs, was also backing Haughey. It was a devastating blow to the Colley camp.[23] Brian Lenihan, Minister for Fisheries, also voted for Haughey, though he did not confirm this until eighteen years later. In the end Haughey won by 44 votes to 38.

In the following days Fianna Fáil came perilously close to an irreversible split. The Colley camp were shocked by their defeat. Frank Dunlop describes calling into Colley's office to commiserate and finding there also "a sulphurous Dessie O'Malley, a reflective Bobby Molloy, a Gauloise-smoking Jim Gibbons and an incandescent Des Hanafin."[24] Dermot Keogh captures the naïveté that permeated Colley's efforts to win the leadership.

In the autumn of 1979 Haughey had one major tactical advantage, his victory in a leadership race was unthinkable to his opponents. They could not conceive of a campaign in which there would be no rules, no boundaries, no depths to which their opponents would not sink to secure victory for their candidate.[25]

After his election Haughey emerged to a press conference surrounded entirely by back-benchers and announced that Colley had pledged him "total and fullest co-operation in my new task." This so angered Colley that two weeks later, in a speech published to the media, he said that while in his role as a minister he was constitutionally obliged to give loyalty to Haughey as Taoiseach, no such obligation existed as far as the leader of the party was concerned. As Colley and his supporters saw it, the way in which Lynch had been forced out, and in which Haughey had bullied and cajoled his way to the leadership, meant that the latter could no longer expect to rely on the traditional party loyalties to the leader.

In the days following Haughey's election there were rumours that Colley and some of his supporters might not even vote for Haughey as Taoiseach, such was their antipathy to him and their concern at the implications of his elevation. Some of these rumours reached the ears of Garret FitzGerald, leader of the opposition, who in the early hours of the morning of 11 December wrote a speech for the debate on the nomination for Taoiseach that included the suggestion that Haughey had "a flawed pedigree". This personal attack was criticised not only by Fianna Fáil but, privately, by some senior Fine Gael politicians. When it came to the vote, however, Haughey did indeed receive the support of all Fianna Fáil deputies and was comfortably elected Taoiseach.

As a man and as Taoiseach, Haughey presented a striking contrast with his predecessor. He was clearly "part of the Irish *nouveaux riches*, expensively dressed, with a taste for fine wines, modern Irish art and life in the fast lane."[26] He flaunted his apparent wealth and shortly before he took over as party leader had bought the small island of Inishvickillane, part of the Blasket Islands, off the Kerry coast.

Although there was speculation at this time about how he financed his extravagant life-style, the true basis of Haughey's wealth did not emerge for almost two decades. Most in Fianna Fáil assumed that he had invested wisely and benefited from land speculation, but the truth was that Haughey, both before and, even more so, after he became Taoiseach was the recipient of large payments from a number of prominent business people, and had extraordinarily tolerant bankers. Testimony before judicial tribunals in the 1990s would reveal that from about 1960 his former accountancy colleague Des Traynor had managed Haughey's financial affairs through a complex web of companies and offshore bank accounts. It also emerged that during the 1970s Haughey wrote cheques totalling approximately £12,000 a month on already overdrawn accounts, that by December 1979 he owed Allied Irish Banks about £1.14 million and that shortly afterwards they wrote off more than half of it. The balance was cleared using, among other things, a £300,000 non-returnable deposit from the developer Patrick Gallagher for an option to purchase lands at Kinsealy, Co. Dublin, which was never exercised. Though there were occasional rumours about all this, and an article in the *Evening Press* in 1983 by the journalist Des Crowley mentioned long-standing rumours in financial circles that Haughey owed £1 million to a bank, concerns about libel meant that the story was never expanded upon or followed up in that or other publications.

When he became leader of Fianna Fáil, Haughey's priorities included establishing who the big donors to the party were and the removal of the Lynch loyalist Senator Des Hanafin from his position as the party's chief fund-raiser. Haughey would subsequently divert to his own use at least £1 million in party funds.

From the moment he became leader Haughey's focus was on preparing for an election in which he hoped to contain Fianna Fáil losses and gain his own mandate. All his actions over the following year and a half should be seen in that context.

Maintaining a semblance of party unity was an essential part of his strategy. This explains why Haughey agreed, at a private meeting with Colley the day before he became Taoiseach, that he would not only make Colley Tánaiste but would grant him a veto over who would be Minister for Defence and Minister for Justice. The former post went to Pádraig Faulkner, while Gerry Collins retained the latter. Indeed Haughey retained all but three of Lynch's ministers in his first Government, dropping only Jim Gibbons, who was a sworn enemy, Bobby Molloy, who was relatively junior at that time, and Martin O'Donoghue, who had said in a newspaper interview in 1977 that he would never serve in a Government under Haughey.[27] Ray MacSharry was promoted to become Minister for Agriculture. Of the "Gang of Five" only Albert Reynolds was promoted, becoming Minister for Posts and Telegraphs two-and-a-half years after he entered the Dáil. Paddy Power from Co. Kildare took over Fisheries and Forestry. In a typically dramatic gesture Haughey appointed the young Galway West deputy Máire Geoghegan-Quinn Minister for the Gaeltacht, making her the first woman minister since Constance Markievicz in 1919. The other surprise promotion was that of the chief whip, Michael Woods, who, although a Colley supporter, was made Minister for Health and Social Welfare. Michael O'Kennedy was promoted from Foreign Affairs to Finance; a year later he would become Ireland's member of the European Commission, with Gene Fitzgerald taking over at Finance.

Haughey's insecurity about his position in the party and his anxiety about an imminent election probably account for his failure to live up to the expectation that he would do what was necessary to tackle the increase in the national debt from £4,220 million in 1977 to £6,540 million in 1979.

On Wednesday 9 January 1980, four weeks after becoming Taoiseach, Haughey delivered a televised address to the country in which he said:

> We have been living at a rate which is simply not justified by the amount of goods and services we are producing. To make up the difference we have been borrowing enormous amounts of money, borrowing at a rate which just cannot continue. A few simple figures will make this very clear.
>
> At home, the Government's current income from taxes and all other sources in 1979 fell short of what was needed to pay the running costs of the state by about £520 million. To meet this and our capital programme we had to borrow in 1979 over £1,000 million. That amount is equal to one-seventh of our entire national output for the year. This is just too high a rate and cannot possibly continue.

In his contribution to the budget debate eight weeks later he stated:

Nobody can argue that it is wise to continue to engage in deficit budget-
ing year after year, when these deficits are contributing to inflation and
to our balance of payments difficulties . . .

A principal aim to this budget was to start the process of reducing
the annual budget deficit as the most important contribution we can
make to keeping the limit of overall borrowing at an acceptable level.
There can be no argument about this being the right thing to do.

However, this was merely rhetoric, and in his first Government Haughey
did exactly the opposite of what he had said was necessary.

In his memoirs the opinion-pollster Jack Jones tells of private research he
conducted for Fine Gael in mid-January 1980 to assess Haughey's impact as
leader.

The findings brought little comfort to Fine Gael. Haughey had
succeeded in creating a new mood of optimism among Fianna Fáil
supporters, despite the by-election defeats of two months earlier, and
had also made a very favourable impression across the electorate
generally. In party support terms, Fianna Fáil was now back to its June
1977 level.[28]

Jones notes, however, that there was slippage in Fianna Fáil's and
Haughey's ratings over the course of 1980 as it became apparent that Haughey
was not implementing the policies he had advocated in his television address.

Inflation and unemployment continued to rise and so too did public-
sector borrowing. The public-sector pay bill also rose, not least because
Haughey agreed to a pay increase for teachers that actually exceeded the initial
arbitration award.[29] The result was that the public-sector borrowing
requirement was 14½ per cent of GNP by early 1981. By the time of the election
in June, borrowing for current purposes had already reached more than 80
per cent of the amount projected for the whole year.

Haughey was tough in his rhetorical stance on Northern Ireland,
describing it at his first ard-fheis as a "failed political entity", but in practice
he followed much the same policy as Lynch had done. He did, however,
initiate a series of regular meetings with the British Prime Minster, Margaret
Thatcher, and on 21 May 1980 he travelled to meet her in London, giving her an
Irish Georgian silver teapot. In their communiqué the two leaders spoke of a
"mutual desire" to "develop new and closer political co-operation between their
governments." On 8 December 1980 Thatcher paid a return visit to Dublin at
the head of a high-level delegation that included her Foreign Secretary and
Chancellor of the Exchequer. After this meeting the leaders spoke to the media
of "joint Anglo-Irish studies" and of "possible new institutional structures" as
part of "an overall review of the totality of relationships between these

islands." It was a significant meeting, but when Haughey and more particularly the Minister for Foreign Affairs, Brian Lenihan, later suggested that the constitutional position of Northern Ireland as part of the United Kingdom was now in the melting-pot and that the partition question was on the verge of being solved, they provoked Thatcher's ire.

This summitry, and the suspension of the first H-block hunger strikes (although this proved temporary), played well for Haughey politically. The economic and budgetary position was less impressive, but he cushioned some of the effect of the recession by maintaining an unsustainable level of public expenditure. In November 1980 a Fianna Fáil victory in a by-election in Co. Donegal also augured well for the party. Speculation intensified that Haughey might call a general election early in the new year.

At the Friday night opening session of the ard-fheis in February 1981 it was clear from the atmosphere that it was shaping up to be a triumphant occasion for the leader and the perfect launching-pad for an election campaign. Then, as a result of a horrific fire at a disco that night in the Stardust night-club in Artane, Dublin, in Haughey's own constituency, the remainder of the ard-fheis was postponed.

The election was delayed by several months, by which time the IRA prisoners had initiated a further round of hunger strikes in the H blocks. On 5 May one of the hunger-strikers, Bobby Sands, died. He had been elected to the British Parliament in a by-election twenty-five days earlier. The election in the Republic was finally called on 21 May, the same day on which two more H-block hunger-strikers died, and would take place on 11 June.

Fianna Fáil had 83 of the 148 seats in the outgoing Dáil; Fine Gael had 45 and the others had 20. In the campaign period the main issues of concern to the electorate were unemployment and inflation. 41 per cent of those interviewed for the first *Irish Times* MRBI opinion poll felt that Haughey had done well in government. At the outset of the campaign Fianna Fáil had an estimated support of 45 per cent, Fine Gael 38 per cent, the Labour Party 11 per cent and others 6 per cent.[30]

FitzGerald had revitalised Fine Gael since he became leader in July 1977, and in 1981 the party ran a "highly personalised, presidential campaign"[31] built around him. Fianna Fáil's campaign was also built around its leader. Haughey helicoptered around the country to lively rallies, which featured not only the leader's addresses but live performances by the Morrisseys of their hit "Charlie's Song". It was to become the party's anthem for the remainder of the decade.

The Labour Party ran an independent campaign, leaving the decision on coalition to a special national conference to be called after the election. It was clear, however, that it favoured government with FitzGerald. The atmosphere of the campaign was almost sulphurous, so intense was the rivalry between Haughey and FitzGerald and the tension surrounding protests and events organised by the National H-Blocks Committee in support of the hunger-strikers.

In the election Fianna Fáil received 45 per cent of the first-preference vote, the same proportion that it had in the first opinion polls; Fine Gael obtained 37 per cent, the Labour Party 10 per cent and others 8 per cent. The result was 78 seats for Fianna Fáil, 65 for Fine Gael, 15 for the Labour Party, 1 for Sinn Féin, and 8 others; these included two H-block prisoners who would not take their seats. FitzGerald was elected Taoiseach as head of a coalition with the Labour Party, with the support of the independent Jim Kemmy. Another independent, Dr John O'Connell, was Ceann Comhairle, and the other three independents abstained. Frank Cluskey, who had lost his seat, was replaced as leader of the Labour Party by Michael O'Leary, who now became Tánaiste.

Haughey was now leader of the opposition, and Fianna Fáil began a short spell out of government.

Chapter 13 ∽

"RISE AND FOLLOW CHARLIE," 1981–7

Fine Gael had promised tax cuts during the 1981 election campaign, but the disastrous fiscal position it and the Labour Party found when they entered office meant that instead they had to introduce a harsh emergency budget in July. The steps to control the spiralling national finances announced by the new Minister for Finance, John Bruton, included an embargo on recruitment to the public service, the introduction of a bank levy, and an increase in value-added tax from 10 to 15 per cent.

Charles Haughey's position had been damaged by the election result. He had come to the leadership as the saviour of Fianna Fáil's fortunes after the debacles in the by-elections and European Parliament elections of 1979, and expectations were high. This meant that the party's failure to win an absolute majority was bound to be a disappointment, although he had managed to shore up its position to the extent of winning seventy-seven Dáil seats. Media commentary about the state in which his Government had left the public finances further undermined his position, and he faced renewed criticism for his stance on the economy, most notably, and surprisingly, from Charlie McCreevy. When McCreevy made his disillusionment plain to Geraldine Kennedy in an interview in the *Sunday Tribune*, Haughey immediately put forward a motion that he be expelled from the parliamentary party; but McCreevy forestalled him by resigning the whip before the question could be debated.

Although Haughey was quick to quell dissent, even among former loyalists, he was slow to reshuffle his front bench, leaving outgoing ministers shadowing their original briefs until the end of the year. The delay can probably be explained by his insecurity about his position. Over these months he held a series of meetings with critics as part of an effort to heal party divisions. This led to a few surprises in the new front bench when it was finally announced in January 1982, the most startling of which was the naming of Martin O'Donoghue as the party's new spokesperson on finance.

Both before and after the reshuffle the front bench struggled with the question of what the party's attitude should be to the FitzGerald Government's measures to tackle the public finances. Haughey had been dismissive of suggestions from economic commentators and the coalition

Government that tough actions needed to be taken. He had attacked John Bruton's emergency budget as both unnecessary and deflationary. Not only O'Donoghue, O'Malley and Colley but also Reynolds and MacSharry were among those urging Haughey to accept the need to get the public finances under control. Within weeks of his new appointment O'Donoghue led for the party in the Dáil debate on Bruton's second budget and accepted that some corrective action was needed. Indeed the appointment of O'Donoghue as finance spokesperson suggested that Haughey was signing up to a more responsible approach, but in his public utterances he continued to confuse the party position.

Bruton's 1982 budget included a proposal to reduce food subsidies and to impose VAT on children's shoes. Among those on whom the Government relied for its slim majority was the Limerick socialist Jim Kemmy, who was appalled at these proposals and was not persuaded by FitzGerald's contention that unless the tax was extended to children's shoes, women with small feet could evade it. Kemmy voted that night against the initial budget motions, as did the Workers' Party deputies, with the result that FitzGerald's first Government became the shortest in the history of the country.

Amid scenes of high drama around Leinster House and Government Buildings, FitzGerald made arrangements to go to Áras an Uachtaráin to ask President Hillery to dissolve the Dáil. The Fianna Fáil front bench decided to call on Hillery to exercise his constitutional power to refuse FitzGerald's request for a dissolution and instead to invite Haughey to explore whether he could form an alternative Government. Haughey issued a statement calling on the President "to consider the situation which has arisen now that the Taoiseach has ceased to retain the support of the majority of Dáil Éireann" and pointing out that Haughey was "available for consultations by the President should he so wish."[1] Several Fianna Fáil ministers also tried unsuccessfully to contact President Hillery by telephone to urge this course.[2] In issuing the statement the Fianna Fáil front-benchers were acting with constitutional propriety, but it has been strongly suggested that they showed a lack of respect for the independence of the President's office in making these persistent efforts to talk to him about the situation. That was certainly how Hillery himself saw it.

It also emerged many years later that when the army officer on duty in Áras an Uachtaráin refused to put Haughey through to the President, Haughey verbally abused him and threatened his career prospects in such strong terms that Hillery immediately wrote to the chief of staff to ensure that the officer would be protected against any interference from Haughey.

These phone calls, and in particular Brian Lenihan's involvement in or recollections about them, were to become the subject of controversy years later during the 1990 presidential election campaign.

Hillery granted the dissolution, and the election was set for 18 February. The Bruton budget and the crisis in the public finances dominated the campaign, and the divisions within the Fianna Fáil front bench became public.

On the night the election was called, and again the following morning, Haughey attacked what he described as the outgoing Government's obsession with the level of foreign borrowing, accusing it of being hypnotised by the debt. He argued that the current budget deficit could be tackled when there was a return to growth. This trivialising of the situation horrified even some of his closest allies in the party, including Reynolds, who joined others in making their views known at an angry front-bench meeting later that day. Haughey was forced to accept the more responsible line now favoured by the majority of his spokespersons.[3] In a radio interview the following weekend O'Donoghue contradicted Haughey's earlier campaign utterances and pointedly avoided answering questions about whether he supported Haughey's leadership. Later in the campaign Haughey announced that Fianna Fáil would accept the current budget deficits and borrowing requirements set out in the coalition budget but would not implement Bruton's harshest proposals.

That budget became Fine Gael's election manifesto, and to some extent also that of the Labour Party. Indeed in his memoirs Garret FitzGerald describes how he experienced "a moment of total exhilaration" when he realised that his Government was going to lose the budget vote. "This was it, we were going into battle on a budget that we could defend with conviction and enthusiasm."[4] Later in the campaign a revised version of the budget was published by Bruton, which bowed to pressure from the Labour Party and abandoned the proposal to tax children's shoes.

Apart from the budget, press coverage of the election campaign focused on the personality and suitability of the two party leaders. In the last week they faced each other in the first televised party leaders' election debate. Haughey got the upper hand in the debate itself; however, reports from Fianna Fáil canvassers suggested that they were meeting—and Fine Gael and the Labour Party were stoking—a " Haughey factor" at the doorsteps.

Abortion emerged as another issue during the campaign. The Pro-Life Amendment Campaign suggested that this was about to be legislated for and secured a commitment from both Haughey and FitzGerald to introduce a referendum that would insert an additional provision in the Constitution. The wording the two leaders agreed would, among other things, "recognise the life of every unborn child from conception."

On polling day there was one last dramatic development when Haughey's election agent and friend, Pat O'Connor, was arrested on suspicion of attempting to vote twice. The moratorium on the broadcast media meant they could not cover the story, but the *Evening Herald* published it on its front page.

On 19 February it became clear as votes were being counted that, although Fianna Fáil would win some additional seats, it had again failed to gain an absolute majority. It was a huge disappointment, especially given the circumstances in which the coalition Government had collapsed.

During the televised coverage of the count, Jim Gibbons, who had just been returned to the seat he had lost the previous June, told reporters in Carlow-Kilkenny and the presenter Brian Farrell on RTE that "the question of the leadership will be raised at the first meeting of the parliamentary party."[5] The outgoing chairperson of the parliamentary party, William Kenneally, who had just lost his seat, told reporters in Waterford that Fianna Fáil would have done better under a more popular leader, and that he too "would not be surprised" if the party leadership became an issue "in the near future." That afternoon the *Evening Herald* hit the streets with the headline "Leadership fight facing Haughey."[6]

The following day the final results came in. Fianna Fáil had pushed up its share of the first-preference vote to 47 per cent and would have 81 deputies in the new Dáil—three short of an absolute majority. That very afternoon several prominent anti-Haughey members of the parliamentary party gathered to plan a further challenge to his leadership. The gathering, which included Des O'Malley, George Colley, Martin O'Donoghue and Séamus Brennan, discussed several alternative strategies. One was that they would put down another motion of no confidence in Haughey which would force him out so that a new leadership election would be required. O'Donoghue favoured sounding out the parliamentary party and, if there was a majority against Haughey, forming a delegation that would include former Haughey loyalists to persuade him to step down. They settled instead, with varying degrees of enthusiasm, on a third option, whereby O'Malley would challenge Haughey at the parliamentary party in the vote on who would be the party nominee for Taoiseach.

In response to the various public and private machinations, Haughey, for whom Brian Lenihan and Ray Burke had also sounded out opinion within the parliamentary party, decided to bring forward the first post-election meeting to 25 February. He hoped to disorient the conspirators and to clarify the situation so that negotiations could begin with the independents. There was intense speculation about whether Haughey could win the vote. Jack Lynch, in one of his rare public comments since retiring from Dáil Éireann, was quoted as saying that he had always regarded O'Malley as one of the most able members of Dáil Éireann and of Fianna Fáil Governments; he was certain that he would be a future leader of the party and a future Taoiseach.[7]

Despite the media support, O'Malley's heave was badly organised and incoherent, in part because those supporting him were divided on how to oust Haughey. Most deputies, even those now lukewarm about him, felt the time was not right and that Haughey, as the incumbent leader and a former Taoiseach, was better positioned to persuade the independents to support Fianna Fáil's return to government.

In the event, O'Malley's challenge dissipated at the parliamentary party meeting. Among the crucial interventions was that of Pádraig Faulkner, now a former Ceann Comhairle and a long-time opponent of Haughey. In his memoirs Faulkner explained his thinking at the time.

> I feared that an attempt to replace Haughey after such a short period in office whether successful or not would destroy the prospects of stability. I still hoped it might not be too late to heal divisions in the

party. I was anxious to help to put a stop to the constant bickering that went on. I wanted to give the party time to settle down ... At the party meeting I said that I was very concerned that the party was split down the middle. I pointed out that many Fianna Fáil deputies looked on one another as enemies, conversations among groups of party deputies often ceased immediately on the approach of another Fianna Fáil deputy—that this was not the Fianna Fáil party I had joined. I proposed that an all out effort had to be made to restore genuine unity and confidence if the party was to have a future. I appealed to Des O'Malley to withdraw his name and I asked Haughey to consult with O'Malley, Colley and Brennan on the formation of a cabinet.[8]

O'Donoghue also stunned deputies on both sides of the divide when he too called for there to be no contest. He had always favoured a broadly based consensus to topple Haughey, and when that failed to emerge he called for party unity.[9] O'Malley withdrew, and Haughey was selected by acclamation as the party nominee for Taoiseach.

The meeting lasted less than an hour, and many journalists waiting around Leinster House for the result were stunned when the outcome was announced. In the days leading up to the meeting Vincent Browne had published in *Magill* a list of thirty deputies who he expected would oppose Haughey; Bruce Arnold in the *Irish Independent* listed thirty-six. At one point the bookies had O'Malley at 2 to 1 to win, with Haughey at only 7 to 4.[10] All of this gave some credence to Haughey's repeated contention that the opposition to him was "media-generated".

Secure as leader, at least for the time being, Haughey set about obtaining the support of the independents for his election as Taoiseach. His principal target was the new deputy for Dublin Central, Tony Gregory. Over the following two weeks Haughey conducted detailed negotiations with Gregory and his team of community activists. He secured his support in return for a list of promises that became known collectively as the Gregory Deal, with a price tag estimated variously between £50 and £175 million.[11] It included a commitment to providing substantial funds for creating employment in the inner city, the acquisition of a 27-acre docks site, 440 new local authority houses in the inner city and 1,600 in the rest of Dublin, free medical cards for all pensioners, and the nationalisation of Clondalkin Paper Mills.

The deal was denounced by Haughey's opponents and by most commentators then and since as a cynical exercise in purchasing individual support, but many of its provisions were of merit. As Joe Lee points out,

what was disgraceful in this case was less the deal than the fact that it needed a deal to win some attention for one of the most deprived areas of the country, an inner city constituency ravaged by poverty and neglect and their concomitants, unemployment, bad housing and a vicious drugs problem.[12]

On 9 March 1982 Haughey was elected Taoiseach for the second time, now at the head of a minority Government. Gregory supported him, as agreed; so too did the three Workers' Party deputies, technically making Gregory's support surplus to requirements and the deal unnecessary. Haughey actually won the vote for Taoiseach by 86 to 79.[13]

In his new Government, Haughey appointed Ray MacSharry Tánaiste and Minister for Finance. George Colley had been offered other ministries but declined, returning instead to the back benches for the first time in two decades. Des O'Malley and Martin O'Donoghue, however, did accept places in the Government, becoming Minister for Trade, Commerce and Tourism and Minister for Education, respectively. Albert Reynolds returned to the Government, this time as Minister for Industry and Energy. Among Haughey's new ministers was the Roscommon deputy Seán Doherty, a former Garda detective, who was appointed Minister for Justice. Ray Burke went to Environment, Gerry Collins to Foreign Affairs, Brian Lenihan to Agriculture, Gene Fitzgerald to Labour and the Public Service and John Wilson to Transport, Posts and Telegraphs.

The intensely personalised nature of the contest between Haughey and FitzGerald seen during this election, the divisions in Fianna Fáil revealed in the aborted heave, the nature of the deal with Tony Gregory and the wafer-thin majority on which he had to rely were far from ideal circumstances for a return to power. Haughey's second Government was to last only nine months and was to prove extremely controversial.

While simultaneously fighting off a challenge to his own leadership and negotiating with Gregory, Haughey had also been busy trying to reduce the Fine Gael numbers in the Dáil by persuading the former European Commissioner Dick Burke TD to return to the EU Commission. Michael O'Kennedy had left the Irish seat there vacant by returning to contest the Dáil election. After first declining because of pressure from his own party, Burke ultimately accepted Haughey's offer on 29 March, thereby occasioning a by-election in Dublin West, which the former Fianna Fáil deputy Eileen Lemass was the clear favourite to win.

A few days later the Argentine military junta invaded the nearby Falkland Islands, a British colony since 1833 but consistently claimed by Argentina. Ireland, as one of the rotating members of the UN Security Council, initially supported British motions for an immediate Argentine withdrawal and the imposition of sanctions.

On 20 April the charge of double-voting against Haughey's election agent, Pat O'Connor, was dismissed at Swords District Court because, although he had sought ballot papers at two polling stations, it could not be proved whether he voted in either of them.

As the crisis over the Falkland Islands developed and the British armada sent to reclaim them reached South American waters, the Haughey Government adopted a more neutral, some said crudely anti-British position. Ireland withdrew from the European Community sanctions and at the United

Nations called for an immediate cessation of hostilities and the retention of the status quo—i.e. Argentine occupation—until a resolution could be negotiated. If this stance was designed to assist Fianna Fáil's efforts in the Dublin West by-election it proved counter-productive. On 25 May the Fine Gael unknown Liam Skelly sensationally defeated Eileen Lemass. Three weeks later the Fianna Fáil deputy for Galway East, John Callanan, died, further weakening the Government's position.

In late June, during the by-election to choose Callanan's successor, the former Fine Gael Minister for Justice Jim Mitchell claimed that when Haughey had become Taoiseach in 1980 he had installed an override facility on the telephone system in Government Buildings that would have enabled him to listen to any calls made through the Leinster House exchange. Haughey denied any knowledge of such a facility, and official and media investigations showed Mitchell's accusation to be groundless.

Meanwhile the new Minister for Finance, Ray MacSharry, together with Haughey and the Government, was struggling to come up with a coherent response to the deteriorating public finances. MacSharry had at first poured scorn on the purveyors of doom and gloom, promising that the new Government would bring "boom and bloom" instead. He introduced his budget on 25 March and it passed with relative ease. It was not enough, however. In July the Government announced a freeze on public-service pay for the remainder of 1982.

Over the summer months MacSharry, who was clearly on a steep learning curve as Minister for Finance, persuaded the Government to write a new national plan that would commit it to phasing out the budget deficit over five years. This plan, which in the light of the Dáil numbers the party knew would soon double as an election manifesto, was worked on over the summer months by a Government sub-committee chaired by Haughey and was published as "The Way Forward" in October.

Over the summer recess the Government was also damaged by a peculiar controversy. On 16 August the Attorney-General, Patrick Connolly, was forced to resign following the arrest in his flat in Dalkey the previous Friday of a murder suspect, Malcolm MacArthur. MacArthur was suspected of killing a nurse, Bridie Gargan, in broad daylight in the Phoenix Park two weeks earlier. He was a friend of a friend of Connolly's, who had innocently let him stay at the flat, not realising he was the subject of a Garda manhunt. The day after the arrest Connolly left the country on a previously arranged holiday, with Haughey's approval, neither of them seeming to appreciate the importance of the event.

In a press conference after Connolly's resignation Haughey inadvertently made a statement about MacArthur's arrest that could be interpreted as prejudging his guilt. An immediate apology was made by the Government Information Service, and the High Court later rejected a contention that contempt was involved. At the same press conference Haughey described this incident as grotesque, unbelievable, bizarre and unprecedented. From this

Conor Cruise O'Brien, then a columnist, coined the acronym GUBU, sub-sequently used to describe various controversies surrounding this Haughey Government.

In the aftermath of these events, and amid enduring criticism about the failure to tackle the budgetary crisis, Charlie McCreevy, on the evening of Friday 1 October, in a surprise move tabled a motion of no confidence in Haughey, and Fianna Fáil was once more convulsed by a nasty internal struggle over the leadership. Haughey again dismissed the challenge as media-driven and yet again mobilised his grass-roots support. He also demanded a commitment of loyalty from all his ministers. Des O'Malley and Martin O'Donoghue felt unable to do this and resigned their ministries.

On 6 October, when the parliamentary party met to consider the motion, Haughey insisted on an open roll-call vote. Twenty-two deputies, who later became known as the "Club of 22", voted no confidence, out of a total of eighty-one. After the meeting there were dramatic and unpleasant scenes outside Leinster House. Crowds of Haughey supporters, many of whom had clearly been drinking, surged forward as McCreevy made his way to his car, jostling him and verbally abusing him. The crowd became even rowdier with Jim Gibbons, who was physically attacked and knocked to the ground. Reports of the event served only to further discredit the Government party. Bertie Ahern, who at the time was briefing the media nearby as chief whip, describes it as "one of the nastiest days I've witnessed in Irish politics."[14]

Years later McCreevy was sanguine about the hostility he faced that night, suggesting that it should be seen in the context of Fianna Fáil's tradition of loyalty.

> What I did in 1982, my outspokenness, was totally unheard of at the time ... [Fianna Fáil] were a closely knit group and that's how it had been for the previous sixty years ... the organisation's members were aghast and appalled at what I had done because that was not in the tradition of the party ... For very genuine reasons, whole lots of well-meaning people would gladly have taken me out and strung me up to the nearest lamppost. Even my own mother had she been alive would have come out against me because she was brought up in the tradition of Fianna Fáil and you just did not do that.[15]

Gibbons could not afford to be as sanguine. He was deeply affected by the night's events, and he suffered a severe heart attack a few weeks later; as a result he was unavailable for Dáil votes for several weeks. On 18 October, Bill Loughnane, the Fianna Fáil TD for Clare, died of a heart attack. Fianna Fáil's Dáil strength was now reduced to 79—four votes short of an absolute majority.

On 20 October the Government unveiled "The Way Forward". Many of the assumptions on which the plan was based were dismissed by economic commentators as unrealistic, but the cuts and commitments contained in it were severe enough to provoke Gregory and the Workers' Party to withdraw their support for the Government. Two weeks later they voted against Haughey in a motion of confidence, and the Government fell.

The economy inevitably dominated a low-key and depressing election campaign. The parties had run out of money and their organisations were worn out. The campaigns ran for the legal minimum of three weeks.

A few weeks before the election was called the Labour Party leader, Michael O'Leary, not only resigned but defected to Fine Gael when his party conference rejected his proposal for a coalition agreement. Dick Spring, the 32-year-old former Irish rugby international, became leader, and the party declared that it was not committed to any coalition arrangement, although it was generally assumed that it favoured going back into government under FitzGerald.

Polling was on 24 November 1982. Fianna Fáil's first-preference vote fell from 47 to 45 per cent. Fine Gael's rose from 37 to 39 per cent. The Labour Party rose only slightly, from 9.1 to 9.4 per cent. Fianna Fáil lost six seats, Fine Gael gained seven and the Labour Party gained one. With Fine Gael on 70 and Labour on 16, the FitzGerald-Spring coalition had 86 of the 166 seats.

Immediately after the election the *Irish Times* published a series of articles reporting that the phones of two journalists, Geraldine Kennedy of the *Sunday Tribune* and Bruce Arnold of the *Irish Independent*, had been tapped. When asked to comment on the articles the new Minister for Justice, Michael Noonan, said he had nothing to say on the matter for the time being. Eight weeks later, however, on 20 January 1983, Noonan announced that investigations since he had taken office had confirmed that the two journalists' phones had indeed been tapped by the Garda Síochána, at the instigation of the previous Minister for Justice, Seán Doherty, unlawfully using a system intended for authorised intercepts. In another dramatic twist Noonan also revealed that Ray MacSharry, then Minister for Agriculture, had been provided the previous October with the loan of Garda recording equipment so that he could secretly tape a conversation with the then Minister for Education, Martin O'Donoghue. He also revealed that the Gardaí had provided MacSharry with a transcript of the tape recording. The two stories caused a sensation, and the Garda Commissioner and an Assistant Commissioner resigned.

Rumours that Haughey had also known about the phone-tapping were widespread, and on the night of 26 January media speculation suggested that he was close to resignation—indeed it was suggested that he had a resignation statement drafted. However, Bertie Ahern, who, as chief whip, was close to events, suggests that Haughey never considered doing this. Ahern had spent that day assessing the mood of the parliamentary party and says that the message he was getting, "and not just from the usual 'Club of 22' suspects," was that it was time for a change. He went out to Kinsealy that evening and told Haughey that if there was a vote that day a majority would vote against him. "They can do what they like," Haughey had replied. "I'm staying." "In that case," Ahern says he told Haughey, "there is only one option. Play for time."[16] Ahern also claims in his autobiography that he told Haughey that if he lost, Michael O'Kennedy had the numbers to be the next leader.[17]

The next morning, 27 January, the *Irish Press* published a detailed account of Haughey's career, which read as a political obituary. The then editor, Tim Pat Coogan, says its publication was due to a production error rather than an editorial one.

> It was arranged that two pages detailing [Haughey's] career would be preset, complete with pictures, and then kept separate to run should news of his departure come at short notice. But somehow the 'keep separate' stipulation did not travel down the line. By a ghastly application of Murphy's law not merely were the two pages prepared in the lull after the country edition, but some 16,000 copies of the city edition appeared with 'Charlie's obituary' included in it.[18]

The exaggerated stories of Haughey's demise greatly assisted his fight back. So too did the fact that Seán Doherty not only took responsibility for initiating the tapping of the journalists' phones but said that it had never been discussed with Haughey. A decade later, in 1992, Doherty was to reveal that he had personally provided transcripts of some of the recordings of the journalists' conversations to Haughey shortly after they were recorded. This revelation would be the straw that broke the back of Haughey's leadership. At this time, however, Doherty stayed silent.

At a parliamentary party meeting MacSharry again defended his taping of the conversation with O'Donoghue, reminding colleagues that this had occurred the previous October, within days of McCreevy's failed motion of no confidence in Haughey, and rumours had been circulating within the party concerning his financial circumstances. O'Donoghue, who was in the middle of a campaign for the Seanad, having lost his seat in the November election, was allowed to attend the parliamentary party meeting. He had no particular recollection of the conversation, and, unlike MacSharry, did not have access to a transcript. A special committee was set up to investigate the events. Several deputies spoke openly at the meeting against Haughey's continued leadership, but Haughey persuaded them he needed time to reflect.

In the following days a race to succeed Haughey began, even though he had not in fact resigned. A number of the putative contenders were encouraged by the Haughey camp in the hope that confusion about a successor would shore up his position.

On Monday 30 January the Donegal Fianna Fáil deputy Clement Coughlan was killed in a car accident. At the parliamentary party meeting the next day a tribute was paid by Haughey, and then after a minute's silence the meeting was adjourned by the chairperson, Jim Tunney, as a mark of respect. Because it was done so abruptly, many of the deputies did not realise the meeting was over until the leader, the chairperson and the chief whip had left the room. The move, appropriate in the circumstances, had the effect of buying Haughey the necessary time.

In the following days forty-one deputies signed a motion seeking a special meeting, and it was arranged for the following Monday. Ben Briscoe, formerly a close supporter of Haughey, put down a motion of no confidence in him. On that Sunday's "This Week" radio programme Haughey told the interviewer, Gerald Barry, that he had

> the overwhelming support of the vast majority of our members and supporters throughout the country. They want me to stay on, they want me to fight on, and it is for them that I am staying on. And, in addition, I am staying on because I don't believe any small rump in the party, combined with friends in the media and other people outside the party, should be in a position to dictate who is the leader of Fianna Fáil.[19]

The appeal to the grass roots worked. Head office was flooded with messages of support for the leader, some orchestrated but many spontaneous.[20] A group of members even organised a picket in support of Haughey outside the party offices in Mount Street for the evening of 31 January. Their placards reflected the arguments being advanced for why Haughey should not be forced out: "Fianna Fáil is not for sale," "Don't forget the crown of thorns," "Don't capitulate to the media." Addressing the protesters and the assembled reporters, the Dublin South deputy Niall Andrews—who, unlike his brother, was an ardent Haughey loyalist—claimed that Haughey was being executed in a manner akin to the men of 1916.

At the parliamentary party meeting the report from the sub-committee was the first item on the agenda. So fearful were they of releasing copies that might be leaked to the media that Ahern read out the committee's conclusions in full. It was no more than a summary of evidence given to the committee in interviews with the main protagonists, and it concluded that Haughey knew nothing about the phone-tapping. In a minority insertion in the report David Andrews held that, although "Mr Haughey while in office was not aware of the telephone tapping of the journalists it seems to me, however, that on the principle of ultimate responsibility, he should have been aware."[21]

The committee's outline conclusion placed more blame on O'Donoghue than on either Doherty or MacSharry. Haughey then announced that he proposed to move a motion to expel Doherty and MacSharry from the parliamentary party. It was 8 p.m. before they came to debate Briscoe's motion. At the previous meeting, on the 26th, Briscoe had told Haughey: "I love you, Charlie." "I love you too, Ben," had been the answer. David Andrews was heard to groan at the back of the room, "I hope the papers don't hear about this!" but the exchange was published in the following day's *Irish Press*.

At this meeting Haughey survived the secret ballot on Briscoe's motion, by 40 votes to 33. The simple fact of his survival gave his position a massive boost. For the remaining five years of his leadership Haughey faced no serious challenge to his position. Most of his opponents were simply beaten and battle-weary and settled down to the reality of serving under Haughey.

The stress of the repeated convulsions over the leadership had taken a heavy toll on the party's capacity to govern during those months it was in power, on its capacity to campaign, and on its standing with the electorate. It also exerted a toll on the health of many of the parliamentarians. Bertie Ahern, whose job included counting the party numbers for Dáil votes, has reported:

> A few months after Bill Loughnane had passed away, Clem Coughlan, who drove backwards and forwards to his Donegal constituency every week, was killed in a car crash on his way to the Dáil. Liam Hyland suffered a heart attack in the Lobby of Leinster House when he heard the news. Paddy Power collapsed after a Fianna Fáil parliamentary party meeting. Jim Fitzsimmons got an ulcer. Paddy Lalor needed a pacemaker fitted. Within a year George Colley would die of a heart attack aged 57, Ber Cowen, Brian's father died of a heart attack at just fifty-one. You would convince nobody that these were not in some way related to the pressure of political life in the 1980s. People were exhausted. Tempers were short. The stakes were high. That made it a dangerous lifestyle, and hardly any wonder when colleagues paid the ultimate price.[22]

The party settled down to a pattern of opposition in which as much energy was spent on consolidating Haughey's position as on seeking to redevelop the party or to undermine the Government. Among those centrally involved in these tasks were Frank Wall and P. J. Mara. Wall, a former official of the party at the European Parliament and then an adviser to Ray MacSharry, had been hand-picked by Haughey to become general secretary in succession to Séamus Brennan in 1982. In 1982 Mara became party press secretary and began to repair Haughey's reputation with the media, and to develop his own reputation for colourful phrases. His efforts to suggest that a line had been drawn under the leadership issues would produce two of his most memorable turns of phrase, once telling political correspondents that it was now "*Uno duce, una voce*" in Fianna Fáil and on another occasion that "there will be no more nibbling at my leader's bum."

Among the more difficult issues to raise its head for the FitzGerald Government had been its commitment to holding a referendum for a "pro-life" constitutional amendment, and to doing so with wording proposed by the Pro-Life Amendment Campaign and also adopted by Fianna Fáil. In government, FitzGerald, on the advice of his Attorney-General, Peter Sutherland, decided that there were substantial legal difficulties with the proposed wording. He put forward an alternative wording, but several conservative Fine Gael deputies rejected it, and the Dáil voted for the original form of words.

The Government did not campaign for the proposal. Fianna Fáil did, though the bulk of the campaign effort for a Yes vote was carried by the Pro-Life Amendment Campaign itself and by the Catholic Church. The referendum was held on 7 October 1983, and the amendment was passed with a Yes vote of 67 per cent. The wording was thereby inserted in the Constitution, where it sat primed as a political time-bomb for several subsequent Governments.

FitzGerald also struggled to persuade some in the Fine Gael parliamentary party to support the Government's commitment to removing the constitutional prohibition on divorce. He and Dick Spring did manage, however, to get legislation through the Dáil, and the referendum was held on 26 June 1986. Fianna Fáil adopted an official policy of neutrality during the campaign, but in reality many in the party were active in the No campaign. The resounding defeat of the proposal, with 63 per cent voting No, suggests that almost all Fianna Fáil supporters also opposed it in the ballot box. However, the Government's lack of legislative preparation on the tax, social welfare and inheritance implications of the divorce proposal was probably the primary reason for its defeat.

Haughey's strengthened position did not mean that he was free of internal criticism. Once again Northern Ireland policy was the issue on which divisions centred. In 1983 the New Ireland Forum had been established to agree a common position between the nationalist parties north and south, excluding Sinn Féin, on progress in the North. After many months of hearings and deliberations the three main parties in the Republic and the SDLP agreed a report, published in May 1984, that proposed a united Ireland as the preferred option but went on to advance a federal approach and joint authority as other options. At the press conference at which the report was published, however, Haughey, to the visible annoyance of the other parties, announced that for Fianna Fáil a united Ireland was the only option that could bring peace to Ireland.

There was criticism, particularly from Senator Eoin Ryan, that Haughey had announced this position without consulting the parliamentary party, but a subsequent meeting gave almost unanimous support to Haughey's stance. Des O'Malley claimed that debate in the party on Northern policy had been stifled. Haughey now used the opportunity to move against him. A motion was put removing the parliamentary whip from O'Malley; it was carried by 56 votes to 16.

In June 1984 Fianna Fáil and Fine Gael both made gains in the European Parliament elections, Fianna Fáil increasing the number of its seats from 5 to 8 while Fine Gael won 6. On the same day the Fianna Fáil candidate, Brian Cowen, won a by-election in Laois-Offaly occasioned by the death of his father.

Later that year the Minister for Health, Barry Desmond of the Labour Party, proposed a new Family Planning Bill that provided for the sale of "non-medical contraceptives", i.e. condoms, without a prescription, in pharmacies, family planning clinics and surgeries. The bill was opposed by Fianna Fáil in the hope of defeating the Government, as a number of conservative Fine Gael TDs had stated that they would also oppose it.

The crucial debate took place in February 1985. O'Malley made a passionate contribution to the debate, which ranged wider than contraception and warned of the effect that legislation on this social issue might have on partition. The speech has been described by Richard Aldous as O'Malley's apologia, a statement of his basic political creed and how it differed from Haughey's. O'Malley concluded his Dáil speech by saying:

> The politics of this would be very easy. The politics would be to be one of the lads—the safest way in Ireland. But I do not believe that the interest of this state, of our constitution and of this Republic would be served by putting politics before conscience in regard to this. There is a choice of a kind that can only be answered by saying that I stand by the Republic, and accordingly I will not oppose this bill.[23]

Having spoken for the bill, O'Malley then, curiously, abstained. It was passed by 83 votes to 80.

Haughey then proposed that O'Malley be expelled from Fianna Fáil. The party's constitution provided for this to be done by the Ard-Chomhairle for "conduct unbecoming," a provision last used for the expulsion of Neil Blaney. At a special meeting of the Ard-Chomhairle on 26 February 1985 the motion to expel O'Malley was carried on a roll-call vote by 73 votes to 9.

Although the proposals in the report of the New Ireland Forum were dismissed by Margaret Thatcher in her "out . . . out . . . out" speech in November 1984, Garret FitzGerald and his Minister for Foreign Affairs, Peter Barry, persisted throughout 1985 in seeking a new departure in Northern Ireland policy. Their negotiations with the Thatcher government culminated in the Anglo-Irish Agreement signed at Hillsborough, Co. Down, on 15 November. For the first time it gave the Irish Government a guaranteed role in Northern Ireland and provided, among other things, for the establishment of a joint British-Irish secretariat in Belfast. The announcement of the agreement was met with inevitable outrage among unionists but obtained widespread international endorsement and overwhelming popular approval in the Republic. Haughey, however, denounced it in trenchant terms. In Dáil contributions on the issue he said:

> We are deeply concerned that by signing this agreement the Irish Government are acting in a manner contrary to the Constitution of Ireland by fully accepting British sovereignty over a part of the national territory and by purporting to give legitimacy to the British administration in Ireland.

Haughey also despatched the party's foreign affairs spokesperson, Brian Lenihan, to Washington to denounce the agreement to Irish-American politicians. Described at the time and often since as an act of national treachery, this Fianna Fáil response to the Anglo-Irish Agreement, even when viewed through contemporary eyes, defies constitutional, political and even party-political understanding. The action may have been motivated purely by short-term considerations and was typical of a pattern of instinctive opposition to every policy announced by the FitzGerald Government. It may in part be explained by Haughey's jealousy, because FitzGerald had succeeded with Thatcher where he himself had promised much but failed. He may also have simply been re-emphasising his republican credentials, something he was always anxious to do in order to shore up his position with the grass roots.

Politically it made no sense. An MRBI opinion poll on 15 November showed public approval for the Anglo-Irish Agreement at 59 per cent; by the following February that figure had risen to 69 per cent. In both opinion polls those surveyed were also asked whether they approved of Haughey's stance. 56 per cent said No in November and 63 per cent in February.[24]

Even though willing to fight with him on economic policy, it seems that none of those on Haughey's front bench felt able to stand up to him on Northern policy. It is also striking how little those who were, or at least should have been, involved in that front-bench decision have said about it subsequently. In his memoirs Albert Reynolds mentions the matter in passing, admitting that he "personally regretted" the decision to oppose the Anglo-Irish Agreement but saying nothing about how it came to be made. Bertie Ahern does not mention the agreement at all in his autobiography. Pádraig Faulkner, who was by then a back-bencher, recalls Ahern, who was the guest speaker at a function in Faulkner's constituency the night the agreement was signed, being distracted and having to leave the table to take or make various phone calls to Dublin, where, presumably, discussions on the party's position were continuing. Faulkner tells of his shock when Ahern finally told him that the party was going to oppose it. Faulkner later played a small part in toning down Haughey's opposition.

Brian Lenihan's biographer, James Downey, maintains that Lenihan had advised Haughey not to take a stand against the agreement, though he went to Washington to argue against it. He claims that Lenihan made no real effort to change the Irish-American leaders' minds.[25]

Another central figure in shaping Haughey's view on Northern policy was Martin Mansergh, an official in the Department of Foreign Affairs who had been seconded to Haughey's department when he was Taoiseach and then left the civil service to head Fianna Fáil research in opposition. Mansergh appears to have been instrumental in giving intellectual support to the constitutional basis relied upon by Haughey in his opposition to the agreement. They both appear to have taken the view that the agreement constituted a legal recognition of Northern Ireland and therefore was incompatible with articles 2 and 3 of the Constitution of Ireland. Later, in 1990, the unionist brothers Chris and Michael McGimpsey launched a legal challenge in Dublin based on a similar suggestion, only to have it roundly rejected by the Supreme Court.[26] Kevin Rafter describes his actions at this time as "the biggest blemish on

Mansergh's record in Northern Ireland policy."[27] Mansergh was to get the opportunity to make up for this in his later work on Northern Ireland for subsequent Taoisigh.

Apart from this republican Fianna Fáil stance, the majority of opposition to the agreement came from the unionist side. In the South this was reflected in the decision of Senator Mary Robinson to resign from the Labour Party, because she said the agreement did not take unionist opinion into account. The agreement was, however, warmly welcomed by the former Fianna Fáil leader Jack Lynch and by the now independent deputy Des O'Malley.

It was also supported by Mary Harney, an O'Malley ally on the Fianna Fáil back benches, who was expelled from the parliamentary party after she voted for it in the Dáil. In the months after O'Malley's expulsion, and even more intensely in the weeks after her own expulsion, Harney was among those strongly encouraging O'Malley to set up a new party. Others involved were the former chairperson of Fine Gael in Dublin South-East, Michael McDowell, the former treasurer of Fianna Fáil in Haughey's Dublin North-Central constituency, Paul Mackay, and the former Labour Party Tánaiste Michael O'Leary. Séamus Brennan was also among those later revealed to have been privately involved in these explorations. His involvement included organising an opinion poll on the prospects for a new party.

The new party, the Progressive Democrats, was launched at a press conference on 21 December 1985. The event was chaired by McDowell and included also O'Malley as leader and the Fine Gael deputy Michael Keating, who had defected to become deputy leader of the new party.

The response within Fianna Fáil to the establishment of the Progressive Democrats was to see it as a breakaway by an O'Malley rump. Early in the new year, however, things took a more dramatic turn. The Progressive Democrats placed advertisements in the national press seeking donations and members. More than a thousand people attended the party's first public meeting, held in Sutton, Co. Dublin. Crowds flocked to more public meetings in the constituencies of its original deputies and to large recruitment meetings in universities. Large sections of Fianna Fáil in O'Malley's Limerick base also defected.

Concerns then began to concentrate on the Cork South-Central deputy Pearse Wyse, who was rumoured to be about to join the new party before its first rally in Cork. Bobby Molloy was among those who agreed to talk to Wyse, at Haughey's request, to persuade him not to leave. All entreaties were unsuccessful, and on 20 January, Wyse's defection was announced at the Cork rally.

The next rally was scheduled for Salthill, Galway, three days later. Molloy had left Dublin at lunchtime that day to return to Galway but stopped half way to phone his secretary in Leinster House. He told her to take a letter out of the filing cabinet and bring it over to Haughey. The letter was notice that he was resigning from the party. That night Molloy was unveiled at the Progressive Democrats' Salthill rally as the party's newest recruit.

The Molloy move rocked Fianna Fáil, which now began to panic about whether its party was breaking up. It gave credence to rumours that other prominent figures, including Joe Walsh, Charlie McCreevy, David Andrews and Séamus Brennan, were about to jump. In the event all four stayed, after intense agonising on their part and trauma for Fianna Fáil. Molloy was to be the last defector from the parliamentary party. However, others with strong family traditions in the party left and would subsequently be Dáil candidates for the PDS, most notably Anne Colley, daughter of George Colley, in Dublin South and Martin Gibbons, son of Jim Gibbons, in Carlow-Kilkenny.

The first *Irish Times* MRBI opinion poll gave the new party 25 per cent support, putting it ahead of Fine Gael, at 23 per cent. Fianna Fáil had slipped down to 42 per cent, and the Labour Party had a mere 4 per cent. Although its leadership and much of its membership consisted of breakaway Fianna Fáil members, the figures from the opinion poll suggest that the new party quickly drew disproportionate support from Fine Gael, and indeed it can be suggested that Fianna Fáil was the long-term beneficiary of the split.

While the emergence of the Progressive Democrats was sucking up much of the media oxygen, the Fine Gael-Labour Government was struggling to maintain its majority and its cohesion. In June 1986 the FitzGerald Government technically became a minority Government. Over the following months the Labour Party and Fine Gael ministers could not agree on the annual estimates process, and they came to a realisation that they could not continue much longer. The 24th Dáil never reconvened after the 1986 Christmas recess.

Chapter 14 ∾

CROSSING THE COALITION RUBICON, 1987–9

After four years of implementing cuts and battling a hugely difficult economic situation, Garret FitzGerald's Government was weary and on its last legs. The end came in January 1987 when the Labour ministers could not agree with the measures for that year's budget and left the Government.

An election was called for 17 February. Given the high levels of unemployment and emigration, the punitive tax increases that FitzGerald's Government had felt compelled to introduce and the state of the public finances, the general economic circumstances seemed to favour Haughey in his pursuit of the elusive absolute majority.

The first opinion poll of the campaign had Fianna Fáil on course for a decisive victory, with 52 per cent. FitzGerald's tactic was to try to peg Fianna Fáil back, and he consistently challenged Fianna Fáil to set out its policies and to spell out exactly how it would manage the gap in the public finances, insisting on hard figures. The Fianna Fáil manifesto was vague and the party refused to make any commitments. Its main electoral strategy was to try to capitalise on the anger with the Government. One very effective poster featured a frail elderly woman with the slogan "Must the old and the sick suffer more vicious cuts?"[1]

FitzGerald sought to convince the electorate that Fianna Fáil's manifesto was a confidence trick, describing it as "a grotesque mishmash of economic buzzwords, blind faith, pulled punches and invented employment targets."[2] Meanwhile the president of the Irish Farmers' Association, Joe Rea, also attempted to place the focus on Fianna Fáil and what policies it would pursue as an alternative Government. He described Fianna Fáil's economic strategy as "something like spot the ball and hope to win."[3]

While the opposition and the media pursued Fianna Fáil—attempting to get the party to explain what cuts it would have to implement—Fianna Fáil spokespersons stuck rigidly to their strategy of appealing to different segments of the electorate but not getting into an overall fiscal framework. In one RTE interview Brian Lenihan stonewalled, repeatedly refusing to get into the specifics of where cuts in expenditure might fall, by insisting that he would not do so "because we're not playing games."

As Fianna Fáil and Fine Gael fought it out, the Progressive Democrats were mounting a strong challenge in their first election. Many of their candidates and canvassers came from a Fianna Fáil background, but as the campaign progressed it became clear that Des O'Malley's party was picking up votes from both main parties.

The PDS campaigned on the slogans "Breaking the mould" and "Dessie can do it." O'Malley was critical of both of the alternatives for Taoiseach. He memorably described the Haughey-FitzGerald leaders' debate on television as "a nil-all draw". O'Malley argued that "the mood of the country is for someone to take over who has never been Taoiseach before." This brought a strong riposte from Haughey, who rejected O'Malley's attempt to repackage himself as a fresh political face and pointed the finger of blame at him for the calamitous state of the national finances. "It would be no harm to point out that Deputy Desmond O'Malley was one of the prime architects of the infamous 1977 election manifesto which has caused so much opprobrium these days."[4]

The outcome of the election was that Fianna Fáil won 81 seats, six more than in November 1982. Fine Gael suffered badly, winning 50 seats, twenty less than in the previous election. The Labour Party lost four seats, to return to the 25th Dáil with 12. The big story of the count was that the Progressive Democrats, and not Fianna Fáil, were the main beneficiaries of the collapse in support for FitzGerald's Government. They won 14 seats, which went beyond their best projections and was a triumph for a small party in its first election.

Fianna Fáil was three seats short of an absolute majority and the mood in the party was one of grave disappointment. This was the fourth time the party had failed to secure an outright victory under Haughey's leadership, and mutterings about this began once again. The disappointment was compounded by the fact that it was the existence of the PDS that had soured the election for them. As T. Ryle Dwyer points out,

> Charlie was again blamed for the failure, this time with real justification. After all he was responsible for driving Des O'Malley out of Fianna Fáil, and he was thus indirectly responsible for the formation of the Progressive Democrats, who won 14 seats. Four of those were former Fianna Fáil Deputies and at least another half dozen were former members of the Party. There could be little doubt that the advent of the Progressive Democrats had denied Fianna Fáil an overall majority. As Charlie sought to form a Government, the media again concluded he was fighting for political survival. If he failed to cobble together a Government, it was generally believed that he would be toppled as Party leader.[5]

Haughey's survival instincts now kicked in. He announced that he believed he could form a Government and made it clear that he would do so without doing deals with anyone else. His chances were also boosted because the PDS did not hold the balance of power and he could still make up the numbers with the support of independents. Stephen Collins writes:

> Many in the [Progressive Democrats] had harboured the ambition of holding the balance of power so that they could force Fianna Fáil to ditch Haughey as the price of their support. They narrowly failed and though Haughey was deeply disappointed he did not show it. Instead, he acted as if he had won an overall majority and as if there was no question but that he would succeed FitzGerald as Taoiseach.[6]

Haughey was confident of the support of the Independent Fianna Fáil deputy Neil Blaney, and he inched even closer to the office of Taoiseach when the independent deputy for Tipperary South, Seán Treacy, acquiesced in Fianna Fáil's offer of the position of Ceann Comhairle. Tony Gregory now held the balance of power, but this time Haughey, reading the public mood, insisted there would be no Gregory Deal part 2. Gregory's response was to tell the press that he would therefore not support Haughey in the vote.

At this point some of Haughey's opponents both inside and outside the party began to float the idea that the only way to prevent another election would be to see whether an alternative candidate from within Fianna Fáil could secure the numbers in the Dáil. Haughey and his supporters moved quickly to batten down the hatches. Bertie Ahern recalls:

> A few days before the 25th Dáil met, Ray Burke went on the radio to warn off anyone who was thinking of using the situation to oust Haughey. "Let nobody outside Fianna Fáil have any feeling that since they've left the party they can influence our leadership," he said. "They tried that when they were on the inside and they're not going to do it from the outside."[7]

To copperfasten the warning, on the day the Dáil reconvened Haughey told his front bench to prepare for an election in the event of the Dáil not electing him Taoiseach, even though it would not have been his prerogative to seek a dissolution. All this became irrelevant when Tony Gregory, anxious to avoid another election, decided to abstain on Haughey's nomination. The vote was now tied, 82 to 82; but the new Ceann Comhairle gave his casting vote to the Fianna Fáil nominee. Charles Haughey was elected Taoiseach for the third time.

In offering his congratulations, the outgoing Taoiseach, Garret FitzGerald, told Haughey that if the new Government took corrective action to restore the public finances Fine Gael would "not oppose such measures or legislative action required to implement the necessary budgetary provisions."[8] Although FitzGerald resigned as leader of Fine Gael shortly thereafter, this stance would later be adopted by his successor, Alan Dukes, and was formalised as the Tallaght strategy.

The composition of the new Fianna Fáil Government contained few surprises. Haughey appointed Brian Lenihan as his Tánaiste and Minister for Foreign Affairs. Other notable appointments were Pádraig Flynn to Environment, Ray Burke to Energy and Communications, Mary O'Rourke to Education, Albert Reynolds to Industry and Commerce and Bertie Ahern to Labour. The one appointment that did cause some surprise turned out to be Haughey's most inspired. Ray MacSharry had been elected to the European Parliament in 1984, and that was where he saw his future in politics. He did run in the 1987 general election, helping Fianna Fáil to secure three out of four seats in Sligo-Leitrim. However, after the election he returned to Strasbourg to continue his duties as a member of the European Parliament, although now with a dual mandate. Haughey persuaded him to take up the position of Minister for Finance, a post he had previously held very briefly in 1982.

The situation that confronted MacSharry and the country was a bleak one. He has recalled the depressing scenario that confronted him on his first day in Merrion Street.

At the time, the efforts of the outgoing coalition to stop the debt/GNP ratio rising had met with little success. The national debt had soared to £22 billion during Fine Gael and Labour's four-year term in office. When the coalition finally broke up in January 1987, it left the public finances in a far worse state than it had found them. The debt mountain I faced had nearly doubled in size since my earlier brief tenure as Minister for Finance in 1982. The budgetary arithmetic was chilling. By 1986, one in every four pounds of current spending represented the interest owing on past debt. But since those payments had to be financed from tax-revenue, one-third of all taxes were required simply to pay those annual debt charges. In other words, some four out of every five pounds raised in income tax were needed to pay the interest from the outstanding national debt. Since servicing the debt had a prior claim on current spending, it meant higher interest payments also required higher taxes to finance them. The result was less money available to pay for day-to-day services, in areas like health, education and welfare.[9]

MacSharry recognised that the country's level of borrowing was unsustainable and the only way to begin to rectify this was to cut spending. Such an approach would severely affect public services, but MacSharry felt there was no other option. He was backed strongly by Haughey, who on 17 May 1987 wrote to all Government departments asking them to give priority to "identifying the specific programmes and expenditures for further cuts now if we want to get results for the remainder of 1987 and 1988."[10]

Fianna Fáil, whose manifesto had been vague to the point of vacuous on cuts, now, in government, embraced the cuts agenda as the only way to solve the crisis in the national finances. In his budget speech on 31 March 1987, only three weeks after taking office, MacSharry told the Dáil:

The message I have to deliver is unpalatable but it is critical to the revival of our economic prospects. We cannot be content to announce our intention to curtail spending, while at the same time deferring action. We have to act now.[11]

It was an extremely severe budget. In it MacSharry set the current deficit at a rate even lower than Fine Gael had proposed. Tax bands were not indexed against inflation. Public-service pay was frozen and the recruitment ban was maintained. Furthermore, the Government introduced a new 35 per cent withholding tax on professional fees. In short, what Fianna Fáil had done was to adopt Fine Gael's policy of fiscal rectitude and then add some more. Michael Noonan, the new Fine Gael spokesperson on finance, pointed out Fianna Fáil's recent conversion. "I have great pleasure today in welcoming Fianna Fáil's acceptance of the Fine Gael analysis of the problem and of the targets which we have set down. This is grand larceny of our policy as put before the electorate."[12]

Fine Gael supported MacSharry's budget, and indeed was left little choice, given that it was very much along the lines of the draft budget it had produced in January 1987. This, however, only mildly alleviated the concerns in Fianna Fáil about having to deal with such a disastrous economic situation while in a minority Government. With the first budget of the new Government completed, MacSharry recalled:

The only question was how the minority government might fare later, when the second and further instalments of tougher austerity measures had to be delivered. Would Fine Gael continue to underwrite the government—where it mattered most—in the division lobbies in the Dáil. The government knew, and all the ministers readily accepted, that the only way to proceed was to turn our parliamentary weakness into a political strength. This meant refusing to do deals with any party, or with independents, in return for their voting support. In that sense the fate of the government rested in the hands of the opposition. For my part, I felt a bit like a high-wire artist performing without the reassurance of a safety net underneath.[13]

Fianna Fáil's fears that its harsh policy on the economy might come unstuck because of the parliamentary arithmetic were eased dramatically and unexpectedly on 2 September 1987 by Alan Dukes. At the Tallaght Chamber of Commerce he committed his party to ensuring that the Government would not be "tripped up" on economic issues, provided "the central thrust of policy" was going "in the right direction" and would resolutely tackle the deficit in the public finances and the mounting public debt.[14]

Fianna Fáil had not been informed in advance that this commitment would be made, and MacSharry recalls learning of the speech with "a mixture of bewilderment and delight."[15] Dukes had been Minister for Finance for most of Garret FitzGerald's Government and was intimately acquainted with how serious the crisis in the public finances was. There is no doubt that in running with the Tallaght strategy he was motivated by the interests of the country and the need for drastic action if Ireland was to be put back on an even financial keel, but there was also an element of political calculation. Fine Gael needed to renew itself after a difficult period in Government and a poor election. Dukes also needed time to play himself in as the new leader. He did not need an election, and in a sense the Tallaght strategy bought him time. Ray MacSharry's assessment in 2000 was:

> The Tallaght Strategy was designed to serve the party and the country. It combined altruism with a degree of political self-interest, and, in fairness to Alan Dukes, perhaps more of the former than the latter. For Fine Gael it served two purposes: the strategy bought time for the party to reorganise itself, while it gave the government no excuse to call a snap general election. And by underwriting, conditionally, the government's economic approach, it also served the country. On balance, Fine Gael put the national interest in restoring financial stability ahead of any short-term political party advantage. In doing so, no doubt there was an element of political calculation: that Fianna Fáil, in embracing fiscal rectitude and taking the tough measures needed to clear up the economic mess, would make itself highly unpopular.[16]

Following Dukes's Tallaght speech there was a significant amount of weekly co-operation between the Fianna Fáil whip, Vincent Brady, and his Fine Gael counterpart, Fergus O'Brien, on the organising of Dáil business. MacSharry also kept the Fine Gael finance spokespersons, Michael Noonan and John Boland, in the know about what he was doing and the measures he was taking. This meant that the main opposition party was not only informed of the thrust of Government policy but could discreetly make a contribution to it. This helped to maintain Fine Gael's support for a bipartisan approach to economic policy. It also allowed the Fianna Fáil minority Government to get on with the job of taking necessary but unpopular budgetary decisions, free from the fear of provoking an election.

MacSharry took to the job of cutting public expenditure with relish, so much so that he became known as "Mac the Knife". His determination to get the public finances under control was also aided by the emergence of social partnership. MacSharry, Haughey and Bertie Ahern, the new Minister for Labour, were the main architects in bringing about this new consensus-driven approach, which saw the Government, trade unions and employers' groups work together on issues such as pay and the economic model the country would follow to move beyond the crisis.

Ahern, who had solid union contacts, came into his own during this period. He hit the ground running as Minister for Labour, and he was energetic and popular with the public. Strikes and fractured labour relations were a major drain on the economy, but Ahern quickly got to grips with the issue. He had a number of notable early successes in reforming the industrial relations architecture and in negotiating settlements in some difficult disputes, including those at the ESB, CIE, RTE and Irish Steel.[17]

The Programme for National Recovery was published in October 1987 and it brought in its train wage restraint and industrial peace. The impact of the advent of partnership, combined with MacSharry's dogged approach to rectifying the public finances, quickly began to pay dividends. Bertie Ahern observed:

> The results were almost immediate. The national debt peaked that year and the new partnership agreement, with strong trade union support, undoubtedly facilitated the difficult political and financial decisions made to put the economy back on track. Public expenditure and borrowing were cut dramatically. Confidence in our economy began to return and a rapid fall in interest rates followed. A sign of its success was that initially zero growth was forecast for 1987. In fact, almost 5 per cent was achieved.[18]

With a chink of light beginning to appear at the end of the tunnel, the Fianna Fáil Government continued with the programme of cuts and financial retrenchment that was slowly but surely returning the public finances to good health throughout 1988. At the end of 1988, with the roadmap now firmly fixed, MacSharry departed for the European Commission, being succeeded in Finance by Albert Reynolds. Haughey meanwhile was showing what a capable and determined politician he could be, and in this period he pushed through the plan for the International Financial Services Centre in the Custom House Docks area of Dublin, which was to bring significant benefits to the national economy very quickly.

As it became clear that progress was being made on the economy, Haughey's public standing was never higher. Fianna Fáil also did extremely well in opinion polls: by the spring of 1989 its standing was over 50 per cent.

On 26 April 1989 Haughey returned from a visit to Japan to discover that the Government was likely to be defeated on a private members' vote on a Labour Party motion on compensation for haemophiliacs. The jetlagged Taoiseach caused a sensation when he stated that if the Government was defeated he was strongly considering seeking a dissolution of the Dáil.

With the Tallaght strategy in operation, private members' motions were the main parliamentary opportunity for the opposition parties to inflict embarrassment on the Government. As a minority Government, Fianna Fáil had lost a number of private members' motions, but these did not constitute a no-confidence vote, so there was no danger to the Government's survival. It is still not clear what prompted Haughey to suddenly raise the stakes on the motion concerning haemophiliacs. One school of thought is that he had made his election threat in a fit of pique after returning from a successful trip abroad to discover that the Government was facing an embarrassing Dáil defeat. Another viewpoint is that Haughey wanted to take advantage of the opinion polls, which were running in his and Fianna Fáil's favour, and that he wished to cash in electorally in the hope of finally securing an absolute majority.

Most of the Government were against an election, but Haughey, egged on by Ray Burke and Pádraig Flynn, decided to go to the country. Revelations in more recent times from the Flood Tribunal (later the Mahon Tribunal) and the Moriarty Tribunal show that Flynn, Burke and Haughey collected substantial amounts of money in donations during that election campaign and that some of these appear to have been used for their own ends.

Albert Reynolds made a determined effort to talk Haughey out of what he thought was a disastrous move for Fianna Fáil's prospects. As a former whip, Bertie Ahern believed a minority Government had to expect to lose a few votes along the way. He too tried to persuade Haughey not to go to the country. Ahern gives an illuminating account of the crisis meeting of the Government convened after its defeat on the private member's motion.

> Albert Reynolds . . . was against an early election. He knew the economy was improving and thought we should wait. Others were more bullish. Padraig Flynn was his usual loud self in demanding that the party take advantage of the good poll numbers. Ray Burke argued the same. That seemed short sighted to me. Everyone knows that you can't rely on opinion polls once a campaign starts, and I knew there was no appetite in the country for an election. That was certainly the case on the doorstep in Dublin Central. If people are not up for an election, they usually punish the ones who've brought it about. That was why later on I always took my governments to their full term. Do what you're elected to do, then ask the people to put you back in. I think that in the end Haughey just found it a personal affront to his dignity that he had to rely on the goodwill of the opposition to keep him Taoiseach. In 1989, he had read the polls, thought he had a chance for the elusive overall majority, and went for it.[19]

The election was eventually called for 15 June, the same date as the European Parliament elections. Fianna Fáil's high level of support began to melt away as the campaign progressed. Some commentators argued that Haughey had forced an unnecessary election so he could escape from the grip of the opposition, who were making him pursue responsible policies. The opposition also relentlessly attacked the shortcomings in the health service. The manner in which Fianna Fáil dealt with this criticism caused some public disquiet. Damian Corless noted:

> Fianna Fáil's initial response to this line of attack was one of flat denial. Health Minister Rory O'Hanlon informed the nation that: "Waiting lists are a very unreliable measure of the availability of hospital services."

His party colleague, Dr John O'Connell pointed out that just because patients found themselves on trolleys didn't mean that there was a shortage of beds. A trolley, he patiently explained, was simply a bed with wheels.[20]

The anger that this response caused was intensified when Haughey changed tack and acknowledged that there were indeed real problems in the health service but that before the election campaign he "personally wasn't aware of the full extent of the problems and difficulties and hardships it was causing."[21] This was an extraordinary admission and was milked to the full by the opposition, who insisted that Fianna Fáil was either out of touch or just didn't care about the concerns of ordinary people.

The election results were the source of further disquiet in Fianna Fáil, which lost four seats and was now down to 77. Fine Gael gained five and returned with 55, while the Labour Party gained three to take 15. The PDs had a bad election and lost more than half their seats, coming back to the 26th Dáil with only 6 deputies. Enmity against the PDs was still strong within Fianna Fáil; for many in the party the only consolation from a disappointing election was the bloody nose the electorate had inflicted on the Progressive Democrats. Ray Burke, commenting on the implosion of the PDs, said, "It couldn't happen to a nicer bunch of people."[22]

Fianna Fáil's problems were bigger than the PDs. Haughey was seven seats short of a majority, but as soon as the count concluded he was quickly out of the traps to announce that he believed he would be able to form a Government. He said he intended to consult other party leaders and met Alan Dukes. However, any notion he may have had that the Tallaght strategy could be resumed was shot out of the water by Dukes. He made it clear that Fianna Fáil's decision to force an election meant that all bets were off, telling Haughey that if Fianna Fáil wanted Fine Gael's support in forming a Government his party would have to get seven of the fifteen ministries, and the office of Taoiseach would have to be rotated between the two leaders.

Haughey's options were narrowing, particularly as the Labour Party ruled itself out of the equation. The Progressive Democrats were the only alternative if he was to avoid another election. If the Ceann Comhairle were returned to his position, Fianna Fáil's seventy-seven seats plus the six seats of the PDs would provide a working majority. This, however, seemed a remote possibility, as some of the PD deputies were extremely hostile to Haughey. One of them, Pearse Wyse, who had previously been a Fianna Fáil TD, said after the election, as speculation began to mount about the permutations for forming a government, "In no circumstances could I bring myself to vote for [Haughey] as Taoiseach."[23]

When Haughey met the PDs, in the persons of O'Malley and their newly elected member of the European Parliament, Pat Cox, he spoke to them on the grounds that they would support a minority Fianna Fáil Government from outside, along the lines of the Tallaght strategy. O'Malley, who now had to try to salvage his party from the wreckage of the election, made it clear that the only way they would support Fianna Fáil would be as part of a formal coalition arrangement.

Both O'Malley and Haughey knew that vehement opposition to coalitions had been a core value for Fianna Fáil from the party's earliest days. According to T. Ryle Dwyer, "when Haughey said he could 'never sell' that to Fianna Fáil, O'Malley smiled. He said that Haughey should not 'make a mistake in underestimating his ability to sell anything to his party.'"[24]

The Dáil reconvened on 29 June, and for the first time in its history it failed to elect a Taoiseach. Charles Haughey, Alan Dukes, Dick Spring and Des O'Malley were all nominated, but no-one could command a majority. A procedural side show developed when Haughey refused to resign as Taoiseach, which, though legally correct, was politically questionable. In the end he did resign but continued with his Government responsibilities as "acting Taoiseach". The Dáil then adjourned for four days, with no solution in sight to the constitutional impasse.

In Fianna Fáil the mood was strongly against any form of coalition. The Ard-Chomhairle had voted unanimously against a coalition arrangement, and on 2 July Haughey went on national radio, again ruling out the possibility of Fianna Fáil entering a coalition Government. The following day the Dáil again assembled, but it was no closer to electing a Taoiseach and adjourned until 6 July. In the Fianna Fáil parliamentary party speculation that another election would be called was intense. However, others in the party were coming to the view that if Haughey stepped down a new leader, who would not attract the same level of hostility from the other parties, might be able to put together a minority Government.

Haughey could smell which way the wind was blowing, and on 4 July he moved to break the deadlock. He phoned O'Malley that morning and arranged to meet him that evening while in the meantime convening a Government meeting, where he asked his ministers for their views on coalition with the PDS. They were stunned. According to Stephen Collins,

> a clear majority of the cabinet, led by Reynolds, was strongly opposed to a coalition arrangement of any kind. Padraig Flynn, Michael O'Kenendy, Rory O'Hanlon, John Wilson, Michael Noonan and Brendan Daly all spoke against a deal. Flynn was the most vehement and shocked everybody by accusing Haughey of opting for coalition out of a personal pursuit of power. Two key ministers, Gerry Collins and Ray Burke, took the opposite view and in coded language spoke in favour of a deal with O'Malley, even if the price was coalition. As ever, Brian Lenihan supported Haughey and said they would be able to sell coalition to the organisation, if that was the ultimate decision.[25]

The meeting broke up without taking any decision; but Flynn, who had been one of the main cheerleaders for an election, now took to the radio to draw the line against any coalition agreement. "The National Executive [Ard-Chomhairle], the Parliamentary Party and the grass roots have indicated [that] this is a core value which we must preserve."[26]

At about the same time Haughey met the PDs and agreed to form a coalition subject to a programme for government being agreed. When Pat Cox suggested that Flynn's remarks showed substantial opposition in Fianna Fáil to any coalition arrangement, Haughey brazenly replied: "It's all right, I just haven't told them yet."[27]

The next day Haughey sent out Bertie Ahern, his most popular minister, to sell the deal to Fianna Fáil. Ahern recalled:

> On the 5th of July, acting on Charlie's instructions, I did a ground-breaking interview on the News at One, saying for the first time that we were prepared to consider a coalition. The negotiations began the following day in the Berkeley Court Hotel. "Let us never negotiate out of fear," I said on the way in, quoting Kennedy, "but let us never fear to negotiate."[28]

Ahern and Reynolds were the Fianna Fáil negotiators; their PD counterparts were Cox and Bobby Molloy. The talks were difficult and tense, with Molloy taking a hard line and angering the normally unflappable Ahern. The mood was not helped on the Fianna Fáil side by the fact that Haughey, in his determination to get a deal, was prepared to pull the rug from under his own negotiators.

> Our annoyance [with the PD negotiators] was nothing in comparison to the anger we felt at the treatment by our party leader. I had got on very well with Albert during the negotiations. We felt we were making real progress in getting a good deal for Fianna Fáil. That's why we were so aggrieved when it became obvious that Haughey had gone behind our backs in dealing directly with the PD leader, Des O'Malley. Talking to O'Malley was Haughey's prerogative as leader. Failing to tell us was not. Albert and I only learnt that Haughey was prepared to concede two cabinet places to the PDs when we heard it on the radio. Both of us were as annoyed as hell.[29]

Haughey had proceeded to furtively implement what he was and was not prepared to concede to the PDs. He was mindful of the resentment in his party towards the PDs and the bubbling anger at the fact that a core value was being jettisoned. He managed this fraught situation ably as he worked towards a deal that would keep him in the Taoiseach's office. His first action was to hold individual meetings with ministers to ascertain their views on coalition. This had the effect of damping down any dissent, as individuals were not sure what their colleagues had told Haughey. Of course all those interviewed by Haughey in this way would also have been conscious that Haughey might soon be appointing a new Government, perhaps with fewer Fianna Fáil ministers; they were less likely therefore to disagree with whatever decisions they felt Haughey was coming to.

Pádraig Flynn was one minister who confronted Haughey head on. He told him that he should step down as leader of Fianna Fáil and let someone else try to form a Government, rather than entering into a coalition agreement with the Progressive Democrats.[30]

After consulting his ministers, Haughey told the parliamentary party that his negotiators had not concluded their talks, and he avoided mention of how many Government places the PDS would get. According to Stephen Collins,

> the anti-coalitionists, Noel Dempsey, Geoghegan-Quinn and Noel Treacy from Galway East, spoke against any deal. Geoghegan-Quinn said that she had sold a number of U-turns to the organisation on extradition, the Anglo-Irish Agreement, the Single European Act, and spending cutbacks, but she drew the line at selling this one. She refused to accept that what the Taoiseach was doing was in the national interest.[31]

Those who raised their voices against a coalition deal were, however, a small minority. Most back-bench TDS were now afraid of the prospect of another election, which they wanted to avoid at all costs. "They're more enlightened than some of my cabinet," Haughey remarked. "They're only a crowd of gobshites."[32]

On 12 July, Haughey met O'Malley and the PD negotiators. He unilaterally agreed to appoint O'Malley and Molloy to the Government, that Mary Harney would be appointed a minister of state, and that the PDS would get three of the Taoiseach's eleven Seanad nominees.

The Rubicon had been crossed. Fianna Fáil, for the first time in its history, was definitely going to participate in a coalition Government. With the deal done, Haughey shook hands with his old nemesis O'Malley and remarked: "Nobody but myself could have done it."[33]

Fianna Fáil's entry into coalition caused great distress and ill feeling in the party. Ahern and Reynolds were unhappy with the manner in which Haughey had manoeuvred behind their backs; indeed Ahern, who was a stalwart Haughey supporter, had an angry row with him over his subsequently implying that the negotiators—and not he himself—were responsible for the PDS' two Government seats. In his memoirs Ahern says that he eventually got over this, but Reynolds never did.

Certainly Reynolds's relationship with Haughey was never the same. Reynolds had been one of the original cadre of back-benchers working for Haughey before Lynch stepped down. He had backed Haughey strongly through the heaves in the early 1980s, but now there was a distinct cooling in relations. Pádraig Flynn, who was one of Haughey's inner circle, was also vehemently opposed to coalition and was seriously disillusioned with him.

Máire Geoghegan-Quinn, then a minister of state, was said to have considered resigning at one point, such was her opposition to seeing her constituency colleague, Bobby Molloy, being appointed to the Government. She had held the line for Fianna Fáil in Galway West for many years; now she was furious at being leap-frogged in the ministerial pecking order by Molloy, who had defected from the party.

Throughout Fianna Fáil there was a sullen resentment that the party was now dependent on the Progressive Democrats. There was anger that people who had opposed majority decisions of the party in the past and then left it were now in influential positions in the Government. There was also a real unease about the ditching of a core value. Under de Valera, Lemass and Lynch a coalition had been unthinkable, yet now Fianna Fáil members were being asked to unlearn years of opposition to coalition. For some senior members of the party it was just too much to swallow. Albert Reynolds said: "It was the moment I lost all faith and made up my mind—enough of Charlie Haughey!"[34]

Haughey's coalition agreement with the PDs had kept him in office after his disastrous decision to call an election. The price he paid was the further division of Fianna Fáil and increased strains on his leadership. From this point on, Haughey would be fighting a protracted internal war to remain as leader of Fianna Fáil.

| NINE LIVES, 1989–92

A s part of the Fianna Fáil-PD coalition arrangement, Charles Haughey appointed Des O'Malley as Minister for Industry and Commerce and Bobby Molloy as Minister for Energy. Séamus Brennan, who had been the party's director of elections in the recent campaign and who Haughey had used during the period after the election as a conduit to the PDS, was promoted to the Government as Minister for Tourism and Transport. The three casualties were Brendan Daly, who as Minister for the Marine had become the focus of a lot of criticism over a controversial policy on rod licences, Michael J. Noonan, and Michael Smith. Smith would soon become a vocal critic of Haughey.

The Tánaiste, Brian Lenihan, who had been abroad for most of the 1989 election campaign, having a liver transplant in the United States, was moved from the Department of Foreign Affairs to the less demanding post of Minister for Defence.

Gerry Collins had supported Haughey's case for coalition and was rewarded with Foreign Affairs, while Ray Burke, another supporter and north Dublin neighbour, not only got Collins's old job in Justice but also retained responsibility for Communications, which he had held in the previous Government. Haughey left the two most outspoken critics of the deal with the PDS, Reynolds and Flynn, in their portfolios of Finance and Environment, respectively. Bertie Ahern remained in Labour and John Wilson moved to the Department of the Marine.

The tensions in Fianna Fáil that had been simmering since the coalition deal were again evident when Haughey appointed his ministers of state. Jackie Fahey, the Waterford TD who had helped Haughey to his leadership victory in 1979, resigned from the parliamentary party when he did not receive an appointment. He felt he needed and deserved promotion because his constituency rival, Martin Cullen, was likely to get one of the three Seanad places Haughey had promised to the Progressive Democrats. Cullen got the Seanad appointment and Fahey remained outside the parliamentary party for a number of months.

In the Seanad there was further tension between the coalition partners when the Progressive Democrats refused to support Seán Doherty, the Fianna Fáil nominee, as Cathaoirleach. Doherty was a controversial figure, and the three PD senators, who had all been appointed by the Taoiseach, voted for the Fine Gael nominee. Because of Fianna Fáil's strength, this did not prevent Doherty's election, but the refusal was interpreted by many in the party as showing bad faith.

The earlier contest to determine who would be the Fianna Fáil nominee for Cathaoirleach was of more significance for the party in the long run. The other candidate had been Des Hanafin, a long-time Haughey opponent. Haughey, however, stood back from the contest, which ended in a tie that was settled only by Doherty's name being drawn from a hat. Though Doherty was victorious he was angry that Haughey had not done anything to help him. In time that would make him a very dangerous opponent.

Meanwhile Haughey and O'Malley had established a businesslike, if never warm, relationship and were determined to make the Government work. Haughey treated O'Malley with respect and made sure he had a real role. Brian Lenihan said in an interview: "I am nominally Tánaiste in this Government, but the reality of the situation is that O'Malley is the real Tánaiste. He is the actual number two in the Government."[1]

At the Government level the only blip in the Fianna Fáil-PD relationship came at the beginning of 1990. Fianna Fáil was reluctant to reappoint Michael Mills as Ombudsman, but the PDs insisted and Haughey eventually agreed. Though the parliamentary party were not happy, the wider Fianna Fáil membership seemed to move on quickly from the debate about coalition. T. Ryle Dwyer writes:

> This was the first time in government that Haughey had been openly forced to give in to the Progressive Democrats, but it would not be the last. Each time the Progressive Democrats compelled him to make a concession, this rankled with members of the Fianna Fáil parliamentary party, even though the whole idea of abandoning the party's "core values" in joining a coalition had not weighed very heavily with Fianna Fáil supporters. A public-opinion poll found that 85 per cent of those who had voted for Fianna Fáil approved of the compromise on coalition. Haughey had clearly overcome that hurdle and again seemed firmly in control as party leader.[2]

Haughey's star was in the ascendant, and Ireland's presidency of the European Council gave him the opportunity to display his political talents on the international stage. As events transpired, the Irish presidency came at a time of crucial importance for the future of Europe. The fall of the Berlin Wall and the subsequent collapse of the Soviet bloc put Haughey at the hinge of world events. He revelled in the challenge and performed magnificently. Thatcher was deeply wary of German reunification and had even asked Gorbachev to do all he could to prevent it.[3] Haughey, however, used Ireland's presidency to support German unity, taking the opportunity of developments in Europe to beat the anti-partition drum so beloved of so many of his

Fianna Fáil activists. In December 1989, as Ireland prepared to formally take over the EC presidency, Haughey told the Dáil what Ireland's approach would be: "Coming as we do from a country which is also divided, many of us would have sympathy with any wish of the people of the two German states for unification."

In the early months of the Irish presidency Haughey and his Minister for Foreign Affairs, Gerry Collins, worked closely with Helmut Kohl to create a groundswell of support for a speedy reunification of Germany within the EC. In April 1990 Haughey, as president of the EC, convened a summit meeting of the member-states in Dublin Castle. This was of huge significance, as it secured agreement that German unification would be a positive factor in the development of the European Union. At its conclusion an ecstatic Chancellor Kohl made a point of praising the diplomacy of Collins and the Taoiseach and the role they had played in opening the door to "the dream of all Germans."[4]

The Irish presidency was seen as a triumph for Haughey, and Fianna Fáil was cock-a-hoop about its leader's success. An excited Brian Lenihan, with characteristic hyperbole, said that "Charlie would lead Fianna Fáil into a united Ireland, a united Europe, a united world and then into the next century."[5]

Not long after the EC summit the soccer World Cup championship began. This was an extraordinary period in the life of the country, with a carnival atmosphere surrounding each of Ireland's games. Jack Charlton's team rose to the occasion, reaching the quarter-final and losing only narrowly at that stage. Haughey and a number of Fianna Fáil ministers attended the crucial game against Italy in Rome. Bertie Ahern recalled:

> At the end of the game, I watched from the stands as Charlie took to the field to acknowledge the Irish supporters, who had been great ambassadors for our country throughout that World Cup. He got a rousing reception.[6]

President Hillery had quietly been refused permission by the Government to travel to the game. As Hillery's official biography put it, the Taoiseach was not prepared to "relinquish his starring role as the spectator-in-chief" and risk being overshadowed by the President.[7] Ironically, as Haughey basked in the supporters' cheers, with his public standing at a record high and the country enjoying a sport-induced feel-good factor, the election to succeed President Hillery was about to cause turmoil within Fianna Fáil.

There had not been a presidential election since 1973, when the Fianna Fáil nominee, Erskine Childers, was the successful candidate. In the period before Ireland's presidency of the EC there had been speculation that Haughey might retire as Taoiseach after he completed his European duties and be a candidate for the Áras. Haughey was quick to pour cold water on this story. At the Cairde Fáil dinner in December 1989 he appeared to give Lenihan, who was eager to do the job, his seal of approval.

Haughey seemed to encourage the rumours of Lenihan's interest in the office at an annual Fianna Fáil dinner. "He will still be one of us, whatever high office he is called to during the next decade," the Taoiseach said, to tremendous applause. Lenihan further encouraged the speculation by declaring publicly, "I would be honoured, as any Irishman would be honoured, to run for the Presidency."[8]

By the end of the summer of 1990, however, Haughey seemed to have had second thoughts. There had already been rumours that Fianna Fáil emissaries had been making approaches to Fine Gael about an agreed candidate, with T. K. Whitaker being one of the names mentioned. Dick Spring, however, scuttled the idea of an agreed candidate. He was determined that there would be an election after a seventeen-year gap, and the Labour Party duly nominated Mary Robinson, a former Labour Party and later independent senator.

John Wilson, Minister for the Marine, then joined the race, seeking the Fianna Fáil nomination. Some of Lenihan's supporters speculated that Haughey had covertly encouraged Wilson's candidacy. Given the Dáil arithmetic, Haughey was certainly concerned that the Government's term would be radically shortened should Lenihan win the contest and if Fianna Fáil were to lose the resultant by-election in Dublin West. The memory of a recent by-election there when, following the appointment of Dick Burke to the European Commission, Eileen Lemass had been rebuffed by the electorate, was still fresh. Wilson's Cavan-Monaghan constituency was much safer territory for Fianna Fáil if the party had to fight a by-election.

Lenihan's candidacy was boosted by the fact that he was extremely popular in the party, and he had declared a long time before Wilson. He had momentum, but this was tested when Albert Reynolds, who was increasingly asserting himself in the parliamentary party, considered giving public support to Wilson. Bertie Ahern, who was close to Lenihan, persuaded Reynolds to remain silent, and in September 1990 Lenihan easily secured the Fianna Fáil nomination, by 51 votes to 19. The selection was done at a parliamentary party meeting convened for the purpose and was approved the same night at an Ard-Chomhairle meeting. The latter event was an emotional gathering, with a series of delegates rising to pay tribute to Lenihan and his work for the party and saying how much he would be missed now that he could no longer play a role in party affairs. It was an indication of how confident Fianna Fáil was of victory.

The Fine Gael candidate was another Dublin West TD, Austin Currie, better known as a former civil rights leader and politician in Northern Ireland. He was a reluctant candidate, and although Mary Robinson, who was supported by both the Labour Party and the Workers' Party, had been running an energetic campaign for months, Lenihan was considered an easy winner. He had more than twice the support of Robinson, his nearest rival; and as the campaign went on, opinion polls suggested that if Lenihan did not win on the first count he was so far ahead that he would easily win on transfers.[9]

But suddenly Lenihan's campaign collapsed. On the television programme "Questions and Answers" on 22 October 1990 he was challenged by Garret FitzGerald and a Fine Gael activist in the audience to say whether, following the collapse of the Government in January 1982, he had telephoned President Hillery in an attempt to persuade the President not to dissolve the Dáil. The accusation was categorically denied by Lenihan. "That never happened. I want to assure you that never happened," he said.[10]

The problem for Fianna Fáil was that Lenihan had clearly forgotten that in May he had told a UCD research student and Fine Gael activist, Jim Duffy, in a taped interview that he had phoned President Hillery on the night in question. "I got through to him," Lenihan had said. With hindsight, he said the whole thing was a mistake, because Hillery was not the type of man who would break new ground. "But, of course," he added, "Charlie was gung-ho."[11] Events rapidly spiralled out of control for the Fianna Fáil campaign when Duffy made his tape available to the *Irish Times*. On 25 October the *Times*, which was now sitting on an exclusive story, bizarrely decided to hold a press conference to share it with other media organisations.

The Fianna Fáil campaign was rattled. Lenihan rushed to RTE to defend himself without having heard the entire tape. Ahern, Lenihan's director of elections, recalled:

> It was a disaster. We had walked right into it. Brian got hold of Mara on the phone. "I want to do an interview now," he apparently told him. "All right," Mara said, "but you've only got one shot at this. Remember, you're talking to the Irish people, so look them straight in the eye and just tell them what happened." Brian would take that advice literally.[12]

Lenihan's interview on that evening's six o'clock television news was a disaster. T. Ryle Dwyer has given a damning assessment of it.

> Rather than candidly admit that he had no recollection of the interview, he tried to bluff his way out by looking straight into the camera. "My mature recollection at this stage is that I did not ring President Hillery. I want to put my reputation on the line in that respect," he said. The interviewer, Seán Duignan, realised that Lenihan could not have it both ways. Either he wasn't telling the truth now, or else he didn't tell the truth to the student . . . "They are all going to come after you demanding that you pull out of the race," Duignan suggested . . . "I will not pull out of the race. I am not going to do so on the basis of a remark made to a university student, to whom I was doing a very great service in providing background for the material he was making on the Presidency." It was a pathetic performance, made all the worse by Lenihan's ridiculous efforts to project sincerity by looking straight into the camera and using the phrase "mature recollection" four different times. Either he was lying now, or else he had spun a cock and bull story

to the student. If the latter was true, it was certainly ludicrous to describe the interview as "a very great service".[13]

As far as most of the public were concerned, Lenihan had been caught in a lie; by continuing to insist on his innocence he was perceived to be insulting the intelligence of the electorate. Bertie Ahern explains the dilemma that the Fianna Fáil campaign now faced.

> The problem for Brian was that he wasn't sure in his own mind. He was talking about two events—the phone calls and the Duffy interview— neither of which he recalled. Interviews with Duignan were hard enough at the best of times. Brian was defending what he thought was the correct position but still he could not be sure. In fact, he had no idea. Around this time I got a phone call from a medical friend in the Mater. "Bertie, would you not just look at the dates for that student's interview," he implored me. "Look at the dates." That made sense. Brian had been very sick in the Mater just beforehand when it looked like his transplanted liver was rejecting. He must have been completely out of it, heavily drugged up. But that was as much a problem as it was a solution. How the hell do you go out and say, "Sorry, my candidate was so out of it on his medication that he can't remember a thing."[14]

The whole controversy was a tragedy for Brian Lenihan, a decent and sincere politician. In his book *For the Record*, published in 1991, Lenihan confirmed that at the time of the Duffy interview he had indeed been taking anti-rejection tablets, which can cause memory loss. But in the middle of an election he was given no quarter from his political opponents.

In the Dáil the morning after Lenihan's television interview Jim Mitchell said: "Brian Lenihan should be hauled in here and hung, drawn and quartered."[15] Fine Gael then put down a motion of no confidence in the Government. That evening things went from bad to worse for Fianna Fáil when O'Malley stated that the Progressive Democrats could not continue in government if Lenihan remained a minister. For the PDs it was now an issue of standards in government.

Haughey was placed in an invidious position. Publicly and in the Dáil he strongly defended Lenihan and, turning defence into attack, accused Garret FitzGerald of lying on "Questions and Answers".[16] Haughey's anger reflected his lack of options. He could either sacrifice a loyal and decent colleague and save the Government or he could back Lenihan and face a general election.

Haughey held a meeting of his ministers but did not invite Lenihan or his sister, Mary O'Rourke, who was Minister for Education. The outcome was a consensus that Lenihan should be prevailed upon to resign, to prevent a general election. Haughey told Ahern to get Lenihan to come to Kinsealy so they could discuss the situation. Ahern has given a fly-on-the-wall account of this dramatic meeting.

Charlie took Brian into his office to talk. He asked me to join them. I was really uncomfortable. I would rather have been anywhere else than in that room. These two men had been friends and allies for decades. They knew each other's strengths and weaknesses to a fault. Even now the banter between them was easy. But nothing could disguise the tension. The strain was apparent on both of them. And no wonder. Charlie needed Brian to resign from the government in order to avoid a general election. It was obvious that Brian thought he had done nothing wrong and didn't want to go. Even if he had made those phone calls to the President—a fact he was unclear about—the tape suggested he had done so at Haughey's insistence. Brian certainly wasn't going to take the fall for Charlie in the middle of the campaign. None of this was actually said. Charlie did not ask Brian to resign. He only wanted him to "reflect on the situation." Brian promised to do that. Stalemate. I hardly said a word throughout the entire meeting. Apparently there was another meeting later that day in Government Buildings when Charlie took the gloves off and presented Brian with a draft resignation statement.[17]

Though in private Haughey was pushing Lenihan to resign, publicly he told journalists at Dublin Airport, as he awaited the arrival of Queen Beatrix of the Netherlands on a state visit, that the issue of resignation was "a matter for my old friend" and that he "would not exert pressure on him in that regard."[18]

Albert Reynolds and Mary O'Rourke were urging Lenihan not to resign. Reynolds had wanted John Wilson to be the Fianna Fáil candidate, but the main focus of his ire was the coalition of Haughey and the PDS, with whom he had become increasingly disenchanted. He therefore encouraged Lenihan to stand firm. This was Lenihan's gut political instinct too. He believed that his resignation would be "tantamount to an admission that I had done something wrong as Tánaiste and Minister for Defence which rendered me unfit to serve as a member of the cabinet."[19] If this were true, Lenihan argued, it would hardly be credible for him to say he was fit to serve as President. Haughey's counter-argument was that people would respect Lenihan for standing down in the national interest. Haughey also suggested that Lenihan's resignation would generate sympathy for his campaign.

At this point Haughey was apparently expecting the Government to fall, because he did not believe he could weather the storm within the party if he sacked Lenihan.[20] But then there was a crucial event that was to refocus minds in the parliamentary party. T. Ryle Dwyer reports:

Then came word of a poll to be published in the *Irish Independent* the next day. The survey found that Lenihan was trailing very badly, with just 31 per cent support against 51 per cent for Mary Robinson. With those kind of figures, it was obvious that fighting a General Election so that Lenihan could retain his job would be extremely risky, and there is nothing more likely to concentrate the minds of politicians than the possibility of losing their seats.[21]

P. J. Mara and Charlie McCreevy urged Haughey to sack Lenihan.[22] The issue went to a meeting of the parliamentary party only hours before the confidence motion was to be taken. The atmosphere was incredibly tense, with everyone in attendance aware that if Lenihan had not resigned from the Government before the Dáil vote on the motion the Progressive Democrats would bring down the Government.

Lenihan did not attend the meeting, but his constituency colleague Liam Lawlor read a letter from him. In it Lenihan confirmed that he would not resign and emphasised his personal integrity and the loyalty he had always shown to his party. Lenihan was not without support at the meeting, and he later wrote:

> After this statement was read a number of deputies spoke, among them Seán Power, Síle de Valera, Noel Dempsey and M. J. Nolan, all indicating that if the choice was to be between sacrificing Brian Lenihan and facing a general election, they were in favour of going to the polls. Seán Power from Kildare put it bluntly when he put it to the Taoiseach that if it were Brian Lenihan's head they were looking for today, what would happen in six months' time when they looked for the Taoiseach's head on a plate. Others who apparently did not favour capitulation to the PDS' demands included Ned O'Keeffe, John Browne, Dick Roche, Séamus Cullimore and Joe Jacob.[23]

According to Lenihan there were a number of other deputies, including Charlie McCreevy, who were telling the meeting that "a Taoiseach must do what a Taoiseach must do." Lenihan said that none of these TDS "explicitly spelt out what they meant and perhaps they didn't want to either."[24] Lenihan was a respected and well-liked figure in Fianna Fáil, and it is clear that none of his colleagues were comfortable in calling for him to be sacked, but it was obvious to the meeting that he must either resign or be dismissed. If anyone had doubts about what the outcome of a general election would be, these were dispelled by Ahern with news of more opinion polls.

> Bertie Ahern induced even more gloom when he outlined the prospects facing the party in both the presidential election and in a possible general election. He told the TDS that the party's private polls put Mary Robinson at 45 per cent of the vote with Brian Lenihan trailing behind on about 39 per cent . . . He predicted that an election caused by the current circumstances would see a big slump in party support and another hung Dáil where nobody would be able to put a government together.[25]

Haughey told the meeting that a cold decision would have to be made, and Jim Tunney, chairperson of the parliamentary party, drew it to a close, saying it should now be left to the Taoiseach to do what was necessary to avoid an election. Nobody demurred.

Afterwards Haughey and Lenihan spoke on the phone. Lenihan's account of this call is as follows:

> It was just before six o'clock in the evening with one hour to go in the confidence debate. When he asked me to directly resign, I replied "No."
>
> "It would have helped your campaign, you know," Mr. Haughey said from Leinster House.
>
> "We'll agree to differ on that," I replied.
>
> He then explained he would be exercising his constitutional prerogative to dismiss me. The telephone conversation lasted a little over a minute.[26]

The Government would now survive, but it would do so by throwing one of Fianna Fáil's favourite sons overboard. Lenihan, in typical literary style, described his arrival in the Dáil bar after his dismissal was announced as "almost as if I were Banquo's ghost."[27]

The Dáil debate was acrimonious. For Dick Spring, Lenihan was a sideshow and the main target was Haughey. Spring's speech, dripping with indignation, caused fury on the Fianna Fáil benches.

> Brian Lenihan is liked and admired on all sides of this house on a personal basis, but he cannot be regarded as being immune from the need for high political standards simply because he is a nice man . . . This debate is not about Brian Lenihan, when it is all boiled down. This debate, essentially is about the evil spirit that controls one political party in this Republic, and it is about the way in which that spirit has begun to corrupt the entire political system in our country. This is a debate about greed for office, about disregard for truth and about contempt for political standards. It is a debate about the way in which a once-great party has been brought to its knees by the grasping acquisitiveness of its leader. It is ultimately a debate about the cancer that is eating away at our body politic—and the virus which has caused that cancer, An Taoiseach, Charles J. Haughey.
>
> There is an ethos underlying Fianna Fáil politics now. It is that ethos that forced Des O'Malley and others out of Fianna Fáil. It is not the ethos of Seán Lemass, Jack Lynch or George Colley. It is, instead, the ethos so clearly illustrated on the Brian Lenihan "Late Late Show" when the audience was invited to chuckle at stories of how Brian dealt with "a sharp little bitch", who happened to be a nun, or of how gardaí were threatened with disciplinary action for trying to carry out their jobs . . .
>
> This last week would not have happened in the days of Seán Lemass or of Jack Lynch. It would not have happened if there had been a George Colley or any person of stature and honour left on the Fianna

Fáil benches. How can anyone conceive of all this happening in the days of the founder of Fianna Fáil and the author of our Constitution, Éamon de Valera? But they have all gone, and the party is now dedicated to the greed and unprincipled behaviour of its present leader, who is bent on creating a party entirely in his own image. When the world watched Ceaușescu and Honecker fall, we knew it was because people could no longer tolerate tyranny, but how much longer will the members of Fianna Fáil tolerate the internal tyranny that rules their party with an iron hand and that has brought it to a point where it is an object of shame and revulsion for so many?[28]

In Fianna Fáil, emotions were running high. Lenihan's sacking was a painful experience for many of his colleagues. Stephen Collins observed from the political correspondents' gallery that many Fianna Fáil TDs walked through the voting lobbies with tears in their eyes, but their pragmatism ensured that they still voted confidence in Haughey.[29]

Fianna Fáil TDs were furious with the Progressive Democrats for forcing Lenihan's dismissal. Reynolds recalled that he was "soured" by "Haughey's treatment of Brian when things did not go according to plan."[30] Many other TDs who had acquiesced in Lenihan's sacking were now making it clear that they were not happy. Their stance seemed to be that they were in favour of the execution but appalled by the executioner. Collins again observed:

After the vote, Haughey, his face like a mask, sat stonily on his seat, many of his colleagues avoiding contact with him. Afterwards he asked Lenihan to meet him and the two old friends had an emotional get-together for a few minutes.[31]

Some of the pent-up anger spilled over when Lenihan's son, Conor, at the time a radio reporter, ran into Des O'Malley in the precincts of Leinster House. He asked O'Malley, "Are you happy now, Des, you got your pound of flesh?"[32]

While there was much emotion and anger in the corridors of Leinster House, the calmest man of all appeared to be Brian Lenihan. An admiring Bertie Ahern wrote:

The night Haughey announced Brian's dismissal to the House was very emotional. Mary O'Rourke was still agitated, shooing people away who wanted to offer their commiserations. Her face was like thunder as she went through the Tá lobby to vote for the government on the confidence motion. Brian on the other hand was calm and dignified. He was deeply hurt by what had happened, but he had been in politics long enough to know that there's nothing to be gained by throwing a wobbly. I think he was glad it was settled. For the first time in days, he seemed focused on the election. Immediately afterwards, he gave an accomplished press conference in Kildare House. When it was over, he pulled me to one side and said, "You can't win every day, but make sure we win the big one." Even in adversity, he was ever the statesman.[33]

Lenihan's resignation was predictably used by the press as a means to exert further pressure on Haughey, who was accused of disloyalty and betrayal. But what was more perturbing for many Haughey loyalists was that these same sentiments were being expressed within the party as well. T. Ryle Dwyer, who is often critical of Haughey, argues that this was unfair.

> Charlie was castigated for abandoning his old friend, but in this instance he really had little choice. He made mistakes in the affair, but his biggest mistakes were not that he did not give Brian enough support, but that he overstepped the bounds of propriety in the way in which he supported him—both by his attack on Garret FitzGerald and his statement to the press at Dublin airport. Lenihan had put his own personal considerations before the Government and the Party. It was he who got into the mess. He really had only himself to blame, but he tried to blame a whole range of people from Charlie, to FitzGerald, to Duffy and the *Irish Times*.[34]

In the public mind, however, Lenihan was now a victim, and there was an outpouring of sympathy for him. Ahern, who was on the campaign trail with him, believed this was translating into votes and that there was still "a good chance we might win."[35] The first opinion poll published after Lenihan's sacking showed that he had cut Robinson's lead of 21 per cent to 5 per cent.[36] If this trend continued, Lenihan had a real chance of snatching victory from the jaws of defeat. The sacking certainly provoked an emotional surge for Lenihan within Fianna Fáil. The crowds that gathered at the various points on his tour became much larger than they had been before the "Duffy tapes controversy" and indeed were dangerous at times.

Fianna Fáil now threw everything in its armoury at Robinson. Full-page advertisements were taken out that asked, "Is the Left right for the Park?" Haughey also pounded out this theme on the final weekend to a rally of about a thousand supporters in the National Boxing Stadium in Dublin. Haughey—who, significantly, was booed by a small number of Fianna Fáil supporters—maintained that Robinson would not be able to escape from her backers and that the allegedly Marxist Workers' Party would have an influence in the Áras if she was elected.[37]

In the end, however, Lenihan's come-back was spectacularly derailed by a combination of Pádraig Flynn and Michael McDowell. Flynn erred badly when, during the final weekend of canvassing, he allowed the attack on Robinson's political backers to degenerate into what most voters viewed as male-chauvinist abuse. Speaking from Castlebar as a member of a radio panel on the lunchtime programme "Saturday View", Flynn said:

She was pretty well constructed in this campaign by her handlers, the Labour Party and the Workers' Party. Of course it doesn't always suit if you get labelled a socialist, because that's a very narrow focus in this country. So she has to try and have it both ways. She has to have new clothes and her new look and her new hair-do, and she has the new interest in family, being a mother and all that kind of thing. But none of us, you know, none of us who knew Mary Robinson well in previous incarnations ever heard her claiming to be a great wife and mother.[38]

Michael McDowell immediately demanded that Flynn withdraw his remarks. Suddenly it was Robinson who was the victim. Stephen Collins commented:

There was outrage up and down the country, particularly among women. Flynn was forced to issue a fulsome apology and the episode had a damaging effect on Lenihan's campaign. Flynn has always maintained that his comments were not intended to reflect on Robinson in a personal way . . . In the final days of the campaign, however, it was the perception and not the precise wording that counted. By pouncing on Flynn, the chairman of the PDs helped to bury Lenihan and the Fianna Fáil campaign.[39]

When the votes were counted, Lenihan topped the poll, with 44 per cent of first-preference votes, which shows how effective the come-back had been. Robinson secured 39 per cent, and Currie was left bringing up the rear with 17 per cent. However, when Currie's votes were redistributed Robinson won by more than 86,000. Another 2 per cent and Lenihan would have pulled off a remarkable come-back. The assessment of his national director of elections, Bertie Ahern, is clear: "There is no doubt in my mind that Flynn's outburst killed us."[40]

Lenihan's defeat left the party shocked and angry. There were reports of ten cumainn passing resolutions of no confidence in the party leadership. In an interview Haughey accused RTE of stirring the issue up, saying: "Stop trawling around the country and trying to get a cumann here or a councillor there to say negative things."[41]

Much of the anger within Fianna Fáil was directed at the PDs and how they had shafted Lenihan, or how Haughey had let them do it. Reynolds now sought to capitalise on this. He had put Haughey's future as leader to the top of the political agenda on the day of the presidential count by saying he would be a contender for the leadership when a vacancy arose.[42] Not long afterwards an aggrieved Lenihan put further pressure on Haughey when he too suggested he would contest any vacancy.[43] Fianna Fáil was now openly talking about the post-Haughey era.

While Lenihan's comments may have been provoked only by the disappointment of having lost the election, Reynolds's declared intention was a much more serious proposition. Even before the PDS had contributed to Lenihan's defeat Reynolds had set himself up as one of the party's most virulent opponents of coalition. In February 1990 his remark that the coalition with the PDS was only "a temporary little arrangement" had gained much coverage. It was also music to the ears of the Fianna Fáil grass roots. After the presidential election Reynolds kept up his internal opposition to the PDS, placing himself on the side of the angels as far as the wider Fianna Fáil membership was concerned. This also contributed to a rapidly deteriorating relationship between Reynolds and Haughey that was obvious to others. Reynolds recalled:

> The tension, bordering on animosity, between us was clear when we shared the same stage at an EC summit in Rome. When asked a question about British financial policy, Haughey deliberately and maliciously responded: "We all know that Chancellors of the Exchequer and Ministers for Finance are neurotic and exotic creatures whose political judgement is not always the best."[44]

During the review of the Programme for Government in October 1991 Reynolds adopted a truculent approach to the PDS. The talks, with the Government's future in the balance, were rescued by Ahern, who managed to bridge the gap between Reynolds and the PD negotiators. Ahern recalled: "The hardest bit was persuading Albert, because he had got seriously annoyed with the 'pie in the sky' demands the PDS were talking, which didn't tie in with all the estimates he was getting from Finance."[45]

Haughey was delighted with Ahern for his part in renewing the deal with the Progressive Democrats and paid him a back-handed compliment, which would subsequently become infamous in Irish political culture. Ahern wrote of this:

> [I was] giving a briefing to political correspondents in Government Buildings about the deal, the Taoiseach put his head round the door. "He's the man," said Charlie, pointing at me. "He's the best, the most skilful, the most devious and the most cunning of them all." I just looked at the journalists—Sam Smyth, Stephen Collins and Gerry Barry. Each of them was scribbling away, getting that very quotable quote down in their notebooks. "Jesus, that's all I need," I said after Haughey left. I think I asked if there was any chance they might forget that one. They just laughed. It's dogged me ever since.[46]

At about this time Haughey hinted to Ahern that he intended to retire the following Easter, i.e. early April. His position had been steadily undermined by a series of controversies in state-sponsored companies over the course of the summer. While Haughey was not directly involved, many of those to the forefront of the controversies were closely associated with him. It was guilt by association, but it was damaging to Fianna Fáil. T. Ryle Dwyer notes:

He was known to have been friendly with people like [Larry] Goodman, Desmond, Smurfit and Bernie Cahill, who was the chairman of the boards of Greencore, Aer Lingus and Feltrim, a mining company largely owned by Haughey's son Conor. These people were part of what was being called "the golden circle"—a group of top businessmen to whom the government seemed particularly helpful.[47]

The local elections in June 1991 were Fianna Fáil's worst performance to date. The party's vote declined to 37 per cent and Fianna Fáil was left in control of only three local authorities. Haughey was increasingly seen as a political liability. When further controversies relating to the state-sponsored companies emerged in the autumn, as well as concerns about the purchase of Carysfort Training College in Blackrock, Co. Dublin, to which Haughey was indirectly linked, rumours of plots to replace him shook Fianna Fáil once again.

Haughey had done himself few favours in a radio interview when he had insisted—in spite of his private admission to Ahern—that he intended to lead Fianna Fáil into the next election. "Some of these Chinese leaders go on till they are eighty or ninety—but I think that's probably a bit long," he had said, half in jest. But many Fianna Fáil TDs, thoroughly disillusioned with Haughey, were not impressed.

Reynolds's supporters were strongly urging him to make a move against Haughey. Noel Dempsey, Seán Power, Liam Fitzgerald and M. J. Nolan—who were quickly dubbed the "Gang of Four"—had already issued a statement expressing concerns about Haughey's leadership and the way in which he was dealing with the controversies surrounding the state-sponsored companies. This increased the pressure on Haughey and showed that discipline within the party was close to breaking down. To head them off Haughey, on Ahern's advice, revealed on 23 October 1991 that he had a retirement date in mind. He told a meeting of the parliamentary party that he wanted to be allowed to leave in dignity and at a time of his own choosing. He spoke about a time limit for his departure, stating that he would go after overseeing the budget in January.[48] This was not good enough for some TDs, who wanted Haughey gone immediately, before he could do any more damage. Having talked to Reynolds, Ahern arrived at the view that "Albert wouldn't wait."[49]

In early November further hostilities broke out at a meeting of the parliamentary party. Charlie McCreevy expressed the view that the uncertainty regarding the leadership should be dealt with one way or another as soon as possible. He tried to suggest that Haughey should table a motion of confidence in himself but was cut off by the chairperson, Brian Lenihan, who by now was firmly back in the Haughey camp. He ruled McCreevy out of order, pointing out that the leadership was not on the agenda for the meeting.

Seán Power resolved to put the matter on the agenda there and then. The same day he formally tabled a motion of no confidence in Haughey. Reynolds now came out into the open, declaring that he would support Power's motion.

Haughey's response was to sack him from the Government. The following day Pádraig Flynn, Minister for the Environment, and three ministers of state, Geoghegan-Quinn, Smith and Treacy, all said they could not support Haughey. They too were sacked. Others, including Mary O'Rourke, Ray Burke and Gerry Collins—who memorably called on Reynolds during a television interview not to "burst up the party"—took to the air waves to declare their loyalty to Haughey. Brian Lenihan also gave him strong public backing.

Haughey fought a characteristically doughty rearguard action and began to meet individual back-bench TDS. At the same time Ahern took responsibility for marshalling the troops and ensuring that Haughey had the numbers to see off the challenge. Ahern recalled:

In the past, I had helped rally around the leader, but the principal role in organising had been taken by more senior guys like Brian Lenihan. This time I was the senior guy. Haughey came to me, told me again that he would be going soon, but that he would not be pushed out by Reynolds. I think a lot of TDS had expected Charlie to go without a fight. They misjudged him.[50]

Haughey won the vote of confidence easily, 55 to 22, but already his mind was moving to the succession. Ahern was given the crucial position of Minister for Finance from which Reynolds had been sacked. A short time later Haughey again confirmed to Ahern that he would be retiring soon, making it clear that he wanted Ahern to succeed him, rather than Reynolds.

That Christmas, Charlie confirmed it to me. "I'm going next year," he said, "and you need to be ready." That was the first time he had said that he thought I should have a crack at the leadership. I told him I thought Reynolds would get it and that he had the numbers. Charlie wasn't so sure. "Albert's not a vote winner," he said, and he reminded me about a recent MRBI poll that said I would be the popular choice for leader.[51]

Haughey's political problems had not ended with his victory in the parliamentary party. His reshuffle had led to controversy over his proposal to appoint Jim McDaid as Minister for Defence. The Workers' Party raised questions about McDaid's presence at an extradition hearing involving one of his constituents. Fine Gael enthusiastically joined in the criticism, and McDaid was forced to defend himself from some dubious allegations made under the protection of Dáil privilege. One comment by Madeleine Taylor-Quinn, Fine Gael spokesperson on defence—"I wonder now, given the proposed appointment, will the terrorist organisations of this country be privy to very secret matters"[52]—caused particular offence in Fianna Fáil. The Progressive Democrats, while accepting that McDaid had no sympathy for any terrorist organisation, moved to block his appointment, arguing that he had compromised himself by his actions. McDaid subsequently withdrew his nomination, generating much sympathy within Fianna Fáil and further anger at the PDS.

Like Lenihan's dismissal, the fiasco of McDaid's non-appointment damaged Haughey's credibility within his party, and he seemed to his own TDS to be losing his touch. Reynolds's supporters were particularly strong in their questioning of his judgement and criticised his failure to stand up to the PDS. According to Reynolds, "McDaid had actually done nothing wrong: but Haughey, instead of supporting his man, once again had simply caved in to the PDS' intervention."[53]

The journalist Gerry Barry had labelled the continuous controversies that had engulfed Haughey since the summer of 1991 a "death of a thousand cuts." It was ironic that Seán Doherty would inflict the final wound.

Doherty had been smarting since Haughey had failed to support his candidacy as Cathaoirleach of the Seanad. In January 1992, on the television programme "Nighthawks", he claimed that Haughey had been fully aware of the tapping of journalists' phones a decade earlier. He followed this with a carefully organised press conference at which he said he was making the revelations because Haughey had succumbed to pressure from the PDS to introduce legislation on phone-tapping "at a time when it could only do maximum embarrassment to me as Cathaoirleach of the Seanad."[54] According to T. Ryle Dwyer,

> [Doherty's] announcement undoubtedly had a lot more to do with the leadership struggle within Fianna Fáil. He had the power to deliver a fatal political blow by telling what he knew about the events of 1982. He declared that he had not only lied for Charlie but surrendered his Front Bench position and had even given up the party whip voluntarily.[55]

At his own press conference Haughey categorically rejected Doherty's claims and insisted that he knew nothing about the phone-tapping. His performance was a strong one and he pointed out a number of inconsistencies in Doherty's story, including the fact that Doherty was now saying the exact opposite of what he said a decade previously.

> Are the Irish people more entitled to believe me, who has been consistent in everything I have said about this affair from the beginning, or someone who has been inconsistent and by his own words untruthful on countless occasions with regard to it?[56]

Haughey also made it clear that he regarded the allegations as part of a plot by disaffected elements in Fianna Fáil, whom he contemptuously labelled the "Country and Western Alliance" (a reference to Reynolds's musical preference and promotions). Haughey's future now depended on the reaction of the Progressive Democrats. After some deliberation the PDS issued a carefully worded statement that, while not explicitly demanding Haughey's resignation, turned up the heat. It said that they could not, and would not, adjudicate between the conflicting accounts of Haughey and Doherty but were "anxious to see that the acute dilemma facing the Government is speedily resolved."[57]

Soon afterwards Bobby Molloy privately approached Ahern, setting out how the PDS expected the matter to be resolved. As far as they were concerned there could only be one solution. Ahern then communicated this to Haughey. It was to be an epoch-changing conversation.

> Eventually Bobby Molloy came to see me. It was the usual story. "Listen, this is a problem for us," he said. "It will put us in a difficult position if it goes to a confidence motion." I went out to Kinsealy afterwards to see Haughey. I told him about the rumblings in the PDS. He just shook his head. They weren't going to make any difference to him. I knew immediately that he had made up his mind. All the fight had gone out of him. This was one battle too many. Normally he would have talked about arranging briefings with the press to get his message out there, asking whose spine needed stiffening, who we could rely on. This time he didn't ask any of those things. There would be no more arguing. He had already made the decision last Christmas that he would go. It was only a question of what day or on what issue. This seemed as good a time as any. "I've had my nine lives," he said as I was leaving.[58]

On 30 January, Charles Haughey announced his intention to resign as Taoiseach; and so the Haughey era ended with a whimper, not a bang. Many people had expected Haughey not to go without a fight or to attempt one last great escape. Instead he chose to quietly retreat into retirement, but not before aiming a thinly disguised kick at his critics within the party. At his final meeting of the Ard-Chomhairle, where a lot of hostility was expressed towards the PDS, Haughey swiped at a different target. "We have nothing to fear from our enemies without. It is the enemies within we must fear," he said before closing the meeting.[59]

Haughey desperately wanted Ahern to become the new leader. Stephen Collins writes:

> When it came to the succession, Haughey informed his TDS that he would not take sides in the leadership contest but his intense antipathy to Reynolds was obvious. Ray Burke, Gerry Collins and all the others who had stood by Haughey through thick and thin also wanted to block Reynolds at any cost and they egged on Bertie Ahern to go for the job. Haughey, too, wanted Ahern to take over from him but now he would no longer be around to instil that mixture of awe and fear that made the parliamentary party bend to his will in every crisis. Haughey did provide covert support for his protégé but essentially it was up to Ahern himself to win the big prize.[60]

Ahern was cautious. As soon as Haughey resigned, Reynolds had announced his candidacy, while Ahern hedged his bets. It was clear that Reynolds had strong numbers in the parliamentary party, and Ahern was conscious that it would be a gamble to take him on. But Ahern also had considerable support of his own. Lenihan had been doing tallies on his behalf and was convinced Ahern would win. Yet, as far as Ahern himself was concerned, it would be "a very tight vote" and possibly "a divisive contest."[61] His instincts were telling him to remain in Finance.

Eventually he and Reynolds met to discuss the situation. Stephen Collins gives a good account of this vital meeting.

> "You know I'll win it," Reynolds told his younger colleague immediately. He went on to tell Ahern that he would not remain in the leadership indefinitely and wouldn't try to do a Haughey on it and hang on. The message to Ahern was clear. If he dropped his challenge he would become the number two and anointed successor. If he insisted on a fight and lost he would have to suffer the consequences. Ahern went for the safe option and agreed to withdraw from the race, which he had never even formally entered.[62]

Mary O'Rourke and Michael Woods offered token resistance to Reynolds's leadership, but in the end he won by a landslide. On 6 February 1992 he obtained 61 votes, compared with 10 for Woods and 6 for O'Rourke, to make him the fifth leader of Fianna Fáil.

Haughey was gone, but he would continue to cast a long shadow over Fianna Fáil.

Chapter 16 ～

BACK FROM THE BRINK, 1989–92

On 11 February 1992 Charles Haughey nominated Albert Reynolds for Taoiseach. The motion was seconded by the Tánaiste, John Wilson, and the Dáil elected Reynolds Ireland's eighth Taoiseach by 84 votes to 78.

The fact that Haughey had nominated Reynolds had more to do with political protocol and decorum than anything else. The wounds from the manoeuvring in the period before the change of leadership in Fianna Fáil ran deep; and in his first formal act as Taoiseach, Reynolds did little to foster reconciliation. His Government appointments (and non-reappointments) sent shock waves through Fianna Fáil. On returning from Áras an Uachtaráin after receiving his seal of office from President Robinson, Reynolds sacked eight of Haughey's ministers. This was unprecedented; but to the new Taoiseach, in the circumstances of the time, it made perfect sense.

Reynolds, who was approaching his sixtieth birthday when he was elected leader of Fianna Fáil and Taoiseach, always behaved like a man in a hurry. He had been a late starter in national politics, having first been elected to the Dáil in 1977, but his journey to the summit was relatively rapid. He also knew when he took office that his spell in the top job was going to be "a limited one". In his own mind he was going to remain Taoiseach for six years at the most, and he had even given Bertie Ahern a private commitment to this effect during the leadership race. He was also a politician who believed in following his instincts and was not averse to taking risks. He had come to the office of Taoiseach after a long-drawn-out leadership battle within his party and knew that he could not expect loyalty from many of the outgoing Government. As he later put it in his autobiography,

there had been bad blood between Haughey and me at the end, and I knew that I was unlikely to get 100 per cent commitment from his old followers. Also, with some of them—not all of them, of course—I felt their day was done: I was a man with things to do and I wanted people in government who would do things with me. It was time to inject new blood into the party, to bring in people who would restore faith in the party.[1]

He further explained:

> I knew there would be resentment from many of the old guard. What I
> was about to do was unprecedented. I knew it would cause uproar and
> I also knew that it would make enemies. The changes I was about to
> make were drastic and went against all the traditions of Fianna Fáil,
> which was used to people holding on to their ministerial positions and
> remaining in power for a very long time. I wanted to bring a new public
> face to the operation, a new team who would best suit the objectives I
> had in my mind for my new administration. True, I might lose con-
> tinuity and there would be political fallout; but I was prepared to risk
> that to have the right people around me.[2]

The ministerial casualties included some of the biggest names in Fianna
Fáil. Reynolds dropped Gerry Collins, Michael O'Kennedy, Ray Burke, Mary
O'Rourke, Noel Davern, Rory O'Hanlon, Brendan Daly and Vincent Brady,
and he followed this up by sacking nine of the twelve ministers of state,
including Haughey's chief whip, Dermot Ahern. Fianna Fáil had never before
experienced such a purge.

According to Reynolds's biographer Tim Ryan, the new Taoiseach told
Gerry Collins he found it hard to envisage a Fianna Fáil Government without
him, but there would be no place for him in this Government. When Reynolds
told another long-serving minister, Ray Burke, that he was being dropped, he
added that his door would always be open. "That's all right," Burke replied. "I
won't be needing it."[3]

Reynolds's own account gives some idea of the brutality of the purge.

> Before I left Government Buildings to go to Áras an Uachtaráin I gave
> my secretary, Donagh Morgan, a long list of names of senior and junior
> ministers I wished to see on my return. Many on the list were well-
> known figures. Donagh reminded me that there would only be half an
> hour before I was due to lead my cabinet into the Dáil, and presumed
> I wanted to see them all together. I told him I would see them
> individually. It was over in fifteen minutes. I called them in one by one
> and I said, "You won't be appointed, thank you." And they went out,
> most of them too shocked even to question me. It was all so fast I could
> have done with a revolving door! Only two queried my decision, Mary
> O'Rourke and Dermot Ahern, who asked me: Why? Why was I doing it
> to them? I told them quite simply: "Nothing personal, you just backed
> the wrong horse!"[4]

Even the beneficiaries of what became known as a "massacre of ministers"
could appreciate the consequences of Reynolds's reshuffle. Reflecting on it a
decade and a half later, David Andrews wrote:

The whole experience was Ireland's equivalent of the Great Purge or the Night of the Long Knives—a bloodletting the likes of which had never been seen before in Irish politics. It engendered great bitterness against Reynolds, some of which has still not dissipated.[5]

After years of being sidelined in the party under Haughey, Andrews got one of the most senior jobs. When he called him in Reynolds jokingly told him that he was getting "FA"; it took Andrews a moment to realise he was going to Iveagh House as Minister for Foreign Affairs. Other prominent anti-Haughey TDs plucked from the back benches were Charlie McCreevy, who was appointed to Social Welfare, and Noel Dempsey, who became chief whip. Reynolds also appointed some of his principal allies to the Government, such as Máire Geoghegan-Quinn, Michael Smith and Pádraig Flynn, each of whom had lost their ministerial post in November 1991 for supporting the failed heave. The other new faces in the Government were Joe Walsh, at Agriculture, and Brian Cowen, then thirty-two, who became Minister for Labour. Reynolds repeatedly described the young Cowen to party and media audiences as "a future leader of Fianna Fáil."

The appointment that generated most comment was that of Dr John O'Connell as Minister for Health. O'Connell, who had first been elected to the Dáil in 1965, had spent several years as a Labour Party deputy and then as an independent before he joined Fianna Fáil in 1983. He had been close to Haughey but is believed to have supported the challenge against him in late 1991.

Although it was not known at the time, O'Connell had played a significant role in Haughey's departure, having actually secured a letter of resignation from him in January 1992 at a meeting in the home of Dermot O'Leary, a prominent businessman who was also chairperson of Fianna Fáil in O'Connell's constituency of Dublin South-Central. This was in the period immediately before Seán Doherty's "Nighthawks" interview. According to an *Irish Independent* investigation in 2002,

> Haughey arranged the meeting to seek O'Connell's silence on Haughey's relationship with a colourful Saudi Arabian businessman. In fact, O'Connell turned the tables on his party leader, insisting that he resign or face the consequences of this Saudi connection becoming public. Haughey acquiesced, agreeing to resign forthwith. He subsequently gave O'Connell an undertaking in writing to quit as Taoiseach and President of Fianna Fáil shortly after the encounter.[6]

When this revelation was made public in 2002, Reynolds said he did not know that O'Connell had privately met Haughey to ask him to resign only a couple of weeks before Reynolds had appointed him to his first Government. In his recently published autobiography Reynolds does not comment on O'Connell's appointment, but he told Tim Ryan: "John O'Connell is a kind and caring man and anybody who wanted that job as badly as he did I felt should be given a run."[7]

As Minister for Finance, Bertie Ahern was the only member of Haughey's Government to retain the same portfolio under Reynolds. Ahern, always a reconciler, was not impressed by the sweeping changes Reynolds had implemented. "Personally, I felt it was a disaster. I wanted to put the divisions of the Haughey years behind us. Instead, Albert had made them worse."[8]

The Government was not the only place where Reynolds effected dramatic changes. He also conducted a clearing out of the former Taoiseach's office. While he retained many of the civil servants, he dispensed with the services of Haughey's personal appointees, including the Government press secretary, P. J. Mara. Instead he approached RTE's senior political correspondent, Seán Duignan, asking him to take on the job. After some reflection, and being anxious for a new challenge, Duignan accepted. In his memoir, *One Spin on the Merry-Go-Round*, Duignan gives a colourful and nearly contemporary account of his dramatic years with Reynolds. His assessment of Reynolds's dramatic reshuffle was similar to that of Ahern.

> If you're going to do something like that you have got to be sure that when they're down, they stay down and they don't crawl off into the long grass, and that may have been the only problem for Albert, that they kind of existed out there and naturally gravitated over to Bertie's wing of the house. Albert had fired them, so they moved over to Bertie's side and to that extent they were waiting.

If ill-feeling and internal rivalries provided the mood music within Fianna Fáil for much of the Reynolds era, the atmosphere in the Government and, in particular, relations between Fianna Fáil and its coalition partners, which had always been tense, now became dysfunctional.

Des O'Malley may not have been unhappy to see his old political nemesis Charles Haughey ride off into the sunset, but this did not mean he was in any way enamoured with Reynolds. With regard to the stability of the Government, O'Malley was not impressed with Reynolds's decision to drop so many experienced ministers.[9] The Progressive Democrats were also conscious that over the previous couple of years Reynolds had been a vocal critic of the coalition within the Fianna Fáil parliamentary party, and that this had done his leadership ambitions no harm. The concept of being part of a coalition was still a new phenomenon for Fianna Fáil and so far the experience had not been a happy one for the party. Many members blamed their Government partners for the political demise of Brian Lenihan, Jim McDaid and ultimately Haughey himself. Reynolds had boosted his leadership credentials by rallying the Fianna Fáil organisation against coalition, once memorably referring to the coalition as "a temporary little arrangement". Now, as Taoiseach, he had to ride two horses at once, keeping his party content while keeping the Progressive Democrats on board.

Under Reynolds, Fianna Fáil enjoyed a honeymoon period that extended into the summer of 1992. There was a genuine sense of excitement in the party after the years of Haughey's dominance.

When Reynolds faced his first ard-fheis a few weeks after becoming leader he and his fresh team received a rapturous reception. The deposed Haughey faction mostly stayed away. Some of the former ministers, most notably Mary O'Rourke, dusted themselves off and tackled their role as minister of state or back-bencher with energy; others simply nursed their anger in silence and waited for their opportunity to exact revenge. The public also appeared to enjoy the change and warmed to the new leader. Opinion polls put Fianna Fáil's standing at 50 per cent or more.

Reynolds's more instinctive, blunt and open style as Taoiseach and party leader contrasted sharply with that of his predecessor; and while it was welcomed by most it did make for more unstable day-to-day political management. Decisions on party matters that would normally have been made by Haughey within minutes now piled up while Reynolds deliberated or was distracted by other concerns. After ten years Haughey's Government and party administration had become regimented; the various politicians and personnel who reported to him had defined roles. Haughey might occasionally seek advice, but he made most party and political decisions on his own. When Reynolds became leader he had very few such systems. He entertained views from many quarters, even outside the party, and relied ultimately on a small kitchen cabinet of ministers, particularly Pádraig Flynn.

However, he did make one party-related decision promptly: this was to transfer responsibility for a range of party accounts from the leader's private office to Fianna Fáil head office. On his second day he sent for Seán Fleming, then Fianna Fáil's full-time financial controller. He showed him a range of books and documents relating to the state-funded party leader's account and other party finance matters, which had been left behind by the Haughey secretaries and advisers. He told Fleming to "take all these over to Mount Street. I want all the party finances dealt with over there from now on." There were suspicions in the party at the time that Haughey had intermingled party and personal finances, though the true extent would not be apparent until it was explored by a tribunal of inquiry many years later.

From its very beginnings this first Reynolds Government seemed constantly overwhelmed by a series of unpredictable events. The first was a controversy relating to abortion. Charlie McCreevy recalls:

That first real cabinet meeting I remember Albert saying, "Before we go on to any other business, the Attorney General has something to tell us." And Harry Whelehan, the Attorney General, explained the history of the "X girl", as she was called. I remember clearly turning to Michael Smith, a close friend of mine, and saying, "Jesus, Mick, I know this is going to haunt us."[10]

The "X case" concerned a fourteen-year-old girl who had been raped and had become pregnant. She was prevented from having an abortion abroad after the intervention of the Attorney-General. The case created an array of legal issues that resulted in Fianna Fáil and the Progressive Democrats pulling in diverging directions. There were tensions within the Government as Fianna Fáil sought to safeguard the "pro-life" provisions in the Constitution while the Progressive Democrats placed more emphasis on the right to travel and the right to information about abortion. The differing points of view led to rows over the wording of a proposed referendum, which eventually resulted in three constitutional amendments being put to the people in November 1992: on the right to travel, the right to information, and the right to life. The first two were easily passed, but the amendment that would have made abortion illegal in all circumstances, except where the life of the mother was in danger, was rejected by the voters.

Abortion was only one of the many issues over which the two coalition parties argued during these months. The same opinion polls that were showing high approval ratings for Reynolds and Fianna Fáil showed the Progressive Democrats on a mere 4 per cent. This lulled many senior people in Fianna Fáil into a false sense of security. There was a growing sense within the party that the Progressive Democrats could not afford to risk leaving the Government, and as a result Fianna Fáil members of the Government were insensitive to the position of the Progressive Democrats.

Stephen Collins, one of the most senior members of the political correspondents' lobby, assessed the state of the Fianna Fáil-PD relationship at this point.

[The] provocation had started almost as soon as Reynolds had taken over. At the Fianna Fáil Ard Fheis in March [1992], he had an unambiguous message for his coalition partners. "Fianna Fáil does not need another party to keep it on the right track or act as its conscience," he declared . . . His young cabinet favourite, Brian Cowen, was even more blunt in his warm-up to the leader's address. "What about the Progressive Democrats?" he asked rhetorically, before providing an answer the delegates loved. "When in doubt leave out," he declared to great applause. It was good crowd-pleasing stuff but it was bad politics. It helped to lock Reynolds and O'Malley on a collision course that was in the long-term interest of neither.[11]

From its earliest days, Reynolds's Government was hampered by an increasingly difficult relationship with the press. This was not what Reynolds may have expected, given that before he became Taoiseach his relations with the press were generally good, though this probably had a lot to do with the fact that he was seen within the party as a rival to Haughey. When he became Taoiseach he suddenly found himself the primary target. His cause was not helped by the fact that on becoming Taoiseach, before hostilities had really begun, he decided to give the press a weekly on-the-record briefing to, in his own words, "let in the light." When Seán Duignan told his counterpart in the British Government, Gus O'Donnell, John Major's press secretary, that every Thursday Reynolds met the press for an hour for a free-ranging question-and-answer session, O'Donnell was shocked. "It doesn't matter how you do it," said O'Donnell. "Find a way to break out of that system before it breaks the Taoiseach." Stephen Collins, who also attended these weekly press briefings, says:

> It was a decision [Reynolds] lived to regret. No Taoiseach, before or since, provided such access to the media and, given the Reynolds experience, it is not difficult to see why. The journalists harried him week in, week out on the abortion issue. It was a subject about which he was clearly uncomfortable as he tried to find a path through the legal and political morass that would not conflict with his own traditional Catholic views and those of his supporters. Committed to giving the briefings, he found himself making unwanted headlines again and again just as the story began to die down. He also discovered that the free-and-easy relationship he had with journalists no longer translated into the same level of positive media coverage. As Taoiseach he was regarded as fair game and he had some difficulty in coming to terms with the fact.[12]

Reynolds's deteriorating relationship with the press resulted in his taking a number of libel actions against media organisations. This bred further hostility, but Reynolds, who was very protective of his good name, was unrepentant. He told Seán Duignan, who was urging caution rather than litigation:

> I don't care, Diggy. I am not going to take that kind of thing lying down. Charlie felt there was nothing he could do about it, but if they tell lies about me, I will sue them, and to hell with the consequences.[13]

Reynolds's battles with the press were viewed sympathetically within Fianna Fáil, but his public perception was taking a battering. The feeling among Fianna Fáil members was that he was being unfairly attacked by what they derisively labelled "Dublin 4", who were viewed as long-standing opponents of the party. Conor Brady, editor of the *Irish Times* (who would later acknowledge that he had been unfair to Reynolds in an unpleasant editorial published the day Reynolds left office), says the uneasy relationship between Reynolds and the media arose in part because of a clash of cultures. "[Reynolds] had come from a background that few of the Dublin press corps understood or empathised with: show-bands, ballrooms and his successful pet-food factory near Longford."[14]

Stephen Collins is more blunt in his assessment. He suggests that some journalists looked down their noses at Reynolds, either because of his rural roots or because they felt he was their intellectual inferior.

Some elements of the media treated him with the same snobbish disdain as that displayed by Haughey and his Dublin north-side mafia. [The] *Irish Times* columnist Fintan O'Toole reflected this negative approach: "When Mary Robinson said, Come Dance with me in Ireland, and the people accepted the invitation, knowing what would fill a ballroom on a wet Tuesday night in Rooskey was not part of the equation." It was ironic that the urban liberals and the Haughey toughs found common cause in sneering at Reynolds as an "unlettered culchie" from Longford. Reynolds was more wounded than he ever cared to admit by the sneers but he pressed on regardless, confident that the majority of Fianna Fáil TDs would back him. However, the sneering did colour his generally benign attitude towards the media.[15]

If Reynolds's determination to defend his personal integrity at all costs harmed his relations with the media, it was also a central factor in the break-up of Fianna Fáil's coalition with the Progressive Democrats. Reynolds and O'Malley crossed swords bitterly at the Beef Tribunal, which in the summer of 1992 was dealing with the way in which Reynolds had handled the export credit insurance scheme as Minister for Industry and Commerce. He was certain that the policy he had introduced was correct. He was obsessive about being vindicated on this issue at the tribunal. When O'Malley, who had succeeded Reynolds in that department, described the decisions taken by Reynolds on export credit as "wrong . . . grossly unwise, reckless and foolish," Reynolds saw red. He followed the daily news coverage of O'Malley's testimony at the tribunal in detail, even cutting short one Ard-Chomhairle meeting so that he could watch the latest update on the nine o'clock news.[16] Stephen Collins writes of his reaction: "Reynolds was livid. Although he did not let that show in public, those around him had a sense of foreboding as he spoke of a day of reckoning when he would set the record straight."[17]

The day of reckoning came in October 1992 when the Taoiseach appeared at the Beef Tribunal to give his evidence. He had been urged by his lawyers and his senior civil servants to proceed with caution, but in the cut and thrust of his cross-examination by Adrian Hardiman, counsel for O'Malley, he described O'Malley's evidence as "puffed up" for "cheap political gain" and "reckless, irresponsible and dishonest."[18]

Seán Duignan, who had accompanied Reynolds to the tribunal, gives a dramatic account of what happened next. Hardiman gave Reynolds the opportunity to withdraw the word "dishonest" and even suggested to him the option of reclassifying O'Malley's evidence as "incorrect". Reynolds, however, did not budge.

> Hardiman . . . asked him if he was now saying that O'Malley's evidence had merely been incorrect as distinct from dishonest. I kept willing him to say yes, to get back to defending his own decisions, to leave O'Malley out of the damn thing, get the show back on the road. Albert paused for

what seemed ages (we all held our breath) and then he said that one word—"dishonest!" I think we're bollixed.[19]

Duignan's assessment was an accurate one as far as the life of that Government was concerned. The Progressive Democrats announced that they would support a motion of no confidence in the Government, and on 5 November 1992 the Dáil was dissolved and Fianna Fáil was thrown headlong into an unexpected election. In his memoir, Duignan poses and answers the question:

> Why did Albert Reynolds do it? Despite what many opposition and media observers maintained, it was not because he wanted to provoke an election (at least not arising from the wretched beef affair) and he never intended to be drawn into battle on the high moral ground, traditionally treacherous terrain for Fianna Fáil. The problem was that he couldn't let it go with Des O'Malley, firstly for his declared determination to harass him on beef from within [the] government, even after he became Taoiseach, and then for the relentless manner in which he gave effect to that threat when he went into the witness box in July. Like a footballer badly fouled in the first round of a cup-tie, Reynolds nursed his wrath until the second leg, and then put the boot in. Unfortunately, as often happens in such circumstances, it instantly earned him the red card.[20]

After a mere nine months as Taoiseach, Reynolds had precipitated an election on terms most unfavourable to Fianna Fáil. Opinion polls showed that the electorate believed O'Malley's account at the tribunal rather than the Taoiseach's. The first opinion poll of the campaign in the *Irish Independent* confirmed the party's worst fears, as it showed a massive drop of 20 per cent in satisfaction with Reynolds. It was predicted that Fianna Fáil would lose seats, and the media prodded Reynolds relentlessly, introducing the term "the Albert factor" to explain Fianna Fáil's unpopularity. On one of the days when opinion polls showed support for Fianna Fáil still declining, the *Irish Press* gave over most of its front page to the headline "Nightmare on Mount Street".

When Reynolds used the word "crap" in a radio interview, the press had a field day, and some of his political opponents even made the ridiculous claim that the use of the word was grounds for impeachment.[21] According to Duignan, the media storm generated over the use of the word cost Reynolds dearly during the campaign, "primarily because it perfectly fitted the grotesque Reynolds caricature being drawn by his opponents, that of a coarse and boorish man."[22]

Fianna Fáil was not prepared for an election, and its organisation was in disarray. Attendances at events on Reynolds's national tour were dismal for the first week. A campaign of phone calls from head office to rally the troops for the party leader's visit to each constituency improved the situation only slightly. Bertie Ahern memorably claimed that the disorganised nature of the campaign proved that it was the Progressive Democrats, not Fianna Fáil, who were responsible for causing an unnecessary election. "The unreadiness shows that we didn't want an election," Ahern said. "All we want to do is run the country."[23]

The election came at a time when the economy was still sluggish and the Government had alienated substantial numbers of people by introducing twelve new eligibility rules for certain social welfare payments. The Labour Party named these "the Dirty Dozen". Together with a number of voluntary and community organisations, the Labour Party protested vocally and effectively about these changes. Charlie McCreevy, the Minister for Social Welfare, refused to budge. When the election came it was clear that this issue was now eating into Fianna Fáil's support. As Frank Dunlop later wrote,

> the canvass feedback was that the public didn't like McCreevy's approach. I was with Albert on his way to an RTE interview with Pat Kenny when he had a telephone conversation with McCreevy about the measures. Seán Duignan and I flinched when he said, "Just fucking withdraw them," and slammed down the car phone so violently we both thought he had broken it.[24]

While allowances must be made for Dunlop's tendency to add colour, his account of the Reynolds-McCreevy exchange is indicative of the way in which important policy decisions were made on the hoof during the campaign. The party manifesto was only completed at a chaotic meeting of ministers that continued into the early morning of the day it was due to be launched. Party officials had deliberately chosen a printer in Longford to produce the document, because they knew the final decisions on its content would be late and hoped that these printers would work flat out to ensure that their local deputy and Taoiseach was not embarrassed at that afternoon's press conference.[25]

As the party continued to slump in the opinion polls, Reynolds sought to put the best gloss on events, insisting: "In the past our strategy has been to start high and finish low. This time we will start low and finish high."[26] To the press he was in denial, and he was mercilessly ridiculed. Stephen Collins observes:

> Some of the old Haughey gang could not disguise their glee at the fact that Reynolds's strategy had come so spectacularly unstuck, but they did not have much time to enjoy his discomfiture. It was every man for himself in the battle to hold on to Dáil seats as the tide moved against Fianna Fáil.[27]

The party's campaign was now in meltdown. Seán Duignan, whose father had been a Fianna Fáil TD in the 1950s, was shocked by the breakdown in the party's organisation.

I was struck by signs of indiscipline and even insubordination in the organisation at large. A steady stream of HQ instructions to FF notables, recommending particular responses to opposition criticisms, were being widely ignored. Certain Ministers and other personages who had been requested to represent Fianna Fáil on various TV and radio election programmes were begging off with all manner of specious excuses.

It seemed the prevailing party wisdom in the teeth of the storm was to remain well below decks. Heads dutifully poked through constituency portholes as we passed by, but were as quickly retracted. There was rarely any outright dissent, mostly regrets and evasions, but it struck me that the much vaunted iron discipline of Fianna Fáil was a myth. Many of the party warlords fought the election within their own territorial fastnesses—in their own way—with little or no reference to Mount Street.[28]

Reynolds was increasingly seen as a liability within the organisation, and even some of his close supporters now ran for cover. Brian Cowen was stunned when he learnt from the party press office that many senior figures in the party were refusing to go on television or radio. Cowen's response, with characteristic loyalty, was to make himself available at any time, anywhere, to defend his leader and to present the Fianna Fáil position.[29] Mary O'Rourke, who Reynolds had demoted, and Bertie Ahern were also prominent; indeed the commitment and enthusiasm O'Rourke showed in this campaign was a factor in Ahern's later decision to make her deputy leader of Fianna Fáil.[30]

Half way through the campaign Reynolds asked Frank Dunlop, who had served as Government press secretary under both Lynch and Haughey, to come on board and help steady the campaign. Dunlop paints a vivid picture of the chaos that was the Fianna Fáil set-up.

When I arrived at Fianna Fáil's Upper Mount Street headquarters, I discovered that the building looked like a sub-office of the Law Library, with cigar-smoking junior and senior counsel proffering, mostly uninvited, opinions on matters about which they hadn't the faintest knowledge and junior HQ staff being unable, or unwilling to contradict them.[31]

Dunlop showed the barristers the door. He then set his mind to working out how Fianna Fáil could tackle the fall-out from the opinion polls, which were becoming progressively worse and were resulting in Fianna Fáil canvassers deserting the battlefield.

Borrowing from American jargon, we decided to invent what we called "tracking" polls. When we were confronted by media queries about our response to the less than encouraging message coming from the

national opinion polls, we merely said that this did not accord with
what we were finding in our tracking polls. It was an outrageous
subterfuge on our part, but one that was both condoned by the party
hierarchy and considered necessary to prevent Fianna Fáil supporters
sliding into a resigned acceptance of the inevitable and doing nothing
to counteract the perception that all was lost. There were many calls for
the party to make these tracking polls available for public scrutiny, both
during the election itself and subsequently. Since these polls had never
been conducted, that was an impossibility.[32]

Fianna Fáil and its leader were at a low ebb. When Ahern rang Reynolds to
congratulate him after the traditional leaders' debate, Reynolds told him he
was the only one who had bothered.[33] As the campaign moved into its final
stage, Fianna Fáil strategists increasingly put Ahern to the fore. Damian
Corless notes:

> As it became clear that Labour stood to make big gains in the capital,
> Fianna Fáil switched its focus to Dublin, and on to Finance Minister
> Bertie Ahern . . . Fintan O'Toole in the *Irish Times* found significance in
> the switch of emphasis, writing: "His chummy image, his lack of
> abrasiveness, were what Fianna Fáil needed to counter the harshness
> that has been their keynote since the break-up of the coalition
> government."[34]

In the last week of the campaign Fianna Fáil rallied and in the election it
got its vote up to 39 per cent, though it struggled badly with transfers. When
the seats were counted the result was, by Reynolds's own admission, "a
disaster for Fianna Fáil [and] . . . a real achievement for Dick Spring."[35] Fianna
Fáil lost nine seats in its worst result since 1927, while the Labour Party gained
eighteen, which was quickly dubbed the "Spring Tide". The Progressive
Democrats gained four seats, benefiting from their dispute with Reynolds.
The only consolation for Fianna Fáil was that Fine Gael lost ten seats. The
Fine Gael campaign had been damaged when John Bruton's suggestion that a
"rainbow" alternative would include the Labour Party but exclude
Democratic Left was given a cool response by Dick Spring.[36]

The Fianna Fáil collapse seemed to make it inevitable that the party was
heading for opposition and that Reynolds's short tenure at the helm was
drawing to a close. Reynolds consoled himself with the thought that nobody
had achieved a clear majority and that he might yet cobble together a deal
with the Labour Party. In his speech on the no-confidence motion on the day
the Dáil was dissolved Reynolds had berated the Progressive Democrats, but
he had avoided attacking the Labour Party, though Spring had been scathing
about Fianna Fáil.

In the last week or so of the campaign Reynolds resisted suggestions from
party strategists that Fianna Fáil should intensify its attacks on the Labour

Party, telling some privately that "we may need Labour yet."[37] Despite this, leading party figures, including Pádraig Flynn and Séamus Brennan, had come out publicly against a coalition before polling day. Only Brian Lenihan, who had always favoured a deal with the Labour Party rather than the Progressive Democrats, spoke publicly in favour of such a coalition.[38] Reynolds continued to believe that the Labour Party might yet prove to be his lifeboat for getting back into government, but this was greeted with scepticism within his own party.

As talks on the formation of a new Government began between Fine Gael and the Labour Party, Reynolds held his nerve. His adviser, Martin Mansergh, knew that Fianna Fáil's only option was the Labour Party and had put together a draft of a joint policy platform based on the manifestos of both parties. Reynolds sat tight on this.

Meanwhile the discussions between Fine Gael and the Labour Party were not going smoothly. Spring had raised the issue of rotating the position of Taoiseach, which was ruled out by Bruton. Fine Gael meanwhile was ruling out Democratic Left, while Spring was ruling it in. Both also disagreed on the participation of the Progressive Democrats in a new Government.

Reynolds began to take soundings within his Government about a potential deal with the Labour Party. Bertie Ahern recalls:

> Late on in the campaign, Albert had raised the question with me about sharing power with Labour. Now it came up again. Labour's early talks with Fine Gael were not going well. I said we would benefit from a period in opposition to rebuild the party organisation, but if there was a chance of a deal with Labour, we should take it. "Even if you talk Springer into it," I warned him, "it's our own supporters that'll need convincing."[39]

Within the ranks of the parliamentary party a significant number were advocating that the party should go into opposition. For some this was based on principle, for others it was a means of ditching Reynolds. Among those seen as being against a coalition with the Labour Party were Gerry Collins, Ray Burke, Jim McDaid, Séamus Kirk, Michael J. Noonan, John O'Donoghue, Mary Wallace and Ned O'Keeffe, and even Reynolds loyalists such as Charlie McCreevy and Noel Dempsey were believed to favour going into opposition.[40] Others were openly agitating for a heave. Haughey's former constituency colleague and chief whip Vincent Brady was taking soundings for a revolt. David Andrews recalls:

> Some people were prepared to hang Albert out to dry at the time, which I felt was grossly unfair. He had placed trust in me as Foreign Minister and now I was being asked to desert him when he was at one of his weakest moments. That was why I referred to the suggestion of my candidacy at the time as "unprincipled and obscene". There was a

move to get rid of Reynolds all right, but I had no intention of allowing myself to be used as the instrument.[41]

The plotters then turned their attention to Bertie Ahern, but he made it clear that he too would not involve himself in a heave.[42]

It was at this point that events began to turn in Reynolds's favour. After the longest recount in the history of the country Ben Briscoe took the final seat in Dublin South-Central, at the expense of Eric Byrne of Democratic Left. This meant that Spring's preferred option of a coalition of Fine Gael, the Labour Party and Democratic Left no longer had the numbers. The Labour Party had already begun to make overtures to Fianna Fáil. Lenihan was in communication with Ruairí Quinn about the possibility of a coalition, as was Ahern. When the Labour Party's talks with Fine Gael ran into the ground, Spring sent Reynolds a copy of the Labour Party's proposals for government. Reynolds, who had waited patiently for this moment, now played his hand expertly. He promptly sent the Labour Party a copy of the analysis Mansergh had completed of a programme based on the two parties' manifestos. The document changed the game. The Labour Party was shocked at the speed of the Fianna Fáil response and by the fact that Fianna Fáil had moved such a long way towards its positions.

On the evening that the documents were exchanged, Reynolds, as caretaker Taoiseach, accompanied by David Andrews, Bertie Ahern and Tom Kitt, headed to an EC summit meeting in Edinburgh. This meeting would decide on the allocation of structural and cohesion funds. Reynolds had confidently predicted, during the earlier referendum on the Maastricht Treaty, that he would get at least £6 billion for Ireland, but this claim had been ridiculed by the media. Their scepticism had, if anything, increased now that Reynolds had lost the election. The prevalent view was that, because Reynolds looked as if he was going out of power, his negotiating strength was weakened. But once again Reynolds had kept an ace in the hole.

During the election campaign Reynolds had met the German Chancellor, Helmut Kohl, in Bonn. The British Prime Minister, John Major, had told Kohl that Reynolds was in communication with the IRA in what were then the early stages of the peace process. Kohl asked Reynolds to use his influence with the republican movement to ensure that the IRA stopped killing British soldiers on German soil. In return Kohl pledged to back Reynolds to the hilt at the Edinburgh meeting. Reynolds and Kohl struck a deal.

This allowed Reynolds to go into the negotiations confident of a successful outcome. In Fianna Fáil there was a keen understanding that this was not only vital to the country's economic future but essential to the party's prospects of remaining in government. Ahern encapsulated this when he said the Labour Party was "watching for a sign," and so the negotiations became a matter of political survival.[43]

The last negotiating session of the summit meeting broke up at 10:30 p.m on 12 December, and Reynolds had secured a staggering £8 billion for Ireland.

It was a negotiating triumph for the Taoiseach and an astonishing back-to-the-wall performance. In his memoirs Reynolds relives this extraordinary achievement.

> After a gruelling round of negotiating, I got it: I came out of the conference hall with not £6 but £8 billion! Seán Duignan was there to meet me, and I said to him: "Eight billion, Diggy, eight billion—now watch me put a government together!" The Irish media had gleefully been awaiting my humiliation—so much so that they had no idea how to react to the news that Ireland had been granted the huge sum of £8 billion. I think if I had only come away with £3 billion they would have cheered, but the fact that I had succeeded in getting £8 billion left them with egg on their faces. We got the deal we wanted—and in Germany the bombing stopped.[44]

With this massive funding due to come on stream, opposition was now not an attractive proposition for any party. At the same time Reynolds, as negotiator-in-chief of the eight billion, had seen his political standing transformed almost overnight. On his return from Edinburgh he met Spring in the Berkeley Court Hotel, Dublin, to begin talks about a coalition Government. Reynolds's tail was up, and Fergus Finlay, Spring's trusted adviser, recalls being taken aback by the Taoiseach's buoyant mood.

> I think I expected to meet someone with the hunted and hang-dog look of a politician who had been under immense pressure for several months. There was no doubt that since the election campaign the knives had been out for Albert Reynolds—both in the media and in his own party. If he couldn't do a deal with Dick Spring, he'd be gone in a week. He needed us a lot more than we needed him. The first revelation was how bright and breezy he was, like a man without a care in the world. He had just arrived back from Edinburgh, where he had astonished everyone . . . One way or the other, he was in high good humour as we took the lift to the penthouse suite.[45]

The chemistry between Reynolds and Spring at this meeting was good. Reynolds's pitch was strong. He discussed with Spring the possibilities the eight billion offered for investment in education and infrastructure. He also spoke with conviction about a new style of partnership government, consisting of two strong parties rather than the traditional type of coalition in which the weaker party was forever vying for influence.[46] Reynolds also had one further trump card to play: Northern Ireland.

After Spring's meeting with Reynolds he briefed some of his closest party colleagues on what had taken place. Finlay recalls Ruairí Quinn asking Spring what else Reynolds had said.

"We talked about Northern Ireland," Dick said. "I promised him I wouldn't elaborate, but you can take it there are real possibilities there. The other thing he told me was that I was getting a briefing that Des O'Malley never got!" That was all he told us about Northern Ireland. But I was watching him [Spring] closely, and I knew that whatever he had been told he had found intriguing.[47]

Spring was hooked. On 16 December formal negotiations opened. The Fianna Fáil team consisted of Ahern, Dempsey and Cowen; the Labour Party's team was Ruairí Quinn, Brendan Howlin and Mervyn Taylor. The negotiations were lengthy, but there was never any doubt that a deal was going to be reached. Cowen played the "hard cop" role, insisting that as much Fianna Fáil policy as possible went into the joint programme and holding the line on budgetary targets. Ahern played his customary conciliatory role. Dempsey facilitated the talks by ensuring that the Labour Party team had access to any information they needed from the Department of Finance or other departments.[48]

The draft programme for government was eventually published in January 1993 and contained significant compromises for both parties. The Labour Party had to reverse its fiscal plans and accepted the Maastricht Treaty budgetary guidelines. Meanwhile Fianna Fáil took on board Labour's commitments on divorce, increased spending on health, proposals for new ethics legislation and the decriminalisation of homosexuality. The programme obtained the approval of both parliamentary parties, and Fianna Fáil and the Labour Party were now on course to form a Government.

On 12 January 1993 Albert Reynolds was elected Taoiseach, with a Dáil majority of forty-two. It was the largest parliamentary majority the country had ever seen, and it capped a remarkable turnabout in Reynolds's fortunes.

Reynolds and his party had been on the floor in the immediate aftermath of the election, but he had picked himself up, fought back and now had confounded his political opponents. O'Malley and the Progressive Democrats were consigned to the opposition benches, Fine Gael was in turmoil after a disappointing election, and within Fianna Fáil, Reynolds had pulled the rug from under the "discontented Haugheyite rump who saw their chances of dumping Albert fading fast."[49]

Reynolds had come back from the brink. He had displayed guts and political skill in doing so and had been rewarded with a second chance as Taoiseach. But if his party, or the commentators, thought he was going to proceed more cautiously or alter his style of politics, they would be proved wrong. Reynolds's new partnership with the Labour Party would prove to be even more of a rollercoaster than his first Government with the Progressive Democrats.

Chapter 17 ∿

A ROLLERCOASTER RIDE, 1992–4

There were some murmurings in Fianna Fáil when Albert Reynolds had to concede six Government places to the Labour Party, but in the end this turned out a less painful exercise than it might have been.

The departure of the Progressive Democrats had already created two vacancies, while the Tánaiste, John Wilson, had retired at the election. Pádraig Flynn, who the Labour Party would not have accepted, was to be despatched to the European Commission, while John O'Connell asked not to be reappointed, because of health concerns.

Séamus Brennan was the only minister to be demoted, but he was consoled with an appointment as minister of state. Brennan had been Fianna Fáil's director of elections during a poor campaign, but, as Frank Lahiffe, his special adviser, points out, he had fundamental misgivings about a coalition with the Labour Party, believing that its ideology was not compatible with Fianna Fáil's.[1] Brennan had even ridiculed the idea of such a link during the campaign, and he was an obvious candidate for demotion. The blow was cushioned by the fact that the department in which Reynolds offered him the position of minister of state was Commerce and Technology, a field of responsibility that he had a particular interest in. In addition Reynolds appointed Brennan to the newly created part-time position of national director of Fianna Fáil, which was modelled loosely on the position of chairperson of the British Conservative Party, a senior politician who is given overarching responsibility for head office and organisation matters.

The brief given to Brennan was to revitalise the Fianna Fáil organisation throughout the country. Substantial gaps had become apparent during the disastrous election campaign, which had developed partly because every time Fianna Fáil was in government the leader and other senior politicians had insufficient time to devote to party affairs. This was a real problem in a party as strongly based on centralism as Fianna Fáil. At the time many saw the appointment as a sop to Brennan and a partial compensation for his demotion from the Government. Nevertheless Brennan, working closely with the general secretary, Pat Farrell, and the former *Irish Press* journalist Mary Kerrigan, who was made the party's new director of communications, threw himself into the task with typical energy.

The position of national director was only a partial success, however, as it blurred lines of responsibility, not least those between leader and general secretary. That it worked at all is attributable to Brennan's particular background. The post was discontinued after Reynolds's term ended.

Over the next year or so the Brennan-Farrell-Kerrigan triumvirate toured the comhairlí dáilcheantair in an effort to assess and improve grass-roots organisation. Brennan's particular talent for communication was also reflected in a marked improvement in the presentation of both the party and its leader. Some of these changes were superficial, including the commissioning of a new party emblem. The previous "burger" design—a circle divided into green, white and orange with the letters FF on a white background—was replaced with one that retained the colours and the letters but also depicted a harp.

A series of youth conferences and of regional women's conference were organised. These operated as set-piece opportunities for Reynolds to both rally the troops and deliver speeches on issues such as the Northern Ireland peace process. These events were one element in a strategy designed to put Reynolds's relationship with the media on a more structured footing. His weekly briefing with political correspondents was abandoned. Indeed from the time of the formation of the Fianna Fáil-Labour Government in January 1993 until the party ard-fheis in November that year Reynolds maintained a relatively low profile. The party strategists were anxious to recast Reynolds's image from that of the truculent and impetuous politician revealed in so many bruising encounters before and during the 1992 election. The evolving peace process provided the opportunity to do that.

Charlie McCreevy was the other minister who commentators had expected would be sacked when the new Government was put together with the Labour Party, but his close personal relationship with Reynolds meant that he survived. The Taoiseach did, however, move him from Social Welfare to Tourism and Trade. Michael Woods returned to the Department of Social Welfare, where he had always been regarded as a safe pair of hands in that most politically sensitive of departments. Another minister to switch portfolios was David Andrews, who moved to Defence and the Marine to make room for the new Tánaiste, Dick Spring, in Foreign Affairs. Andrews, who had been one of Reynolds's strongest supporters, was probably one of those most disappointed with the reshuffle. He confessed to

> feeling a bit let down by Reynolds. I felt I had given him a huge amount of support, particularly after the results of the election and when things looked pretty grim for him. While his popularity was going down (even to as low as eleven per cent in the polls), my own was soaring and I was being talked about in many quarters as a possible leader . . . I scotched such talk in no uncertain terms. I felt let down by Albert, because he didn't seem inclined to fight my corner when it came to the Foreign Affairs position. He told me he would have re-appointed me there, had

Labour not insisted that they wanted that portfolio, and that seemed to be that.[2]

Dick Spring had insisted on the Foreign Affairs portfolio, because when Reynolds was seeking to persuade him to come on board, one of his selling points was that there was real scope for developments in the North. Spring had been intrigued by what Reynolds had told him and wanted to ensure that the Labour Party was directly involved in the process. This was why he decided to take the Foreign Affairs portfolio as Tánaiste, rather than Finance, where he felt he would have struggled with economics.

Reynolds had been working on the Northern situation throughout his previous term with the Progressive Democrats. In his first press conference as leader of Fianna Fáil he had said that his priority was peace in Northern Ireland. This surprised both party activists and political commentators, because Northern Ireland was not an issue on which he had had much to say previously. But he told interviewers that he had a lifelong interest in developments north of the border and an extended network of Northern contacts from his business involvements in the midlands. He also revealed that in 1970, when he was running a business in the Liberties in Dublin, he had spent many days in the public gallery of the Four Courts watching the proceedings of the Arms Trial.

Reynolds insisted he was in earnest about making Northern Ireland his priority and that he was going to bring a new approach to the question. He did not see the North in terms of republican goals or historic claims but as a conflict that was holding Irish people back economically and socially. Martin Mansergh, who worked closely with Reynolds and two other Fianna Fáil Taoisigh on Northern Ireland, said: "Albert doesn't come with any hang-ups about Republicanism or this or that, he simply says—there's a problem there, let's deal with it."[3] Seán Duignan had a similar assessment.

I don't believe Albert gives a tupenny damn about Articles 2 and 3. As he says himself, he's a "dealer" . . . I notice he refers to the IRA Army Council without the slightest emotion—they're just there—he might as well be talking about the PLO. He sees killing as the ultimate stupidity—so everything is the deal, the deal, the deal.[4]

Reynolds's approach to the North was rooted deep in his experiences as a pragmatic businessman. Recalling his first press conference as leader of Fianna Fáil, he wrote:

In my first press conference as leader on 6th February 1992, I expressed the objectives I hoped to achieve in my tenure as Taoiseach, however long or short that might be. The first and of prime importance was peace in Northern Ireland . . . People were surprised, shocked even; they had expected me to talk about the economy, but not of my concern for

Northern Ireland . . . However, through my life in business I had gained
a very good grounding in attitudes in the North, I had friends and
colleagues there across the religious spectrum, and I understood their
thinking and concerns . . . This was what I tried to put across in my
speech to the press and to the people on that first night: the background to my way of thinking, the influences and initiatives that had
made me put peace in Northern Ireland at the top of my agenda.[5]

He further elaborated:

Since 1969, I explained, all the outside world was seeing of Ireland was
bombs and bullets. It didn't matter that it was in the North: as far as the
world was concerned it was Ireland . . . Yet here were we trying to
develop an economy where tourism and inward investment were
important. Who was going to holiday in a place where there was
trouble, where atrocities were being committed every day of the week?
Who was going to invest in a country that hadn't a solid political
position? That's why I wanted peace in Ireland, I said. Whatever it took,
that's where I was going. If I get that, I added, whenever I get it, it will
inject investments into the country, investment will create jobs,
emigration numbers will fall, and so will unemployment . . . Asking
American high-fliers to come over here and invest their money when
you have all that trouble just up the road is not a good sales pitch. That
was where I was coming from—a financial, investment and
technological viewpoint—and I knew that there were many in the
North who understood that way of thinking and they too wanted
peace, and I'd made up my mind I was not going to fail.[6]

The quest for peace in Northern Ireland was another of the things about
which Reynolds became obsessive. He set about the task with real energy, with
courage bordering on recklessness and with dogged perseverance. He also
brought to it a particularly good relationship with the British Prime Minister,
John Major, which dated from the time when they had managed the finance
portfolios of the Irish and British Governments.
    During the coalition with the Progressive Democrats, Reynolds felt
restricted in what he could do in breaking the logjam in the North.
O'Malley's agenda seemed strongly anti-republican. In this period Reynolds
concentrated publicly on building relations with the Unionists, something his
predecessor as leader of Fianna Fáil would have found very difficult, given his
Arms Trial baggage. He had some early success in July 1992 when, for the first
time, the Ulster Unionists agreed to talks with an Irish Government. In
private, Reynolds opened a back-door channel of communication with the
republican movement, seeking to persuade them to move towards a more
realistic and solely political agenda. The fact that Reynolds kept the British
Prime Minister up to date with what he was doing is a testament to the strong

relationship between the two. The fact that he felt he could not trust any of his Government colleagues, especially O'Malley, is equally indicative of the instability in the Fianna Fáil-PD Government.

> Obviously the government was aware of my official agenda on Northern Ireland, but I could not divulge to O'Malley or anyone else in government anything of my covert plans. Government policy still endorsed non-communication with those who sought to rule by the gun, or those associated with them. It was too dangerous. O'Malley was already looking for ways to bring down our coalition, and any hint of my being in contact with Sinn Féin or the IRA, or indeed the Loyalists, would have been just the excuse he was looking for. It would not have been acceptable to most members of the government. I simply could not afford to let it be known until I was sure I could get the IRA paramilitaries to agree to a ceasefire—and a permanent one at that.[7]

When the Labour Party replaced the Progressive Democrats as Fianna Fáil's coalition partners it did a lot to change the dynamic. Reynolds is blunt in his assessment, saying he believed that Dick Spring

> would be a more understanding partner in the search for peace in Northern Ireland. O'Malley had never believed in the possibility of peace, and I had deliberately avoided involving him in what was going on. Spring, although reasonably sceptical, was definitely intrigued and I felt I could trust him to go along with my ambitions.[8]

From the beginning of 1993 the peace process gathered real momentum. With the PD monkey off his back, Reynolds threw himself into achieving agreement on a joint Anglo-Irish declaration, which he had been working on since he became Taoiseach. To reach this goal he was prepared to challenge the political orthodoxies of the day. In a series of speeches over the course of 1993, some of them delivered to party conferences, Reynolds set out how he proposed to turn Fianna Fáil policy on the North around. Stephen Collins writes of this:

> The truly original core of the policy pursued by Reynolds was to argue that everybody else had put the cart before the horse in trying to get a political solution in order to bring about peace. He proposed instead to concentrate all efforts on bringing about peace first, in the belief that a political solution would inevitably flow from that. It was an idea whose time had come. Republicans were weary with a campaign of violence that had got them nowhere and the British were weary of a war they could not win.[9]

Reynolds was taking a real political risk, and this was pointed out to him by close political advisers. Seán Duignan wrote in his diary on 4 March 1993:

Albert gives Bart [Cronin] and me sneak preview of draft document on
N.I., plus rundown on what he's up to, which scares the bejasus out of
both of us. He is convinced he can sell it to Major, and he insists Sinn
Féin and the Army Council of the IRA will also buy it. He says: "This is
about the IRA being persuaded to lay down their arms . . ." He says it will
involve the Republican movement accepting Irish unity coming about
only by consent (that doesn't sound like the IRA to me!) but what's really
scary is that he seems to be fixing to contact these guys. Bart and I so
worried we go back in to warn him he could be destroyed if he goes
down that road. He says maybe so, but he's going to go all the way.[10]

Though Reynolds considered Spring to be more in tune with his thinking
on Northern Ireland, Spring was the more cautious of the two. In pursuit of
peace Reynolds was prepared to gamble his political future and back his
instinct that he could achieve a deal. Duignan wrote:

I subsequently asked [Reynolds] if Spring knew about pulling in the
Provos. I made a diary note of how Reynolds responded: "Yes, I told
him." "And what did he say, Taoiseach?" "You're on your own, Albert." I
also jotted down something else Reynolds said when Bart and I were
telling him of our fears: "I'm a dealer—not a wheeler-dealer or a
double-dealer—just a dealer. That's what I do, hard straight dealing.
And that's what I think I can pull off on the North, something they'll
all accept as an even deal."[11]

In working towards a deal Reynolds was not afraid to alter Fianna Fáil's
policy. Haughey had had a firm belief in the primacy of Fianna Fáil's
constitutional republicanism, but Reynolds was more willing to take into
account the alternative viewpoints of other nationalist parties in an effort to
build consensus. Furthermore, Haughey's Fianna Fáil had always been
dubious about the principle of consent. He had rejected the Anglo-Irish
Agreement of 1985 on the grounds that the principle of consent enshrined in
it ran counter to articles 2 and 3 of the Constitution. Haughey was only
comfortable with traditional Fianna Fáil policy, focused on a unitary 32-
county state. Reynolds sought to move Fianna Fáil beyond this cul-de-sac.
Stephen Collins observed that Reynolds

let republicans know that they would get the broad support of
democratic nationalist Ireland if they accepted the principle of consent,
involving the agreement of all the people of Ireland to future political
structures. Effectively what Reynolds did was to synthesise all the
various strands of nationalist policy that had developed since the
outbreak of the Troubles. He accepted the crucial importance of the
consent principle, something Haughey had always refused to do, but he
did so in the context of a new expression of self-determination by all
the people of Ireland, something that was crucial for republicans.[12]

Throughout 1993 Reynolds and his officials kept up constant communication with Gerry Adams and John Hume. He worked continuously to bring about further compromise and agreement so that the Hume-Adams document could form the basis for talks with John Major. However, he changed course when, in November 1993, after an IRA bomb had killed ten people on the Shankill Road and loyalist paramilitaries shot seven people dead in a pub in Gresteel, Co. Derry, in retaliation. There was public revulsion at the upsurge in killing, and there was a further outcry, especially in Britain, when Gerry Adams was pictured carrying the coffin of the Shankill bomber. Reynolds and Major felt compelled to stand back from the Hume-Adams document. Reynolds recognised that if peace was to be brought about Major must be kept on board and that the best way towards a solution was now for the two governments to move matters forward. Reynolds recalls:

> I remember [Major] said over the funeral incident, "I'm going to have to condemn Adams." We agreed that we had to distance ourselves from the Hume-Adams initiative, that it was now so tainted as to be unusable; the only way forward was for the two governments to take matters into their own hands, and we had to make a public statement to that effect. Strictly between ourselves, we agreed that I should try to keep the Irish initiative going to see where it would lead. Major was adamant [that] he could not be seen publicly to wear this. But we reasoned it out between us, the Hume-Adams initiative was being declared dead in order to keep it alive, in the same way as Adams carried the bomber's coffin, because otherwise he couldn't deliver the IRA.[13]

This took political guts on Reynolds's part, because he was subjected to a lot of criticism in nationalist Ireland for being seen to ditch the Hume-Adams initiative. Within Fianna Fáil there was much indignation because the Taoiseach appeared to be siding with a British Prime Minister over the SDLP and Sinn Féin and in particular because he seemed to be at variance with John Hume, who was an iconic figure for the Fianna Fáil grass roots.

The decision to change the status of the Hume-Adams document was made at about the time of the Fianna Fáil ard-fheis in November 1993. Unaware of what was really going on between Dublin and London, and between Reynolds and the Sinn Féin and IRA interlocutors, the delegates reacted angrily to media suggestions that Reynolds was distancing himself from Hume. Once again, however, Reynolds backed his own instinct. He was prepared to bear the wrath of the Fianna Fáil grass roots, and the brickbats of the dispossessed ministers, at least temporarily, in pursuit of what he saw as a bigger prize. For that reason he hung tough, revelling in the cut and thrust of negotiations and the pursuit of a deal. The two governments worked painstakingly on a text for a joint declaration.

By early December, however, when Major came to Dublin, the process had run into a crisis. The British Government produced its own text for a declaration, withdrawing the text that the two governments had been working on. This new text was not acceptable to the Irish Government, and Reynolds realised that he would not be able to deliver the republican movement on those terms. He was determined to get this document off the table. Fergus Finlay, who was an active participant in the exchanges between British and Irish officials, and who has at times been a vocal critic of Reynolds, attended the vital meeting. He has given a dramatic and admiring account of Reynolds's performance at this make-or-break moment in the peace process.

> The two delegations were seated on either side of the Queen Anne table, and Albert got right to the point. "You're making a fool out of me, John" he said, "and I won't have it. We'll do no business on the basis of this thing." And he threw the British paper into the middle of the table. "What are you suggesting?" Major asked him. "Surely we have the right to table important new ideas . . ." "I'm suggesting bad faith, John," Albert snapped. "And we'll do no business that way. We go back to the document we started with, or we're outa here now." John Major had been toying with a pencil as Albert spoke. At the use of the words "bad faith" the pencil snapped in his hands. He looked down at it, bemused, and then looked up at Albert. "I think we should talk privately," he said. He was pale, his lips tight. "Grand so," Albert grinned and I realised with a start he was enjoying this.[14]

The whole peace process now hung in the balance. While the two leaders adjourned for their private talk, the air was thick with tension. Finlay continues:

> Eventually the door to the ante-room opened, and Albert came out, saying to the nearest British official, "he wants to see ye inside." I happened to be standing nearest to the Taoiseach when Albert emerged, and I said "How did it go, Taoiseach?" "It wasn't too bad," Albert replied. "He chewed the bollix off me, but I took a few lumps out of him!" He grinned, as always, but he too was pale, and tense. When John Major returned, it was as if nothing had happened. It was agreed, without any further discussion, that work would resume on the [original] text that was already in hand. Some desultory work was done on some of the paragraphs, before the meeting ended with an agreement to finalise the text as rapidly as possible and hold another summit to announce the outcome as soon as we had an outcome.[15]

Reynolds's hardball paid dividends. Twelve days later, amid continuing speculation that a historic breakthrough in relations between the Irish and British Governments with regard to Northern Ireland was imminent, he went to London, where he and Major signed what became known as the Downing Street Declaration. It was a huge political breakthrough and a triumph for Reynolds's perseverance.

In the declaration the British Government stated, for the first time, that it would "uphold the democratic wish of a greater number of the people of Northern Ireland on the issue of whether they prefer to support the Union or a sovereign united Ireland." It also affirmed that the British Government had

> no selfish strategic or economic interest in Northern Ireland. Their primary interest is to see peace, stability and reconciliation established by agreement among all the people who inhabit the island, and they will work together with the Irish Government to achieve such an agreement, which will embrace the totality of relationships.

This was the type of declaration that Lemass had told Kennedy in 1963 would be very helpful towards resolving the problem. The declaration also confirmed that

> the role of the British Government will be to encourage, facilitate and enable the achievement of such agreement over a period through a process of dialogue and co-operation based on full respect for the rights and identities of both traditions in Ireland. They accept that such agreement may, as of right, take the form of agreed structures for the island as a whole, including a united Ireland achieved by peaceful means on the following basis. The British Government agree that it is for the people of the island of Ireland alone, by agreement between the two parts respectively, to exercise their right of self-determination on the basis of consent, freely and concurrently given, North and South, to bring about a united Ireland, if that is their wish.

There was widespread acclamation in Ireland for the work of Reynolds and Spring in securing this agreement. When they entered the Dáil chamber together after their return from London they received a standing ovation from all sides. In Fianna Fáil the Downing Street declaration was seen as major progress, and Reynolds's achievement was lauded. Throughout the months of negotiations Reynolds had kept his cards very close to his chest. He never shared even the outline of what was being negotiated with his parliamentary party. There was little or no debate on the matter in the parliamentary party or the Ard-Chomhairle, even though the policy shifts had been foreshadowed in Reynolds's public utterances. Throughout the party there was a general sense that "Albert was up to something big with the British"; but when the details were revealed in the Downing Street Declaration even Reynolds's critics were impressed. They too appreciated the significance of what had been achieved. John O'Donoghue, who had been dropped as a minister of state by Reynolds when he came to power, paid him this tribute:

> The present Taoiseach, Deputy Reynolds, has secured his place in Irish history by obtaining a formal, explicit recognition for the first time that

Britain has no economic or strategic interest in this country and that the Irish people, North and South, have the right of self-determination. He deserves the eternal gratitude of the Irish people for that and I believe his initiative will succeed.[16]

The press, which had so often laid into Reynolds, was also generous in its praise. Seán Duignan wrote in his diary:

Albert deified! Even Éamonn Dunphy, Shane Ross, Eoghan Harris join the chorus of praise. He sits for a special photo for the *Sunday Tribune* of himself superimposed on pic of Declaration. They actually wanted to use a live dove in the shot. Albert, the Longford Slasher, looking soulfully heavenwards under a snow-white dove of peace! They seemed disappointed when I said "no thanks."[17]

When Duignan offered the Taoiseach his own congratulations, Reynolds made it clear that he was only warming up.

Reynolds said to me: "They're telling me to stand back now and rest on my laurels, when I'm not even going to have a breather before I take even bigger risks." "What do you mean?" "The Declaration is grand if it works. Otherwise, it doesn't amount to a damn thing. I've now got to find out if it will fly—if it can deliver what it was built for—the peace."[18]

While Reynolds now vigorously pursued a ceasefire in the North, hostilities were breaking out in the Fianna Fáil-Labour Government. Relations between the parties had been difficult from the earliest days of the Government. The Labour Party had become the focus of the press's ire for propping up Reynolds and for going back on the criticisms it had made of Fianna Fáil in opposition. The public mood cooled towards the party in the face of this barrage, especially when the press published stories about Labour Party ministers appointing large numbers of party-political activists, friends and even relatives to government jobs. The Labour Party was not used to having its political morals attacked, and its ministers were not amused, as Duignan records, when Cowen shook his head at them and said, "Jaze, lads, ye're giving us an awful bad name."[19]

Opinion polls showed that the Labour Party's standing with the public was suffering, and this made it more assertive in government. It believed it could pull back lost ground by showing that it was working hard and was the power-house of the Government. This tactic soon had Labour and Fianna Fáil ministers, as well as advisers, at each other's throats. Stephen Collins comments:

Reynolds quickly came to believe that Spring wanted to dominate the partnership, even though Labour had only half Fianna Fáil's number of seats. He saw Finlay's hand in a spate of newspaper stories suggesting that Labour ministers were really running the show in government and he came to resent it.[20]

On 1 March 1993, less than two months after the two parties had sealed the coalition agreement, Seán Duignan wrote in his diary:

> FF getting pissed off. Ruairí [Quinn] boasts "Labour are now in control of foreign affairs." All the corrs [political correspondents] telling me Labour are claiming to control the Programme Managers plus Dempsey says Dame Eithne [Fitzgerald] is driving FF nuts with her endless ethics lectures—"I don't want a Ferdinand Marcos (for Marcos read Reynolds) situation developing here," on top of her self-appointed role as "Minister for the €8 billion." Hardly a wet week in office, and this stuff already. Is it going to be worse than with the PDs?[21]

In fact right from the beginning Fianna Fáil and the Labour Party were at odds. The Labour Party had forced Fianna Fáil to back down on a plan to privatise the state-owned telecommunications service, Telecom Éireann, but the row had gone to the wire and had been resolved only when the Labour Party threatened to pull the plug on the coalition. Further tensions were sown over a tax amnesty. Reynolds had pushed for this, but the Labour Party believed that Ahern, as Minister for Finance, would oppose it in the Government. Ahern didn't, and Spring took much of the blame for not preventing Fianna Fáil from putting a "cheats' charter" through the Government.

Another coalition squabble developed in April 1994, which again took the Government to the brink. This concerned the Finance Bill and proposals regarding residence restrictions for tax exiles. Spring was opposed to part of the legislation, believing it would ease the tax obligation on the super-rich. Reynolds, on holiday in Cyprus, received a fax from Spring warning him that he would not tolerate this measure. Reynolds was livid.

> Taoiseach phones from Limassol, tells me he will not be dictated to— "I will not be a half Taoiseach . . . this could be the breakpoint." Jaysus! I ring John Foley [Labour Party press secretary] who says, "yes, it's a 'principle' thing for Labour and could lead to a general election!"[22]

This dispute was eventually resolved with some hasty amendments to the legislation, but any good will between Fianna Fáil and the Labour Party was fast evaporating. Matters were not helped when a controversy connected to the Taoiseach's family business arose over the so-called "passports for sale" investment scheme. The press turned their guns on Reynolds, who insisted he had done nothing wrong, while the Labour Party agonised over how to react to the revelations. Trust had broken down between Reynolds and Spring, as is clear from Reynolds's account of his engagement with Spring on this issue.

I told Dick Spring that he was welcome to inspect the Department of Justice files on the Masri [passport] deal and was somewhat taken aback when he said he'd already done so! For once I was speechless. Nevertheless, having perused all the papers he was forced to admit that everything had been conducted in an "ethical and above board, arm's-length way."[23]

This brought more denunciation down on Spring's head. The PD deputy Michael McDowell told the Dáil that Spring was now "morally brain dead". To make matters worse for the stability of the Government, all this occurred in the period leading up to the European Parliament elections of June 1994, which were coinciding with by-elections in Dublin South-Central and Mayo. In the elections the Labour vote nose-dived, and Labour Party activists and strategists were quick to attribute this to its association with Fianna Fáil and especially with Reynolds. Seán Duignan noted:

John Foley still saying Spring and his entire team deeply bitter. They insist Dick went to the wall for Albert on passports—I think they now see it as a major blunder that Dick went anywhere near the justice files—and that Albert showed his appreciation by kicking Dick in the balls.[24]

Fianna Fáil had gained a seat in the European Parliament, but what would be more significant, given the atmosphere between Fianna Fáil and the Labour Party, was that Democratic Left and Fine Gael won the two Dáil by-elections. One consequence of this was that there were now sufficient numbers for an alternative coalition to be formed, without the need for a general election, if the Labour Party felt it could not continue in its relationship with Reynolds.

Following the elections another crack in the cohesion of the Government came about with a row about TEAM Aer Lingus (the airline's maintenance subsidiary). Four Labour Party TDs, with an eye on their constituencies, failed to vote with the Government. Cowen, as Minister for Transport, and Dempsey, as chief whip, were furious and viewed Ruairí Quinn's Dáil contribution as a "betrayal" of his Fianna Fáil colleagues. Cowen, possibly Reynolds's most loyal minister, was so incensed that he threatened to resign. Reynolds himself defused the crisis. Duignan noted:

Cowen absolutely livid. Says he'll resign if Quinn is allowed to get away with it. Keeps saying Fianna Fáil held the line on Shannon Airport when Tony Killeen and Síle de Valera jumped ship. Albert comes in and tries to calm the pair of them [Cowen and Dempsey]. Eventually, he gets them to cool down a bit, and they both go away. I relax—just another hiccup—but then Albert says to me, as calmly as if he were making a comment on the weather: "Mark my words, tonight means the beginning of the end of this government!"[25]

That end seemed to have arrived with another row over the report of the Beef Tribunal. With the publication of the report pending in July 1994, the *Sunday Business Post* published a clearly informed article that suggested that the Labour Party would withdraw from the Government if the report was critical of the Taoiseach. Duignan wrote in his diary on 3 July:

> Emily O'Reilly has SBP [*Sunday Business Post*] story headlined "Spring ready to leave Coalition if Tribunal Report Censures Reynolds". It's straight from the horse's mouth stuff. Albert swears it's from an "unidentified, bearded, Labour source" [Fergus Finlay]. Significantly, Labour are not denying the story. More significantly, Albert says: "No government can survive this kind of thing." Why do Labour do these things publicly?[26]

At the last Government meeting in July before the summer recess the Labour Party ministers made it clear that they would not be "frog-marched" into taking an immediate position on the publication of the report. Finlay and two other Labour Party advisers also contacted Duignan and warned him to be careful how he briefed the political correspondents when the report emerged.[27] The report was finally delivered to Government Buildings on the night of 29 July 1994. It was nine hundred pages long, and Reynolds, his legal team, his advisers and senior civil servants ploughed through it to see if the Taoiseach had been criticised in any way. Duignan, who was present, noted:

> Someone said "You're in the clear." "Are you sure?" asked Reynolds. "Yes," came the reply. "OK," said Reynolds, "I've taken this shit long enough. I'm not taking another minute of it. Tell the pol corrs [political correspondents] I'm vindicated, Diggy." I hesitated: "Taoiseach, Labour are going to go spare. They've warned me against this." Teahon [Secretary of the Department of the Taoiseach] rowed in: "You don't need to do this, Taoiseach. You don't need to have a row with Labour. You've won." Reynolds said: "They told the dogs in the street they would bring me down on this if they didn't like the judgement. Now I've been cleared, and I don't need their permission to tell it as it is."[28]

When Duignan proceeded to brief the press that Reynolds had been vindicated, the Labour Party lost the plot. Duignan was confronted by an irate Fergus Finlay, who made it clear that the Government was now in real danger of collapsing.

> The worst part is Fergus. I'm phoning the papers when the door opens and I'm confronted by this old testament whirlwind of wrath, biblical beard quivering, like Moses about to smite the idolators of the Golden Calf . . . All I can clearly remember is him fiercely proclaiming: "This could mean the end of the government—you have been WARNED!"[29]

Reynolds had an equally angry conversation with Dick Spring.

Dick Spring called in the early hours of the morning to express his anger that I had pre-empted the government's perusal of the verdict. Not a word of congratulations, you're in the clear, only more dire warnings and threats. "Would you deny me my hour in the sun, Dick?" I asked him. "There may be no sun," he answered. "This is bad."[30]

While the Labour Party did not walk out of the Government on this occasion, Spring now began to give thought to his options, including the fact that the numbers were now available for a "rainbow" Government, with the Labour Party joining with Fine Gael and Democratic Left.[31]

Meanwhile, though relations within the Government had become more and more fractious, the two parties stood on the brink of a breakthrough. Since the Downing Street Declaration, Reynolds had doggedly pursued the quest for peace in the North. He was determined to bring about an IRA ceasefire; and, following tortuous and lengthy communications, by August 1994 he was on the brink of pulling it off.

An Irish-American delegation, which had been helpful to the process, came to Ireland at this time, and before going to meet Gerry Adams they met the Taoiseach. They raised with him the possibility that the IRA would call a temporary ceasefire, but Reynolds held firm for the bigger prize. He snapped:

Permanent! No pussy-footing. I haven't devoted two years of my life to this in order to be insulted with a temporary ceasefire. And another thing: I want their announcement to be written in language that an eleven-year old can understand. No messing—there's to be no messing.[32]

In the end the IRA ceasefire hinged on Joe Cahill, a former IRA chief of staff, getting a visa for the United States so he could brief Irish-American supporters on the position the republican movement intended to adopt. President Clinton was reluctant to sanction the visa, given Cahill's para-military connections, but Reynolds convinced him that it was a deal-maker. In his memoirs Reynolds describes the phone calls when he played hardball with President Clinton.

"If you don't do it," I warned him, "there will be no peace. I'm talking a permanent ceasefire here. What's that worth to you, for a start, politic-ally now? Let's talk politics. Politically, if it makes a difference between electing you and not electing you, is it worth it or not? All the criticism over Adams's visa will disappear if you pull it off. It's up to you!"

"All my experience tells me," [Clinton] said slowly "that if there's going to be a ceasefire soon, the statement has already been put together by those guys. Do you know if it's been put together?"

I knew I had one last card to play. "I do," I said.

"How do you know?"

"Because," I answered, "I have a copy of it here in my pocket."

"Then read out the paragraph that matters . . ."

I read out the statement—and waited. It was his call.

"Ok," he said. "We'll go for it. But this is the last chance. And if this one doesn't run, I never want to hear from you again! Goodbye."[33]

Cahill got his visa, and within hours, on 31 August, the IRA had announced "a complete cessation of military operations." Twenty-five years of armed struggle had come to an end. It was another unprecedented and astonishing triumph for Albert Reynolds. Nobody had believed he could do it, but Reynolds had done the impossible.

When the Taoiseach attended a meeting of the Fianna Fáil parliamentary party in Leinster House he received two standing ovations. There was a similar reaction from all sides of the Dáil when he entered the chamber accompanied by Dick Spring.

David Andrews, Reynolds's Minister for Defence, has an interesting angle on Reynolds's role in bringing about the ceasefire.

> Historically speaking only a Fianna Fáil Taoiseach could have secured this agreement from the IRA. What I mean is that, if the IRA were to trust anybody—and I have no regard whatsoever for the IRA—they would be much more likely to trust a Fianna Fáil leader, rather than any of the other leaders. I would see it as a question of historical resonance, in that the Provisional IRA would have recognised where we were born and bred, and would therefore have been more inclined to trust us, or at least interface with us as a prelude to trust. Of all the political leaders involved in bringing about this ceasefire, from Garret FitzGerald's Anglo-Irish Agreement onwards, most credit for the Joint Declaration and the subsequent end of the campaign of violence must go to Albert Reynolds. His energy, drive and single-minded commitment, and, indeed, willingness to gamble all, pushed things forward in a way nobody else could have done. Whatever else may have happened in his political life—and it was far from a story of continued triumph, particularly towards the end—what he achieved in Northern Ireland will be a lasting monument.[34]

It was to be the high point of Reynolds's term as leader of Fianna Fáil. Like many people in the country, the majority of his party colleagues and the party grass roots had a mixed attitude towards Reynolds. They respected him most of the time and had some affection for him, but they were always wary of where his words and deeds might lead. In elections he had been a disaster for the party. He seemed to be uninterested in party management, he was frustratingly bad at day-to-day political tactics, he was often gauche in his communications and he appeared blind to the need for either party unity or subtle coalition management. But he could do the big things well.

If there had been admiration within the party for his achievement on the Downing Street Declaration there was adulation when he pulled off the IRA ceasefire. Like most of the public, Fianna Fáil members had become inured to the regular reports of killing in the North; they had not dared to hope that it might somehow be stopped. Now, thanks in large part to the efforts of their leader, the IRA guns and bombs had fallen silent and within days the loyalist guns followed suit. At a press conference given by the "Combined Loyalist Military Command" at Fernhill House in Belfast on 13 October the leading loyalist figure Gusty Spence, flanked by figures from the PUP and UDP, announced that the loyalist organisations would also "universally cease all operational hostilities," and offered apologies to all innocent victims. It was thought at the time that the loyalist move had derived from indirect contacts the Reynolds Government had had through Archbishop Robin Eames and others. What was not known then and was only revealed when Reynolds published his memoirs in 2009 was that he had held a series of direct meetings on his own with Gusty Spence and David Ervine in a Dublin hotel some months earlier. He had done this unknown even to Martin Mansergh, who had been his main contact with the Sinn Féin and IRA interlocutors.

109 days after the high point of achieving the IRA ceasefire, Albert Reynolds was compelled to resign as Taoiseach. Relations between Fianna Fáil and the Labour Party had been teetering on the brink for quite a while, but it was a dispute over the appointment of the Attorney-General to the position of president of the High Court that finally precipitated the collapse of the Government. This followed an earlier disagreement over the appointment of the new Chief Justice. The Minister for Justice, Máire Geoghegan-Quinn, had recommended Liam Hamilton, who had chaired the Beef Tribunal, whereas Spring had wanted Dónal Barrington, then serving in the European Court of Justice.

In the end—but not before another disagreement between Spring and Reynolds—it appeared that the Fianna Fáil choice would prevail. As it happened, Barrington's appointment would not have been possible, because of a provision that prevented a judge moving directly from the European Court of Justice to the Supreme Court; but that emerged later and had no effect on what followed.

Because Fianna Fáil was now going to get its way on the appointment of the Chief Justice, given the tit-for-tat atmosphere now permeating the Government, the Labour Party was insisting on its own choice for president of the High Court. Harry Whelehan, the serving Attorney-General, had made it clear that he was interested in the post, but this did not meet with any enthusiasm in the Labour Party. The party was critical of Whelehan's intervention in the X case during the previous Government and favoured a more liberal and reforming candidate. The Labour Party viewpoint was that

Whelehan was a conservative Catholic, and he was also regarded as very much a Fianna Fáil Attorney-General.

This did not stop Whelehan from approaching Spring and setting out his interest in the job; but Spring had no intention of supporting him. When he told Fergus Finlay of Whelehan's approach Finlay asked Spring whether he had given Whelehan any commitment. "You must be joking!" was Spring's reply. Meanwhile, undeterred, Whelehan had been going around leading members of Fianna Fáil, gathering support, and most of them agreed to back his appointment.[35] Crucially, Whelehan had secured Reynolds's word that he would get the job.

> As far as I was concerned, it was traditional that if the chief constitutional officer of the state and legal advisor to the government indicated an interest in a major position, it was normal that the request should be acceded to, if the Taoiseach was so minded. The Attorney General had indicated his strong interest in being appointed president of the High Court, I had agreed and given him my word, and that was that.[36]

Spring's preferred candidate was Susan Denham, a High Court judge with strong liberal credentials, and he made it clear to the Fianna Fáil ministers that the Labour Party would not accept the appointment of Whelehan. A stalemate ensued, which was heightened by the fact that the newspapers had become aware of the disagreement. David Andrews realised that this could be a breaking point and was of the view that Whelehan should have stepped aside.

> Harry Whelehan, instead of going for the Presidency of the High Court, should have accepted appointment as an ordinary judge of the court. I cannot speak highly enough of his character—one could not ask to meet finer—but his political nous was limited. It is amazing that a highly intelligent man could not see that his appointment was likely to bring down a government. Clearly he should have stood back and settled for the lesser position. Had he done so, he would have been a prime candidate for the Presidency of the High Court when the position next became vacant.[37]

Reynolds, however, decided to proceed with Whelehan's appointment. The judicial appointments appeared on the Government agenda at a time when Dick Spring was in Japan, and—though Reynolds argued that their appearance on the agenda was routine—the timing aroused suspicion in the Labour Party. Before the meeting could begin Ruairí Quinn had contacted Spring on the phone in Tokyo and brought him up to date on developments. Reynolds himself was due to head for Australia after the Government meeting, but his departure was delayed because Labour Party ministers made it clear that they would not support Whelehan's appointment. In his diary for 14 September 1994 Seán Duignan wrote:

Suddenly departure for Australia put back three hours as cabinet crisis develops . . . Appointments of Chief Justice and sequential jobs, President of the High Court and AG [Attorney-General] on cabinet agenda. Ruairí Quinn tells Taoiseach they will walk out if he tries to push it through. Accuse Albert of trying to slip appointments through while Dick out of country. Albert insists they were on last week's cabinet agenda, but not dealt with; therefore go automatically onto this week's agenda. Quinn/Howlin in touch with Spring at Tokyo Airport. They say no deal on Liam Hamilton's appointment as Chief Justice unless it is agreed that Harry doesn't get President of H.C.[38]

Reynolds and the Fianna Fáil ministers were now engaged in a game of political poker with the Labour Party. At one point Reynolds said to Duignan that he was going to proceed to the Government and make the appointments, irrespective of the Labour Party's views. "If they walk out, they walk out. They want to bring the thing down; so be it."[39] Eventually, however—following long negotiations between Reynolds, Howlin and Quinn—the Labour Party agreed to Hamilton's appointment as Chief Justice on the understanding that the other vacancies would be deferred until the Taoiseach and Tánaiste met when they returned to Ireland.

Reynolds, with Duignan in tow, then headed for Australia on Government business, but not before Finlay had issued a stark warning to Duignan. "I'm just telling you, if he tries to force Harry on us we will make the Beef Tribunal row look like a storm in a teacup."[40] In Sydney, reflecting on the political turmoil that he and Reynolds had temporarily escaped from, Duignan wrote in his diary on 23 September 1994:

I think we're all insane. Albert Reynolds is being treated like God down here. He's headline news right across Australia for what he's done on the North. And we're talking about bringing down the Government over Harry and some job people hardly know exists. Madness!!![41]

Most back-bench Fianna Fáil and Labour Party TDs were very much of the view that it would indeed be foolhardy to risk an election on the grounds of judicial appointments that the public were not interested in. The Labour Party TD for Dublin South-Central, Pat Upton, encapsulated this view when he asked sarcastically whether the row would divide the public into "Whelehanite and Denhamite factions".[42] Those closer to the inner sanctum, however, recognised that the Taoiseach and Tánaiste were in no mood to compromise, and that trust had completely broken down at the heart of the Government.

Reynolds was annoyed by what were clearly Labour Party leaks to the effect that it had stopped Fianna Fáil railroading through Whelehan's appointment. He admits to being infuriated by what he regarded as the Labour Party's public abuse.

I was extremely angry, and further irritated at evidence of more Labour briefings when the *Sunday Business Post* of 25th September 1994 printed claims that Spring and his people were describing me, the Taoiseach, as "power-drunk following the IRA ceasefire" and as "the High King of Ireland on a roll!"[43]

Reynolds was not prepared to take this lying down, and he was emboldened by the fact that the media unexpectedly swung in behind him. The *Irish Times* in particular was critical of Spring. An editorial on 26 September 1994 said:

> Those who know Mr Spring recognise that he can be at his most dangerous when he feels taken for granted or condescended to. In those circumstances his aggressive side comes out. It is not beyond the bounds of possibility that he could decide to bring the whole house down simply to teach Albert Reynolds manners, as he might be inclined to put it himself . . . Mr Spring has made a gaffe on the High Court issue. He purported to run a candidate—Mrs Justice Denham—whom he never even consulted and who, it now turns out, is not even interested in the post. And he has blocked the man who, as Attorney General, acts as chief legal advisor to the Government of which Mr Spring is deputy premier. If Mr Whelehan is not fitted for the largely bureaucratic post of President of the High Court, how can Mr Spring have confidence in him as Attorney General? All in all Mr Spring is on shaky ground.

Reynolds says that as far as he was concerned "the gloves were off," and he publicly contradicted the Labour Party claims that had so incensed him.[44] This set alarm bells ringing among some more perceptive Fianna Fáil ministers, including McCreevy and Geoghegan-Quinn.[45]

David Andrews was another Fianna Fáil minister concerned at the direction events were taking.

> Some of us, his Fianna Fáil Ministers, were worried . . . "Why would you bring a government down over a judicial appointment?" was one of the questions being asked. Another question was that, while Harry Whelehan was a good Attorney General, what did we owe him collectively as a government? He should have waited his turn—his time would come.[46]

The pressure on Spring from party colleagues to resolve the dispute and patch up the Government was even more intense than that on Reynolds. The Labour Party was already struggling in the opinion polls and, with the public mood swinging against it, the Labour parliamentary party did not want to risk an election. Spring had a difficult meeting with some Labour Party ministers, who believed matters were getting out of hand.[47] Back-benchers also took to the air waves, saying that the appointment of Harry Whelehan should not cause an election and effectually pulled the rug from under their leader.

Reynolds and Spring held a late meeting in Baldonnel Airport to resolve the issue. They agreed not to allow the situation to spill over into a general election and made an agreement to revamp the whole judicial appointments system. Spring accepted that the issue of judicial appointments could come back to the Government table after the details of the court reforms were worked out in a matter of weeks. According to Stephen Collins, he did not specifically agree to the appointment of Whelehan, but even Labour Party sources concede that it was implicit in the agreement. "As far as Reynolds was concerned he had won, but he was prepared to give Spring time to eat humble pie. It was one of the biggest mistakes of his political career."[48]

Within a week of this meeting a story broke that an extradition warrant for a paedophile priest, Brendan Smyth, had not been dealt with in the Attorney-General's office for seven months. This handed Spring the means to scuttle Whelehan's appointment and to trump Reynolds; but at first the Taoiseach was not alive to the danger. Seán Duignan recalled:

> Reynolds was warned there was a legal link between Smyth and the Attorney General's office. He mentioned it to me as a new and irritating development, but not something he regarded as threatening. For a considerable time afterwards, he failed to appreciate its significance in terms of the Whelehan appointment—"Dick and I have a deal"—but it emerged that Spring and his advisers had understood its potential much sooner. Said John Foley to me: "The priest changes everything."[49]

Reynolds wanted the matter dealt with, and as far as he was concerned Whelehan had acted in good faith. He decided to push ahead with the judicial appointment, believing the Labour Party would back down. Duignan wrote:

> I could not believe this was happening; first of all, that Labour were upping the ante yet again; and, then, that the Taoiseach was not just calling their bluff but betting all he had that they would ultimately fold. Still, I told myself, crafty operators like Bertie, Quinn, McCreevy, Howlin, Cowen, and others, would not let it get to that. And, yet, I had a feeling that things were finally spiralling out of control. I kept recalling the strangely excited, almost challenging, look in Reynolds's eye as he said: "Are you worried, Diggy?"[50]

At the Government meeting at which Reynolds proposed Whelehan's appointment, the Labour Party ministers walked out. The Fianna Fáil ministers then approved Whelehan's appointment.

The results of two Cork by-elections on the day of that Government meeting may have encouraged Reynolds to gamble on resolving an issue that was now a source of great frustration to him. Those by-elections had been won by Kathleen Lynch of Democratic Left and Hugh Coveney of Fine Gael, which meant that the numbers for an alternative Government without an election had been further improved. The Labour Party recognised this, but Fianna Fáil ministers thought that it would not risk a general election because it had done so badly.

As Spring consulted his party colleagues, Reynolds proceeded to Áras an Uachtaráin for Whelehan's appointment. The real possibility that the Government would collapse now seems to have dawned on the Fianna Fáil members. Duignan recalls Reynolds turning to him in Áras an Uachtaráin and saying, "No Taoiseach ever sacrificed so much for an Attorney-General." Whelehan seems to have been the only person not conscious that a political crisis was now under way.

One particularly interesting exchange at Áras an Uachtaráin shows how some Fianna Fáil ministers were increasingly concerned at what Reynolds had done. They had not resisted his actions at that morning's Government meeting but they now blamed Whelehan for putting the Taoiseach and themselves in this position. Máire Geoghegan-Quinn marched over to Whelehan and hissed, "When I am out in the snow on the election trail in Galway and people on the doorsteps ask me, 'What about Harry Whelehan?' I'm going to reply, "Fuck Harry Whelehan."[51]

What followed was an increasingly desperate series of attempts by Fianna Fáil to put the Government back together. Spring had gone to his parliamentary party and made a powerful speech that placed the emphasis on the emotive subject of child abuse and on Fianna Fáil's perceived failures on the issue.

"At the end of the day, when all other questions have been dealt with, one remains. We have allowed a child abuser to remain at large in our community, when we had it in our power to ensure [that] he was given up to justice. Is no one to explain why? Is no one to take responsibility? Is no one to account to the people of this country for so grievous a lapse?" The speech was made in private but when garbled versions were published in the media Reynolds and Fianna Fáil interpreted it as an unfair charge that they were in some way prepared to cover up for a paedophile . . . Spring was [now] backed to the hilt by his backbenchers who vied with each other to express their loyalty and support, just weeks after they had tried to out-do each other expressing the opposite view.[52]

Séamus Brennan began talking to Ruairí Quinn about ways of solving the crisis. He reported back to an emergency meeting of Fianna Fáil ministers that if the Taoiseach were to express regret to the Tánaiste on how the matter had been handled in his Dáil contribution there was a chance that the Government could be saved.

At this same meeting the new Attorney-General, Eoghan Fitzsimons, told the assembled Fianna Fáil ministers about another case, that of an English paedophile priest, Anthony Duggan, who had fled to Ireland. In this case also there were delays in dealing with an extradition warrant. It remains disputed whether Reynolds and his ministers understood the full implications of this case, and the meeting dealt more with trying to persuade Whelehan to get them off the hook. Fitzsimons was despatched to Whelehan's house to see if the current Attorney-General could persuade the former Attorney-General to delay his swearing in as a High Court judge. Whelehan refused, saying he considered it "inappropriate and constitutionally incorrect and improper" that members of the Government should bring pressure to bear on a judge to resign.

A group of Fianna Fáil ministers, including Cowen, Smith, McCreevy and Geoghegan-Quinn, joined Mansergh and Tom Savage, Reynolds's communications adviser, in drafting the Taoiseach's crucial speech. Reynolds refused to use the word "apologise", so it was decided instead to express "regret," while taking into account all the other points the Labour Party was insisting should be included. Duignan records in his diary for 14 November 1994:

> Extraordinary late night (2.30a.m.), session of FF Ministers as Máire Geoghegan-Quinn, Michael Smith and Tom Savage direct operations. Too many cooks? Albert balks at the word "apologise". He tells me in the jacks that other stuff is emerging re AG's office dealing with sexual abuse; that he sent message to him that he should consider his position and at least postpone his swearing in; that Harry responded: "I am President of the High Court." i.e. goodbyeee! Reynolds tells me his gut instinct is that Labour want an election, that they engineered Friday with that in mind. His speech for tomorrow, according to Máire Geoghegan-Quinn/Smith, is brilliant. But Albert is hyper. His instinct is [that] the game is up.[53]

The following day Reynolds went into the Dáil and ate humble pie. He said there was an unacceptable delay in dealing with the Smyth case, he promised to review the workings of the Office of the Attorney-General and he paid generous tribute to the contribution of Dick Spring and the Labour Party in government. Some Fianna Fáil ministers were confident that the speech would be enough to see the Labour Party come back into the Government, but others in the party were working to a different agenda, believing that "if Fianna Fáil dumped Reynolds and installed Bertie Ahern in his place then Humpty Dumpty could be put together again."[54] Duignan noted in his diary for 15 November:

> Albert does the business in the Dáil, Says he's sorry to the Irish people, to Dick Spring et al. Almost immediately, word comes back: "It's not enough." Greg Sparks [Labour Party programme manager] comes over to me and says "It's not enough." I say automatically: "General election?"

He pauses, eyes momentarily glazing, then says: "Prob-ab-ly." Jesus. Probably my arse. Suddenly, it's clear. They're going to go for it. Gambling just like Albert. The trick is no election. Shaft Albert but stick with Fianna Fáil? Albert may have walked into a trap . . .[55]

At this point the attention of the media began to turn to the Duggan case. Reynolds, who by now had grasped the significance of another extradition warrant not being dealt with adequately by the Attorney-General's office, was openly saying he felt betrayed by Whelehan. Meanwhile McCreevy had been talking to Senator Pat Magner of the Labour Party, who was close to Spring and who passed on the message that there was still a chance to save the Government. This was confirmed when Brendan Howlin rang Dempsey and said that if the Taoiseach was prepared to say that, knowing what he now knew, it had been a mistake to appoint Whelehan, and that Spring was right all along, the Labour Party would go back into government with Reynolds. At the same time another attempt was made to get Whelehan off the stage. At the instigation of Michael Woods, Fitzsimons again went to see Whelehan with the message that if the Government fell, the peace process could break down. Whelehan stood firm and again refused to resign.

The following morning McCreevy showed Brendan Howlin a draft of Reynolds's crucial speech for later that day. It included a number of sentences that the Labour Party had insisted on.

I now accept that the reservations voiced by the Tánaiste are well founded and I regret the appointment of the former Attorney General as president of the High Court. I also regret my decision to proceed with the appointment against the expressed wishes of the Labour Party . . . I guarantee that this breach of trust, a trust on which the partnership Government was founded, will not be repeated.

Howlin told McCreevy he believed that if these sentences were uttered, the Labour Party would resume its partnership with Fianna Fáil; but trust had so far deteriorated that Fianna Fáil ministers were prepared to accept this assurance only if they got it in writing. They therefore sought a written assurance from Spring that, if the sentences were used, the Labour Party would come back into the Government.

"Look, do you not trust me?" Howlin asked Dempsey.

"Yes, Brendan, I trust you, but some of my colleagues don't trust some of your colleagues, or some other people in the Labour Party," came the reply . . . Spring was brought in. He read the draft speech and said, "Yes, fine. What do you want me to sign?" Dempsey produced a short note which read, "On the basis of the statement prepared by me being incorporated in the Taoiseach's speech, I will lead my ministerial colleagues back into Government to complete the Programme for

Government." [Spring] took the note from Dempsey and signed it: *Dick Spring, 16th November, 10.22 a.m.*[56]

It looked as if Reynolds had once more done the impossible and had pulled his Government back from the abyss. Spring went to Reynolds's office, and the deal to keep the Government was confirmed "with handshakes and backslaps all round."[57]

Harmony lasted for less than an hour. Spring received an anonymous tip-off that Reynolds had known about the Duggan case all along and had misled the Dáil. Reynolds recalls:

> They came to confront me—Dick Spring, Howlin, Quinn and Mervyn Taylor—and accused me of lying, of deliberately withholding information about the Duggan case and of deceiving the house. Of course I denied it vehemently; but all my explanations—that I had not wilfully misled the house but had been waiting for the Attorney General's definitive advice, as was correct procedure—fell on deaf ears.[58]

It was at this point that Ruairí Quinn made his now infamous remark: "We've come for a head, Harry's or yours; it doesn't look like we're getting Harry's."[59] Reynolds's time as Taoiseach was now almost at an end. The Labour Party had made it clear that it would not continue in Government with him. Seán Duignan records the scene of devastation among the Fianna Fáil ministers as that reality dawned.

> I meet Dempsey who is almost speechless, suddenly aged for such a young guy . . . Máire Geoghegan Quinn like I've never seen her before, utterly shattered; Smith as if he has been hit between the eyes with a hammer. All standing around Albert, beating their breasts, saying: "We let you down." Albert occasionally taking out the sheet of paper [the note signed by Spring] and looking at it bemusedly. A dud cheque.[60]

It was now clear to all in Fianna Fáil that Reynolds could not survive either as Taoiseach or party leader. Over the previous days, as the "will Labour stay, will Labour go?" saga was played out in the media, and as Reynolds's various acts of contrition were broadcast live to the country from the Dáil chamber, the Haugheyites met in open groups around Leinster House. Former ministers such as Ray Burke could not keep a smile off their faces as they enjoyed Reynolds's discomfiture and looked forward to the imminent end of his short-lived era. Almost everyone assumed that Bertie Ahern would be leader soon, and open campaigning for him began as soon as the fall of the Government appeared to be confirmed. Ahern himself was careful not to be seen seeking support until Reynolds had actually resigned: he made sure he did not fall into the trap of being an instrument of revenge for Burke and his fellow-conspirators.

On the evening of 16 November even Reynolds loyalists knew the game was up. He himself appeared to still be in denial. There was a surreal atmosphere in Government Buildings that night. While Reynolds sat quietly in his office, his advisers and ministers and some constituency supporters wandered aimlessly through the corridors of that building and of Leinster House. Occasionally they clustered in small groups, seeking to ease the trauma and discussing how the end would play out. Some of those closest to Reynolds wanted to go to his office and tell him to announce his resignation that night. Others, however, asked that he be given the space to come to the realisation himself. There was a sense that Reynolds needed to go home to his wife and children and talk it through, that if he did not already appreciate it himself they would soon tell him. Everyone expected that his resignation would come in the morning.[61]

And that was what happened. Albert Reynolds resigned as Taoiseach on 17 November 1994, agreeing to stay on as caretaker until a new Government was formed. After making his resignation speech in the Dáil he remarked ruefully to the press gallery as he left: "It's amazing. You cross the big hurdles, and when you get to the small ones you get tripped."

There was one further dramatic twist. After returning his seal of office to President Robinson, Reynolds attended a meeting of the Fianna Fáil parliamentary party, where he tendered his resignation as party leader. News then arrived that Whelehan had resigned as president of the High Court, and the Fianna Fáil meeting broke to consider its implications. Duignan noted:

I'm standing in the corridor as they sweep back. "It's not over yet," says [Noel] Treacy fiercely. "It's not over yet," says Bertie too. They've lost the run of themselves, clutching at straws, they must know that. Everyone talking about "What if Harry had done this earlier?" But he didn't. Albert telling me fellas telling him to hang on and not to resign as leader of FF. But he admits to me that he had, before Harry's resignation news, told the meeting that he would resign "at the wishes of the party." Yet the remnants keep urging him on. This is bunker fever. Where is Wenck [Hitler's last general to try to defend Berlin]? Where is the Ninth Army? Total fantasy. I feel I'm watching from a distance. Stupefying.[62]

It was in this fevered, surreal and confused atmosphere that Albert Reynolds's tenure as Taoiseach and as president of Fianna Fáil drew to a close. It had been an era of real achievements. Employment was at last growing, and the economy had expanded by 8½ per cent over 1993 and 94. There were the great high points of the £8 billion in EC funding and, of course, Reynolds's accomplishments in Northern Ireland.

But there were also real low points for Fianna Fáil, such as a serious election reverse, the break-up of two Governments and poisonous relations with coalition partners. It was rollercoaster stuff, but that was Albert Reynolds's style of politics, as he explained to Seán Duignan.

Early on, he told me: "The main thing to remember about being in this job is that you're here to make the decisions, and that involves taking risks . . . You cannot get all the decisions right, but you'll have no hope at all if you try to play it safe, and duck taking them . . . You've got to be prepared to take the responsibility and also, if you get it wrong, to take the consequences." I was to learn that Albert Reynolds consistently played for high stakes, was prepared to back his hunch to the limit, and preferred to bet on the nose rather than each way. This made for a precarious existence; it left little margin for error, and, when the chips were down, no margin at all for the unexpected. Playing that system, you win big—or you lose big.

Fianna Fáil was dizzy from the ride Reynolds had taken it on. It craved a calmer, quieter atmosphere. After decades of internal divisions under Lynch, Haughey and Reynolds the party needed a rest from acrimony. They wanted their next leader to be someone who could unite the party and safeguard their electoral fortunes. Now, in the age of coalition government, Fianna Fáil needed a leader with the personality and skill to build and sustain relations with other political parties. Bertie Ahern fitted the bill perfectly.

Chapter 18

THE BERTIE BOUNCE, 1995–7

Bertie Ahern was busy on the night before he was elected leader of Fianna Fáil. It was the day after Albert Reynolds had resigned as Taoiseach, and the parliamentary party was due to meet the next morning to elect its new leader. Ahern, like everyone else, knew that he would win comfortably, but that was not enough for him: he needed it to be unanimous—not because he desired a coronation but because it would be a break from almost a quarter of a century of divisions in Fianna Fáil.

The only other candidate who had declared was Máire Geoghegan-Quinn, Minister for Justice. She was a strong Reynolds loyalist and had been at the very centre of the extraordinary events that had brought about Reynolds's demise. Since 1979, when she had become Ireland's first woman minister since Constance Markievicz, MGQ (as she was popularly known) had always been spoken of as a potential leader of Fianna Fáil. But the timing and circumstances of the succession did not suit her. Her initial ringing around on that Friday morning had quickly established that there was a groundswell of support for Ahern. Charlie McCreevy had agreed to propose her, but none of the party's other front-benchers had rallied round. At this point she expected only a handful of votes.

Despite this, Ahern worked the phones into the early morning, talking to back-benchers such as Noel Treacy, Pat "the Cope" Gallagher and John Browne, who were close to Geoghegan-Quinn and might be able to persuade her to withdraw.

When all the deputies gathered in Leinster House shortly after 11 a.m. that Saturday, Geoghegan-Quinn was duly nominated by McCreevy, but she withdrew her name, and, for the first time since June 1959, Fianna Fáil had a leader who enjoyed a unanimous mandate from his parliamentary colleagues.

Ahern's first press conference, held that afternoon in the Burlington Hotel, was a lively celebratory affair at which he emphasised the need for Fianna Fáil to set aside old squabbles. John Downing recounts one particularly tricky question at this event.

[The] veteran tabloid journalist, Paddy Clancy, asked him about his marital status. The new Fianna Fáil leader hushed his supporters' angry

jeers and prevented [the] Parliamentary Party chairman Deputy Joe
Jacob from disallowing the question. Ahern said it was public
knowledge that for several years he had been amicably separated from
his wife Miriam. Even so he said he was glad of the understanding
shown him by colleagues. To loud cheers from supporters, Bertie Ahern
added that Irish society now took a more enlightened view of people in
his situation.[1]

When he succeeded Reynolds as leader of Fianna Fáil it was assumed that
Ahern would also, within a couple of weeks, succeed him as Taoiseach. The
negotiation of a renewed programme for government with Dick Spring and
the Labour Party was expected to be a formality. The negotiations went
relatively smoothly, and when Ahern retired for the night on Monday
7 December 1994 he expected to become Taoiseach, at the head of a
reconstructed Fianna Fáil-Labour Government, when the Dáil reconvened
two days later. He had even spent some time that evening considering his list
of potential Government appointments. There had been some discussion
between himself and Spring earlier in the day about an article in that
morning's *Irish Times*. Geraldine Kennedy had written a detailed account of
the events surrounding the collapse of the Reynolds Government, and one
part of it in particular had upset the former Labour Party ministers. This
paragraph said that all the Fianna Fáil ministers, not only Reynolds, had
known about the Duggan case on Monday 14 November when Reynolds had
continued his support in the Dáil for the appointment of Harry Whelehan as
president of the High Court. The suggestion was not news to most who had
been following the events in detail: the *Irish Times* itself had referred to it in
several previous articles.[2] It had set alarm bells ringing in the Labour Party,
however, and these chimed with a growing desire among some of Spring's
closest advisers not to go back into government with Fianna Fáil but to
explore instead the option of a coalition with Fine Gael and Democratic Left.
    In talking to Ahern that day Spring had asked for further details about the
meeting at which the Duggan case had or had not been discussed; but Ahern
had no inkling of what was about to happen overnight.

The phone upstairs in St Luke's [Ahern's constituency building in
Drumcondra, where he was living] rang around two that morning and
the noise scared the life out of me. It was Spring on the line. "I'm sorry
Bertie," he said. "I've decided to pull out." I was surprised. I told him
that I had been trying all day to get comprehensive information for
him. He accepted that. "It's all too much, Bertie, its all too much," he
said. I asked if there was anything else I could do. He said no. We said
goodnight. The whole conversation had taken five minutes. Nobody
lost his temper. By the end of it I was no longer "Taoiseach-in-waiting".
I had been thirty-six hours away from forming a government. Now it
was "Welcome to life in opposition."[3]

Eight days later the Fine Gael leader, John Bruton, was elected Taoiseach. In the intervening days Ahern had managed to grin and bear the disappointment. His "mask of calm"[4] slipped only once, when he turned on Deputy Gay Mitchell of Fine Gael, who was interrupting his speech in the Dáil, and shouted at him, "You're a waffler, a waffler, and you've always been a waffler!" It was the only public display of the frustration Ahern must have felt at the turn of events. Where he had expected to be tackling the Northern peace process and other national challenges in government he would now have to knuckle down and use the time to reorganise Fianna Fáil and prepare to win his own mandate whenever the next election came along.

Ahern and his party used this unexpected sojourn in opposition extremely well. Of all Fianna Fáil's leading figures he was particularly well suited to the task of revitalising the party organisation and preparing for an election. He was "of the party" and not just "in the party" and was steeped in Fianna Fáil's heritage. He had also been a political organiser all his life.

Bertie Ahern learnt his political campaigning techniques in his teens. The youngest son in a houseful of Fianna Fáil activists, he was appointed director of postering for the local party in Drumcondra at the age of fifteen. Over the following four decades he designed, built and led the most formidable and well-resourced urban political machine ever seen in Ireland. As a dishevelled 25-year-old he won a seat in the Dublin Finglas constituency during the 1977 Fianna Fáil landslide. Four years later, in the newly drawn Dublin Central constituency, he took the first seat, beating his colleague George Colley in the process. He quickly achieved political dominance in Dublin Central, surging ahead of Colley and later seeing off other Fianna Fáil contenders. He had taken the first seat in that constituency in each election since, and from 1982 he had always polled more than ten thousand first preferences.

Once having arrived in Leinster House, Ahern had been favoured by Charles Haughey, who made him first assistant chief whip and then chief whip. By the time he was thirty-five Ahern had not only become one of Dublin's youngest Lord Mayors but was simultaneously sitting at the Government table as Minister for Labour and had begun to build a formidable reputation as the "Red Adair" of Irish industrial relations. He had decided, wisely, not to oppose Reynolds for the leadership in 1992, and as a result, less than three years later, he had become the inevitable and unopposed choice to lead the party.

Ahern now set about the tasks of healing, rebuilding and reconciling Fianna Fáil. A first step in that regard was the selection of his new front bench, which he announced at a lavish press conference in the Royal Hospital, Kilmainham, in January 1995. His new line-up contained an interesting mix of former Haughey ministers and former Reynolds ministers, together with a sprinkling of entirely new faces. None of the outgoing Reynolds ministers was dropped; instead extra room was created by extending the range of portfolios. The most surprising appointment was that of Charlie McCreevy to be Fianna Fáil's finance spokesperson. Not only had McCreevy been Geoghegan-Quinn's

chief advocate during her short-lived leadership campaign but he had also
been close to Reynolds and was not known as a friend of Ahern. Another
ardent Reynolds loyalist, Brian Cowen, was given agriculture. David Andrews
would speak on defence and the marine, and Noel Dempsey became spokesperson on the environment. Michael Smith was also reappointed to the front
line, despite his remarks during the Ahern-Reynolds leadership tussle in 1992
when he had commented to a reporter that people liked to know "where their
Taoiseach sleeps at night," widely taken as suggesting that Ahern was
unsuitable for office because of his separated status.

The Haughey wing was also well represented in the new line-up, most
prominently by Ray Burke, who was given the foreign affairs brief and was to
be a confidant and close adviser to Ahern in these opposition years. Dermot
Ahern and John O'Donoghue, both of whom had briefly been ministers of
state at the end of the Haughey era, now became full members of the front
bench as spokespersons on justice and social welfare, respectively. Other new
faces were those of Síle de Valera, a granddaughter of Éamon de Valera, who
was spokesperson on arts and culture, and Micheál Martin, who was given the
education brief.

Early in 1995 a team of newly recruited senior researchers and *ad hoc*
committees in each policy area were appointed to support the front bench.
This support structure was similar to the one the party had built during its
period in opposition between 1973 and 1977, with the difference that Ahern
was more directly involved than Lynch had been. Ahern also made sure that
all his disparate front bench felt involved. One of them, the late Séamus
Brennan, told John Downing how the Ahern front bench, despite their
previous differences, began to work together in harmony.

> "The party was riven. There was the residual Haughey gang, the Albert
> gang and other gangs. Worst of all, the party had only 69 TDs," Brennan
> recalled. However, he believed that gradually under Bertie Ahern, Fianna
> Fáil became "a genuinely nice place where there wasn't a single cabal."[5]

Brennan's account may be a little rose-tinted. The Ahern people were still
suspicious of those who had been close to Reynolds, who had an office as a
back-bencher on the same floor in Leinster House as McCreevy and
Geoghegan-Quinn. Michael Smith was also not far away, and Ahern associates
fretted about the level of to-ing and fro-ing between these offices. They also
worried about the possibility of a threat from Geoghegan-Quinn, who,
though one of the most effective spokespersons for the party, especially on the
hepatitis C scandal, was not completely trusted. Her decision to give up
politics eventually alleviated any further concerns in that regard.

Apart from the impact that it had during the debates on the hepatitis C
controversy, Fianna Fáil also hurt the Government on the issue of crime. The
new justice spokesperson, John O'Donoghue, ceaselessly, and at times harshly,
attacked the Minister for Justice, Nora Owen, for an alleged failure to clamp

down on criminal gangs. The issue of crime became particularly salient after the murder of the *Sunday Independent* crime correspondent Veronica Guerin and the killing by the IRA of Detective-Garda Jerry McCabe. Fianna Fáil launched a detailed policy document promising a new toughness in tackling crime, which was to form one of the planks of its 1997 manifesto.

The party had to be subtler and more sensitive in its approach to the other controversial issue in this term, divorce. The "rainbow coalition" proposed another constitutional referendum to revisit the issue. In 1986, when the previous divorce referendum had been held, Fianna Fáil had adopted a policy of official neutrality on the proposal, but in reality party activists had formed the core of the No vote campaigners in many constituencies. This time around, Ahern and his front bench announced that Fianna Fáil would support the holding of the referendum and would call for, though not campaign for, a Yes vote. Obviously Ahern's personal circumstances, as a separated man publicly in a second relationship, gave an additional dimension to the party's support for the proposal. At a number of media events during the campaign in November 1995 Ahern, Geoghegan-Quinn and Mary O'Rourke "strongly and unequivocally"[6] urged voters to support the proposal. Fianna Fáil's intervention in the campaign probably proved decisive. The proposal narrowly passed, by 819,000 votes to 810,000.

More generally, Ahern took a while to settle in to his role as leader of the opposition. His first parliamentary performances were faltering and he never managed to rattle John Bruton, whose popularity had soared after he became leader. Where Ahern was strongest was on the subject of Northern Ireland. From the outset Ahern, assisted by Martin Mansergh, who continued to work for him and the party in opposition, mastered the issues. While he and Ray Burke had always maintained the cross-party agreement on Northern policy, Ahern was energetic in keeping contacts alive in Northern Ireland and dogged and sophisticated in reminding Bruton that, as head of the Irish Government, he needed to argue the nationalist case and to push the British Government towards more substantial engagement with those who had given up violence. He was strongly critical of the IRA when the ceasefire collapsed in February 1996 but criticised both the British and Irish Governments for allowing the decommissioning of arms and other hurdles to get in the way of the momentum that the process required.

However, most of Ahern's time in opposition was taken up with party rather than parliamentary matters. He decided not to change any of the head office staff, choosing to work with the existing general secretary, Pat Farrell, who had been close to Reynolds. The two were to work extremely well together, not least during Ahern's nationwide constituency tours. These were not like those that had been conducted by previous party leaders during periods in opposition. Instead of just travelling down to a party meeting in the evenings Ahern would devote the whole day to the constituency. His visit was planned in detail. He might do a studio interview with local radio in the morning, then at lunchtime or in the early afternoon he would do walkabouts in the main towns and spend an hour or two meeting local groups and organisations with the Fianna Fáil deputies. At teatime he would sit down with the local party officers for detailed discussions on the state of the organisation in their area. The final event would be an evening rally of all party members in the constituency. At these events he would drive home a message of renewal and reorganisation. At least one day a week, usually Friday, was devoted to these visits. Even after he became Taoiseach he maintained this pattern, though occasionally rather than weekly and with some official engagements in each area added to the programme.

RTE's chief news correspondent, Charlie Bird, who regularly covered these Ahern road-shows before, during and after the 1997 election, describes their impact.

> During Bertie Ahern's first leader's tour, in 1997 I noticed that Fianna Fáil had got this down to an art form. Every time Bertie went on the road even as leader of the opposition he would be accompanied by a number of media handlers. Maurice O'Donoghue was the tour manager: he went ahead to every location to make sure everything was arranged and nothing was out of place. Marty Whelan from the party press office was there to deal with "us the media."
>
> The party general secretary, Pat Farrell, was also on the road. He watched from a distance to make sure there were no glitches or gaps and that nothing was left to chance. He seemed to have the job of making sure that any images that might make Bertie look stupid or silly . . . were not allowed to happen.[7]

Both Ahern, as party leader, and Farrell, as general secretary, used these visits also to assess potential candidates. Another central figure in this process was Haughey's former press secretary, P. J. Mara, who, having been sidelined during the Reynolds era, was now back at the centre of Fianna Fáil affairs. Mara was designated director of elections in early 1995. This was a break with the tradition of appointing a senior politician to the post. Mara, Farrell, Chris Wall, Ahern's constituency right-hand man, and Charlie McCreevy, who had always had a flair for constituency numbers, were instrumental in persuading Ahern that a tighter, research-led candidate strategy could bring the party more seats for its share of the vote.

To this end Ahern set up a constituency committee to look at each of the forty-one constituencies in detail, with a view to holding early conventions or having the Ard-Chomhairle select candidates in each area well before the likely election date. The former EU commissioner and minister Ray MacSharry chaired this group. Other politicians on it included Michael Smith, Noel Dempsey and the Dublin North-West deputy Jim Tunney. Also involved was Michael Murphy, a long-time party activist who was a master of electoral data. The other members were Farrell, Mara, the party's national organiser, Seán Sherwin, and the director of finance, Seán Fleming.

Over the course of eighteen months the MacSharry committee performed three important functions. They considered the potential candidates in each constituency, identified who might run, and decided when a convention might be held and whether the convention should be allowed pick all or only some of the candidates. The committee also oversaw the conduct of constituency opinion polls, which not only tested the level of support in each area but also, using sample ballot papers, tested particular names to see what support they might attract. Finally, and perhaps most importantly, the committee acted as a shield for Ahern. Although the MacSharry committee nominally reported to the Ard-Chomhairle, in reality the leader had the final say about who would or would not be a candidate. However, it suited Ahern's conciliatory style to be able to blame the MacSharry committee for unpopular decisions. Pat Farrell says of the work of the committee: "Their work was important in itself. But it also bought us a deal of political cover. In situations where disputes arose we were able to point to the committee's work."

As well as agreeing policy and selecting candidates, Fianna Fáil was also planning the minutiae of literature, marketing and events for the election campaign. All of this meant that when Bruton called a general election for 6 June 1997 Fianna Fáil and Ahern were ready. Within hours the lampposts on all main national routes were covered with election posters featuring Ahern, posed in the light and surrounded by black and bearing the slogan *People before politics*. With the help of a style manual issued to all constituencies and candidates, all the party's election material was co-ordinated, using the same design scheme and the same slogan. Later in the campaign the party shifted to another slogan, reiterating the strength of Ahern's appeal: *A young leader for a young country*. Neither the individual campaigns nor the joint events and programme of the three "rainbow" parties—Fine Gael, the Labour Party and Democratic Left—could keep up with the pace of the Fianna Fáil campaign, or of Ahern's highly successful nationwide tour.

The other important feature of the Fianna Fáil campaign was a formal transfer agreement with the Progressive Democrats, which was re-emphasised by means of staged Ahern-Harney meetings and photo calls during the election tour.

The 1997 election saw Fianna Fáil's most successfully executed campaign since 1977. This was due in no small part to the political skill and appeal of Bertie Ahern. In 1995 he had taken over a bruised parliamentary party and party machine. He managed to extend, remodel and ultimately re-energise both his front bench and the party organisation and then presented a reworked policy platform and a tightened candidate strategy that would bring in extra seats in the general election two years later.

When the votes were counted, Fianna Fáil's first-preference vote, 39 per cent, was almost exactly the same as in 1992, but where this had won 68 seats on that occasion it took 77 this time. Unlike the perceived "Haughey factor" or "Albert factor", which had troubled the party in previous elections, Ahern had a strong personal appeal and an approval rating from the electorate that was much more than that of the party itself. Also important was the pre-election pact with the Progressive Democrats. Both these elements increased the rate of transfers available to Fianna Fáil, and this, together with the decision to run fewer candidates in certain constituencies, gave Fianna Fáil the extra seats. Fine Gael lost nine seats and the Labour Party lost sixteen. Ahern and Harney quickly put together a coalition Government that could also rely on the support of the more Fianna Fáil-minded independents.

Chapter 19 ⌒

PEACEMAKER AND POLITICIAN, 1997–2002

In June 1997 Fianna Fáil was back in power for what was to be an unbroken fourteen years. For the bulk of that time the party would enjoy unchallenged domination of the political scene.

Ahern's new Government held few surprises. Most of the senior front-bench personnel were appointed to the portfolios they had shadowed in opposition. These included Ray Burke, who was appointed Minister for Foreign Affairs. It emerged later that this appointment was made only after Ahern had conducted his own inquiries into allegations then circulating that during the 1989 election campaign Burke had received untoward payments from a local building company, JMSE, in his constituency of Dublin North. Ahern was later to describe these investigations as involving him "looking up every tree in north Dublin." His inquiries had included sending Dermot Ahern, who was then chief whip, to London to meet the principals of that company. Drawing a blank, and having been reassured by Burke that there was nothing to the stories, Ahern went ahead with the appointment. Ahern was close to Burke, who had worked hard and effectively in his role in opposition. Northern Ireland was going to be an important part of the Government's work, and the new Taoiseach wanted to have someone he liked and trusted working on it with him. As Ahern saw it, there was no reason not to give Burke the job. It was to prove a bad judgement.

Almost immediately after coming back into power Fianna Fáil was also shaken by developments at a tribunal of inquiry chaired by Mr Justice Brian McCracken. In July 1997, in testimony before the tribunal, Charles Haughey was forced to admit that he had received more than £1 million (€1.3 million) in covert personal payments from the former supermarket owner Ben Dunne. The tribunal had been set up after revelations two years earlier concerning the then coalition minister Michael Lowry, who had extensive business and personal financial dealings with Dunne. In November 1996 the *Irish Independent* journalist Sam Smyth had revealed that Dunne had paid for work to be done on Lowry's house. Smyth and other colleagues later reported that Dunne had also made substantial payments, estimated to be in the region of £1 million, to another politician. Allegations were then published suggesting that this other politician was Charles Haughey.

Haughey issued vehement denials and eventually instructed a legal team to attend the tribunal to fight the suggestion. At this point, as always with allegations involving the controversial Haughey, those who wanted to disbelieve his denials did so, but his supporters accepted them. That changed, however, in July 1997 when the tribunal revealed the outcome of extensive investigations it had conducted in three different jurisdictions into a complex web of money trails connected with Haughey. He was forced to acknowledge both that he had received the money and that he had lied in his denials.

The revelations had an immediate and dramatic impact on the country and sent shock waves through Fianna Fáil. The mood among party activists is well captured by Johnny Fallon, a former delegate to the Fianna Fáil Ard-Chomhairle for Co. Longford, in his book *Party Time*.

> We were disgusted, and so was everyone we talked to in the party. Every member felt let down, completely betrayed. How could a man who had done so much in the service of the country and in truth done a good job, have been so foolish, grubby and dishonest in his own finances. What was worse was that the real people Charlie hurt, the ones who were really hit by what he did were the Fianna Fáil members who travelled to the Ard Fheis every year, those who contributed what they could to alleviate the Party debt, those who slaved year in year out buying and selling raffle and dinner dance tickets when all along Charlie was off buying Charvet shirts with it.[1]

This is a reference to the shirt-maker in Paris where the tribunals found Haughey had spent some of the money obtained from Dunne and other businessmen, and even some of the money meant for Fianna Fáil under the publicly funded party leader's allowance.

The revelations created an immediate problem for Ahern. John Downing sums up Ahern's predicament as follows:

> Just when everything appeared to be falling into place for Bertie Ahern and Fianna Fáil, chaos descended. Charlie Haughey, Ahern's mentor and patron, who had sloped out of public life with dignity in February 1992, was suddenly back in the limelight for all the wrong reasons.[2]

Of course Ahern had had time between late 1996 and the summer of 1997 to deal with the matter, as the allegations had been public knowledge all that time. He had already laid the groundwork for a strategy of distancing himself and the party from Haughey when, on the opening night of the ard-fheis in April 1997, he had said:

> We will not tolerate any deviation from the benchmarks of honour, at local level or in Leinster House, be it in the past, present or future. No one is welcome in this party if they betray public trust. I say this and

mean this with every fibre of my being. We will write new ethics standards and independent enforcement into this island.[3]

Although Ahern had not named Haughey in these remarks, it was generally understood that he was referring to him. Now, in July, the evidence at the tribunal undermined any suggestion that this was all just another conspiracy against Haughey. These were issues that Ahern would have to return to again and again as further revelations emerged from the tribunals about Haughey and other politicians. For the moment, however, he had no choice but to weather the storm. Fianna Fáil had good reason to be grateful to John Bruton for calling the 1997 election before, rather than after, the summer recess.

When he returned from his traditional holiday in Co. Kerry in September 1997 Ahern was faced with another bubbling political scandal, this time involving a current minister. There were repeated stories, particularly in the *Sunday Business Post*, about alleged payments to a minister not yet named but generally understood to be Ray Burke. As the information in print hardened, Burke's position became increasingly difficult. When he was named as the minister concerned, he mounted a combative defence of his position in Dáil Éireann and afterwards in interviews. But further revelations made his position unsustainable. On 7 October 1997 he resigned not only from the Government but also from Dáil Éireann.

While all this was going on, Ahern also had to find a Fianna Fáil candidate for the presidential election, due to be held that autumn. Albert Reynolds had expressed interest and felt he had Ahern's support. Indeed Reynolds maintains that he would have retired at the 1997 election except that Ahern prevailed on him to run again and in so doing dangled the prospect of the presidency in front of him. Many in the party, however, thought that having Reynolds as the candidate was a bad idea. It threatened to reawaken the controversies that had been a feature of his time as Taoiseach, including, but not limited to, the Beef Tribunal and the Harry Whelehan appointment, with its interlinked Smith and Duggan cases.

From September onwards Reynolds began an individual canvass of Fianna Fáil deputies, telling them of a private opinion poll he had commissioned that showed he was in with a real chance of winning. Most Fianna Fáil deputies felt that might change during the campaign itself. Their view hardened when it was leaked that the Labour Party had asked the Chernobyl children's campaigner Adi Roche to be its candidate. Fianna Fáil deputies and strategists worried about how Reynolds might fare in a contest involving himself, Roche and the likely Fine Gael nominee, Mary Banotti.

For all the talk and effort at reconciliation, the bitterness engendered by Reynolds's culling of the former Haughey ministers in 1992 ran deep among those who had been dismissed. Newly restored to power, they felt they owed Reynolds no favours. Electoral logic and the desire for vengeance merged in their minds to generate arguments against Reynolds running for the presidency. Things took a further turn against him when the Belfast academic Mary McAleese, then vice-chancellor of Queen's University, declared an interest in the position and began lobbying Fianna Fáil TDs for the nomination. While living in Dublin and working as Reid professor of criminal law in Trinity College, McAleese had been active in the party. She had also worked for a short while as a current affairs reporter with RTE. The former Minister for Foreign Affairs Michael O'Kennedy was also a candidate but managed to attract only a handful of TDs to publicly support him.

The machinations against Reynolds intensified as the special parliamentary party meeting to select the candidate approached. The night before, at a scheduled meeting of ministers and ministers of state in the party head office, the issue came up for discussion either formally or informally, and the mood against Reynolds was made clear. As a result there was a last-minute co-ordinated attempt to make sure he did not succeed. Ahern has always denied any involvement in these manoeuvres, but those closest to Reynolds felt they saw his fingerprints all over these efforts.

Reynolds, however, continued to believe that he was the leader's favoured candidate for the presidency right up to the important meeting. He later wrote:

> I felt reassured, when on the very morning of the vote, Bertie phoned me at home to ask if I thought I had the required number of votes to win. I said I believed I had, and we discussed who would be my director for the presidential election campaign itself. We even talked about a fund-raising event in America. He also made a point of telling me that there would be no need to give a speech at the meeting before the vote. Imagine my shock, then, when at that very meeting the chairman, Rory O'Hanlon, announced that the candidates would each have five minutes in which to speak! Neither O'Kennedy nor I was aware that we would have to speak, but Mary McAleese was well prepared; she delivered her speech with confidence from an impressive three-page script whereas O'Kennedy and I were completely thrown and forced to speak off the cuff. I believed we had both been set up.[4]

To the surprise of most of the waiting media, and indeed of party officials in head office, McAleese was comfortably selected. After the elimination of O'Kennedy she had beaten Reynolds by 62 votes to 48. Reynolds now feels strongly that Ahern doublecrossed him. In his biography he wrote:

> I was sure that Bertie's pretence of remaining neutral was just that, pretence. He even made a big show that he had cast his vote in my favour—the first vote that is: no one knew how he voted with the second—but I remember Brian Crowley, a Fianna Fáil MEP, sitting next to me and, as Bertie, smiling held up his first vote card with my name on it, whispering "You're fucked!"[5]

Ahern continues to deny that he was involved in stopping Reynolds's candidature. Of Crowley he says:

I don't know why he said that. And I still can't understand the comment, except that it shows the level of paranoia growing up around Albert. That doesn't mean there weren't people in the party out to get him. I believe Gerry Collins, who Albert had sacked from the cabinet, travelled back from the European Parliament to vote, and sat on the front row for the meeting of the parliamentary party. Certainly there were those looking to see Albert defeated. But I wasn't one of them.[6]

Even if its selection process had caused some bruising, Fianna Fáil now set up the same efficient operation for the McAleese election that it had implemented in June for Ahern. An extended nationwide tour was planned. Professional crews erected striking posters of McAleese pictured against a blue background with just her name and the slogan *Building bridges*. While it did not reach the surreal levels of the Lenihan battle in 1990, the 1997 presidential election campaign was to have its own dramatic moments. The first of these was the leak of a Department of Foreign Affairs memo about a conversation between McAleese and an official that some of her opponents distorted to suggest that she was a Sinn Féin sympathiser. McAleese was also the subject of a series of intemperate attacks by the supporters of the independent candidate Derek Nally. One of them, Eoghan Harris, memorably called McAleese "a tribal time bomb".

About ten days before polling there was a stalemate between the McAleese campaign and the media, which culminated in a suggestion that her campaign director, Noel Dempsey, had pushed an RTE reporter aside at the entrance to an event in Galway. After a series of difficult and at times nasty interviews, Fianna Fáil strategists and the candidate simply decided to restrict the number of encounters she had with the media and see how all this would be received by the electorate in a series of opinion polls due to be published on the second-last weekend before polling.

McAleese's prospects were also assisted by the fact that, whereas Mary Banotti put in a solid campaign for Fine Gael, Adi Roche's efforts proved disastrous, in part because she had failed to understand the limitations on the role and power of the presidency. When the opinion polls were finally published they showed a substantial move to McAleese. She had proved to be a formidable campaigner and had attracted much sympathy for the manner in which she had withstood the various onslaughts.

In the election McAleese polled a little over 45 per cent of first-preference votes and on the second count beat Banotti by 706,259 to 497,516. After an efficient and morale-boosting campaign Fianna Fáil had, with some limited assistance from its Government partners, the Progressive Democrats, decisively regained the presidency.

Fianna Fáil's next electoral outing was in the 1999 local and European

Parliament elections. In 1991 Fianna Fáil had also been in government, but that had been during the Haughey era. The party had suffered a punishing electoral backlash then and had lost sixty county council and city council seats, losing control of thirteen councils. In 1999 it was in government again, but on this occasion it did not suffer the traditional mid-term backlash. In 1999 opinion polls showed that more than half the electorate were satisfied with Ahern's Government. This was reflected in Fianna Fáil's vote in the local election, and it did slightly better than it had done in 1991. Its total vote was up 1 per cent and it gained twenty-five seats. In the European Parliament elections the same day the party's performance was only fair: it lost one of its seats, though its national share of the vote was up 3½ per cent.

Ahern's overriding priority in government during his first term was Northern Ireland. At the beginning his emphasis was on securing a restoration of the ceasefire. He had immediately struck up a close working relationship with Tony Blair, who was elected Prime Minister in May 1997. In July that year the IRA ceasefire was restored, and over the following months the two governments sought to persuade the Northern parties to agree to a three-strand settlement that would involve a new power-sharing executive, a North-South dimension and further agreements between the British and Irish governments. The former US senator George Mitchell, who had been charged by the Blair, Ahern and Clinton governments with chairing the talks, conducted the detailed negotiations between the parties. Mitchell was finally forced to put a deadline of Easter (April 1998) on the talks process, telling the parties he was due to return to America on Thursday 9 April, in the hope of concentrating the minds of the negotiators.

When those negotiations stalled, arrangements were made for both the British Prime Minister and the Taoiseach to go to the venue at Stormont Buildings and become directly involved. The same week, as the talks process was coming to its climax, Ahern's mother died. Notwithstanding this he travelled back and forth from Dublin to Belfast to participate in the final stages of the negotiations. After a lengthy overnight session, and seventeen hours after Mitchell's deadline, documents on all three strands, which collectively came to be known as the Belfast Agreement, were finally approved. Ahern himself describes his feelings on the night the agreement was concluded.

Flying back to Dublin that night was strange for me. Someone produced a bottle of champagne and there was a good celebration on the plane. I shared that, because I knew we had achieved something amazing over these few days. I was pleased that I had held it together all week, but I was still in mourning. The intensity of the negotiations; shuttling backwards and forwards between Dublin and Belfast; attending my mother's funeral between meetings. It had all been a strain. When we arrived back at the airport there was a crowd of TDS and supporters waiting to meet us. That was very moving.

The negotiations during the final week played to Ahern's strengths as a negotiator and as someone with shrewd instincts on Northern Ireland policy. The recognition that much of this achievement was Ahern's was reinforced by genuine public warmth and understanding of the personal sacrifice he had made in the week he suffered his bereavement. Above all else, the Belfast Agreement gave him sustained strong approval ratings, because he was seen as having passed his first and most crucial test and, in the words of one commentator after that week, any "gravitas" doubts about Ahern had been dissipated. Approval of the Government and the Taoiseach soared to record levels, as did Fianna Fáil's opinion poll figures during this initial post-agreement phase, the referendum process and the summer. The public view of Ahern and of the importance of the peace process was also sustained by his strong response to the security crisis created by the Omagh bombing in August, the continuing threat from the "Real IRA" and the need to avoid retaliatory action from the loyalists.

The details of the negotiations and the final terms of the Belfast Agreement are obviously beyond the scope of this book. It is worth noting, however, that in its final form the agreement enshrined the principle of consent, which had formed the basis of Fianna Fáil policy and that of the other main parties in the South since the time of Lemass (albeit with some deviations during Haughey's leadership). It is also worth noting that Ahern, like Reynolds before him, had given a commitment that the Republic would abandon its constitutional claim over the North when a final agreement was adopted. It is striking that he was able to do so almost without resistance from within the party.

In May 1998 Fianna Fáil led the all-party campaign for a Yes vote in the referendum that, among other provisions designed to enable the Belfast Agreement, replaced articles 2 and 3 of the Constitution of Ireland. The proposal secured an unprecedented 94 per cent Yes vote. On the same day the Amsterdam Treaty passed with a 62 per cent vote.

Fianna Fáil was to prove less successful in two other referendums, however. In June 2001 the referendum on the Nice Treaty was defeated by 54 to 46 per cent. In that campaign Fianna Fáil ran a badly designed and badly executed marketing effort, which was not supported by a countrywide campaign or by the party organisation. All the main parties supported a Yes vote and they had all taken the result for granted. With the exception of set pieces featuring the Minister for Foreign Affairs, Brian Cowen, and Ahern himself, the Government was largely silent on the main issue in the campaign.

During this first term Ahern's Government also proposed a further abortion referendum. This was politically the most divisive referendum during the lifetime of the 28th Dáil. Following the deliberations of an All Party Committee on the Constitution the Government proposed an amendment whose effect would have been to narrow the grounds on which the Constitution could be interpreted as allowing abortion. While it would have kept the entitlement when there was an obvious physical risk to the life of the mother, it would have removed that entitlement where the only risk was one of suicide. Fine Gael, the Labour Party and the smaller parties strenuously opposed the change, saying it was too restrictive. So too did some of the more conservative elements of the anti-abortion movement, who argued that it was too liberal. Fianna Fáil found it difficult to communicate the precise nature of what it was proposing, and it was narrowly defeated, by 50.4 per cent to 49.6 per cent.

Fianna Fáil had to deal not only with the continuing fall-out from revelations concerning Haughey and the Burke affair but also with a number of other controversies about standards in public life. The stream of revelations at the tribunals of inquiry sometimes appeared unending but did not, in the main, attract much public interest, except on 19 April 2000, when the former Fianna Fáil press secretary Frank Dunlop again appeared in the witness box at the Flood Tribunal and went on to make dramatic revelations about money that, as a lobbyist for developers, he had given to some Fianna Fáil and Fine Gael politicians.

During these years there was also a stream of resignations and controversies among members of the Fianna Fáil parliamentary party. The Kerry back-bencher Denis Foley resigned when he became the subject of inquiries at the Moriarty Tribunal into the Ansbacher deposits, where Charles Haughey had also placed money. The Mayo TD Beverley Cooper Flynn had the whip removed when she voted against a Dáil motion of censure directed at her father's dealings with the Flood Tribunal, which was also investigating allegations that he had received untoward payments. The Dublin West deputy Liam Lawlor resigned from Fianna Fáil when an internal party ethics investigation, established to examine Dunlop's revelations, accused him of non-cooperation with it.

At times the media found it inexplicable that these controversies and resignations did not seem to damage Ahern's standing with the electorate, and they took to calling him the "Teflon Taoiseach". Much to the frustration of the opposition, these various revelations also failed to damage Fianna Fáil itself, and the party's support remained steady in opinion polls. This may be because the events about which evidence was being given were historical, though only by about ten years. The impact may also have been influenced by the fact that, although the allegations were mainly about Fianna Fáil politicians, some also concerned other parties, particularly Fine Gael, and Ahern had been at pains to publicly distance himself from previous unethical practices in the party.

The most peculiar controversy of this period was the one that erupted in the summer of 2000 over the proposed nomination by the Government of the former Supreme Court judge Hugh O'Flaherty to the position of director of the European Investment Bank. O'Flaherty had resigned from the Supreme Court a year earlier because of his involvement in having the case of a man called Philip Sheedy re-listed before a judge in the circuit court. As a result of this re-listing, Sheedy, who had been convicted of dangerous driving causing the death of a young woman, was released prematurely from prison. After an investigation into this court hearing by the then Chief Justice, both O'Flaherty and the Circuit Court judge involved had to resign. The Government's decision a year later to nominate O'Flaherty to the European Investment Bank suggested that in an act of political folly it had either misread, forgotten or was simply indifferent to the reasons why the public had been outraged about the Sheedy controversy itself. This appointment reopened those wounds and gave rise to charges of political arrogance.

The initial political error of making the nomination was compounded by the flippant manner in which the Minister for Finance, Charlie McCreevy, responded to concerns by the Dáil and the public. The controversy dragged on for several months because of the complicated nomination procedure of the European Investment Bank itself and because a lay litigant, Denis Riordan, successfully made application to the High Court for leave to judicially review the procedure by which the nomination was made. For several weeks, in the heightened atmosphere of a by-election in Co. Tipperary, the Government took a pounding on the issue. Fianna Fáil's disastrous showing in the by-election and in published national opinion polls confirmed what radio phone-ins and media comment had correctly read as the public mood. Ahern himself was the first to appreciate that the issue was hurting the Government and the party, and when confronted in September he admitted that the Government had "taken a hit" on the issue. Notwithstanding this, the political wound continued to bleed until the lack of support for the nomination to the European Investment Bank prompted O'Flaherty to withdraw his name and allowed the Government a belated and somewhat undignified exit from a controversy that had caused the only significant dip in Fianna Fáil ratings during this term.

It was Ahern himself who drew up a recovery strategy to restore the party's standing after the damage caused by the O'Flaherty nomination controversy. A combination of a successful and controversy-free budget in December 2001 and a competent and assured handling of the outbreak of foot-and-mouth disease that visited the country the following spring allowed the Government, and Fianna Fáil in particular, to claw its way back up to its original levels of support.

Ahern had said immediately after the 1997 election that his Government would last a full term. He believed, he said, in five-year stable Governments and in summertime elections. He was true to his word, and the election was called for Friday 6 June 2002.

Fianna Fáil ran a campaign that was again remarkable for its precision. In the pre-campaign phase it emphasised its achievements. Speaking to a pre-election ard-fheis in March, Ahern reminded voters that in 1997 Fianna Fáil had promised to restore the peace, create jobs, cut crime and cut taxes. He set out how, within months of its returning to power, the IRA ceasefire had been restored and within a year the Belfast Agreement had been negotiated and approved in referendums in both parts of the country. This message was emphasised in the party's first-phase poster slogan, *Peace, prosperity, and progress.*

Fianna Fáil also emphasised that serious crime has been reduced, that additional prison places and gardaí had been provided and, in particular, that early prison releases had been ended. Lines like "The revolving door has been slammed shut" flowed off the tongue of John O'Donoghue and other speakers over the ard-fheis weekend and were repeated during the election campaign. The publication by the Minister for Health, Micheál Martin, of a detailed health strategy and the extensive public debate on it in the autumn of 2001 had drawn some of the electoral heat out of that issue, but continuing waiting lists and queues in accident and emergency departments meant that, after crime, health was the second-biggest issue in the campaign.

The party also emphasised the tax cuts that the Minister for Finance, Charlie McCreevy, had implemented in his five budgets. With the economy booming and the boom appearing sustainable, the economic context made a Fianna Fáil victory almost inevitable.

When the election campaign proper began, Fianna Fáil set out to build on this theme of achievements with the slogan *A lot done—more to do.* The concept was designed to persuade voters that this Government's projects and policies were work in progress.

Fianna Fáil's biggest electoral asset in the 2002 election, however, was, as it had been in 1997, Ahern himself. He had in fact been in permanent campaign mode since 1997, travelling out of the city at least one day each week and availing of numerous engagements in the capital to reinforce his direct-contact politics. Ahern's personal approval rating, having reached a high point following the Belfast Agreement and a low point during the O'Flaherty nomination controversy, had in general remained consistently high. Indeed he had gone into this election even more popular than he had been in 1997. His period in office had removed any doubt about his ability to do the job.

Chapter 20

BERTIE: FROM BOOM TO BUST, 2002–8

The 2002 election was the closest Fianna Fáil had come to an overall majority in a quarter of a century. It was once more built around Bertie Ahern's popular appeal, and P. J. Mara, again director of elections, launched the manifesto with the cry "It's show time!" According to Ahern, the campaign "wiped the floor with its opponents."[1] Indeed it was so lively and so well executed that it threatened to overheat, while Fine Gael's campaign was disastrous. Panicked by declining opinion poll ratings, the parliamentary party had ousted John Bruton as leader in February 2001. His replacement, Michael Noonan, and deputy leader, Jim Mitchell, destroyed their party's credibility in the months before the campaign began by announcing proposals to compensate those who had lost money on the privatisation of Telecom Éireann and taxi-owners who had lost out because of deregulation. During the three weeks of the campaign Noonan proved a weak campaigner, and Fine Gael's support went into free fall. The Labour Party's campaign, led by Ruairí Quinn, was better organised but low-key. With Fine Gael in trouble there was no realistic alternative Government to which the Labour Party might belong.

As Fianna Fáil's opinion poll figures surged, the main talking-point was whether or not Ahern would be returned at the head of a Fianna Fáil Government with an overall majority. This led to two significant movements in the last week of the campaign. A large number of Fine Gael supporters, some of them long established, gave up on the Noonan-led campaign and instead voted for or at least gave subsequent preferences to PD, independent or Green Party candidates in an attempt to impose some restraint on the presumed Fianna Fáil Government. Meanwhile some of those who had first shown support for Fianna Fáil were also unnerved by the prospect of an overall majority and voted instead for smaller parties and independents.

Much of the credit for engineering these last-minute shifts from Fianna Fáil was given to the president of the Progressive Democrats, Michael McDowell. Though the two parties had been in government together, there was no formal pact between them, and McDowell launched a vicious attack on Fianna Fáil in the first week of the campaign, describing Ahern's pet proposal to build a national stadium at Abbotstown, Co. Dublin, as a "Ceaușescu-era" project. In the last two weeks before polling day the Progressive Democrats engaged in a vigorous and at times dramatic effort to stop Fianna Fáil getting an overall majority. The most significant was a morning photo call on a footpath in Ranelagh, Dublin, when McDowell himself put up posters bearing the slogan *Single party government—No, thanks.*

When the votes were counted, Fianna Fáil was short of an overall majority, though by only three seats, having increased its total from from 77 to 81 in a Dáil of 166. Two of the independents who had supported the Ahern Government between 1997 and 2002 were re-elected, as well as the son of a third. There were also two new independent deputies who had previously been Fianna Fáil activists and whose vote Ahern could count on if required.

Thus the electorate comfortably re-elected the Ahern Government and, as Charlie McCreevy memorably put it, "threw out the opposition," or at least dramatically reconfigured it. Fine Gael suffered a parliamentary meltdown, losing twenty-three seats, including much of its front bench. Instead of benefiting from Fine Gael's losses, the Labour Party had stagnated, returning with 21 deputies, only one more than it had held before the election. The Green Party increased its representation from 2 to 6, Sinn Féin went from 1 to 5, and there were 13 independents, some of them elected on local hospital campaigns and other single issues.

From 1997 to 2002 Fianna Fáil had governed in coalition with the Progressive Democrats but with the support of four independents. Now it could probably rely on five if the need ever arose. When asked by Brian Farrell during the traditional victor's television interview on the night of the count whether Fianna Fáil would now govern as a single-party Government with the support of these independents, Ahern was uncharacteristically definite in his response, declaring that he intended to continue his coalition with Mary Harney.

One of Ahern's central ambitions and party-political achievements during his first term in government had been to show that Fianna Fáil could actually make coalition government work. Previously Fianna Fáil had proved to be a dysfunctional coalition partner, first with the Progressive Democrats under Des O'Malley and then with the Labour Party under Dick Spring. By contrast, the Ahern-Harney partnership had worked smoothly for a full term, from 1997 to 2002. The only hiccup had been at the time of the controversy over the Sheedy case. Ahern was now determined to complete a second full coalition term. He later explained how important making his first coalition last had been to him.

Coalitions are unstable. That was the conventional wisdom in Irish politics. It was something I was determined to change. Throughout my first couple of years as Taoiseach, the question was always how long can the government last. Then it became how long before I took advantage of our popularity and went to the polls. Only right at the end did people realise that when I said we would run the full term all the way to 2002 I really meant it.[2]

An important factor in the stability of the Fianna Fáil-Progressive Democrat Governments had been, and continued to be, the strength of the relationship between Ahern as Taoiseach and Harney as Tánaiste. This bond between the two, aided by the close friendship between Harney and Charlie McCreevy, Minister for Finance until his departure for the European Commission, ensured that the coalition Government was often more cohesive than some previous Fianna Fáil single-party Governments. With an improved majority, a minimal reshuffle and an initial further bounce in the opinion polls after the election, the Ahern-Harney Government settled, over the summer months of 2002, into what seemed destined to be another five-year term.

In the early autumn the ground under the Government shifted. It began to implement a series of what it called "adjustments to public expenditure" but the media quickly dubbed "cutbacks". Ministers maintained that these cuts had been necessitated by the altered state of the public finances, caused, they argued, by the delayed downturn in international economic circumstances after the terrorist attacks on New York in September 2001. They also maintained that this had become apparent only after the 2002 election. However, the inadvertent inclusion of a confidential Government note with documents furnished to the *Sunday Tribune* under the Freedom of Information Act appeared to corroborate an emerging belief that even if the Government had not actually been planning them it had at least been aware before the election of a need for cuts. This revelation sat uneasily with the promises of the Fianna Fáil election campaign and particularly with statements such as that made by McCreevy himself, who, a week before the election, had reassured the electorate that there were "no significant overruns projected, and no cutbacks whatsoever are being planned, secretly or otherwise."[3]

A perception soon formed that either the true extent of the crisis in the public finances had been withheld from the electorate before polling day or, alternatively, that the Government had gone on a spending spree to ensure its re-election, thus causing the crisis. By the spring of the following year this impression, accurate or not, was carved in stone.

In retirement, Ahern remained adamant that in 2002 his Government had not engaged in a pre-election pumping up of the economy for political advantage. His version of what happened is as follows:

The start of my second term, just like that of my first in 1997, got off to a very shaky start. There was a lot of aggravation about the economy. We had tried to stimulate the economy after 9/11 [2001], but when we got the figures for the first six months of 2002, we could see that the rate of growth had slowed down dramatically. That meant that we would have to cut our cloth in the next budget. This would see cuts of around

€250 million from a budget of billions. The media and opposition went mad saying we were only telling everyone now that the election was over. I knew this was rubbish and that decisive action in tightening up now would let the economy roar ahead again the following year. In the event that is exactly what happened. We had acted quickly enough to get on top of things, but we made a mistake in not dealing with the media angle that we had misled people in the run up to the general election.[4]

Many economists take issue with this Ahern narrative, and the fact that his Government repeated the same trick of loosening expenditure before the 2007 election gave further credence to their beliefs. Whatever the truth of the situation, the political reality was that the budgets announced in December 2002 and again in December 2003 were tighter than the electorate and the political system had become accustomed to, and the Government's approval rating suffered as a result.

Over the same period the Government was not only slated for these cutbacks but faced controversies over waste and folly in public spending. The most prominent of these related to a botched and costly attempt to introduce electronic voting in local and Dáil elections and to making a special grant to the National Equestrian Centre at Punchestown, Co. Kildare, in McCreevy's constituency. The Government's position was also damaged by Ahern's stubborn persistence with the proposal to build a stadium at Abbotstown, Co. Dublin, in addition to the redevelopment of the GAA stadium, Croke Park, and a partly state-funded revamp of the rugby stadium in Lansdowne Road. The Abbotstown project was never completely abandoned, despite a shortage of resources.

In the December 2003 budget McCreevy also announced an extensive programme of decentralisation for state bodies, which most commentators regarded as badly thought out and appeared to be designed to shore up support for the Government in those counties where the decentralised departments would be moved in the period before the 2004 local elections.

During the last part of 2002 and most of 2003 Fine Gael remained traumatised. Michael Noonan had resigned as party leader on the night of the election results, and Enda Kenny emerged victorious in the subsequent vote of the parliamentary party. His first year in the job was inevitably concentrated on the task of healing and reorganising his party. The Labour Party leader, Ruairí Quinn, resigned a few weeks later, and, after a direct vote of members, the former Democratic Left deputy Pat Rabbitte replaced him. Rabbitte had acquired much of his support by promising not to go into government with Fianna Fáil after the next election.

The first half of Ahern's second term saw the same issues to the fore. One of these was the Nice Treaty, which was put to the voters for the second time on 19 October 2002. This time the Government and main opposition parties were more energised and were ably assisted by civil society groups and social partners in the campaign for a Yes vote, and the electorate gave a ringing endorsement. 1.4 million went to the poll, almost half a million more than had voted in the first referendum on the treaty. In June 2001 Ireland had rejected the Treaty by 54 per cent to 46 per cent; in the second referendum, in October 2002, the vote changed to 63 per cent in favour and 37 per cent against.

Fianna Fáil's campaign efforts were not helped when the interim report of the Flood Tribunal was published a few weeks before the date of the referendum. It found that Ray Burke had received payments not only from several developers but from the backers of Century Radio, the commercial radio station that had been established when he was Minister for Communications. In January 2005 Burke pleaded guilty to offences arising from his failure to disclose details of these payments when he availed of a tax amnesty, and he was sentenced to six months in prison.

Another prominent issue during the last months of 2002 and the early months of 2003 was the prospect of an invasion of Iraq. On 15 February 2003 in Dublin more than 100,000 people marched in protest, the largest rally in the city since the PAYE marches of the late 1970s. Although the Government was avowedly neutral, on 25 February, as American and British forces massing on the Kuwaiti border made final preparations to invade, the Government had a comfortable majority in a Dáil vote that, among other things, enabled the continuation of controversial landing rights for American air force planes at Shannon Airport. Fine Gael, the Labour Party, Sinn Féin, the Green Party and most independents opposed the motion, but there was no substantial popular backlash. Opinion polls soon established that most of the electorate were as pragmatic and as incoherent on the issue as the Government; though unhappy about the invasion they were largely comfortable with the landing rights and anxious not to alienate the United States or run the risk of affecting its economic ties with Ireland.

This early period of Ahern's second term was also memorable for one dramatic initiative that had not been the subject of any manifesto promises or indeed previous political debate. In January 2003 the Minister for Health, Micheál Martin, announced a ban on smoking in all places of work, including pubs and restaurants, to come into effect on 1 January 2004. Publicans and other tourism interests led a well-resourced campaign against it during the late summer and early autumn of 2003, which reached a crescendo before the Fianna Fáil ard-fheis in early October. There Martin received overwhelming support, and when opinion polls showed this was general, opposition fizzled out. After a few legislative delays the ban came into effect in March 2004.

For the first half of 2004 Ireland held the six-month rotating presidency of the European Union, and it proved a considerable success for the country and for Ahern personally. Among the achievements was the securing of agreement of a final text for a European Constitution. Ahern managed to persuade the March summit of EU heads of state and heads of government that this might be possible. He undertook a tour of the capitals of member-states, a particularly difficult and time-consuming task since enlargement. At the June

2004 summit the Irish presidency, after intensive negotiations, managed to shepherd the various delegations towards a text acceptable to all members.

After this Ahern turned to the task of seeking agreement among the member-states on who should be the next president of the European Council, only to find that some of them felt he should take the position himself. For about ten days there were suggestions in European media and feverish speculation in Ireland that Ahern might accept the post. Had he done so it would certainly have changed subsequent Fianna Fáil history. He later explained his reflections on the position.

> There's no doubt I gave it serious thought. I was confident I had the numbers. I didn't seem to have many enemies and had shown I was capable at doing the job. The big three powers, Britain, Germany, and France all wanted me to run. So I was thinking hard about it the week after the Brussels meeting. I took soundings from a few key people. I had a long chat with [Senator] Tony Kett about it. I spoke to McCreevy and to Gerry Hickey [programme manager]. Naturally I talked to the girls [Ahern's daughters]. There was no one view that emerged. Some people were saying, go on, take it—you've done your bit winning two elections and the party will be fine. Others were asking whether I would be happy living in Brussels and sitting on an airplane travelling round the world non-stop . . . In the end I decided no. Partly it was because I thought there was still a job to be done at home. There was the question of living in Brussels, which didn't appeal much. And then there was the thought that while president of the commission was a good job, it was also a thankless one.[5]

Having declined the position himself, Ahern went on to secure unanimous agreement for the candidature of the Portuguese prime minister, José Manuel Barroso, thereby achieving "a clean sweep for Ireland."[6]

While he was being lauded and headhunted on the European stage, Ahern was about to suffer his most unpopular period domestically. In June 2004 Irish voters went to the polls in the local and European Parliament elections. At 60 per cent, the turn-out for the local elections was only 3 per cent less than in the 2002 general election. The results, the party's worst electoral performance to date, were disastrous for Fianna Fáil. Its share of the vote was down by 7 per cent on the previous local elections, and it lost more than eighty county council and city council seats. In the election for the European Parliament its vote fell significantly in all four constituencies, and it lost two of its six seats.

By comparison, Fine Gael, under its new leader, Enda Kenny, not only managed to halt its slide but increased its number of seats in the local elections while making two dramatic gains in the European Parliament election. The Labour Party's performance was also relatively good in both elections, and it achieved a slight improvement in its representation on local councils. Most of the smaller parties had a geographically patchy performance in the local elections, the only exception being Sinn Féin, which more than doubled the number of its seats on county and city councils and made particularly strong gains in Dublin. It also had a a member elected to the European Parliament for the first time in the capital. The Green Party lost both the seats it had held in the European Parliament.

The results sounded an alarm bell for Fianna Fáil and for Ahern. When he first became leader, during the opposition years of 1995-7, he had revitalised party morale, but he had never really addressed an enduring weakness in the party. The Fianna Fáil organisation, as distinct from the personal machines of deputies or challengers, was depleted in many rural areas and non-existent in much urban territory. The problem was particularly acute in Dublin, where the party structure and membership bore no relation to the population movements and development that had occurred over the previous fifteen years. Instead it had come to rely on professionalised paid-for electioneering and on individualised candidate campaigns, and this was now further endangering the party's base, which had already been loosened by the abandonment of family-led voting patterns. During Dáil elections these candidate machines, together with Ahern's personal appeal and the credit the party attracted for the economic boom, had masked organisational weaknesses. Local and European Parliament elections revealed them.

As a result, a review group was set up to look at the party organisation, headed by the deputy leader, Brian Cowen. Their report, based in part on the results of a nationwide telephone survey of Fianna Fáil cumainn undertaken in the second half of 2004 by head office, laid bare the gaps in the party's operation on the ground and revealed publicly for the first time that Fianna Fáil's roll of nominal membership was very much out of date. This confirmed what the party's senior politicians and officials had known for more than a decade; but, apart from a recruitment drive, no real effort was made to address the problem. Instead, in many constituencies where the organisation was weak the party continued to seek to overcome this by identifying candidates with a wider appeal who could, if necessary, work outside the local party structure to obtain financial resources and election workers. As a consequence, Fianna Fáil essentially became a franchised brand in some constituencies, while in many the Fianna Fáil election campaigns were run by the candidates themselves, with the party organisation's role relegated to policing disputes between candidates in order to avoid mutually destructive warfare between those on the same party ticket.

While the Cowen groups set about this private assessment of the party organisation over time, Ahern himself immediately set about implementing a series of changes that came to be called the "Inchydoney repositioning". Within weeks of the elections in June 2004 there was a surprise announcement that Ahern's closest colleague, the Minister for Finance, Charlie McCreevy, was going to go to Brussels to become Ireland's member of the European Commission. This was seen as part of a strategy of recasting the Government as more caring and left of centre.

In the reshuffle arising from McCreevy's departure, Ahern moved Brian Cowen to Finance, allowed Joe Walsh to retire, demoted Michael Smith, and promoted Mary Hanafin, Dick Roche and Willie O'Dea. Cumulatively this was a shift to a more left-of-centre line-up. Another significant change was Mary Harney's decision to exchange posts with Micheál Martin, moving from the Department of Enterprise to that of Health, where she felt she could tackle obvious systemic difficulties. This was a significant reduction in the Progressive Democrats' influence on economic policy.

In mid-September the economic justice campaigner Father Seán Healy was invited to the Inchydoney Hotel near Clonakilty, Co. Cork, to address the Fianna Fáil parliamentary party's annual "away day". Healy had been one of the fiercest critics of McCreevy's budgets, and his attendance at the event suggested that Fianna Fáil would now listen to voices that said that free-enterprise economic policies were creating an increasingly unequal society. Shortly afterwards Ahern gave a series of interviews to mark his tenth anniversary as leader of Fianna Fáil. He told the *Irish Times* that he "was one of the few socialists left in Irish politics." This remark entertained many commentators and attracted derision from his opponents across the political spectrum. When the Dáil resumed in early October the Socialist Party deputy Joe Higgins, who had been abroad at the time of Ahern's interview, spoke in the Dáil:

> You can imagine, a Cheann Comhairle, how perplexed I was when I returned to find my wardrobe almost empty. The Taoiseach had been busy robbing my clothes. Up to recently the Progressive Democrats did not have a stitch left due to the same Taoiseach, but we never expected him to take a walk on the left side of the street. He said, "I am one of the few socialists left in Irish politics" . . . I thought, Good, Taoiseach. There are two of us in it and we will go down together![7]

In his memoirs Ahern explains what he meant to suggest by the remark.

> I might have meant it slightly tongue in cheek, because I certainly wouldn't be an ideological socialist. But it had a grain of truth. I was genuinely interested in helping the poor and making sure that we distributed wealth to help the low-paid and disadvantaged. I pumped billions into the health service and social service. I worked with the unions on social partnership to deliver a better deal for workers. And I protected and improved the wonderful civil amenities that belong to all of us. I worked hard over the years, to take a local example, to invest in the Botanic Gardens, which were in poor repair and are now one of the glories of Dublin . . . Maybe it was naïve but since I was a child, I had always believed that when places like that were owned by the state, I owned them. These were the places we shared together as a community. Perhaps it was not socialism exactly but it was definitely a belief in society.[8]

In the same *Irish Times* interview Ahern revealed that he had twice read *Bowling Alone* by the Harvard academic Robert Putnam, which discusses the depletion of social capital in modern societies. The book's themes were reflected in many of his speeches. Putnam suggests that Americans have become increasingly disconnected from their families, neighbours, communities and the political system itself, and that this has given rise, among other things, to a dramatic decline in community activism. Putnam was later invited to address the Fianna Fáil parliamentary party pre-season gathering in Cavan in 2005. Active citizenship remained a theme of Ahern's time as Taoiseach, and he later set up a task force on the topic.

The new Minister for Finance, Brian Cowen, demonstrated the repositioning in his first budget in December 2004 when he announced a range of tax measures designed to help those on lower wages and a multi-annual funding package for disability services. All this was initially seen as politically successful. In his book *Showtime*, Pat Leahy assessed the effect of the Inchydoney repositioning and the subsequent budgets as follows:

> Cowen's budgets were hardly Robin Hood take-from-the-rich-give-to-the-poor efforts. He depended on economic growth and increased taxation revenues—not increased rates of taxation or better value in public spending—to pay for the extra teachers, care workers, hospital facilities, social welfare payments and so on. The socialist stuff was about expenditure—not revenue. McCreevy might have gone and his legacy been repudiated, but even the new economic policy engine of the government wasn't forgetting all his lessons. Taxes would remain low, and many tax incentives would remain in place. The change was on the spending side of the ledger, not the tax side. That might seem like good politics but it would store up economic problems for the future.[9]

It certainly looked like good politics at first. An improvement in the Government's fortunes was reflected in the first opinion polls of 2005, but throughout that year it continued to come under fire for perceived incompetence in managing the economic boom. Delays and cost overruns on infrastructural projects, such as the Luas light rail system in Dublin, the Dublin Port Tunnel, the National Aquatic Centre and the health service payroll computer system all gave the opposition much ammunition with which to sustain an attack on the Government.

The main opposition parties got their act together in this phase and, importantly, they began to present a possible alternative Government. In September 2004 Enda Kenny and Pat Rabbitte travelled to Mullingar for the signing of a co-operation agreement between the two parties on Westmeath County Council, using the occasion to announce the start of talks about talks between their national leaderships. They were back in Co. Westmeath a year later to develop this "Mullingar Accord", with the publication of the first in what they promised would be a series of position papers on major issues, this time on social partnership.

During this period health remained the issue on which the Government was most vulnerable to attack from opposition and media. Despite record expenditure and dramatic improvements in treatment, particularly of cancer and heart conditions, public confidence in the Health Service Executive remained low, and anger on health-related issues was intense. The persistent problems of queues in accident and emergency departments in many hospitals and of the MRSA super-bug continued. Public perceptions of mismanagement and lack of political leadership in the health service were reinforced when it was revealed in late 2004 that tens of thousands of people had been unlawfully charged for nursing-home care when, under the law as it stood, it should have been free. It is estimated that this legal oversight cost the exchequer more than €1 billion in refunds.

One issue to which there was very positive reaction, however, was the prospect of a peace agreement in Northern Ireland that would include both Sinn Féin and the Democratic Unionist Party. Repeated attempts to re-establish devolved government in Northern Ireland and to steer the peace process through turbulent times, particularly in late 2004 and early 2005, consumed much of Ahern's time and political attention during his second term. At one point he estimated that he was spending 40 hours in what was typically a 100-hour week working on Northern Ireland. It was, as ever with the peace process, a case of two steps forward and one step back. Setbacks such as the IRA's involvement in the robbery of £26 million from the Northern Bank in Belfast just before Christmas 2004 and the brutal killing by IRA members of Robert McCartney in January 2005 were followed by really significant achievements, including the publication of an IRA statement in July 2005 announcing that it was disbanding, and the completion of IRA arms decommissioning a few weeks later. Ahern worked tirelessly with the British Prime Minister, Tony Blair, to bring about a wider political agreement that would accommodate the new political reality that Ian Paisley's DUP was now the leading unionist party and would make possible the re-establishment of all-party government in Northern Ireland. He also courted Paisley and his party assiduously, developing a cordial relationship that would ultimately result in the establishment of a Northern Ireland Executive comprising the DUP and Sinn Féin.

As Sinn Féin edged closer to integration in mainstream politics and participation in government in Northern Ireland it posed an increasing threat to Fianna Fáil in the Republic. It had won additional seats in both the 2002 Dáil election and the 2004 local elections, many of them in Ahern's own heartland of Dublin's north city. At one point in mid-2004 its opinion poll ratings and political commentary suggested that if the IRA decommissioned, Sinn Féin might take up to twenty seats in the next Dáil election. Ahern was particularly conscious of this threat. He decided that there would be a large state commemoration of the ninetieth anniversary of the 1916 Rising in Dublin in April 2006 and announced this at the 2005 ard-fheis. Ultimately, however, Sinn Féin's capacity for growth was limited by the reaction to the McCartney murder, by foot-dragging on decommissioning and by suggestions that the IRA was laundering the proceeds of the Northern Bank robbery in the Republic.

It was the events of September 2006 that were to have most influence on Ahern's fortunes, on Fianna Fáil, and on the stability of his coalition.

On her return from holidays in early September, Mary Harney surprised all in media and political circles by announcing that she was stepping down as leader of the Progressive Democrats, and the following week Michael McDowell was unanimously elected as her successor. He barely had his feet under the party leader's desk when he had to deal with a completely unforeseen political controversy that was all the more significant because it centred on the Taoiseach himself.

On 21 September 2001 the main front-page story in the *Irish Times*, written by Colm Keena, the paper's public affairs correspondent, was headed "Tribunal examines payments to Taoiseach." It was based on a document from the Mahon (formerly Flood) Tribunal of which the paper had received a copy that revealed that Ahern, then Minister for Finance, had received between €50,000 and €100,000 from a group of businessmen in late 1993 and 1994.

This caused a political sensation that appeared to threaten the stability of the coalition Government and even Ahern's leadership of Fianna Fáil. In a lengthy and at times emotional interview with Bryan Dobson on RTE's six o'clock news a week later the Taoiseach said that all those from whom he had received money—£38,000 in total—were friends who had come together to collect money to help him defray costs and expenses arising at the time of his marital separation. The controversy took a further twist in the same interview when Ahern revealed that he had also received £8,000 in cash from a group of businessmen in Manchester in 1994. He told Dobson that guests had gathered this money for him at an informal dinner he had addressed.

The Progressive Democrats said that Ahern had further questions to answer, particularly on the Manchester payment. It then transpired that one of the Manchester businessmen, Michael Wall, subsequently sold Ahern a house in Dublin. The controversy rumbled on for almost three weeks but abated after Ahern explained the Manchester payment in the Dáil and made a more specific apology at a media briefing for accepting the money.

To the surprise of some, opinion polls published shortly after the controversy showed a sharp rise in support for Fianna Fáil, with both Fine Gael and the Labour Party down significantly. While the same opinion polls revealed that almost two-thirds of the public believed that Ahern was wrong in accepting the payments, support for Fianna Fáil rose by between 4 and 8 per cent. Helped by a successful one-day ard-fheis in early November 2006, and a well-received budget that December, Fianna Fáil managed to sustain its improvement in the opinion polls.

The issue of Ahern's finances had not gone away. Relations with the Progressive Democrats had been fatally damaged, because they simply did not believe his explanation. The controversy would resurface during the following year's general election, but for the moment Fianna Fáil could withstand the storm. The issue of Ahern's finances had been parked and preparations for the election concentrated instead on the economy and other issues.

Although Ahern's explanation of even this first set of curious circumstances had been incomplete, his Government and parliamentary party continued to support him in public. Indeed Ahern enjoyed almost unanimous support within his parliamentary party during all his time as Taoiseach. There were occasional internal tensions, but these usually coincided with reshuffles at the ministerial or minister of state level and arose from disappointments at being demoted or passed over, often because Ahern failed to communicate directly with those he was disappointing. The success of Fianna Fáil's candidate strategy in the two previous elections had led to an influx of new, mainly younger, talented and ambitious deputies, some of whom had forgone a promising career in other walks of life. Many of these back-benchers felt stuck at the wrong side of a bottleneck, unable to discern consistent criteria for political advancement under this Taoiseach.

Of course the traditional Fianna Fáil loyalty to the leader played a role in this solid support for Ahern, but equally important was the recognition that he was still the party's most significant political asset. If they ever doubted it, the bounce Fianna Fáil achieved in the opinion polls published immediately after the controversy surrounding payments to Ahern in October 2006 served to remind them of the extent to which their leader enjoyed popular appeal and even affection.

Although he was absorbed in governmental issues, and now had to deal with the tribunal inquiries into his personal finances, Ahern also found plenty of time for party management matters. He was more involved in day-to-day party affairs than any Fianna Fáil leader before or since. He seldom missed parliamentary party or Ard-Chomhairle meetings and attended many national sub-committees, including the important constituency committee, now chaired by Brian Cowen. He also included numerous party functions and meetings in his extensive schedule of visits around the country. The general secretary, Seán Dorgan, who replaced Martin Mackin in 2003, was often summoned to the fringes of national or international events for side meetings about party matters.[10]

One feature of the management of Fianna Fáil during this period was Ahern's reliance, like many other party leaders, on a close cohort of personal loyalists to keep control of the party. What was different was how many of these were originally operatives in his local political organisation. They included both Chris Wall, his constituency strategist, who also sat on many national campaign committees, and, crucially, Des Richardson. A businessman in the recruitment and engineering industries, Richardson had professionalised Ahern's constituency fund-raising by organising an annual dinner, usually held at the Royal Hospital, Kilmainham, at which prominent local and national business figures contributed and paid homage. When

Ahern was appointed Fianna Fáil's national treasurer in the early 1990s Richardson became full-time national fund-raiser, a role in which he continued throughout Ahern's leadership. It was he, for example, who initiated the most controversial of the party's fund-raising events, a hospitality tent at the annual Galway Races where ministers, party grandees and officials socialised with figures from the business world. As a fund-raiser the "Galway tent" actually raised very little for the party but it generated bad publicity in abundance.

In seeking to understand how both Ahern and Fianna Fáil withstood these controversies and moved confidently into the 2007 election one must consider two factors. The first is that Ahern achieved extraordinary personal appeal, and that the increase in media coverage of politics played to his strengths. He also appeared regularly in the non-political media, where his fondness for soccer and the celebrity status of both his daughters served to increase his popularity. The sheer energy of Ahern's full-time campaigning activity and nationwide touring meant that at least a third of the population had physically met him by that time. Right up to the election in June 2007 Ahern's approval ratings, while slightly lower than they had been before the 2002 election, remained comparatively high. His standing in most of the main opinion polls, at more than 50 per cent, was still unusually positive for an outgoing Taoiseach.

The other, perhaps more important factor was that the country was enjoying an extraordinary economic boom, which not only enabled the incumbent Government to take credit for rapidly rising living standards but also gave it access to a greatly increased tax base. In 2002 Ireland's GNP had grown by a moderately impressive 1.5 per cent; in 2003 this rose to 2.8 per cent, and in 2004 it reached an extraordinary 4.9 per cent. It would stay at this high level for 2006 and the first half of 2007. As Pat Leahy puts it, "this would provide huge growth in taxation revenue for Bertie Ahern and Brian Cowen. They knew what they wanted to do with it, they wanted to win an election."[11]

In the spring of 2007 there was a struggle within the Government between those, including Brian Cowen and Séamus Brennan, who argued that they should not offer tax reductions or other treats for voters but should instead concentrate on providing continuity and stability. The party strategists had proposed that an initial slogan for the campaign would be that Fianna Fáil would "promise less but deliver more." This appears to have become the settled view of the Fianna Fáil ministers, including Ahern himself. However, in early February the Progressive Democrats' leader, Michael McDowell, at his party conference promised dramatic reductions in tax rates and a widening of tax bands. A few weeks later the Labour Party leader, Pat Rabbitte, surprised commentators with a promise of his own to cut the standard rate of tax by 2 per cent.

Even after these announcements Fianna Fáil held firm to its cautious stance, with Brennan, in a briefing before the ard-fheis, attacking auction politics and saying that initiatives to be announced at the ard-fheis would be cautious and low-key.

Exactly the opposite happened, however. In what seems to have been a personal last-minute change of tack, Ahern in his televised ard-fheis address on the Saturday night promised that if Fianna Fáil was returned to power there would be a further cut of two percentage points in the standard rate of tax, a halving of PRSI, an increase in the old-age pension to €300 a week, and the employment of two thousand more gardaí and four thousand more teachers.

His Government members were stunned but supported him. Ahern appeared to have come to the view that he could not win the election with a cautious approach, perhaps because, unlike his colleagues, he knew that further revelations about his personal finances were likely to come to public knowledge just before or at the time of the expected election in June, as a result of the work of the Mahon Tribunal.

If Ahern was apprehensive on this point he had reason to be. He called the election on 29 April, which, unusually for such an event, was a Sunday. He took particular pleasure from getting the political journalists out of their beds in the early morning for his visit to the President before 8 a.m. The dawn dissolution was apparently occasioned by a realisation that the President was to fly abroad later that morning. On the same day the *Sunday Mail*, in a story by Frank Connolly, published details of an initial private interview that the Mahon Tribunal lawyers had conducted with Ahern, which included the suggestion that he had received sterling and dollar cash payments.

The further revelations about Ahern's finances stalled his party's national campaign, on one occasion literally when a question from a journalist about the payments controversy was met with complete silence from Ahern for a full six seconds before a handler asked for another question. Inhibited by the following press pack, which, he claimed, made it impossible for him to meet the public, Ahern cut back on his public appearances during the first two weeks. There was none of the barnstorming that had been a feature of his previous electoral victories.

On the second Sunday of the campaign, fighting for their political survival, the Progressive Democrats demanded that Ahern issue a statement dealing with the latest allegations. A press conference to be addressed by senior Fianna Fáil ministers, Brian Cowen, Micheál Martin and Dermot Ahern, was postponed for an hour to allow them to consult their leader. When they emerged they announced that Ahern would make a detailed statement on the latest allegations later in the campaign. In an interview earlier that morning Ahern had told Adam Boulton of Sky News that he would issue a comprehensive statement before polling day.

When it came, the statement gave details of how Michael Wall had given Ahern the money for remodelling and furnishing a house Wall had bought and was later to sell to Ahern, including receipts itemising the furniture and fittings purchased with some of that money.

However, the focus of the campaign eventually shifted back to the economy. Ahern, in his head-to-head leaders' debate with Kenny, and Cowen, in a series of encounters with the Fine Gael finance spokesperson, Richard Bruton, succeeded in undermining the costing of Fine Gael's election pledges. At the same time public reaction to his performance in the leadership debate, irritation at what some perceived as media hounding and a disposition to gamble on Fianna Fáil's continued economic success all contributed to an appreciable surge to the party in opinion polls at the end of the campaign. Fianna Fáil was also boosted by Ahern's historic address to the British Parliament and by the restoration of devolved government in Northern Ireland, both of which occurred during the campaign. The image of Ahern as peacemaker was driven home by the Fianna Fáil campaign, and a party political broadcast featured Senator George Mitchell, Tony Blair and ex-President Bill Clinton all extolling his virtues as a statesman.

In the 2007 election Fianna Fáil won 78 seats, only three fewer than it had won in 2002—a remarkable achievement in all the circumstances. The Progressive Democrats, however, suffered a near-wipeout, losing 6 of their 8 seats. Among the casualties was McDowell, who resigned as leader that night. Harney, one of the two survivors, resumed temporary leadership. Fine Gael made significant gains, winning a further 20 seats in addition to the 31 it had obtained in 2002. The chances of the "Mullingar Accord" evolving into a programme for government were undermined, however, by the continuing stagnation of the Labour Party. Under Pat Rabbitte it won 20 seats, one fewer than it had won under Ruairí Quinn in 2002. The Green Party held 6 seats, Sinn Féin lost one to return with 4, while there were 5 independents, a small number of whom would again be prepared to support a Government led by Ahern.

The results meant that Ahern just about had a majority with the support of the remaining PDs and his friendly independents. He surprised once more, however. He was again set on proving that Fianna Fáil was coalition-compatible and on ensuring another full-term Government. He announced to his parliamentary party that he had decided to invite the Green Party to join his coalition. After a short period of negotiations, including one complete breakdown, the Fianna Fáil team, led by Brian Cowen and including Séamus Brennan and Noel Dempsey, negotiated a programme for government that incorporated a number of the Green Party's manifesto proposals. The more significant negotiations were between Ahern and the Green Party leader, Trevor Sargent. Ahern agreed not only to give the Green Party two full ministries but to give them the two departments most relevant to their agenda, namely Environment, to which John Gormley was appointed, and Energy and Communications, where Éamon Ryan took charge.

Having created this innovative extended coalition, Ahern then took a significant step towards planning his succession. In a radio interview with Seán O'Rourke the week he was re-elected Taoiseach he stated that he felt that Brian Cowen was his obvious successor. In so doing he put a few other ministerial noses out of joint, including that of Dermot Ahern, who publicly commented that the next leader was properly a matter for the entire parliamentary party when that time would come. In anointing Cowen, however, Ahern was doing no more than recognising the obvious. Deputy leader since 2002, Minister for Finance since 2004 and credited by many of his colleagues with winning the 2007 election, Cowen would have succeeded Ahern whether or not he enjoyed Ahern's public support.

What neither Ahern nor Cowen expected was that the latter would become leader so soon. Ahern later said that before the 2007 election he had decided to retire as Taoiseach and Fianna Fáil leader after the local and European Parliament elections in 2009, but in the event he could not pick his time. It was again controversies about his personal finances that determined the pace and outcome of events.

Over the following autumn, winter and spring the evidence before the Mahon Tribunal revealed an extraordinary story of money moving between a safe in Ahern's constituency office in Drumcondra and a safe in his office in the Department of Finance, of money moving in and out of accounts held in his name or the names of associates at various bank branches around the city, and of money moving to and fro across the Irish Sea, where it was converted to sterling and sometimes back again. Ahern's own explanation for this web of financial transactions was that it was due to his personal circumstances as a man going through a contested judicial separation and a man for whom there was no distinction between his personal and political life or finances. However, the sheer amount of money involved, the circumstances in which the payments were said to have occurred and the manner in which his tortuous explanations emerged left his political position ultimately untenable.[12]

No suggestion that Ahern had done any favours in return for these various payments was ever substantiated. On the contrary, allegations that he had received large payments from the Cork developer Owen O'Callaghan, some of which formed the grounds for the tribunal's initial trawl through his financial affairs, had been disproved in a libel action in July 2001. To the general public Ahern appeared to live a frugal and ordinary existence without obvious trappings of wealth. Nonetheless the effect of the whole affair was politically fatal, revealing as it did a Minister for Finance who lived for several years entirely on cash, a former accountant who had no bank account and kept no financial records, and a cash-rich man with his own separately funded constituency office and living quarters for whom two sets of friends separately organised "dig-outs".

In early 2008 one aspect of the evidence proved particularly damaging to Ahern's relationship with the Fianna Fáil membership when it was revealed that money meant for party purposes in the Dublin Central constituency had been lent to Ahern's former partner, Celia Larkin, for the purpose of buying a house and had not been repaid until just before the matter became public. The final straw for many came when Ahern's former secretary Gráinne Carruth gave tearful evidence, altering what she had previously said about bank transactions she had executed for him. Many were angered because Ahern had placed her in this position. Ahern too saw this as the last straw but laid the blame elsewhere. In his memoirs he wrote:

> The point for me came when my former secretary Gráinne Carruth was called back into the witness box where she broke down. All they had to do was write to her and ask her to clarify her earlier evidence. They threatened her with jail. And she cried on the stand. It was real low life stuff, picking on an ordinary mother of three who by bad luck had found herself right in the middle of a massive story and dealing with issues from fourteen years earlier relating to a job she had long left.
>
> It convinced me. For some time I had been growing more and more concerned that the work of government was being overshadowed. But it was now clear that the incessant publicity about the Tribunal was going to continue unabated. There and then I thought "It's not worth it."[13]

The truth, of course, is more complex. The documentary evidence that the tribunal had been able to obtain about his finances in the relevant period had left Ahern with no political options, and his colleagues were finding it increasingly hard to defend his various explanations. If he had not gone when he did he would have had to go a few weeks later when he claimed, to derision, that one particular lodgement was the winnings on a horse he could not name at a race meeting he could not recall.

Gráinne Carruth's second appearance in the witness box occurred in the week before the Easter recess of 2008. On the morning the Dáil was scheduled to resume after the recess Ahern chaired one of his regular pre-Government meetings with his Fianna Fáil colleagues at 10 a.m. Many of them were distracted by text messages telling them that the Government press secretary had invited the media to a special news briefing for 10:30 and that the air waves were already rife with speculation that Ahern was resigning. It was not until he was asked by some of his colleagues what was going on that he confirmed the rumour. He had made up his mind over the previous week but had shared his decision with only a handful of advisers. At the Government table only the Attorney-General, Rory Brady, and the Minister for Finance, Brian Cowen, were aware of his intention. There were tearful scenes at the gathering, the meeting broke up, and Ahern went to the steps to meet reporters. His remarks there included the following:

> I first sought election to the office of Taoiseach on the pledge that I would put people before politics. I have kept that promise. I have always placed the interests of the Irish people above my own. Therefore I will not allow issues relating to my own person to dominate the body politic, as this would be contrary to the long-term interests of the Irish people. I want everyone to understand one truth above all else. Never, in all the time I have served in public life, have I put my personal

interest ahead of the public good. I have served this country and the people I have the honour to represent in Dáil Éireann honestly.

The weeks between 2 April, when Ahern announced his departure, and 6 May, when he left office, included two events that acknowledged his contribution to the Northern Ireland peace process. On 30 April he addressed a joint session of the US Houses of Congress, becoming the first Fianna Fáil Taoiseach to do so. He told the American parliamentarians:

On St Patrick's Day 2008, a few short weeks ago, I came here to Washington. I came with a simple and extraordinary message. That great day of hope has dawned. Our prayer has been answered. Our faith has been rewarded. After so many decades of conflict, I am so proud, Madam Speaker, to be the first Irish leader to inform the United States Congress: Ireland is at peace.

His theme echoed the address that, at Tony Blair's invitation, he made to a joint meeting of the British House of Commons and House of Lords in May 2007. He had told that gathering:

Now we look back at history not to justify but to learn, and we look forward to the future in terms not of struggle and victories to be won but of enduring peace and progress to be achieved together. In that spirit I [recall] the words of John Fitzgerald Kennedy, the first American President to speak to the Dáil . . . Today I can say to this Parliament at Westminster, as John Kennedy said in Dublin, "Ireland's hour has come." It came, not as victory or defeat but as a shared future for all. Solidarity has made us stronger. Reconciliation has brought us closer. Ireland's hour has come: a time of peace, of prosperity, of old values and new beginnings. This is the great lesson and the great gift of Irish history. This is what Ireland can give to the world.

Ahern's last day as Taoiseach, however, perhaps best demonstrated how much politics in Ireland had been transformed since 1997. Together with Ian Paisley, then First Minister of Northern Ireland, he opened an interpretative centre at the site of the Battle of the Boyne. Paisley heaped praise on Ahern for his role in bringing peace to Northern Ireland, saying:

To the bad old days there can be no turning back. The killing times must end for ever, and no tolerance must be given to those who advocate their return. A strong dedication to peace and an intolerance of murder must drive us forward. This must be the end of all atrocities and the building of the ways of peace.[14]

When asked by reporters what he thought the retiring Ahern should do next, Paisley said: "I think that, after all he has done, he deserves to be the president of the country, if he so desires it."

While the controversy over his finances brought about Ahern's fall from office, it was the subsequent realisations about the unstable basis of national finances and revelations about the health of the country's banks that would finally destroy his reputation. He left the post of Taoiseach and the leadership of Fianna Fáil just before the economic and banking crisis, but in the public mind he has attracted much of the blame for the policies that led to it. The failure to regulate the banks and the reliance of the public finances on the bloated tax receipts of the construction boom are laid squarely at his feet and those of Fianna Fáil.

It may be that, if public anger at the economic crisis is assuaged and a broader appreciation of its complex origins emerges, Ahern's reputation and that of his party will recover somewhat. The success of his Northern Ireland policy stands unblemished, but his later actions undermine the economic achievements of his earlier years. It seems likely, however, that Bertie Ahern will in time be more popular with historians than he is with the public at present, although a lot less popular than he was with the same public in three successive elections.

EPILOGUE

AN APPREHENSIVE ANNIVERSARY

By comparison with other recent anniversaries, Fianna Fáil's celebration of its 85th anniversary was low-key. Only weeks after the disastrous 2011 general election, the party had much to be low-key about.

On the occasion of its 80th anniversary Fianna Fáil, then in power, had organised a lavish commemorative event in the Mansion House, Dublin, which was addressed by the Taoiseach, Bertie Ahern, and included a re-enactment by the actor Barry McGovern of de Valera's address to the inaugural meeting at the La Scala Theatre on 16 May 1926.

For the 70th anniversary in 1996 it had held a similarly grand "Night of Celebration" in the Concert Hall of the RDS, which featured a powerful musical and film tribute to the party, its history and its achievements.

Fianna Fáil was in opposition at that time, and a series of events and publications to mark the 70th anniversary was part of Bertie Ahern's strategy for raising morale and rejuvenating the party in preparation for the 1997 election. Among the publications produced by the party to mark that anniversary was *Taking the Long View,* a collection of essays on different aspects of the party by historians and commentators, most of them from outside the party. The launch of the book at Fianna Fáil head office was attended by three of the party's leaders: Ahern, Reynolds and Haughey.

The 75th anniversary of the party was also commemorated by an official publication: *Republican Days: 75 Years of Fianna Fáil.* It was an attractive paperback notable for the stunning quality of the historical photographs and posters it contained. It was also remarkable for the fact that this expensively produced official party history was paid for by advertising. Of the 276 pages, 70 were given over to advertisements, and more than half of those were from developers or construction-related companies.

The party was understandably in much more sombre mood approaching its 85th birthday. After the 2007 general election Fianna Fáil had 78 seats in the Dáil and 29 in the Seanad; when the 2011 elections were over it had a mere 20 TDS and 14 senators. Only three members of the outgoing Government had been returned to Dáil Éireann: the new party leader, Micheál Martin, Éamon Ó Cuív and Brian Lenihan. At the time of the anniversary Lenihan was Fianna Fáil's only TD in Dublin. Three weeks later he died, finally succumbing to the pancreatic cancer with which he had been diagnosed in December 2009. His death deprived the party of one of those who might have been most effective in its efforts at recovery.

On the evening of the 85th anniversary Micheál Martin addressed a party meeting in Tipperary, but his message was directed at the wider party organisation, to whom the address was e-mailed later that evening. He sought to remind his depleted troops of Fianna Fáil's honourable early history and to use the inspiring tale of its origins to raise their spirits. He also sought to reassure them that Fianna Fáil would survive.

> The fact that from the outset, de Valera and Lemass saw Fianna Fáil as a republican organisation, a unifying force and a vehicle for progressive politics should not be lost on us today as we seek to revitalise this party and bring new energy to it. We can also take inspiration from the fact that when our founders set out on their task to create the great national movement that became Fianna Fáil, they did so from the grass roots up.

Martin emphasised that the struggles faced by the party's founding fathers were exponentially greater than the party's present difficulties.

> Many of our founders had experienced a bitter defeat in the Civil War and had seen comrades lose their lives in that divisive and tragic struggle. They had also lived through the frustration and pain of being imprisoned for their political views during the Civil War or in its immediate aftermath. They had experienced defeat in the 1923 General Election and had come through a rancorous split with former allies in Sinn Féin.
>
> They had every reason to be disillusioned or to turn their back on politics, but they were people of commitment and determination. They were not going to walk away from their responsibilities to the Irish people and, in our generation, nor will we.
>
> If we return Fianna Fáil to the core principles that for so many years won the support and loyalty of the Irish people, we will not only renew our party, we will renew a vital positive force in the life of our nation.
>
> I want Fianna Fáil to be that great party it once was and to be in touch with and responsive to the needs of the Irish people.
>
> I want Fianna Fáil to value the experience and contribution of our current members and public representatives but also to welcome new members, including more women and young people to our ranks.

Shortly afterwards Martin set up renewal committees in each constituency, and a nationwide multimedia consultation with the party membership was established, although the ard-fheis that he promised for the autumn of 2011 was postponed to the spring of 2012.

The forceful rallying cry of this 85th anniversary speech reflected Martin's optimistic nature. Over the summer and early autumn of 2011, however, Fianna Fáil battled to come to terms with the scale of its loss of power, position and prestige. It failed even to field a candidate for the presidency. It remains to be seen whether Fianna Fáil will be around to commemorate any more significant anniversaries. The omens are not good for its recovery.

NOTES

Chapter 1 (pp 9–16)

1. For one account and a discussion of this exchange see Farrell, *Seán Lemass*, p. 17.
2. Lemass's own account of this period is given in *Studies*, 1966; see also Browne, "Seán Lemass."
3. Browne, "Seán Lemass."
4. See Dunphy, *The Making of Fianna Fáil Power in Ireland*, p. 70; Fanning, *Independent Ireland*, p. 96.
5. Bowman, *De Valera and the Ulster Question*, p. 95.
6. Dunphy, *The Making of Fianna Fáil Power in Ireland*, p. 73.
7. De Valera to J. J. McGarrity, 13 March 1926 (National Library of Ireland, McGarrity Papers, ms. 17,441), cited by Bowman, *De Valera and the Ulster Question*, p. 95.

Chapter 2 (pp 17–30)

1. Lemass to MacEntee, 24 March 1929 (UCD Archives, Seán MacEntee Papers).
2. See the commemorative plaque at 23 Suffolk Street.
3. Éamon de Valera, interview with United Press, 17 April 1926.
4. 1927 Ard-Fheis, honorary secretaries' report, quoted by John Horgan in Hannon and Gallagher, *Taking the Long View*, p. 41.
5. Seán Sherwin, interview with the author.
6. For an account of the work of this early research unit see Dunphy, *The Making of Fianna Fáil Power in Ireland*, p. 86–7; documents cited include National Library of Ireland, Gallagher Papers, ms. 18357. For samples of the material published see http://www.whytes.ie/4ImageDisplay.asp?AUCTION=20090314&IMAGE=1533.
7. Briscoe, *For the Life of Me*, p. 230.
8. See Fianna Fáil, *Fianna Fáil: An Chéad Tréimhse*, p. 13–14.
9. See Dunphy, *The Making of Fianna Fáil Power in Ireland*, p. 86–7.
10. Quoted by Coogan, *De Valera*, p. 395.
11. See Briscoe, *For the Life of Me*, p. 231.
12. See Breathnach, *Republican Days*, p. 13.
13. Seán MacEntee, interview with Michael McInerney, *Irish Times*, 23 July 1974.
14. Farrell, *Seán Lemass*, p. 19.
15. Boland, *The Rise and Decline of Fianna Fáil*, p. 18.
16. Ó Beacháin, *Destiny of the Soldiers*, p. 51.
17. Gallagher, *Political Parties in the Republic of Ireland*, p. 10.
18. Michael Mills, "Seán Lemass looks back," *Irish Press*, January 1969.
19. Dunphy, *The Making of Fianna Fáil Power in Ireland*, p. 74.
20. Dunphy, *The Making of Fianna Fáil Power in Ireland*, p. 75.
21. John Horgan, in Hannon and Gallagher, *Taking the Long View*, p. 35.
22. Rafter, *Neil Blaney*, p. 5.
23. Sacks, *The Donegal Mafia*, p. 73.

24. See Carroll, *Seán Moylan*, chap. 24.

25. Andrews, *Man of No Property*, p. 23.

26. Boland, *The Rise and Decline of Fianna Fáil*, p. 21–2.

27. Tom Garvin, "National elites," *Economic and Social Review*, 8/3 (1977), p. 172–9.

Chapter 3 (pp 31–44)

1. See Ó Beacháin, *Destiny of the Soldiers*, p. 54.

2. Coogan, *De Valera*, p. 398.

3. Dónal O'Sullivan, *The Irish Free State and Its Senate: A Study in Contemporary Politics* (1940), p. 193, cited by Coogan in *De Valera*, p. 399.

4. Hill, *A New History of Ireland*, VII, p. 120.

5. Coogan, *De Valera*, p. 399–400.

6. Lee, *Ireland, 1912–85*, p. 152.

7. Quoted by Dwyer, *De Valera*, p. 146.

8. Hill, *A New History of Ireland*, VII, p. 119.

9. Quoted in *Fianna Fáil: An Chéad Tréimhse*, p. 14.

10. *Nation*, 25 July 1927, cited by Ó Beacháin, *Destiny of the Soldiers*, p. 63.

11. O'Sullivan, *Seán Lemass*, p. 45.

12. Longford and O'Neill, *Éamon de Valera*, p. 254.

13. Bourden, *The Emergence of Modern Ireland*, p. 146.

14. Minutes of Fianna Fáil parliamentary meeting, 5 August 1927, cited by Ó Beacháin in *Destiny of the Soldiers*, p. 64.

15. Lee, *Ireland, 1912–85*, p. 155.

16. Longford and O'Neill, *Éamon de Valera*, p. 257.

17. Longford and O'Neill, *Éamon de Valera*, p. 257.

18. Quoted by Longford and O'Neill, *Éamon de Valera*, p. 258.

19. Peter Mair, "De Valera and democracy," in Garvin et al., *Dissecting Irish Politics*, p. 37.

20. Meehan, *The Cosgrave Party*, p. 96–100.

21. See Ó Beacháin, *Destiny of the Soldiers*, p. 67–9.

22. See Longford and O'Neill, *Éamon de Valera*, p. 259.

23. Browne, "Seán Lemass."

24. Michael Mills, "Seán Lemass looks back," *Irish Press*, 28 January 1969.

25. Honorary Secretaries' Report, 1928 (UCD, Fianna Fáil Archives, FF/702), figures for 1927, cited by Martin in *Freedom to Choose*, p. 138.

26. See Horgan, *Taking the Long View*, p. 39.

27. Boland, *The Rise and Fall of Fianna Fáil*.

28. Seán MacEntee Papers (UCD Archives); Dunphy, *The Making of Fianna Fáil Power in Ireland*, p. 80.

29. Dwyer, *De Valera*, p. 152.

30. Collins, *The Power Game*, p. 17.

31. Coogan, *De Valera*, p. 444.

32. Longford and O'Neill, *Éamon de Valera*, p. 270.

33. Quoted by Coogan, *De Valera*, p. 444.

34. Quoted by Coogan, *De Valera*, p. 421.

35. Ó Beacháin, *Destiny of the Soldiers*, p. 58.

36. Feeney, *Seán MacEntee*, p. 56.

37. Farrell, *Seán Lemass*, p. 24.

38. Farrell, *Seán Lemass*, p. 24.
39. *Nation*, February 1929, quoted by Coogan, *De Valera*, p. 421–2.
40. Garvin, *Judging Lemass*, p. 97.
41. Bowman, *De Valera and the Ulster Question*, p. 102.

Chapter 4 (pp 45–62)

1. Skinner, *Politicians by Accident*, p. 308.
2. Coogan, *De Valera*, p. 429.
3. Bourden, *The Emergence of Modern Ireland*, p. 148.
4. *Irish Independent*, 7 February 1932, cited by Moss in *Political Parties in the Irish Free State*, appendix 2.
5. Dwyer, *De Valera*, p. 157.
6. Collins, *The Cosgrave Legacy*, p. 52–3.
7. Coogan, *De Valera*, p. 425.
8. See Ó Beacháin, *Destiny of the Soldiers*, p. 122 and illustrations; also Dwyer, *De Valera*, p. 157.
9. Coogan, *De Valera*, p. 432.
10. Collins, *The Cosgrave Legacy*, p. 54; Manning, *James Dillon*, p. 153.
11. Browne, "Seán Lemass."
12. Jordan, *Éamon de Valera*, p. 177.
13. Peter Mair, "De Valera and democracy," in Garvin et al., *Dissecting Irish Politics*, p. 37.
14. Coogan, *De Valera*, p. 435.
15. Peter Mair, "De Valera and democracy," in Garvin et al., *Dissecting Irish Politics*, p. 38.
16. Bromage, *De Valera*, p. 122.
17. Dwyer, *De Valera*, p. 161.
18. See Garret FitzGerald, "Éamon de Valera and the price of achievement," in Doherty and Keogh, *De Valera's Irelands*, p. 192.
19. Fanning, *Independent Ireland*, p. 109.
20. *Irish Press*, 24 April 1933; Longford and O'Neill, *Éamon de Valera*, p. 289.
21. Jordan, *Éamon de Valera*, p. 205.
22. Moss, *Political Parties in the Irish Free State*, p. 189.
23. Brian Girvin, "The republicanisation of Irish society, 1932–1948," in Hill, *A New History of Ireland*, VII, p. 131.
24. Moss, *Political Parties in the Irish Free State*, p. 194.
25. Cabinet minutes, 18 March 1932 (National Archives, D/T 6230); discussed in Horgan, *Seán Lemass*, p. 73.
26. O'Sullivan, *Seán Lemass*, p. 76.
27. Dwyer, *De Valera*, p. 202.
28. Moss, *Political Parties in the Irish Free State*, p. 192.
29. See Farrell, *Seán Lemass*, p. 40.
30. O'Leary, *Irish Elections*, p. 27.
31. Dwyer, *De Valera*, p. 179.
32. Mulcahy Papers, undated memo in file Mar./May 1933 (P7b/90), 310; see Girvin, "The republicanisation of Irish society, 1932–1948," in Hill, *A New History of Ireland*, VII.

33. O'Leary, *Irish Elections*, p. 40.

34. Manning, *Blueshirts*, p. 97.

35. Keogh, *Twentieth-Century Ireland*, p. 84.

36. O'Leary, *Irish Elections*, p. 29.

37. Jordan, *Éamon de Valera*, p. 201.

38. Browne, "Seán Lemass."

39. *Parliamentary Debates: Dáil Éireann: Official Report*, 11 May 1937.

40. Bourden, *The Emergence of Modern Ireland*, p. 153.

41. Jordan, *Éamon de Valera*, p. 212.

42. Referred to by Bowman in *De Valera and the Ulster Question*, p. 183.

43. *Irish Times*, 30 June 1937.

44. Gallagher, *Political Parties in the Republic of Ireland*, p. 14.

45. See Girvin, "The republicanisation of Irish society, 1932–1948," in Hill, *A New History of Ireland*, *VII*, p. 139.

46. Dwyer, *De Valera*, p. 198.

47. Farrell, *Seán Lemass*, p. 40.

48. Horgan, *Seán Lemass*, p. 68.

49. Horgan, *Seán Lemass*, p. 67.

50. Minutes of Fianna Fáil Ard-Chomhairle, 1932–48; see Ó Beacháin, *Destiny of the Soldiers*, p. 142.

51. See Brian Farrell, "De Valera: Unique dictator or charismatic chairman?" in O'Carroll and Murphy, *De Valera and His Times*.

52. The term used by Bowman to describe those who wanted Fianna Fáil to organise in Northern Ireland or be more active on the issue of partition.

53. Bowman, *De Valera and the Ulster Question*, p. 133; *Dictionary of Irish Biography*.

54. See Bowman, *De Valera and the Ulster Question*, p. 134; also Ó Beacháin, *Destiny of the Soldiers*, p. 142.

Chapter 5 (pp 63–78)

1. Quoted in *Fianna Fáil: An Chéad Tréimhse*, p. 38.

2. Dwyer, *De Valera*, p. 241–2.

3. Dwyer, *De Valera*, p. 227–8.

4. Dwyer, *De Valera*, p. 228.

5. Dwyer, *De Valera*, p. 242.

6. Dwyer, *De Valera*, p. 244.

7. Coogan, *De Valera*, p. 535–6.

8. Garret FitzGerald, "Éamon de Valera: The price of his achievements," in Doherty and Keogh, *De Valera's Irelands*, p. 193.

9. Dwyer, *De Valera*, p. 244.

10. *Parliamentary Debates: Dáil Éireann: Official Report*, vol. 37, col. 592 (29 September 1939); see Longford and O'Neill, *Éamon de Valera*, p. 349.

11. Bowman, *De Valera and the Ulster Question*, p. 211.

12. Keogh, *Twentieth-Century Ireland*, p. 109.

13. See Ó Beacháin, *Destiny of the Soldiers*, p. 166.

14. Ó Beacháin, *Destiny of the Soldiers*, p. 166.

15. Ó Beacháin, *Destiny of the Soldiers*, p. 179.

16. See Farrell, *Seán Lemass*, p. 56.

17. O'Sullivan, *Seán Lemass*, p. 96.
18. Skinner, *Politicians by Accident*, p. 139–43.
19. Keogh, *Twentieth Century Ireland*, p. 124.
20. Memorandum, Minister for Co-ordination of Defensive Measures to Taoiseach, January 1940 (National Archives, Department of the Taoiseach, SI 1586A), quoted by Fisk, *In Time of War*, p. 484–5; see also Keogh, *Twentieth-Century Ireland*, p. 124.
21. Skinner, *Politicians by Accident*, p. 254–5.
22. Keogh, *Twentieth-Century Ireland*, p. 136.
23. Jordan, *Éamon de Valera*, p. 229.
24. Jordan, *Éamon de Valera*, p. 229.
25. Dónal Ó Drisceoil, "Keeping the temperature down: Domestic politics in Emergency Ireland," in Keogh and O'Driscoll, *Ireland in World War Two*; see also Ó Beacháin, *Destiny of the Soldiers*, p. 188.
26. O'Leary, *Irish Elections*, p. 35.
27. Breathnach, *Republican Days*, p. 79.
28. Speech in Ranelagh, 8 June 1943 (UCD Archives, Seán MacEntee Papers, P67/364/9).
29. Speech in Ranelagh, 8 June 1943 (UCD Archives, Seán MacEntee Papers, P67/364/9).
30. Lemass to MacEntee, 10 June 1943 (UCD Archives, Seán MacEntee Papers, 67/363/6); Ó Beacháin, *Destiny of the Soldiers*, p. 188; see also Dunphy, *The Making of Fianna Fáil Power in Ireland*, p. 287.
31. See Keogh, *Twentieth-Century Ireland*, p. 138.
32. Lee, *Ireland, 1912–85*, p. 241.
33. Lee, *Ireland, 1912–85*, p. 241.
34. O'Leary, *Irish Elections*, p. 34–5.
35. Garvin, *The Evolution of Irish Nationalist Politics*, p. 169.
36. Dunphy, *The Making of Fianna Fáil*, p. 284.
37. Dunphy, *The Making of Fianna Fáil Power in Ireland*, p. 284.
38. Gallagher, *Political Parties in the Republic of Ireland*, p. 106.
39. Tom Garvin, *The Evolution of Irish Nationalist Politics*.
40. Dunphy, *The Making of Fianna Fáil Power in Ireland*, p. 287.
41. Ó Beacháin, *Destiny of the Soldiers*, p. 186.
42. For a detailed account of the rise and fall of the Labour Party in these years see Puirséil, *The Irish Labour Party*, chap. 4.
43. See Puirséil, *The Irish Labour Party*, chap. 7.
44. Quoted by Jordan, *Éamon de Valera*, p. 246.
45. See, for example, Breathnach, *Republican Days*, p. 83.
46. See *Irish Press*, 25 and 29 May 1943; Keogh, *Twentieth-Century Ireland*, p. 143–4.
47. Lee, *Ireland, 1912–85*, p. 241.
48. Jordan, *Éamon de Valera*, p. 237.
49. Aldous, *Great Irish Speeches*, p. 92.
50. De Valera used the words "comely maidens" in the broadcast, but confusion has been caused by the substitution of "happy maidens" in a recording made later for HMV.
51. Collins, *The Power Game*, p. 19.
52. Keogh, *Twentieth-Century Ireland*, p. 137.
53. See "Hyde (and de Valera) offered condolences on Hitler's death," *Irish*

Independent, 31 December 2005, at http://www.independent.ie/national-news/hyde-and-de-valera-offered-condolences-on-hitlers-death-228426.html.

54. Longford and O'Neill, *Éamon de Valera,* p. 414.

Chapter 6 (pp 79–95)

1. Lee, *Ireland, 1912–85,* p. 289.
2. Bardon, *A History of Ireland in 250 Episodes,* p. 499.
3. Hill, *A New History of Ireland,* VII, p. 264.
4. Dwyer, *De Valera,* p. 295.
5. Dwyer, *De Valera,* p. 295; Bardon, *A History of Ireland in 250 Episodes,* p. 499.
6. P. Dempsey, "Tom Derrig," in *Dictionary of Irish Biography.*
7. O'Sullivan, *Seán Lemass,* p. 108.
8. Keogh, *Twentieth-Century Ireland,* p. 167.
9. Dwyer, *De Valera,* p. 291.
10. "A number of prominent party members are said to have gone to de Valera." Browne, "Seán Lemass."
11. Dunphy, *The Making of Fianna Fáil Power in Ireland,* p. 297.
12. Dunphy, *The Making of Fianna Fáil Power in Ireland,* p. 296.
13. Bardon, *A History of Ireland in 250 Episodes,* p. 500.
14. Horgan, p. 5, working notes for *Lemass.*
15. See MacBride, by-election literature, October 1947; also Keogh, *Twentieth-Century Ireland,* p. 188.
16. Bowman's adjective; see also Ó Beacháin, *Destiny of the Soldiers,* p. 211.
17. See Ó Beacháin, *Destiny of the Soldiers,* p. 211.
18. John Whyte in Hill, *A New History of Ireland,* VII, p. 267.
19. O'Leary, *Irish Elections,* p. 38.
20. MacDermott, *Clann na Poblachta,* p. 164.
21. Farrell, *Seán Lemass,* p. 79.
22. Coogan, *De Valera,* p. 637; *Parliamentary Debates: Dáil Éireann: Official Report,* October 1947.
23. Longford and O'Neill, *Éamon de Valera,* p. 430.
24. Corless, *Party Nation,* p. 116.
25. Corless, *Party Nation,* p. 117.
26. Ó Beacháin, *Destiny of the Soldiers,* p. 207–9.
27. Dunphy, *The Making of Fianna Fáil Power in Ireland,* p. 295.
28. Ó Beacháin, *Destiny of the Soldiers,* p. 214.
29. Dwyer, *De Valera,* p. 299.
30. John Whyte, in Hill, *A New History of Ireland,* VII, p. 268.
31. O'Leary, *Irish Elections,* p. 39.
32. Farrell, *Seán Lemass,* p. 79; see also Michael Mills, "Seán Lemass looks back," *Irish Press,* 28 January 1969.
33. See Jordan, *Éamon de Valera,* p. 259–60.
34. Fianna Fáil, *Fianna Fáil: An Chéad Tréimhse,* p. 101.
35. Fianna Fáil, *Fianna Fáil: An Chéad Tréimhse,* p. 101.
36. Gallagher, *Political Parties in the Republic of Ireland,* p. 160.
37. Childers to Mullins (UCD Archives, Seán MacEntee Papers, p67/299); Keogh, *Jack Lynch,* p. 189.

38. Childers to MacEntee; see Keogh, *Twentieth-Century Ireland*, p. 184.
39. Lee, *Ireland, 1912–85*, p. 321.
40. Niamh Puirséil, "Political and party competition in post-war Ireland," in Girvin and Murphy, *The Lemass Era*, p. 14.
41. Horgan, *Seán Lemass*, p. 144.
42. Lynch, "My life and times."
43. Farrell, *Seán Lemass*, p. 84.
44. John Horgan, notes for Lemass biography.
45. Longford and O'Neill, *Éamon de Valera*, p. 435–6.
46. Bowman, *De Valera and the Ulster Question*, p. 274.
47. Hugh Delargy, "The man who outlived his memory," *New Statesman*, 5 September 1975; Bowman, *De Valera and the Ulster Question*, p. 275.
48. Longford and O'Neill, *Éamon de Valera*, p. 433.
49. O'Sullivan, *Seán Lemass*, p. 121.
50. Longford and O'Neill, *Éamon de Valera*, p. 437.
51. Bowman, *De Valera and the Ulster Question*, p. 276.
52. Farrell, *Seán Lemass*, p. 81.
53. See, for example, Browne, "Seán Lemass."
54. Michael Mills, "Seán Lemass looks back," *Irish Press*, 28 January 1969.
55. See Farrell, *Seán Lemass*, p. 84.
56. Feeney, *Seán MacEntee*, p. 171.
57. See P. Dempsey and L. W. White, "Erskine Childers," *Dictionary of Irish Biography*.
58. Corless, *Party Nation*, p. 121.
59. Keogh, *Jack Lynch*, p. 37, quoting *Cork Examiner*, 26 May 1951.
60. Jordan, *Éamon de Valera*, p. 265.
61. Farrell, *Seán Lemass*, p. 84–5; Michael Mills, "Seán Lemass looks back," *Irish Press*, 28 January 1969.
62. John Whyte, in Hill, *A New History of Ireland*, VII, p. 281.
63. John Whyte, in Hill, *A New History of Ireland*, VII, p. 282.
64. See, for example, Dwyer, *De Valera*, p. 30.
65. Browne, "Seán Lemass."
66. See Keogh, *Twentieth-Century Ireland*, p. 221.
67. Murphy, *In Search of the Promised Land*, p. 98.

Chapter 7 (pp 96–116)

1. O'Leary, *Irish Elections*, p. 43.
2. Corless, *Party Nation*, p. 126.
3. John Whyte, in Hill, *A New History of Ireland*, VII, p. 282.
4. Horgan, *Seán Lemass*, p. 160.
5. See Farrell, *Seán Lemass*, p. 89.
6. Fianna Fáil parliamentary party minutes, 17 August 1954; see also Horgan, *Seán Lemass*, p. 160.
7. Horgan, *Seán Lemass*, p 160.
8. Yeats, *Cast a Cold Eye*, p. 76–7.
9. Yeats, *Cast a Cold Eye*, p. 77.
10. Fianna Fáil parliamentary party minutes, 18 June 1954 (Fianna Fáil Archives, FF/440A); see Horgan, *Seán Lemass*, p. 160.

11. Chubb, *A Source Book of Irish Government*, p. 231.
12. Chubb, *A Source Book of Irish Government*, p. 233.
13. Chubb, *A Source Book of Irish Government*, p. 236.
14. O'Sullivan, *Seán Lemass*, p. 141.
15. Downey, *Lenihan*, p. 22.
16. Downey, *Lenihan*, p. 22.
17. Horgan, *Seán Lemass*, p. 161.
18. Faulkner, *As I Saw It*, p. 32–3.
19. Faulkner, *As I Saw It*, p. 34.
20. Downey, *Lenihan*, p. 27.
21. *Irish Times*, 29 October 1953, quoted by Horgan, *Noël Browne*, p. 176–7.
22. Horgan, *Noël Browne*, p. 178.
23. See Browne, *Against the Tide*, p. 220–26. For Lenihan's viewpoint on the same events see Downey, *Lenihan*, p. 28.
24. Horgan, *Noël Browne*, p. 185.
25. Browne, *Against the Tide*, p. 222.
26. Horgan, *Seán Lemass*, p. 162.
27. Horgan, *Seán Lemass*, p. 163; *Irish Press*, 18 January 1955.
28. Horgan, *Seán Lemass*, p. 165.
29. McCarthy, *Planning Ireland's Future*, p. 26.
30. McCarthy, *Planning Ireland's Future*, p. 26.
31. Aldous, *Great Irish Speeches*, p. 107.
32. McCarthy, *Planning Ireland's Future*, p. 26–7.
33. McCarthy, *Planning Ireland's Future*, p. 27.
34. Browne, "Seán Lemass."
35. Longford and O'Neill, *Éamon de Valera*, p. 444.
36. Ó Beacháin, *Destiny of the Soldiers*, p. 237.
37. *Cork Examiner* and *Irish Times*, 7 January 1957, quoted by Ó Beacháin, *Destiny of the Soldiers*, p. 244.
38. *Anglo-Celt* (Cavan), 23 February and 2 March 1957; see Ó Beacháin, *Destiny of the Soldiers*, p. 242.
39. McCarthy, *Planning Ireland's Future*, p. 35.
40. McCarthy, *Planning Ireland's Future*, p. 36–7.
41. John Whyte, "Economic crisis and political cold war," in Hill, *A New History of Ireland*, VII, p. 293.
42. Patrick Hillery, interview with John Horgan.
43. Walsh, *Patrick Hillery*, p. 54–5.
44. Arnold, *Jack Lynch*, p. 40–41.
45. Farrell, *Seán Lemass*, p. 95.
46. McCarthy, *Planning Ireland's Future*, p. 50.
47. McCarthy, *Planning Ireland's Future*, p. 51.
48. McCarthy, *Planning Ireland's Future*, p. 52.
49. McCarthy, *Planning Ireland's Future*, p. 52.
50. O'Sullivan, *Seán Lemass*, p. 144.
51. Kevin Boland, interview with John Horgan.
52. G. Kimber, Dublin, to G. W. Chadwick, Commonwealth Relations Office, 3

December 1958 (Public Records Office [London], PRO DO35/7906); see Horgan, *Seán Lemass*, p. 185.

53. See Horgan, *Seán Lemass*, p. 185.
54. Patrick Hillery, interview with John Horgan.
55. Charles Haughey, interview with John Horgan: see Horgan, *Seán Lemass*, p. 184.
56. Faulkner, *As I Saw It*, p. 41.
57. Yeats, *Cast a Cold Eye*, p. 71.
58. Farrell, *Seán Lemass*, p. 96.
59. Yeats, *Cast a Cold Eye*, p. 71.
60. O'Sullivan, *Seán Lemass*, p. 148.

Chapter 8 (pp 117–140)

1. Patrick Hillery, interview with John Horgan.
2. Charles Haughey, interview with John Horgan.
3. Horgan, *Seán Lemass*, p. 196.
4. Walsh, *The Party*, p. 147.
5. See Walshe, *Patrick Hillery*, p. 70–71, and Rafter, *Neil Blaney*, p. 24–5.
6. Tadhg Ó Cearbhaill, interview with John Horgan.
7. Charles Haughey, interview with John Horgan.
8. Based on an account given by Eoin Ryan in an interview with John Horgan; see also Horgan, *Seán Lemass*, p. 197–8.
9. See Farrell, *Seán Lemass*, p. 102.
10. Report, 18 June 1959.
11. Michael Mills, "Seán Lemass looks back," *Irish Press*, 28 January 1969.
12. Lynch, "My life and times," p. 41.
13. Walsh, *Patrick Hillery*, p. 55.
14. Patrick Hillery, interview with John Horgan.
15. See Farrell, *Seán Lemass*, p. 102.
16. John Horgan, notes for Lemass biography, p. 15; Irish Representation fortnightly summary, 19 June and 2 July 1959.
17. *Parliamentary Debates: Dáil Éireann: Official Report*, 3 June 1959.
18. *Parliamentary Debates: Dáil Éireann: Official Report*, vol. 175, 3 June 1959, Committee on Finance, vote 50: Industry and Commerce (resumed).
19. O'Sullivan, *Seán Lemass*, p. 169.
20. Horgan, *Seán Lemass*, p. 197. See Lemass, interview with Dermot Ryan; Downey, *Lenihan*, p. 46.
21. See Lemass, interview with Dermot Ryan.
22. O'Sullivan, *Seán Lemass*, p. 169.
23. Horgan, *Seán Lemass*, p. 226.
24. Horgan, *Seán Lemass*, p. 245.
25. T. Desmond Williams, "Irish foreign policy, 1949–69," in Lee, *Ireland, 1912–85*.
26. R. Fanning, "Frank Aiken," *Dictionary of Irish Biography*.
27. R. Fanning, "Frank Aiken," *Dictionary of Irish Biography*.
28. Joannon, *De Gaulle and Ireland*, p. 87; see also Horgan, *Seán Lemass*, p. 225.
29. Farrell, *Seán Lemass*, p. 120.
30. See, for example O'Sullivan, *Seán Lemass*, p. 169.
31. Faulkner, *As I Saw It*, p. 44.

32. Browne, "Seán Lemass."
33. Farrell, *Seán Lemass*, p. 122.
34. Dwyer, Short Fellow, p. 60–61.
35. Farrell, *Seán Lemass*, p. 103.
36. O'Sullivan, *Seán Lemass*, p. 167.
37. Ó Beacháin, *Destiny of the Soldiers*, p. 254.
38. Farrell, *Seán Lemass*, p. 122.
39. Horgan, *Seán Lemass*, p. 207.
40. Keogh, *Jack Lynch*, p. 91.
41. David Thornley, "The Fianna Fáil party," *Irish Times*, 1 April 1965.
42. O'Leary, *Irish Elections*, p. 65.
43. Corless, *Party Nation*, p. 152.
44. Corless, *Party Nation*, p. 151
45. Corless, *Party Nation*, p. 154–5.
46. Corless, *Party Nation*, p. 154.
47. Corless, *Party Nation*, p. 155.
48. Collins, *The Power Game*, p. 21.
49. Keogh, *Jack Lynch*, p. 92.
50. Lynch, "My life and times," p. 41.
51. Daly and O'Callaghan, *1916 in 1966*, p. 27.
52. Keogh, *Jack Lynch*, p. 113.
53. Keogh, *Jack Lynch*, p. 114.
54. Browne, *Unfulfilled Promise*, p. 83.
55. Downey, *Lenihan*, p. 41.
56. Ó Beacháin, *Destiny of the Soldiers*, p. 279.
57. Faulkner, *As I Saw It*, p. 35.
58. Downey, *Lenihan*, p. 43.
59. Bourden, *The Emergence of Modern Ireland*, p. 193.
60. See Farrell, *Seán Lemass*, p. 123.
61. Walsh, *Patrick Hillery*, p. 146.
62. Faulkner, *As I Saw It*, p. 54.
63. Arnold, *Haughey*, p. 66.
64. Rafter, *Neil Blaney*, p. 36.
65. Rafter, *Neil Blaney*, p. 36.
66. Rafter, *Neil Blaney*, p. 37.
67. Walsh, *Patrick Hillery*, p. 146.
68. See, for example, O'Sullivan, *Seán Lemass*, p. 187.
69. Lynch, "My life and times."
70. See, for example, Horgan, *Seán Lemass*, p. 336.
71. See Arnold, *Charles Haughey*, p. 74–5.
72. See, for example, Rafter, *Neil Blaney*, p. 40.
73. Faulkner, *As I Saw It*, p. 56.

Chapter 9 (pp 141–153)

1. McMorrow, *Dáil Stars*, p. 194.
2. Rafter, *Neil Blaney*, p. 39.
3. Rafter, *Neil Blaney*, p. 40.

4. Dwyer, *Nice Fellow,* p. 139.
5. Lynch, "My life and times."
6. Faulkner, *As I Saw It,* p. 56.
7. James Dillon in Dáil Éireann, 19 November 1966, quoted by Dwyer, *Nice Fellow,* p. 139.
8. Dáil Éireann, 10 November 1966.
9. Downey, *Lenihan,* p. 67.
10. Arnold, *Jack Lynch,* p. 84.
11. Dwyer, *Short Fellow,* p. 88.
12. Dywer, *Haughey's Forty Years of Controversy,* p. 15.
13. See, for example, Keogh, *Jack Lynch,* p. 135.
14. Keogh, *Jack Lynch,* p. 135.
15. Sacks, *The Donegal Mafia,* p. 196–7.
16. Rafter, *Lenihan,* p. 27.
17. See Dwyer, *Nice Fellow,* p. 159.
18. Dwyer, *Fallen Idol,* p. 33.
19. See Dwyer, *Nice Fellow,* p. 173.
20. Rafter, *Lenihan,* p. 41.
21. Faulkner, *As I Saw It,* p. 55–6.
22. Keogh, *Twentieth-Century Ireland,* p. 204.
23. See Collins, *The Power Game,* p. 41.
24. Downey, *Lenihan,* p. 83.
25. Rafter, *Neil Blaney,* p. 43.
26. Lynch, "My life and times."
27. Quoted by Keogh, *Jack Lynch,* p. 153.
28. Keogh, *Jack Lynch,* p. 155.
29. *Irish Times,* 1 February 1969, p. 13, quoted by Arnold, *Jack Lynch,* p. 79.
30. John Whyte, in Hill, *A New History of Ireland, vII,* p. 318.
31. Keogh, *Jack Lynch,* p. 127.
32. Hanafin to Collins.
33. Dwyer, *Short Fellow,* p. 91; Corless, *Party Nation,* p. 160.
34. Corless, *Party Nation,* p. 160.
35. Keogh, *Jack Lynch,* p. 154.
36. Quoted by Dwyer, *Nice Fellow,* p. 169.
37. Quoted by Dwyer, *Nice Fellow,* p. 170.
38. See Dwyer, *Nice Fellow,* p. 169.
39. Dwyer, *Fallen Idol,* p. 34.
40. *Irish Independent,* 21 September 1999.
41. Keogh, *Jack Lynch,* p. 161; *Parliamentary Debates: Dáil Éireann: Official Report,* vol. 241, col. 148 (2 July 1969).
42. Collins, *The Power Game,* p. 39; information from Paddy Creamer, Limerick hurler.

Chapter 10 (pp 154–174)

1. See Collins, *The Power Game,* p. 42.
2. Faulkner, *As I Saw It,* p. 89.
3. Keogh, *Jack Lynch,* p. 168.
4. Keogh, *Jack Lynch,* p. 170.
5. Faulkner, *As I saw It,* p. 90.

6. Keogh, *Jack Lynch*, p. 170.
7. Faulkner, *As I Saw It*, p. 91.
8. Keogh, *Jack Lynch*, p. 172.
9. Donnacha Ó Beacháin, "We Asked for guns: The question of military intervention in Northern Ireland," UCD *History Review*, 1993.
10. See Collins, *The Power Game*, p. 51; Keogh, *Jack Lynch*, p. 180–81.
11. Boland, *The Rise and Decline of Fianna Fáil*, p. 67.
12. Boland, *The Rise and Decline of Fianna Fáil*, p. 68.
13. Interview with Paddy Lalor.
14. Keogh, *Jack Lynch*, p. 211–12.
15. Rafter, *Neil Blaney*, p. 57.
16. Collins, *The Power Game*, p. 59.
17. See Dwyer, *Charlie*, p. 103–4.
18. Keogh, *Jack Lynch*, p. 219; Browne, "The Peter Berry Papers."
19. Dáil Éireann, 25 November 1980.
20. See, for example, Collins, *The Power Game*, p. 77.
21. Keogh, *Jack Lynch*, p. 261.
22. Collins, *The Power Game*, p. 79; Aiken Papers (UCD Archives, 82341).
23. Faulkner, *As I Saw It*, p. 96.
24. Faulkner, *As I Saw It*, p. 99.
25. Walsh, *The Party*, p. 120, quoted by Collins, *The Power Games*, p. 83.
26. Collins, *The Power Game*, p. 84.
27. Arnold, *Jack Lynch*, p. 143.
28. Collins, *The Power Game*, p. 88.
29. Faulkner, *As I Saw It*, p. 104–5.
30. See http://www.youtube.com/watch?v=eKpByXL1Xxo.
31. Walsh, *Jack Lynch*, p. 284.
32. Dáil Éireann, 11 May 1971.
33. Patrick Hillery, interview with Dermot Keogh: see Keogh, *Jack Lynch*, p. 286.

Chapter 11 (pp 175–192)
1. Lee, *Ireland, 1912–85*, p. 466.
2. Gallagher, *Political Parties in Ireland*, p. 118.
3. Faulkner, *As I Saw It*, p. 108.
4. O'Leary, *Irish Elections*, p. 77.
5. Quoted by Collins, *The Power Game*, p. 101.
6. Faulkner, *As I Saw It*, p. 112.
7. O'Leary, *Elections in Ireland*, p. 78.
8. Lee, *Ireland, 1912–85*, p. 468.
9. O'Leary, *Irish Elections*, p. 78.
10. Keogh, *Jack Lynch*, p. 374.
11. O'Leary, *Irish Elections*, p. 79.
12. Lynch, "My life and times."
13. Downey, *Lenihan*, p. 91.
14. Faulkner, *As I Saw It*, p. 117.
15. Lynch, "My life and times."
16. Browne, "How Haughey won," p. 25.

17. Dunlop, *Yes, Taoiseach*, p. 8.
18. Dunlop, *Yes, Taoiseach*, p. 9.
19. Keogh, *Jack Lynch*, p. 382.
20. Lahiffe, *Séamus Brennan*, p. 5.
21. Browne, "How Haughey won."
22. Faulkner, *As I Saw It*, p. 121.
23. Browne, "The making of a Taoiseach."
24. Keogh, *Jack Lynch*, p. 407.

Chapter 12 (pp 193–206)

1. To Geraldine Kennedy, cited by Dwyer, *Haughey's Forty Years of Controversy*, p. 78.
2. See Downey, *Lenihan*, p. 105.
3. Keogh, *Jack Lynch*, p. 410.
4. Brian Farrell, in Penniman and Farrell, *Ireland at the Polls*, p. 3.
5. See Keogh, *Jack Lynch*, p. 409; also Martin O'Donoghue, "Irish economic policy, 1977–79," *Studies*, vol. 79, no. 315 (autumn 1990), p. 313.
6. Browne, "The making of a Taoiseach."
7. Faulkner, *As I Saw It*, p. 124.
8. Faulkner, *As I Saw It*, p. 125.
9. Faulkner, *As I Saw It*, p. 126.
10. Mansergh, *The Spirit of the Nation*, p. 261.
11. See also Dwyer, *Charlie*, p. 122.
12. Browne, "The making of a Taoiseach."
13. Browne, "The making of a Taoiseach."
14. Keogh, *Jack Lynch*, p. 417.
15. Browne, "The making of a Taoiseach."
16. For a list of those said to have attended this caucus meeting see Browne, "The making of a Taoiseach."
17. Browne, "The making of a Taoiseach."
18. See Keogh, *Jack Lynch*, p. 42.
19. Brian Farrell, in Penniman and Farrell, *Ireland at the Polls*, p. 5.
20. Collins, *The Power Game*, p. 113.
21. Faulkner, *As I Saw It*, p. 150.
22. Dunlop, *Yes, Taoiseach*, p. 131.
23. Faulkner, *As I Saw It*, p. 150.
24. Dunlop, *Yes, Taoiseach*, p. 141.
25. Keogh, *Jack Lynch*, p. 425.
26. Dermot Keogh, in Hill, *A New History of Ireland*, VII, p. 379.
27. Collins, *The Power Game*, p. 134.
28. Jones, *In Your Opinion*, p. 30.
29. Collins, *The Power Game*, p. 139.
30. Jones, *In Your Opinion*, p. 32.
31. Brian Farrell, in Penniman and Farrell, *Ireland at the Polls*, p. 8.

Chapter 13 (pp 207–223)

1. Hill, *A New History of Ireland*, VII, p. 384.
2. FitzGerald, *All in a Life*, p. 398.

3. Browne, "The making of a Taoiseach."
4. Smith, *Garret*, p. 397; Keogh, *Twentieth-Century Ireland*, p. 368.
5. Quoted by Dwyer, *Charlie*, p. 154.
6. Dwyer, *Charlie*, p. 155.
7. Keogh, *Jack Lynch*, p. 440.
8. Faulkner, *As I Saw It*, p. 164–5.
9. Brian Farrell, in Penniman and Farrell, *Ireland at the Polls*, p. 16–.
10. Dwyer, *Charlie*, p. 157.
11. See, for example, Keogh, *Twentieth-Century Ireland*, p. 369; Brian Farrell, in Penniman and Farrell, *Ireland at the Polls*, p. 17.
12. Lee, *Ireland, 1912–85*, p. 508.
13. Brian Farrell, in Penniman and Farrell, *Ireland at the Polls*, p. 17.
14. Ahern, *The Autobiography*, p. 68.
15. Reynolds, *My Autobiography*, p. 138.
16. Ahern, *The Autobiography*, p. 73.
17. See Ahern, *The Autobiography*, p. 72–3.
18. Coogan, *A Memoir*, p. 259.
19. Collins, *The Power Game*, p. 55.
20. See, for example, Faulkner, *As I Saw It*, p. 178.
21. Quoted by Ahern, *The Autobiography*, p. 75.
22. Ahern, *The Autobiography*, p. 68.
23. Aldous, *Great Irish Speeches*, p. 155.
24. Jones, *In Your Opinion*, p. 63.
25. See Downey, *Lenihan*, p. 140.
26. See Rafter, *Martin Mansergh*, p. 176, 177.
27. Rafter, *Martin Mansergh*, p. 177.

Chapter 14 (pp 224–236)

1. Corless, *Party Nation*, p. 232.
2. Corless, *Party Nation*, p. 223.
3. Corless, *Party Nation*, p. 223.
4. Corless, *Party Nation*, p. 225.
5. Dwyer, *Fallen Idol*, p. 131.
6. Collins, *The Power Game*, p. 168.
7. Ahern, *The Autobiography*, p. 96.
8. Dáil Éireann, 10 March 1987.
9. MacSharry and White, *The Making of the Celtic Tiger*, p. 46–7.
10. Collins, *The Power Game*, p. 177.
11. Dáil Éireann, 31 March 1987.
12. Dáil Éireann, 31 March 1987.
13. MacSharry and White, *The Making of the Celtic Tiger*, p. 66–7.
14. http://research.finegael.org/learn/c/q/article.
15. MacSharry and White, *The Making of the Celtic Tiger*, p. 75.
16. MacSharry and White, *The Making of the Celtic Tiger*, p. 75–6.
17. Ahern, *The Autobiography*, p. 100.
18. Ahern, *The Autobiography*, p. 102.
19. Ahern, *The Autobiography*, p. 105.

20. Corless, *Party Nation*, p. 232.
21. Corless, *Party Nation*, p. 233.
22. Collins, *The Power Game*, p. 193.
23. Dwyer, *Fallen Idol*, p. 137.
24. Dwyer, *Short Fellow*, p. 358.
25. Collins, *The Power Game*, p. 197.
26. Dwyer, *Fallen Idol*, p. 140.
27. Collins, *The Power Game*, p. 191.
28. Ahern, *The Autobiography*, p. 107–8.
29. Ahern, *The Autobiography*, p. 108.
30. Collins, *The Power Game*, p. 199.
31. Collins, *The Power Game*, p. 200.
32. Dwyer, *Fallen Idol*, p. 141.
33. Collins, *The Power Game*, p. 200.
34. Reynolds, *My Autobiography*, p. 156.

Chapter 15 (pp 237–254)

1. Dwyer, *Short Fellow*, p. 363.
2. Dwyer, *Short Fellow*, p. 366.
3. *Times* (London), 11 September 2009.
4. *Irish Times*, 29 April 2010.
5. Dwyer, *Short Fellow*, p. 366.
6. *Sunday Independent*, 5 April 2009.
7. Walsh, *Patrick Hillery*, p. 495.
8. Dwyer, *Short Fellow*, p. 366.
9. Dwyer, *Fallen Idol*, p. 143.
10. Dwyer, *Fallen Idol*, p. 144.
11. Dwyer, *Fallen Idol*, p. 144.
12. Ahern, *The Autobiography*, p. 115.
13. Dwyer, *Fallen Idol*, p. 145–6.
14. Ahern, *The Autobiography*, p. 116.
15. Dwyer, *Fallen Idol*, p. 146.
16. Dáil Éireann, 25 October 1990.
17. Ahern, *The Autobiography*, p. 117–18.
18. Dwyer, *Fallen Idol*, p. 148.
19. Dwyer, *Fallen Idol*, p. 147.
20. Dwyer, *Fallen Idol*, p. 147.
21. Dwyer, *Fallen Idol*, p. 148.
22. Collins, *The Power Game*, p. 208.
23. Lenihan, *For the Record*, p. 176.
24. Lenihan, *For the Record*, p. 174.
25. Collins, *The Power Game*, p. 210.
26. Lenihan, *For the Record*, p. 179.
27. Lenihan, *For the Record*, p. 180.
28. *Dáil Éireann*, 31 October 1990.
29. Collins, *The Power Game*, p. 212.
30. Reynolds, *My Autobiography*, p. 156.

31. Collins, *The Power Game*, p. 212.
32. Collins, *The Haughey File*, p. 193.
33. Ahern, *The Autobiography*, p. 119.
34. Dwyer, *Fallen Idol*, p. 150.
35. Ahern, *The Autobiography*, p. 120.
36. Collins, *The Haughey File*, p. 194.
37. Collins, *The Haughey File*, p. 195.
38. Collins, *The Haughey File*, p. 194.
39. Collins, *The Haughey File*, p. 194.
40. Ahern, *The Autobiography*, p. 121.
41. Dwyer, *Short Fellow*, p. 387.
42. Collins, *The Power Game*, p. 214.
43. Dwyer, *Short Fellow*, p. 388.
44. Reynolds, *My Autobiography*, p. 165.
45. Ahern, *The Autobiography*, p. 128.
46. Ahern, *The Autobiography*, p. 128–9.
47. Dwyer, *Short Fellow*, p. 400.
48. Dwyer, *Fallen Idol*, p. 161.
49. Ahern, *The Autobiography*, p. 129.
50. Ahern, *The Autobiography*, p. 129–30.
51. Ahern, *The Autobiography*, p. 131.
52. Dwyer, *Fallen Idol*, p. 172.
53. Reynolds, *My Autobiography*, p. 170.
54. Dwyer, *Fallen Idol*, p. 176.
55. Dwyer, *Fallen Idol*, p. 176.
56. Collins, *The Haughey File*, p. 230.
57. Collins, *The Power Game*, p. 222.
58. Ahern, *The Autobiography*, p. 132.
59. Collins, *The Power Game*, p. 230.
60. Collins, *The Power Game*, p. 230–31.
61. Ahern, *The Autobiography*, p. 137.
62. Collins, *The Power Game*, p. 239.

Chapter 16 (pp 255–270)

1. Reynolds, *My Autobiography*, p. 176.
2. Reynolds, *My Autobiography*, p. 178.
3. Ryan, *Albert Reynolds*, p. 164.
4. Reynolds, *My Autobiography*, p. 178–9.
5. Andrews, *Kingstown Republican*, p. 188.
6. *Irish Independent*, 26 January 2002.
7. Ryan, *Albert Reynolds*, 163.
8. Ahern, *The Autobiography*, p. 139.
9. See Ryan, *Albert Reynolds*, p. 162.
10. Reynolds, *My Autobiography*, p. 181.
11. Collins, *The Power Game*, p. 245.
12. Collins, *The Power Game*, p. 243.
13. Duignan, *One Spin on the Merry-Go-Round*, p. 40.

14. Brady, *Up with the Times*, p. 224.
15. Collins, *The Power Game*, p. 229–30.
16. Witnessed by the author.
17. Collins, *The Power Game*, p. 246.
18. Corless, *Party Nation*, p. 238.
19. Duignan, *One Spin on the Merry-Go-Round*, p. 52.
20. Duignan, *One Spin on the Merry-Go-Round*, p. 49.
21. Corless, *Party Nation*, p. 242.
22. Duignan, *One Spin on the Merry-Go-Round*, p. 53.
23. Corless, *Party Nation*, p. 238.
24. Dunlop, *Yes, Taoiseach*, p. 322.
25. Witnessed by the author.
26. Corless, *Party Nation*, p. 242.
27. Collins, *The Power Game*, p. 248.
28. Duignan, *One Spin on the Merry-Go-Round*, p. 59.
29. Collins, *The Power Game*, p. 242.
30. Ahern, *The Autobiography*, p. 147.
31. Duignan, *One Spin on the Merry-Go-Round*, p. 59.
32. Dunlop, *Yes, Taoiseach*, p. 321–2.
33. Ahern, *The Autobiography*, p. 147.
34. Corless, *Party Nation*, p. 244.
35. Reynolds, *My Autobiography*, p. 202.
36. Collins, *The Power Game*, p. 249.
37. Witnessed by the author.
38. See Collins, *The Power Game*, p. 250.
39. Ahern, *The Autobiography*, p. 148.
40. Duignan, *One Spin on the Merry-Go-Round*, p. 69–70.
41. Andrews, *Kingstown Republican*, p. 214.
42. Duignan, *One Spin on the Merry-Go-Round*, p. 70.
43. Collins, *The Power Game*, p. 253.
44. Reynolds, *My Autobiography*, p. 208.
45. Finlay, *Snakes and Ladders*, p. 138.
46. Reynolds, *My Autobiography*, p. 209.
47. Finley, *Snakes and Ladders*, p. 140.
48. Collins, *The Power Game*, p. 249.
49. Andrews, *Kingstown Republican*, p. 216.

Chapter 17 (pp 271–296)

1. Lahiffe, *Séamus Brennan*, p. 53.
2. Andrews, *Kingstown Republican*, p. 216.
3. Reynolds, *My Autobiography*, p. 12.
4. Duignan, *One Spin on the Merry-Go-Round*, p. 100.
5. Reynolds, *My Autobiography*, p. 173–4.
6. Reynolds, *My Autobiography*, p. 174–5.
7. Reynolds, *My Autobiography*, p. 233.
8. Reynolds, *My Autobiography*, p. 209.
9. Collins, *The Power Game*, p. 261.

10. Duignan, *One Spin on the Merry-Go-Round,* p. 96–7.
11. Duignan, *One Spin on the Merry-Go-Round,* p. 97.
12. Collins, *The Power Game,* p. 261.
13. Reynolds, *My Autobiography,* p. 320.
14. Finlay, *Snakes and Ladders,* p. 202.
15. Finlay, *Snakes and Ladders,* p. 203.
16. Dáil Éireann, 17 December 1993.
17. Duignan, *One Spin on the Merry-Go-Round,* p. 127–8.
18. Duignan, *One Spin on the Merry-Go-Round,* p. 128.
19. Duignan, *One Spin on the Merry-Go-Round,* p. 88.
20. Collins, *The Power Game,* p. 264.
21. Duignan, *One Spin on the Merry-Go-Round,* p. 90.
22. Duignan, *One Spin on the Merry-Go-Round,* p. 92.
23. Reynolds, *My Autobiography,* p. 263.
24. Duignan, *One Spin on the Merry-Go-Round,* p. 94.
25. Duignan, *One Spin on the Merry-Go-Round,* p. 95.
26. Duignan, *One Spin on the Merry-Go-Round,* p. 112.
27. Duignan, *One Spin on the Merry-Go-Round,* p. 112–13.
28. Duignan, *One Spin on the Merry-Go-Round,* p. 113.
29. Duignan, *One Spin on the Merry-Go-Round,* p. 114.
30. Reynolds, *My Autobiography,* p. 431.
31. Collins, *The Power Game,* p. 272.
32. Collins, *The Power Game,* p. 273.
33. Reynolds, *My Autobiography,* p. 405.
34. Andrews, *Kingstown Republican,* p. 228–9.
35. Reynolds, *My Autobiography,* p. 433.
36. Reynolds, *My Autobiography,* p. 437.
37. Andrews, *Kingstown Republican,* p. 239.
38. Duignan, *One Spin on the Merry-Go-Round,* p. 116.
39. Duignan, *One Spin on the Merry-Go-Round,* p. 116.
40. Duignan, *One Spin on the Merry-Go-Round,* p. 117.
41. Duignan, *One Spin on the Merry-Go-Round,* p. 117.
42. Collins, *The Power Game,* p. 278.
43. Reynolds, *My Autobiography,* p. 435–6.
44. Reynolds, *My Autobiography,* p. 434.
45. Collins, *The Power Game,* p. 279.
46. Andrews, *Kingstown Republican,* p. 239.
47. Finlay, *Snakes and Ladders,* p. 250.
48. Collins, *The Power Game,* p. 279.
49. Duignan, *One Spin on the Merry-Go-Round,* p. 135.
50. Duignan, *One Spin on the Merry-Go-Round,* p. 154.
51. Quoted by Collins, *The Power Game,* p. 281.
52. Collins, *The Power Game,* p. 282.
53. Duignan, *One Spin on the Merry-Go-Round,* p. 156.
54. Collins, *The Power Game,* p. 278.
55. Duignan, *One Spin on the Merry-Go-Round,* p. 157.
56. Based on the account by Collins in *The Power Game,* p. 288–9.

57. Reynolds, *My Autobiography*, p. 455.
58. Reynolds, *My Autobiography*, p. 455.
59. Reynolds, *My Autobiography*, p. 455.
60. Duignan, *One Spin on the Merry-Go-Round*, p. 162.
61. Witnessed by the author.
62. Duignan, *One Spin on the Merry-Go-Round*, p. 165.

Chapter 18 (pp 297–304)

1. Downing, *Most Skilful, Most Devious, Most Cunning*, p. 135–6.
2. See, for example, Leahy, *Showtime*, p. 20.
3. Ahern, *The Autobiography*, p. 166.
4. Downing, *Most Skilful, Most Devious, Most Cunning*, p. 139.
5. Downing, *Most Skilful, Most Devious, Most Cunning*, p. 142.
6. Downing, *Most Skilful, Most Devious, Most Cunning*, p. 149.
7. Charlie Bird, in McGuire, *The Election Book*, p. 52–3.

Chapter 19 (pp 305–314)

1. Fallon, *Party Time*, p. 90.
2. Downing, *Most Skilful, Most Devious, Most Cunning*, p. 152.
3. Downing, *Most Skilful, Most Devious, Most Cunning*, p. 155.
4. Reynolds, *My Autobiography*, p. 500.
5. Reynolds, *My Autobiography*, p. 501.
6. Ahern, *The Autobiography*, p. 205.

Chapter 20 (pp 315–333)

1. Ahern, *The Autobiography*, p. 257.
2. Ahern, *The Autobiography*, p. 251.
3. In response to a letter from the Fine Gael finance spokesperson during the campaign.
4. Ahern, *The Autobiography*, p. 260.
5. Ahern, *The Autobiography*, p. 275.
6. Ahern, *The Autobiography*, p. 276.
7. Quoted by Leahy, *Showtime*, p. 230.
8. Ahern, *The Autobiography*, p. 286.
9. Leahy, *Showtime*, p. 244.
10. See, for example, Leahy, *Showtime*, p. 217.
11. Leahy, *Showtime*, p. 250.
12. For a detailed account of the revelations about Ahern's finances in evidence at the tribunal see Clifford and Coleman, *The Drumcondra Mafia*, chap. 10–18.
13. Ahern, *The Autobiography*, p. 329.
14. *Guardian*, 7 May 2008.

BIBLIOGRAPHY

— Ahern, Bertie, *The Autobiography,* Dublin: Arrow Books, 2010.

— Aldous, Richard, *Great Irish Speeches,* London: Quercus, 2008.

— Andrews, C. S., *Man of No Property: An Autobiography,* Dublin: Mercier Press, 1982.

— Andrews, David, *Kingstown Republican: A Political Memoir,* Dublin: New Island, 2008.

— Arnold, Bruce, *Haughey: His Life and Unlucky Deeds,* London: Harper-Collins, 1993.

— Arnold, Bruce, *Jack Lynch: Hero in Crisis,* Dublin: Merlin Publishing, 2001.

— Bardon, Jonathan, *A History of Ireland in 250 Episodes,* Dublin: Gill & Macmillan, 2008

— Boland, Kevin, *The Rise and Decline of Fianna Fáil,* Dublin: Mercier Press, 1982.

— Bourden, Patricia, *The Emergence of Modern Ireland, 1850–1966,* Dublin: Folens, 1986.

— Bowman, John, *De Valera and the Ulster Question, 1917–1973,* Oxford: Clarendon Press, 1982.

— Brady, Conor, *Up with the Times,* Dublin: Gill & Macmillan, 2005.

— Breathnach, Máirtín, *Republican Days: 75 Years of Fianna Fáil: Ceiliúradh 75 Bliana,* Dublin: Ashville Media Group, 2001.

— Briscoe, Robert (with Alden Hatch), *For The Life of Me,* London: Longmans, 1959.

— Bromage, Mary C., *De Valera and the March of a Nation,* London: Four Square Illustrated, 1956.

— Bromage, Mary C., *De Valera: The Rebel Gunman Who Became President of Ireland,* London: Four Square Books, 1967.

— Browne, Noël, *Against the Tide,* Dublin: Gill & Macmillan, 1986.

— Browne, P. J., *Unfulfilled Promise: Memories of Donogh O'Malley,* Dublin: Currach Press, 2008.

— Browne, Vincent, "Seán Lemass: A Profile," *Nusight,* November 1969.

— Browne, Vincent, "The making of a Taoiseach," *Magill,* January 1980.

— Browne, Vincent, "The Peter Berry Papers: The top-secret memoirs of Ireland's most powerful civil servant," *Magill,* 1980.

— Carroll, Aideen, *Seán Moylan: Rebel Leader,* Cork: Mercier Press, 2010.

— Chubb, Basil, *A Source Book of Irish Government,* Dublin: Institute of Public Administration, 1983.

— Clifford, Michael, and Coleman, Shane, *Bertie Ahern and the Drumcondra Mafia,* Dublin: Hodder Headline Ireland, 2009.

— Collins, Stephen, *Breaking the Mould: How the PDs Changed Irish Politics,* Dublin: Gill & Macmillan, 2005.

— Collins, Stephen, *The Cosgrave Legacy,* Dublin: Blackwater Press, 1996.

— Collins, Stephen, *The Haughey File: The Unprecedented Career and Last Years of the Boss,* Dublin: O'Brien Press, 1992.

— Collins, Stephen, *The Power Game: Ireland under Fianna Fáil* (revised edition), Dublin: O'Brien Press, 2001.

— Coogan, Tim Pat, *A Memoir,* London: Weidenfeld and Nicolson, 2008.

— Coogan, Tim Pat, *De Valera: Long Fellow, Long Shadow,* London: Hutchinson, 1993.

— Corless, Damian, *Party Nation: The Strokes, Jokes, Spinners and Winners,* Dublin: Merlin, 2007.

— Daly, Mary E., and O'Callaghan, Margaret (eds.), *1916 in 1966: Commemorating the Easter Rising,* Dublin: Royal Irish Academy, 2007.

— Doherty, Gabriel, and Keogh, Dermot (eds.), *De Valera's Irelands,* Dublin: Mercier Press, 2003.

— Downey, James, *Lenihan: His Life and Times,* Dublin: New Island, 1998.

— Downing, John, *Most Skilful, Most Devious, Most Cunning: A Political Biography of Bertie Ahern,* Dublin: Blackwater Press, 2004.

— Duignan, Seán, *One Spin on the Merry-Go-Round,* Dublin: Blackwater Press, 1995.

— Dunphy, Richard, *The Making of Fianna Fáil Power in Ireland, 1923–48,* Oxford: Clarendon Press, 1995.

— Dwyer, T. Ryle, *Charlie: The Political Biography of Charles J. Haughey,* Dublin: Gill & Macmillan, 1987.

— Dwyer, T. Ryle, *De Valera: The Man and the Myths,* Dublin: Poolbeg Press, 1991.

— Dwyer, T. Ryle, *Éamon de Valera,* Dublin: Gill & Macmillan, 1980.

— Dwyer, T. Ryle, *Fallen Idol: Haughey's Controversial Career,* Cork: Mercier Press, 1997.

— Dwyer, T. Ryle, *Haughey's Forty Years of Controversy,* Cork: Mercier Press, 2005.

— Dwyer, T. Ryle, *Nice Fellow: A Biography of Jack Lynch,* Cork: Mercier Press, 2001.

— Dwyer, T. Ryle, *Short Fellow: A Biography of Charles J. Haughey,* Dublin: Marino, 1999.

— Fallon, Johnny, *Party Time: Growing Up in Politics,* Cork: Mercier, 2006.

— Fanning, Ronan, *Independent Ireland,* Dublin: Helicon, 1983.

— Farrell, Brian, *Seán Lemass,* Dublin: Gill & Macmillan, 1983.

— Faulkner, Pádraig, *As I Saw It: Reviewing Over 30 Years of Fianna Fáil and Irish Politics,* Dublin: Wolfhound Press, 2005.

— Feeney, Tom, *Seán MacEntee: A Political Life,* Dublin: Irish Academic Press, 2009.

— Ferriter, Diarmaid, *Judging Dev: A Reassessment of the Life and Legacy of Éamon de Valera,* Dublin: Royal Irish Academy, 2007.

— Ferriter, Diarmaid, *The Transformation of Ireland, 1900–2000,* London: Profile Books, 2005.

— Fianna Fáil, *Fianna Fáil: An Chéad Tréimhse: The Story of Fianna Fáil: First Phase,* Dublin: Fianna Fáil, 1960.

— Finlay, Fergus, *Snakes and Ladders,* Dublin: New Island, 1998.

— Fisk, Robert, *In Time of War: Ireland, Ulster and the Price of Neutrality, 1939–45,* London: Deutsch, 1983.

— FitzGerald, Garret, *All in a Life: An Autobiography,* Dublin: Gill and Macmillan, 1991.

— Gallagher, Michael, *Political Parties in the Republic of Ireland,* Dublin: Gill & Macmillan, 1985.

— Garvin, Tom, *The Evolution of Irish Nationalist Politics*, Dublin: Gill & Macmillan, 1981.
— Garvin, Tom, *Judging Lemass: The Measure of the Man*, Dublin: Royal Irish Academy, 2010.
— Garvin, Tom, *Preventing the Future: Why Was Ireland So Poor for So Long?* Dublin: Gill & Macmillan, 2004.
— Garvin, Tom, Manning, Maurice, and Sinnott, R. (eds.), *Dissecting Irish Politics: Essays in Honour of Brian Farrell*, Dublin: UCD Press, 2004.
— Girvin, Brian, and Murphy, Gary (eds.), *The Lemass Era: Politics and Society in the Ireland of Seán Lemass*, Dublin: UCD Press, 2005.
— Hannon, Philip, and Gallagher, Jackie, *Taking the Long View: 70 Years of Fianna Fáil*, Dublin: Blackwater Press, 1996.
— Hill, Jacqueline R. (ed.), *A New History of Ireland*, VII: *Ireland, 1921–84*, Oxford: Oxford University Press ,2003.
— Horgan, John, *Noël Browne: Passionate Outsider*, Dublin: Gill & Macmillan, 2000.
— Horgan, John, *Seán Lemass: The Enigmatic Patriot*, Dublin: Gill & Macmillan, 1999.
— Joannon, Pierre (ed.), *De Gaulle and Ireland*, Dublin Institute of Public Administration, 1991.
— Jones, Jack, *In Your Opinion: Political and Social Trends in Ireland through the Eyes of the Electorate*, Dublin: Town House, 2001.
— Jordan, Anthony J., *Éamon de Valera, 1882–1975: Irish: Catholic: Visionary*, Dublin: Westport Books, 2010.
— Joyce, Joe, and Murtagh, Peter, *The Boss: Charles J. Haughey in Government*, Dublin: Poolbeg Press, 1983.
— Keena, Colm, *Haughey's Millions: Charlie's Money Trail*, Dublin: Gill & Macmillan, 2001.
— Keogh, Dermot, *Jack Lynch: A Biography*, Dublin: Gill & Macmillan, 2008.
— Keogh, Dermot, *Twentieth-Century Ireland: Nation and State*, Dublin: Gill & Macmillan, 1994.
— Keogh, Dermot, and O'Driscoll, Mervyn (eds.), *Ireland in World War Two: Diplomacy and Survival*, Cork: Mercier Press, 2004.
— Lahiffe, Frank, *Séamus Brennan: A Life in Government*, Dublin: Liffey Press, 2009.
— Leahy, Pat, *Showtime: The Inside Story of Fianna Fáil in Power*, Dublin: Penguin Ireland, 2009.
— Lee, Joseph, *Ireland, 1912–85: Politics and Society*, Cambridge: Cambridge University Press, 1989.
— Lee, Joseph, *Ireland, 1945–70*, Dublin: Gill & Macmillan, 1975.
— Lee, Joseph, and Ó Tuathaigh, Gearóid, *The Age of de Valera*, Dublin: Ward River Press, in association with Raidió-Teilifís Éireann, 1982.
— Lenihan, Brian, *For the Record*, Dublin: Blackwater Press, 1990.
— Longford, Frank Pakenham, Earl of, and O'Neill, T. P., *Éamon de Valera*, Dublin: Gill & Macmillan, 1970.
— Lynch, Jack, "My life and times," *Magill*, November 1979.
— McCarthy, John F. (ed.), *Planning Ireland's Future: The Legacy of T. K. Whitaker*, Dublin: Glendale Press, 1990.

— McCullagh, David, *A Makeshift Majority: The First Inter-Party Government, 1948–51,* Dublin: Institute of Public Administration, 1998.
— MacDermott, Eithne, *Clann na Poblachta,* Cork: Cork University Press, 1998.
— McGuire, Tom (ed.), *The Election Book,* Dublin: O'Brien Press, 2007.
— McMorrow, Conor, *Dáil Stars: From Croke Park to Leinster House,* Dublin: Mentor, 2010.
— MacSharry, Ray, and White, Padraic, *The Making of the Celtic Tiger: The Inside Story of Ireland's Boom Economy,* Cork: Mercier Press, 2000.
— Manning, Maurice, *James Dillon: A Biography,* Dublin: Wolfhound Press, 1999.
— Mansergh, Martin (ed.), *The Spirit of the Nation: The Speeches and Statements of Charles J. Haughey (1957–1986),* Cork: Mercier Press, 1986.
— Martin, Micheál, *Freedom to Choose: Cork and Party Politics in Ireland, 1918–1932,* Cork: Collins Press, 2009.
— Meehan, Ciara, *The Cosgrave Party: A History of Cumann na nGaedheal, 1923–33,* Dublin Royal Irish Academy, 2010.
— Mills, Michael, *Hurler on the Ditch: Memoir of a Journalist Who Became Ireland's First Ombudsman,* Dublin: Currach Press, 2005.
— Moss, Warner, *Political Parties in the Irish Free State,* New York: Columbia University Press, 1933.
— Murphy, Gary, *In Search of the Promised Land: The Politics of Post-War Ireland,* Cork: Mercier Press, 2009.
— Ó Beacháin, Donnacha, *Destiny of the Soldiers: Fianna Fáil, Irish Republicanism and the IRA, 1926–1973,* Dublin: Gill & Macmillan, 2010.
— O'Brien, Justin, *The Arms Trial,* Dublin: Gill & Macmillan, 2000.
— O'Byrnes, Stephen, *Hiding Behind a Face: Fine Gael under FitzGerald,* Dublin: Gill & Macmillan, 1986.
— O'Carroll, John P., and Murphy, John A. (eds.), *De Valera and His Times,* Cork: Cork University Press, 1983.
— O'Leary, Cornelius, *Irish Elections, 1918–77: Parties, Voters, and Proportional Representation,* Dublin: Gill & Macmillan, 1979.
— O'Mahony, T. P., *Jack Lynch: A Biography,* Dublin: Blackwater Press, 1991.
— O'Sullivan, Michael, *Seán Lemass: A Biography,* Dublin: Blackwater Press, 1994.
— Peck, John, *Dublin from Downing Street,* Dublin: Gill & Macmillan, 1978.
— Penniman, Howard R., and Farrell, Brian (eds.), *Ireland at the Polls, 1981, 1982, and 1987: A Study of Four General Elections,* Durham (NC): Duke University Press, 1987.
— Puirséil, Niamh, *The Irish Labour Party, 1922–73,* Dublin: UCD Press, 2007.
— Rafter, Kevin, *Martin Mansergh: A Biography,* Dublin: New Island, 2002.
— Rafter, Kevin, *Neil Blaney: A Soldier of Destiny,* Dublin: Blackwater Press, 1993.
— Reynolds, Albert, *My Autobiography,* Dublin: Transworld Ireland, 2009.
— Ryan, Tim, *Albert Reynolds: The Longford Leader,* Dublin: Blackwater Press, 1994.
— Sacks, Paul Martin, *The Donegal Mafia: An Irish Political Machine,* New Haven (Conn.): Yale University Press, 1976.
— Skinner, Liam C., *Politicians by Accident,* Dublin: Metropolitan Publishing, 1946.
— Smith, Raymond, *Charles J. Haughey: The Survivor,* Dublin: Aherlow Publishers, 1983.

— Smith, Raymond, *Garret: The Enigma: Dr Garret FitzGerald*, Dublin: Aherlow Publishers, 1985.
— Smyth, Sam, *Thanks a Million, Big Fella*, Dublin: Blackwater Press, 1997.
— Walsh, Dick, *The Party: Inside Fianna Fáil*, Dublin: Gill & Macmillan, 1986.
— Walsh, John, *Patrick Hillery: The Official Biography*, Dublin: New Island, 2008.
— Whelan, Ken, and Masterson, Eugene, *Bertie Ahern: Taoiseach and Peacemaker*, Dublin: Blackwater Press, 1998.
— Whelan, Noel, *Showtime or Substance? A Voter's Guide to the 2007 Election*, Dublin: New Island, 2007.
— Yeats, Michael B., *Cast a Cold Eye: Memories of a Poet's Son and Politician*, Dublin: Blackwater Press, 1998.

INDEX